CAREER-FOCUSED COUNSELING

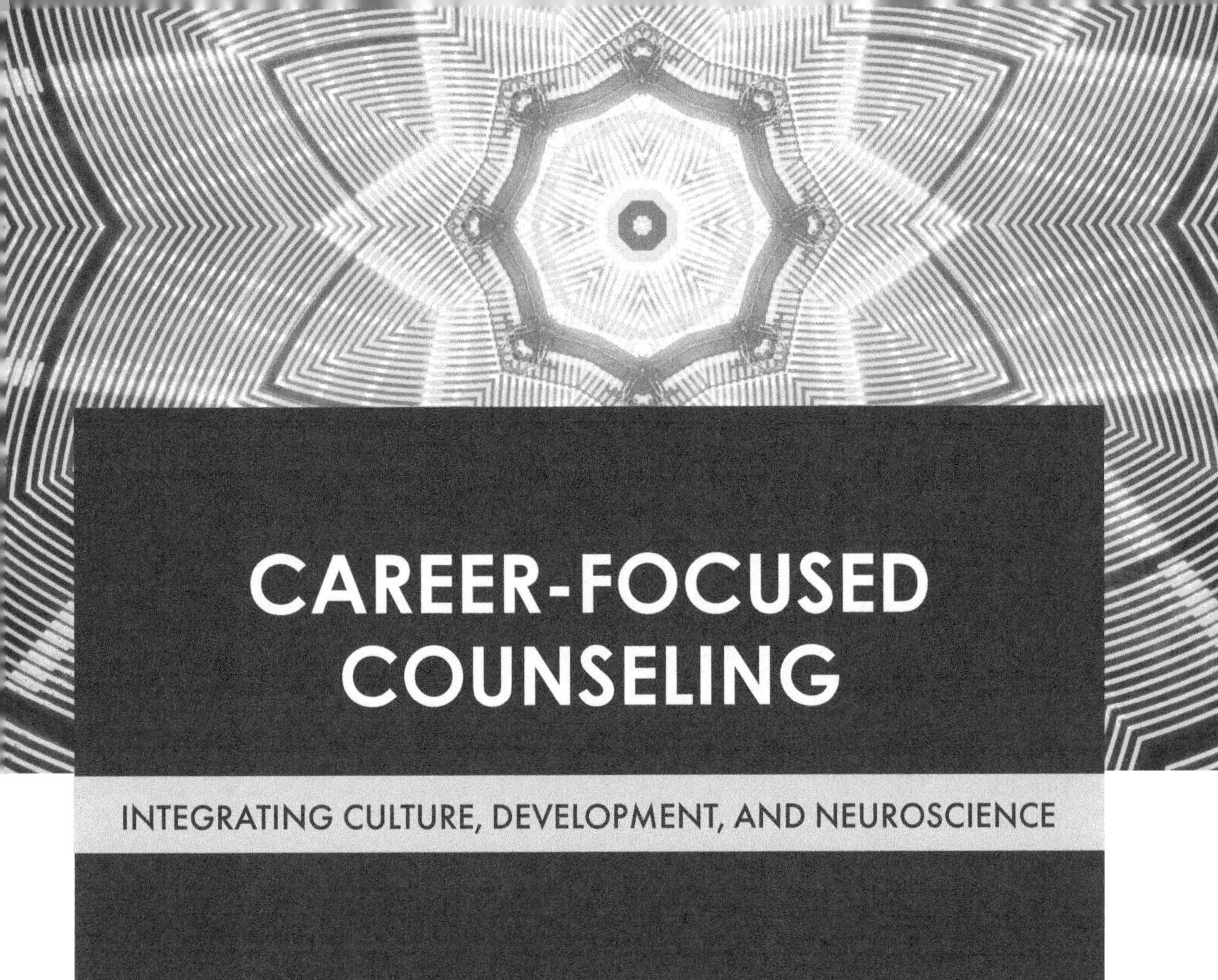

CAREER-FOCUSED COUNSELING

INTEGRATING CULTURE, DEVELOPMENT, AND NEUROSCIENCE

CHAD LUKE

Saint Bonaventure University

MELINDA M. GIBBONS

The University of Tennessee, Knoxville

Bassim Hamadeh, CEO and Publisher
Amy Smith, Senior Project Editor
Alia Bales, Associate Production Manager
Emely Villavicencio, Senior Graphic Designer
Natalie Piccotti, Director of Marketing
Kassie Graves, Senior Vice President, Editorial
Jamie Giganti, Director of Academic Publishing

Printed in the United States of America.

This book is dedicated to my wife, Erinn, and our daughter, Gretchen. They have been my beloved supporters throughout this whole process.

Chad

This book is dedicated to my husband, Tony, and our two sons, Ben and Ryan. It is also in memory of my mom, who was so proud when she heard her daughter was writing a textbook. I wish she could have been around to see the finished product.

Melinda

BRIEF CONTENTS

DETAILED CONTENTS

Preface

Career counseling is counseling. Career-focused counseling is counseling for career-related concerns, typically performed by counselors who do not necessarily intend to be career counselors. The purpose of this *career-focused counseling* textbook is to aid in the training of counselors working—or planning to work—in school, agency, and community settings. The text is intended to be a practical guide based on theory, research, and practice. It focuses on understanding the individual and applying counseling skills to career-related concerns, while focusing on the whole person. Further, the text takes an andragogical approach to writing to readers: it assumes the lived experiences of readers inform their understanding and integration of the material, rather than "writing down" as if to children with limited knowledge. This approach assumes that readers are responsible for taking in and digesting the information contained and then reflecting and practicing that information to improve their skills in career-focused counseling.

Features and Benefits

The features of this text are intended to provide readers with the resources to be apply this material to their counseling practice. There emphasize the theoretical and the practical, guiding readers through the nuances of the work of addressing work and career in the lives of their students and clients. We describe them briefly below.

ETHICS AND CULTURE EMPHASIS

Chapters 1 and 3, in particular, highlight the importance of ethical practice and the development of cultural competence. However, ethical and cultural considerations are carefully woven throughout each chapter. The text emphasizes the ethics of social justice counseling and the implications of and for cultural factors.

THEORY TO PRACTICE

The text contains five separate chapters on career theory. Each chapter contains case vignettes to give the reader a concrete look at the types of presenting concerns that counselors encounter in career-focused counseling. Further, the cases include sample transcript excerpts to provide readers examples of how a career conversation or intervention may look in practice. This aids in building their confidence in applying the material when the time comes.

ASSESSMENT

The coverage of assessment and assessments in career-focused counseling in this text is application based. It eschews extended discussions of validity, reliability, test construction, and the like that can bog down readers. Instead, it demonstrates how and when to use career assessments and to do so in ways that empower students and clients.

NEUROSCIENCE

One of the many features of this text is the incorporation of neuroscience research into career-focused counseling. Chapter 2 is dedicated to an overview of neuroscience principles used throughout the book. It is largely jargon free and offers a natural process for application to students and clients with career-related concerns.

INTEGRATION OF CAREER AND MENTAL HEALTH

This text assumes that career-focused counseling is counseling for career-related concerns. It is performed by counselors in school, agency, and community contexts. It incorporates literature from counseling and psychology to assist readers in being better counselors—not necessarily career counselors. Several chapters are dedicated to clinical issues that interrelate with career.

INTEGRATION OF CAREER AND SCHOOL

The authors have been very intentional in this text to provide a text that is practical for both mental health and school counselors. It focuses heavily on development of the individual throughout childhood, adolescence, emerging adulthood, and beyond. School counselors (and those in training) will note the applicability of the content to their current or future work. It is a career-inclusive text.

CONTEMPORARY ISSUES

The world has changed significantly since the publication of the *Essentials of Career-Focused Counseling* text in 2018. As such, the career and mental health issues that have emerged in the last five years have been carefully covered. It includes coverage of the COVID-19 pandemic, the Great Resignation, trauma-informed care, and other contemporary issues in career-focused counseling.

Organization of This Book

Chapter 1 offers introductory material to the study of career-focused counseling, including ethical and historical considerations. Chapter 2 covers the basics of neuroscience that are integrated throughout the book. Chapter 3 presents a detailed discussion of culture and diversity in career-focused counseling. Chapter 4 covers the nuts and bolts of career-focused counseling that every counselor needs to know. Chapter 5 is a primer on theory and assessment.

Chapters 6–10 cover leading career theories and their application to career-focused counseling. Chapter 11 covers career-focused counseling in K–12 settings, while Chapter 12 addresses career-focused counseling in emerging adulthood, and Chapter 13 covers career-focused counseling with adults. Chapters 14–16 cover a myriad of concerns in career-focused counseling, describing the interplay of career, mental health, and modern life. The text concludes with Chapter 17 as a brief call to action.

PART I

Foundations of Career-Focused Counseling

CHAPTER 1

Job, Work, Career, and Vocation

Clarifying the Counselor's Role

Please take a moment to identify (a) a reason this topic should not take up a whole course in the program (and what course should replace it for you) and (b) a reason this should be a whole course.

CHAPTER GOALS

- Present a perspective on "career" and its use throughout the text.
- Discuss career in its past, current, and future contexts.
- Describe the role of work in people's lives.

OPENING VIGNETTE

Sarah is a first-year master's student in a counseling program. She is excited to learn about counseling theories and skills. When signing up for spring classes, she notes that she has to take a career counseling course. At first she believes the course is a personal one, intended to help her own career develop, and she likes the thought of that. However, in speaking with her adviser, she learns the course is designed to help her work effectively with students and clients in their career development. She confides with a friend that she does not understand why she has to take this course, since she does not plan to be a career counselor. She resigns herself that it's a program requirement, so she'll do her best to just get through it.

Introduction

Writing a textbook is hard. Writing a textbook on a topic few people are truly passionate about is really hard. We both care deeply about understanding the impact of work on the lives of our clients, students, and others with whom we work. Our goal for this book is to help future counselors understand the relevance and importance of career-focused counseling.

Most people are mostly ambivalent about most change. This is a foundational component of counseling. Students approaching a career counseling course may also be ambivalent or reluctant to take this course. This is understandable because it does feel like a specialty area that one has to have an interest in (e.g., "I don't want to be a career counselor or specialize in career"). So the purpose of this reflection is to demonstrate a basic motivational interviewing technique: The first part is to draw out strong feelings of reluctance to take the course by providing permission to speak freely. These feelings, and many others, are already present in students, so it is important to acknowledge them. This is drawing out ambivalence (remember that "resistance" in a client or student is the counselor's responsibility because they pushed them beyond their stage of readiness for change). Next, instead of us, as authors, trying to convince you that this course is vital for ethical, effective practice, we ask you to tell us why it's important to *you*. In doing so, the rationale you provide is your own—not ours.

Consider a high school student who does not want to complete the career assessment program at their school. The school counselor can lecture them about the value or can draw out the student's own arguments against doing it and for doing it. Talking folks into things is rarely effective in the long term and undermines their own agency. Now consider a client in residential treatment for alcohol or drug misuse. They know they need a job when they complete the program but are reluctant to develop a résumé, look for job postings or even consider relocating to find work in a healthier environment. The counselor can try to "make them see" that a good job is necessary for them to stay clean, but most clients in treatment have heard this also before. Instead, the counselor can invite the client to reflect on (a) the ways in which it's better not to worry about a job now (they're already thinking about it anyway) and (b) the possible benefits of doing this while still in treatment. The responses are more likely to be real and true for the individual if they are self-generated (with the support of the counselor).

It is our contention that career or work issues should be incorporated widely in our work with students or clients, but that's our reality. We can try to tell you that or we can try to lead you into this reality to experience for yourself, recognizing that it's you who is ultimately in charge of the degree to which you value the material and process.

The term *career* has been in use for over half a millennium, but its meaning and use have not stayed static. In its current form, career seems to mean something more than work but less than calling or vocation (as if these things can be listed hierarchically). In the original Latin (we know—stay with us for a minute longer), *carrus* meant a wheeled vehicle. You might picture a career as a means of moving a person from one place to another, like a modern day car. In the mid-16th century, the term took on a nuanced meaning in Italian, where instead of referring to a conveyance, it referred to the course or track a conveyance moved upon; the focus shifted from the vehicle to the roadway. So why the language lesson? These early meanings help us describe what we mean in this book by "career-focused counseling" (Luke, 2018). For us, career means both the vehicle *and* the road. It is not as lofty as vocation (though both words have similar histories) or calling, nor is it as banal as terms like job and employment. It does, in fact, subsume all of these terms for this reason: Career is the vehicle of one's agency that moves them down a path toward some end goal.

In 2012, Mary Sue Richardson, a counseling psychologist, published an article offering a new view of the way to address work in counseling. Grounded in social justice and recognizing the unpredictability of the world of work, Richardson argued for a shift to counseling for work and relationships. She noted that we could no longer ignore cultural context in our discussions about career development and highlighted that work looks different for different people. She suggested that career-focused counseling needed to be contextual, culturally centered, and connected to the overall work of counselors. In other words, career and personal counseling are one and the same; we help clients construct lives and see career as a critical part of holistic counseling. Richardson (2012) asserted that all counselors need to be competent in both career-focused and general counseling practice if they are to meet the needs of their clients. Her approach forms the foundation for this textbook. Another reason we use the term *career* as an umbrella term is to remain consistent with the language used in professional associations, namely, ACA, ASCA, and CACREP.

History

The surest way to remain stuck in the past is to remain fixated on it. One of the critiques of contemporary career counseling is its fascination with its own past. While we appreciate the history of career development, we want to encourage readers to strive to step outside their current context to observe the trends of the moment and make certain predictions regarding what comes next.

Pope (2000) provided an impressive overview of the history of career development. He pulled from numerous sources (see Pope, 2000 for reference list) and then used the development of career-related organizations to frame his social transitions stage model. His model covers six 10- to 20-year epochs in the development of career and vocational organizations. Table 1.1 summarizes his model.

TABLE 1.1 POPE'S SOCIAL TRANSITIONS STAGE MODEL

Stage	Time Period	Name	Description	Key Names and Dates
1	1890–1919	Job placement services	• confluence of social and industrial factors forced rethinking the world of work—a move from an agrarian to industrial society • influx of workers from farms to factories (and cities) • WWI veterans returning and needing work • increasing role of psychological testing • social reform movements • job placement was key	• 1909: Parson's *Choosing a Vocation* published posthumously • 1913: National Vocational Guidance Association (NVGA) established • 1917: Smith-Hughes Act of 1917 established secondary school vocational training

(Continued)

TABLE 1.1 POPE'S SOCIAL TRANSITIONS STAGE MODEL *(Continued)*

Stage	Time Period	Name	Description	Key Names and Dates
2	1920–1939	Educational guidance in schools	• increased need for literacy • continued advancement in psychometric testing, including vocational assessment • reformers Jesse B. Davis and Eli Weaver	• 1929: stock market crash, leading to Great Depression of the 1930s • 1933: Civilian Conservation Corps (CCC) established • 1935: Works Progress Administration
3	1940–1959	Colleges and universities and the training of counselors	• WWII resulted in Truman's Fair Deal (veteran employment) • Sputnik launch scared the United States into drafting National Defense Education Act (1957) • NVGA becomes founding division of American Personnel Guidance Association; this dramatically diminished NVGA membership, as APGA became the American Association for Counseling and Development and later the ACA	• 1939–1945: WWII • 1944: Army GI Bill • 1957: Russia launches Sputnik
4	1960–1979	Meaningful work and organizational career development	• Civil Rights Movement • Vietnam Conflict • press to find work that "matters" • explosion of social legislation focused on employment, including Head Start and Job Corps	• 1963 (1968, 1976): Vocational Education Act • 1962: Manpower Development and Training Act—to adjust for job loss from automation • 1966: Anne Roe receives inaugural Eminent Career Award from NVGA • 1967: Vocational Education Act initiated the development of the Bureau of Labor and Statistics
5	1980–1989	Independent practice career counseling and outplacement services	• shift from industrial to information and technology • career counseling as private practice work • outplacement (i.e., downsizing, laying off, and firing) takes center stage, as companies try to adjust to transitions	• 1976: *ACES Position Paper on Counselor Preparation for Career Development* • c. 1982: National Certified Career Counselor Credential by NVGA • 1984: Carl D. Perkins Vocational Education Act • 1984: NVGA becomes the National Career Development Association (NCDA)

(Continued)

TABLE 1.1 POPE'S SOCIAL TRANSITIONS STAGE MODEL *(Continued)*

Stage	Time Period	Name	Description	Key Names and Dates
6	1990–Present	A focus on the school-to-job transition, internalization of career counseling, multicultural career counseling, and increasing sophistication in the use of technology	• continued expansion of career counseling services • Americans with Disabilities Act of 1990 is in this column because of the significant impact of access and opportunities to work for all—covers physical and mental disabilities • increase in technology and "instant" communication and implications for world of work came into great focus • Soviet Union dissolves during this period, increasing global economy, global workforce, and great international career counseling • increase in multicultural considerations in career counseling • women continue to be marginalized in workplace/workforce	• 1998: Workforce Initiative Act • 1994: School-to-Work Opportunities Act • 1994: One-Stop Career Centers Act
7*	1999–Present (2017)	Globalization and an aging workforce	• shifts in worker demographics, as Americans live and work longer • increasing numbers of retirees not fully replaced by successive generations • outsourcing of jobs reaching global (and epidemic?) proportions • increased pressures on school counselors to prepare and push students toward college	• 2001: No Child Left Behind Act (NCLB) • 2014: Workforce Innovation and Opportunity Act (WIOA) • Reach Higher Initiative: https://www.whitehouse.gov/reach-higher

Note. From Pope, 2000.

In Table 1.1, we have included the period from 2000 to the present to address globalization and the global economy—a factor that has changed the vocational landscape in the U.S. and around the world for workers. Pope, Briddick, and Wilson (2013) summarized the objectives of the early days of the vocational guidance movement, which is a view he invites modern day readers to compare with contemporary career and vocational objectives:

> During the 1913 convention, papers were presented that provided insight on the most critical issues that vocational counselors were facing at the time. Many of these issues still resonate 100 years later.

- Implementing some form of vocational guidance within the school system throughout the country and abolishing child labor.
- Reforming education to make it more relevant to students by infusing vocational material throughout the curriculum.
- Developing new psychological tests for vocational guidance to "choos(e) persons for positions rather than ... positions for persons" (Ayres, 1913, p. 37, in Pope et al., 2013).
- Expanding the training of vocational counselors to include the use and interpretation of psychological tests and gaining the knowledge that would allow them to be able to work with diverse populations.
- Developing the skills of vocational counselors to conduct research in order to stay current in the field.
- Preparing vocational counselors to challenge each industry regarding wages, hours, working conditions, and unemployment and to advocate for workers. (pp. 371–372)

Earlier on, career counseling and vocational guidance, as it was called prior to the 1950s, struggled regarding the role of professionals in career guidance (Super, 1955). Super illuminates the discrepant views between guidance professionals and counseling psychologists: "[I]n the 1920s, of educators such as John Brewer (1932) with his stress on exploratory experiences in guidance, and of psychologists such as Clark Hull (1928), with his hopes for psychological tests as the basis of vocational counseling" (p. 3). The difference is significant, and the enduring influence of this philosophical perspective can be seen today. Career counseling is largely dominated by a proliferation of career-based psychometric tests and assessments. Rogers's (1942) book strongly influenced the "push back" of guidance as psychometrics to that of relationship, such that "one counsels people rather than problems, of the fact that problems of adjustment in one aspect of living have effects on other aspects of life, and of the complexity of the processes of counseling concerning any type of individual adjustment, whether in the field of occupation, of group living, or of personal values" (Super, 1955, p. 4). This history provides a contextual understanding through with to view contemporary career-related issues and developments.

More recent events have also impacted the world of work and the ways people think about work, including the Fourth Industrial Revolution (Schwab, 2016); the Great Recession; the pandemic-induced recession; and what has been dubbed the Great Resignation. These current

TAKE A MINUTE

Imagine it is 25 years in the future (that would make the year 2047, at the time of this publication). Now, imagine you are describing this time in history to those much younger than your future self. How would you describe the time period we are currently in, in terms of work, life, social events, and other aspects of life? In other words, in the year 2047, how would you describe the past, circa 2022?

What came to mind about this epoch in the world? How do you think the world of work now will be discussed in 25 years?

events have challenged how individuals and corporations think of working and workers, even as remote, work-from-home positions not only become more prevalent but are also demanded by employees.

Trends

Much has been written regarding the changing world and the shifting landscape of the world of work. There are several trends of note that we address at various points throughout the text: globalization, the global pandemic, racial unrest and the advent of a second Civil Rights Movement, technology and remote working, the intersection of career and culture, the so-called "gig" economy, and even shifts in career theories themselves. As we think through these things together, it is important to keep one immutable reality in mind: an individual's connection to work still comprises Parsons's (1909) century-old formula that includes self-knowledge, occupational knowledge, and true reasoning. The trends in this regard we find most inspiring are how self-knowledge is obtained and understood, especially in the context of a brain renaissance; how one accesses occupational information in the digital age, where little is what it seems; and how models for true reasoning draw upon the latest scientific research on decision-making.

SELF-KNOWLEDGE

Self-knowledge was Parsons' view that the youth with whom he worked needed to understand their likes and dislikes, their personal characteristics, and their interests. This was beyond revolutionary at the time, and it is difficult to fathom, as the world today looks very different than it did then. As the shift from agrarian to industrial economy changed the work landscape, Parsons encouraged self-understanding to add in selection of work. Many of the dominant categories of self-knowledge assessment include skills, interests, personality, and values. It is predicted, and demonstrated empirically, that self-knowledge plays a vital role in matching a person with work.

OCCUPATIONAL KNOWLEDGE

The second part of the matching equation is occupational knowledge. *Occupational knowledge* includes types of work, skills needed to perform the work, and where to find information about available work. Without the skills needed to sort between occupational information and knowledge, seekers can feel more lost and spend a lot of time exploring paths based on spurious information. Another way of saying this is: Occupational information is data, but knowledge is the discernment of data and incorporating it into one's experience. In cognitive development terms, occupational knowledge is the assimilation and accommodation of new data and information (Piaget, 1952). There is a further dimension to occupational knowledge that deserves attention here. Occupational knowledge is obtained, assimilated, and accommodated through the lens of self-knowledge.

TRUE REASONING

Parsons passed away before he was able to fully develop—in writing—his concept of true reasoning, but today it is taken to mean decision-making. It addresses the process of reconciling self-knowledge with occupational knowledge leading to wise career choice. It becomes clearer in this process just how important it is for an individual to possess accurate self- and occupational knowledge. Otherwise, the decision-making process in this context is unlikely to be as successful as it otherwise would be.

However, to this we must now add a fourth ingredient to Parson's formula. Our understanding of *cultural and environmental context* has evolved to the point where we can never ignore or overlook their impact on career development. Access to career options, opportunities for learning and development, and equity in hiring are not equal for all. Systemic oppression runs deep in our world, including the world of work. Power and privilege are defined by those who have it, and at times, those with power are reluctant to change or even acknowledge that inequity exists. As counselors, it is vital that we consider these issues when providing career-focused counseling.

To self-knowledge, we can add the source of our knowledge: identity. Identity is essentially the accumulation of memory storage and recall over time that results in more stable traits. This understanding provides counselors with the resources to further explore how individuals arrived at their particular self-understanding (e.g., assessment results). Culture and the course of development affect self-perception and, therefore, influence self-knowledge and assessment results. Furthermore, the earlier an individual is in the developmental process (often independent of their chronological age), the more suggestible their interests will be. In a similar vein, cultural expectations influence interests and other facets of self and, therefore, self-knowledge. As we will see, memory of self in context is vulnerable to the state of mind a person is in when they recall those memories.

In career-focused counseling, offering occupational information on careers that do not fit with an individual's identity is essentially answering a question that no one asked. It is primarily for this reason that occupational knowledge is predicated on self-knowledge. In career-focused counseling, therefore, it is vital that we not get the proverbial cart (i.e., occupational information) before the horse (i.e., self-knowledge). Counselors are uniquely trained and positioned to guide clients and students in this particular work.

One of the benefits inherent to true reasoning is the ways in which a skilled counselor leads a client or student through the decision-making process in recursive fashion with the two knowledge domains. For instance, when self-knowledge or identity is limited, leading to difficulty in making decisions, the counselor can use that frustration to bring the individual back to reflection on who they are and how this "who" formed through the eight factors described above. This recursive process uses client or student barriers and frustration to move them through career-related stages of change.

CONSTANT CONNECTION (WIRELESS DEVICES)/TECHNOLOGY

Regardless of how an individual feels personally about wireless techologies, we live in a connected world that shows no sign of slowing down. Social media—the use of techology to share thoughts and ideas with friends and the wider world—has ushered in a new form of communication. There is certainly a perspective that argues that social media and constant connection have resulted in personal disconnection. While this argument is outside the scope of the goals here, there are some palpable changes to the world of work as a result. One prominent effect is the reality that many workers today are always available, depending on the culture of their work environment. Many times, there is an expectation that, because there is the possibility of instant contact via text and email, it can and should be required. Because of this, workers today have a trickier path to boundary setting between their personal self and their work self.

RECESSION

Until about 2007, a large proportion of the young workforce, as well as middle and high school students, had little experiential knowledge of national and global economic collapse. The certainty—the privilege of not having to think about it—of ready work and resources was replaced with fear and uncertainty. This generation of prospective and young (career-wise) workers have now lived through a national and worldwide economic trauma that changes both retirement prospects and attitudes toward work.

WHITE HOUSE INITIATIVES

From No Child Left Behind (NCLB) to Reach Higher to the Every Student Succeeds Act (ESSA), the United States government continues to pump funds and legislation into initiatives to train and educate the American workforce. Now more than ever, America and Americans need to be able to compete in a global economy, where knowledge and skills become outdated at an increasingly rapid pace.

MIDDLE CLASS "GAP"

The working poor, or what have been called wage-dependent earners (also often referred to as those working paycheck to paycheck), is a growing group in the current economic climate. Debates regarding "the one percent" and "the point zero one percent" highlight the distance between the "haves" and the "have-nots," but in a way, that feels increasingly insidious to a shrinking middle class. Skyrocketing college student loan debts push retirement planning and estate building further out from the reach of early career workers, while cost of living increases limit what minimum and low wages can purchase. At the same time, the public perception is that the wealthiest group of Americans continues to build wealth and influence public policy. Another trend involves dual-income families, which impose different stressors. These challenges all impact engagement in the world of work.

COVID-19 and the Great Resignation

In Chapter 15 we discuss this in greater detail, so briefly, the age in which this book is penned is one in transition. Luke (in press) summarizes the challenges associated with this time in history:

> The early effects of COVID-19 on the physical, mental, social, financial, and vocational health of millions around the world is well documented (Brooks et al., 2020;

Sauer et al., 2020) but the impact continues to unfold. Many adults have lost their employment and livelihood, while others face the specters of lay-offs and reduced work (Pfefferbaum et al., 2020). High school students are delaying college, while those who do attend face a campus environment very different from their predecessors; new graduates enter a workplace fraught with uncertainty—that is, if they can find a workplace (Haleem, 2020). Displaced and unplaced workers must find an alternative to their daily routine; many spend their time at home, social distancing, and waiting to see if their government or the scientific community can intervene (Dubey et al., 2020). Others have managed their stress and disbelief through unbelief—choosing to deny that COVID-19 is any more dangerous than the flu (Rutjens et al., 2021). Those most vulnerable to the negative effects are those with lower socioeconomic status, less education, un- and under-employment, and pre-pandemic mental health issues (Xiong et al., 2020).

Career and the Field of Counseling

Career-focused counseling includes three components: vocational guidance, career education, and career counseling (Savickas, 2015). All are incredibly important, but each component is quite different. Vocational guidance is where career counseling began, focusing on providing concrete data, measurement of values, skills, interests, and offering connections between results and possible work opportunities. Tasks include employment, fit, satisfaction, and matching (Savickas, 2015). Career education embeds the concept of career development, where career is understood as a lifelong journey. Counselors offer education, both formal and informal, to help people understand themselves better while concurrently learning about the world of work. Tasks of career education include decision-making, exploration, self-concept, transition, and choice. And finally, there is career counseling, where people consider their past experiences and build on their prior successes to create new positive outcomes. Here clients construct, author, adapt, prepare, and consider meaning-making (Savickas, 2015). You will learn ways to provide all three types of career-focused counseling in this text.

CACREP

Our primary accreditation body, CACREP, requires coverage of career development content. In most programs, this occurs in a single course focused on career development and counseling. As of publication of this book, the topics that must be covered include the following (CACREP, 2016):

1. Career Development
   a. theories and models of career development, counseling, and decision making

b. approaches for conceptualizing the interrelationships among and between work, mental well-being, relationships, and other life roles and factors
c. processes for identifying and using career, avocational, educational, occupational and labor market information resources, technology, and information systems
d. approaches for assessing the conditions of the work environment on clients' life experiences
e. strategies for assessing abilities, interests, values, personality and other factors that contribute to career development
f. strategies for career development program planning, organization, implementation, administration, and evaluation
g. strategies for advocating for diverse clients' career and educational development and employment opportunities in a global economy
h. strategies for facilitating client skill development for career, educational, and life-work planning and management
i. methods of identifying and using assessment tools and techniques relevant to career planning and decision making
j. ethical and culturally relevant strategies for addressing career development

TAKE A MINUTE

How do you imagine yourself responding to a client or student who comes to your office in a near panic, asking for help getting a job? What feelings are aroused in you as you sense their urgency and need for help? If you are like many students and counselors, you may feel some anxiety about how to help this individual, caught between merely reflecting their difficulty and trying to fix their work-related problem. This, too, reflects a core belief in counseling and, in particular, career-focused counseling: The goal of this work is for a student or client to *make a decision*. Career guidance and career coaching or facilitation are examples for which information is delivered to help individuals make a career decision. This is also true in counseling, where clients often feel stuck. But it is also the case that counselors use specific strategies to allow clients and students the space to explore barriers, understand motivation, learn more about themselves, and so forth, such that they arrive at a better understanding of themselves and the process. In career-focused counseling, then, making a decision is often a side effect of the work. Counseling for career-related issues fits well into the American Counseling Association's 20/20 definition of counseling, "Counseling is a professional relationship that empowers diverse individuals, families, and groups to accomplish mental health, wellness, education, and *career goals*" (Kaplan et al., 2014; emphasis added).

Ethical Considerations

Ethics are both cross-cutting, generally applied to the field of counseling, and site-specific, tied to the type of counseling being done. As a result, the American Counseling Association (ACA), along with many of its current and previous divisions, includes ethical codes.

Although there is great value in the ethical codes specific to career counseling (National Career Development Association [NCDA], 2015), school counseling (American School Counselor Association [ASCA], 2016), and clinical mental health counseling (American Mental Health Counselors Association [AMHCA], 2020), for the purposes of this book, we will focus on *ACA Code of Ethics* (2014).

In the preamble for the *ACA Code of Ethics* (2014), the 20/20 definition of counseling reminds counselors that a key part of counseling is to help with client goals, including career goals. Next, the code lists the following basic principles for ethical behavior: autonomy, nonmaleficence, beneficence, justice, fidelity, and veracity. You probably learned about these and how to apply them using an ethical decision-making model as part of your professional orientation and ethics course. Regardless of setting or type of client, all counselors consider these ethical principles when deciding how to best serve their clients.

Throughout the *ACA Code of Ethics* (ACA, 2014), counselors are reminded of the importance of maintaining ethical boundaries, relationships, and overall practice with clients. Counselors consider cultural identities, developmental level, legal requirements, and client vulnerability as they engage in counseling relationships. Sections about respecting client rights, keeping clients safe, maintaining appropriate records, practicing with competence, avoiding discrimination, and honoring diversity help counselors understand best practices. These same topics are covered in the other ethical codes noted above.

The takeaway here is that ethics don't stop when counselors provide career-focused counseling. We continue to abide by our ethical code. In this way, career-focused counseling is the same as any other type of counseling; that is, to provide clients with ethical, legal, and client-focused services designed to help them address their goals and increase overall quality of life.

Career Counseling *Is* Counseling

As we have been alluding to throughout this chapter, our view is that career-focused counseling *is* counseling. What this means is that you will use your basic counseling skills in career-focused counseling as well. This seems like a silly point to make, but sometimes, counselors view career counseling as something different from counseling. Perhaps they see it only as information provision, as testing and interpretation, or simply as helping someone create a résumé. As you read through this text, however, you will find it is so much more than this. Counselors—all counselors—use basic attending skills. Understanding the role of work in people's lives requires active listening, a theoretical frame, and a therapeutic relationship. You may recall from your introductory courses that effective helpers share various characteristics. They view clients as worthy and able, they communicate acceptance of others, they are honest and empathic, they are self-aware, they demonstrate ethical behavior, and they demonstrate cultural humility and competence. Effective counselors also use certain skills, such as nonverbal behaviors, open-ended questions, paraphrasing, reflection of feeling and meaning, clarifying, and minimal encouragers. These skills are used to help demonstrate they are listening and ensure they actually understand what the client is sharing. They are also used to help clients consider alternate perspectives, identify underlying emotions, or consider how they might be getting in the way of their own success.

So use of your basic counseling skills is part of the work of career-focused counseling. You will use these to build a strong therapeutic relationship with your clients. The connection with your client will be based on their developmental level, the setting in which you work, and their salient cultural identities. The amount of time you have with your client may be directly impacted by your setting; if you work in a school, you may only have one or two formal counseling sessions with a student but see them regularly in the hallway, lunchroom, or classroom during guidance lessons. Alternatively, if you work in an inpatient substance abuse facility, you may see your clients daily but only for the 28-day period for which they are there. Or you may have the luxury of working with a self-paying client over a six-month period. In all cases, you will engage in an authentic and supportive relationship with your clients to help them navigate their current challenges and find more satisfying alternatives.

In addition to using attending skills and creating therapeutic connections, you will also identify a career-focused theory that connects to your personal theoretical orientation. As we discuss later in this textbook, most of you will use career theories as a supplement to your work with clients rather than as your primary theoretical frame. You will need to select a career-focused theory that aligns with your view of how people grow and change, so you can easily shift to it as needed with your clients. The career counseling and development theories found in this text connect to a variety of general counseling theories, so you should be able to find the one that makes sense to you and aligns with your worldview. Whichever theory you choose, utilizing a theory is part of effective career-focused counseling.

Neuroscience, Culture, and Development

A unique and significant feature of this book is the ways in which neuroscience, culture, and development are woven throughout and described in more detail in this section of each chapter. Luke (2018) first incorporated neuroscience into the work of career-focused counseling, and we extend that work here to include culture and development. These three components are linked to one another and certainly to counseling for career-related issues. The neuroscience of development (see Jones, 2017), the neuroscience of culture (see Luke et al., 2020), and the broader implications of culture and development on career-focused counseling are highlighted throughout, as they form the foundation of the transformative work of career-focused counseling.

The literature on the areas of neuroscience, culture, and development is each voluminous on its own. To make the information manageable, we will use the frame of reference offered by Luke (2016; 2020) to understand how each of these is related to one another and then to career-focused counseling. Neuroscience has established that humans are nothing if not relational, so relationships are core to the work of career-focused counseling. One of the purposes in understanding career-focused counseling is the recognition that when we talk about a career decision, so much more is involved than "just do it." It's similar to a spiderweb. Touch one side of the web with a probe, and the web reverberates throughout. Likewise, a neuroscience-informed, developmentally and culturally relevant, career-focused counseling perspective helps identify barriers to the process—in part by viewing the person as a unified whole instead of parts (the part needing only to make a career decision). At the same time, this perspective can assist counselors working with individuals with career-related presenting concerns by addressing what, on the surface, appears to be unrelated components of the person and process. Just as with the spiderweb, all is connected.

Another way in which we explore the connections among neuroscience, culture, and development is through the lens of Parsons's tripartite model. Self-knowledge, occupational knowledge, and decision-making are all linked to brain, culture, and development, which we explore throughout. Because Parsons's model has influenced every major career theory (Luke, 2018), it is useful to briefly describe the three components here and their relation to the components of this section and direction of this text.

TAKE A MINUTE

Consider a career-related decision you have recently made or have to make in the near future. What was your approach to making that decision? Researchers have explored this process and identified several stages in approaching making a change. As you think about these for yourself in light of your own career decision-making, consider how it might look to work with students or clients at these different stages.

STAGE 1

Is there even a problem—a decision to be made? Many students and clients can experience "true reasoning as irrelevant" because "it will all work out." There is simply no thought given to work after school or the implicit assumption that a career comes with the degree (i.e., high school diploma, college degree, or advanced degree). These individuals are least invested and least likely to seek counseling for career issues. When they do, it tends to be for a collateral issue, like family pressure and tension, or other mental health issues or psychosocial stress. Counselors work to understand the client's perspective on the "nonproblem" and to enhance the client's reflection on their situation.

STAGE 2

In contemplation, there is an awareness that a problem exists, such as the need for employment, or to make a career-related decision. However, there is little if any ownership for resolving the problem or concern. There is a belief that it is someone else's concern, and things will just work out. This mindset, as we have seen in many years of professional practice, is a sort of magical thinking: "I'll find a job when I need it." At this stage there is a rising tension that the concern exists but that no action is yet needed to resolve it. Counselors can carefully inquire about how the individual pictures the issue resolving, in concrete terms. This process can easily evoke defensiveness, as it is likely not something they are comfortable thinking about or discussing. Empathy at this point is key in limiting the amount of judgment they feel as they confront their externalization of their career-related concern.

STAGE 3

At this point, the student or client has begun to experience the realization that there is a problem, and it is their responsibility to resolve it. Preparation is a challenging stage of readiness for change because it can be intimidating to entertain a sense of agency over one's life, particularly when there is limited experience in doing so. Counselors can aid in the transition to preparation by sitting with clients and students in their ambivalence and uncertainty about how to proceed, being mindful to draw out these experiences from their student or client without giving them the answers. *Suggestion* is a technique that is useful here, in which, as opposed to advice-giving, provides a framework for exploration. For example, questions like, "Have you considered how you will take action?" or "I wonder if you have done any research into this area of concern" can open them to new possibilities for resolution and give them confidence to take the next step.

STAGE 4

As the name implies, action means engaging in a behavior or set of behaviors that will move the client or student forward toward their goal. Action, in this sense, is targeted—not haphazard. In a general sense, any movement is good movement for a "sedentary" person, but is not self-sustaining without purpose and intention. Counseling can assist with action by helping the client assess the practicality of the action and, often, helping to break the big actions down into smaller, more manageable steps.

It is helpful to understand where a client or student is in their awareness of an issue, disposition toward it, and motivation for taking meaningful action on their behalf. Counselors who are less familiar with this approach can use the relatively brief psychotherapy version of the URICA found at the following URL: https://habitslab.umbc.edu/files/2014/07/University-of-Rhode-Island-Psychotherapy-Version-for-site.pdf.

Take Away and Use Today

Whatever term we use—job, work, career, vocation—counselors must be prepared to respond to the needs of the students or clients they serve in this life domain. The purpose of this book is to support readers in mapping out a strategy to work individually and in groups with students and clients for whom career is a concern. As you read through this book, we challenge you to keep in mind three things: (a) how have you seen career-related concerns affect yourself and those you know and love; (b) how can you harness the skills and training in your other learning experiences to bring to bear on career-related concerns; and (c) how can having a career-focused mindset in your training and work as a counselor help to bring about change in the lives of those you serve?

References

American Counseling Association. (2014). *2014 ACA code of ethics.* https://www.counseling.org/resources/aca-code-of-ethics.pdf

American School Counselor Association. (2016). *ASCA ethical standards for school counselors.*

Ayres, P. L. (1913). *Psychological tests in vocational guidance.* Paper presented at the meeting of the Vocational Guidance Association, Grand Rapids, MI.

CACREP Board. (2016). *CACREP standards.* http://www.cacrep.org/for-programs/2016-cacrep-standards/

Hull, C. L. (1928). *Aptitude testing.* World Book Co.

Jones, L. K. (2017). Anatomy and brain development. In T. Field, L. K. Jones, & L. A. Russell-Chapin, Neurocounseling: Brain-based clinical approaches (pp. 3–24). Alexandria, VA: American Counseling Association.

Kaplan, D. M., Tarvydas, V. M., & Gladding, S. T. (2014). 20/20: A vision for the future of counseling: The new consensus definition of counseling. *Journal of Counseling & Development, 92*(3), 366–372. https://doi.org/10.1002/j.1556-6676.2014.00164.x

Luke, C. (2018). *Career focused counseling: Integrating theory, research and neuroscience.*

Luke, C. (in press). Principles for post-pandemic humanistic responsiveness to children and adolescents. *Journal of Humanistic Counseling.*

Luke, C., & Redekop, F. (2016). Supervision of co-occurring career and mental health concerns. *Career Planning and Adult Development Journal, 32*(1), 130–140.

Luke, C., Redekop, F., & Moralejo, J. (2020). From microaggressions to neural aggressions: A neuro-informed counseling perspective. *Journal of Multicultural Counseling and Development, 48*(2), 120–129. https://doi.org/10.1002/jmcd.12170

National Career Development Association. (2015). *NCDA code of ethics.*

Parsons, F. (1909). *Choosing a vocation.* Brousson Press.

Piaget, J. (1952). *The origins of intelligence in children.* (M. Cook, Trans.). W W Norton & Co. https://doi.org/10.1037/11494-000

Pope, M. (2000). A brief history of career counseling in the United States. *Career Development Quarterly, 48*(3), 194–211.

Pope, M., Briddick, W. C., & Wilson, F. (2013). The historical importance of social justice in the founding of the national career development association. *The Career Development Quarterly, 61*(4), 368–373.

Richardson, M. S. (2012). Counseling for work and relationship. *The Counseling Psychologist, 40*(2), 190–242. https://doi.org/10.1177%2F0011000011406452

Savickas, M. L. (2015). Career counseling paradigms: Guiding, developing, and designing. In P. Hartung, M. Savickas, & W. Walsh (Eds.), *The APA handbook of career interventions.* APA Press.

Schwab, K. (2017). *The fourth industrial revolution. Currency.*

Super, D. E. (1955). Transition: From vocational guidance to counseling psychology. *Journal of Counseling Psychology, 2*(1), 3.

Schwab, K. (2016). *The fourth industrial revolution.* Crown Business.

CHAPTER 2

Neuroscience-Informed, Career-Focused Counseling

CHAPTER GOALS

- Present the neurobiology that underlies work in the lives of people.
- Identify the neurobiological correlates of self and identity, taking in information (based on understanding of self), work-related decision-making, stress, and transitions.
- Outline the neurobiology of social stressors like poverty and racism and their effects on career development.
- Describe an intervention strategy that uses neuroscience-based metaphors for components of career development.

OPENING VIGNETTE

Temeka is a 30-something-year-old woman, who has been working as a bank teller for the past three years. She has worked in a number of these entry-level positions since completing high school and one-and-a-half years of junior college. She has three children, aged four, six, and 11. She has lived with her current fiancé for the past seven years. Temeka was referred by her primary care provider to a community counseling center because her stress level is affecting her physical health. In her first session with the counselor, Temeka describes feeling overwhelmed managing her roles as a mother, partner, employee, and caregiver to her elderly parents. She expresses frustration at her "dead-end" job; she shares that she cannot be promoted unless she has a bachelor's degree, and she does not enjoy the work or environment enough to want to stay, either way. Her life is full, so the thought of returning to school to complete her degree only adds to her stress.

REFLECTION QUESTIONS

- Before you would consider a mental health diagnosis, what role do you see Temeka's work life playing in her situation?
- If you read this same vignette for another course, what consideration would you give to Temeka's work life?

- If you do view Temeka's work life as relevant to her treatment, how would you begin to address this in your work with her? Furthermore, what possible contribution could neuroscience make to Temeka's situation?

Introduction

This book is about the role of work in people's lives; it is not a neuroscience text. Therefore, the coverage of neuroscience in this chapter and throughout the book will be presented in an integrative, applied approach for counselors working with career or work concerns. We explore four dimensions of the role of work in the lives of clients from a neuroscience perspective. But first, a quick tour.

TOUR OF THE BRAIN

The brain has been described using a 1, 2, 3, 4, 5 mnemonic (Luke, 2020):

1. *One* brain: Figure 2.1 shows the brain as a unified whole, comprised of billions of neurons that make up many networks of networks working synchronously to produce behavior.
2. *Two* hemispheres: Figure 2.2 highlights the two complimentary parts of the whole working together and connected by nerve fibers (corpus callosum) to aid and speed up communication.

FIGURE 2.1. One Brain

FIGURE 2.2. Two Hemispheres

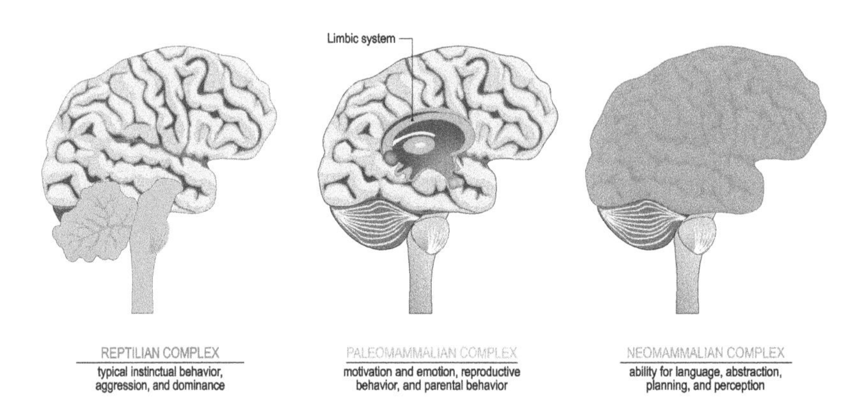

FIGURE 2.3. Three Functional Levels

3. *Three* functional levels: The ancient brain (reptilian) is responsible for reflexes; the old mammalian brain is responsible for regulated reactions; the newer mammalian brain is responsible for relationship-based responses.
4. *Four* lobes: Figure 2.4 shows the four separate, but tightly interconnected, regions of the brain that connect the inner world of the individual with the outer world.

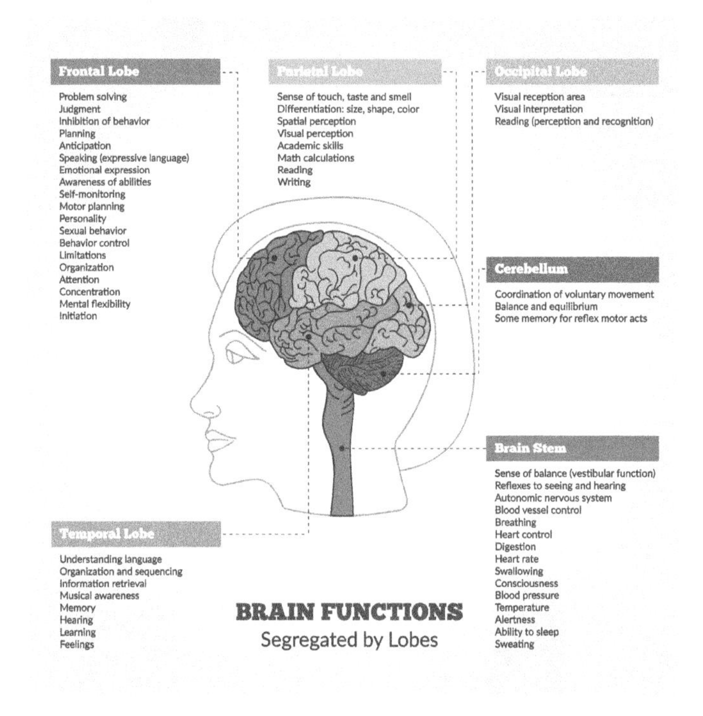

FIGURE 2.4. Four Lobes

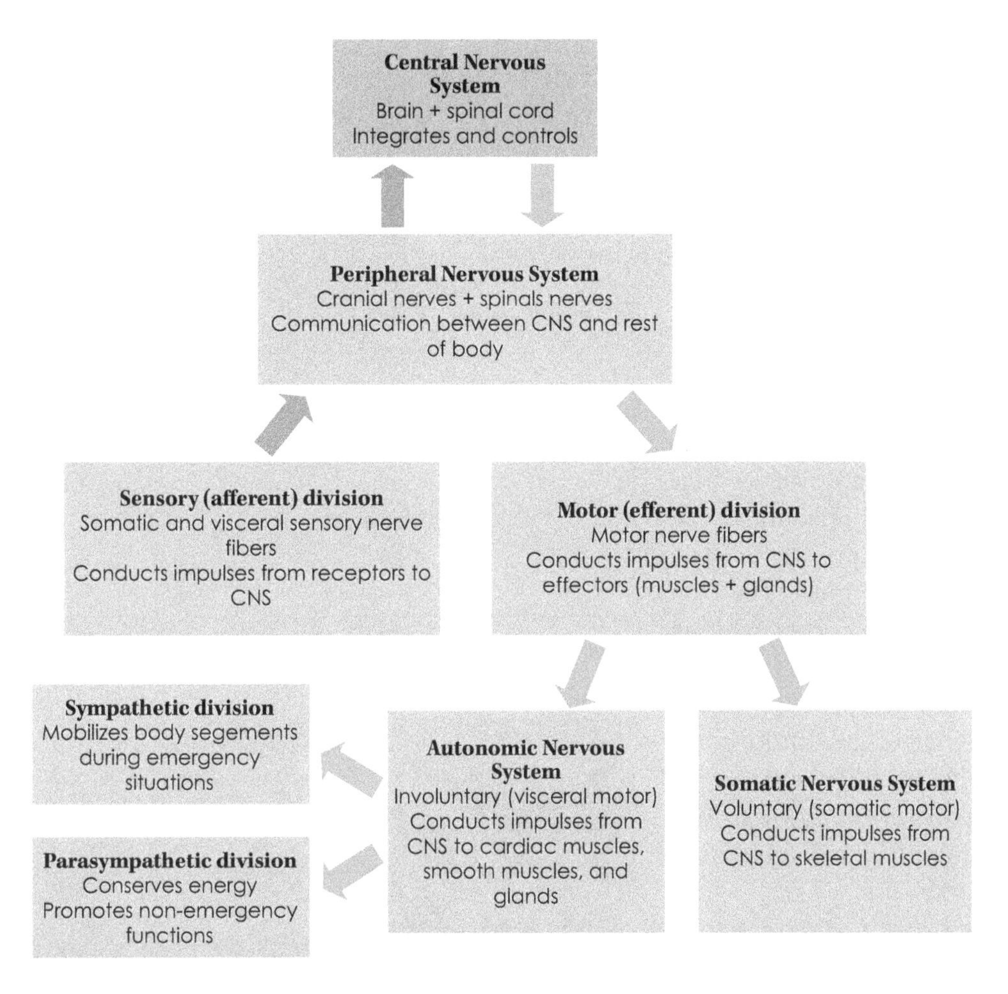

FIGURE 2.5. Five Regulatory Systems

5. *Five* regulatory systems: Figure 2.5 shows one of five (out of many) systems in the brain-body that regulate conscious and unconscious responses to the internal and external environment: central, peripheral, sympathetic, parasympathetic, and enteric nervous systems.

Using Neuroscience to Enhance Career-Focused Counseling

In the following sections, we will explore four areas in which neuroscience integrates with work-related issues. These include career identity, obtaining and using occupational information, making work- and career-related decisions, and managing work-related stress. After each section, the information will be applied to the case of Temeka to illustrate its usefulness in practice.

PREFRONTAL CORTEX

The brain is best understood as a system of systems, a network of networks, that overlap in their functions, so it is not possible to dissect a brain and observe the decision-making structure. Instead, multiple systems work in synchrony to produce decisions and, subsequently, behavior. The most dominant brain region associated with executive functioning is the prefrontal cortex (PFC). Its name denotes its location, the front of the front of the cerebral cortex, which is highlighted in Figure 2.6. The PFC is thought to be responsible for higher-order thinking and complex problem-solving and decision-making, including social-based behaviors and personality.

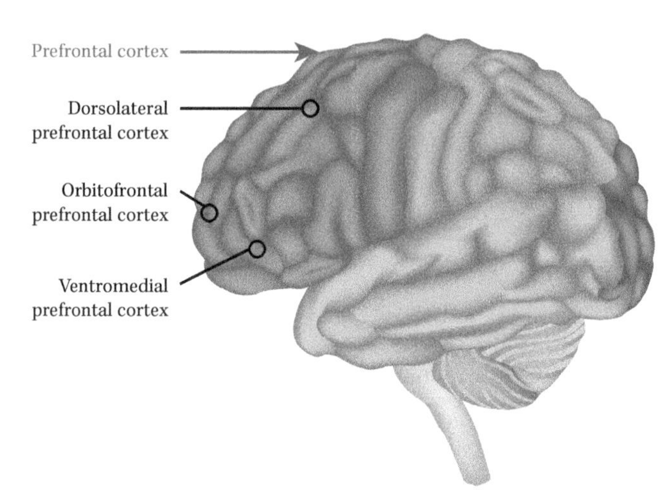

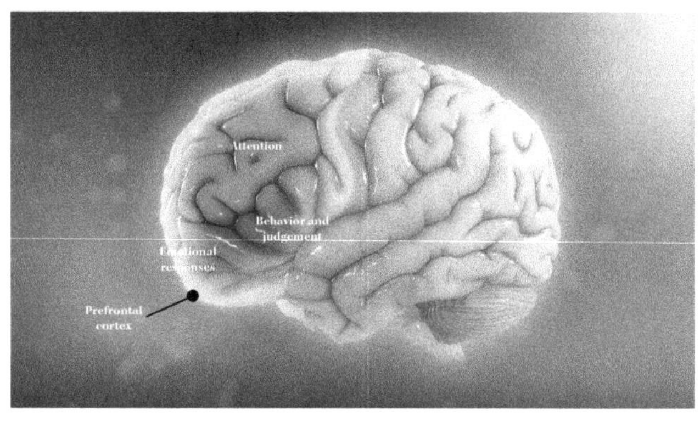

FIGURE 2.6. Prefrontal Cortex

ORBITOFRONTAL CORTEX

Surrounding the PFC is the orbitofrontal cortex (OFC). This part of the PFC coordinates signals coming from all sensory inputs, including visual, auditory, somatic, olfactory, and gustatory sensations. Here, in the OFC, these inputs are assigned value representations and conveyed to other parts of the PFC, the medial (middle) and lateral (side) PFC. These signals are then sent to the premotor and parietal cortices to prepare for some action and then on the motor cortex for execution of the behavior. In addition, these structures and networks are connected to the amygdala for emotional processing and the hippocampus for memory via neurotransmitters like dopamine, serotonin, and acetylcholine. The OFC seems to play a role in reward and evaluation. "Estimating the value of an option involves perceiving sensory properties, identifying the situation, and retrieving information about past experiences with similar contexts from memory" (Purves et al., 2018, p. 727).

VENTROMEDIAL PREFRONTAL CORTEX

The ventromedial prefrontal cortex (vmPFC) works in concert with the OFC to value options based on comparing them with memories of past choices as well as making subjective valuations. It works to evaluate multiple value criteria separately but simultaneously. One example is the selection of a college to attend, wherein price, location, community, and reputation may all have to be evaluated separately but in concert to inform decision-making.

DORSOLATERAL PREFRONTAL CORTEX

The dorsolateral prefrontal cortex (dlPFC) is involved in flexible, future-oriented behaviors that are highly complex. It connects with the OFC, anterior cingulate cortex (ACC), and premotor cortex. The dlPFC also plays a role in regulating short-term memory, which, as we have seen, is vital for decision-making.

TAKE A MINUTE

You just read several Latin terms for structures and their location in the brain. The purpose of the preceding content is to provide background information about the brain and career. As you consider how you can use this in your current and future work, how might you translate this into practice in language that makes sense to students and clients? What analogies or metaphors can you think of for work the brain is involved in career development that can be useful for your students or clients?

Career Identity and the Brain

This section is adapted from Luke (2018) and Luke and Field (2017) and is informed by key neuroscience textbooks by Bear et al. (2016) and Purves et al. (2018). Additionally, special attention is given to research highlighting two brain-based aspects of identity. The first involves memories of self that are retrieved from a first-person versus third-person perspective. The second involves neural processes underlying self-referential thinking when considering the future. We could, of course, follow many paths since this area is one of intense focus for cognitive neuroscientists, social and affective neuroscientists, and personality psychologists and neuroscientists. However, these two have been selected from among many as guides for informing the application of neuroscience to career-focused counseling. Super (1990) described the role of self (identity) related to work as a complex interaction of characteristics that includes inherited aptitudes, neural and endocrine make-up, roles, and evaluations existing in a social space with important others. This is a view of self-knowledge as a deep understanding of how one's environment, experiences, and relationships have shaped the self.

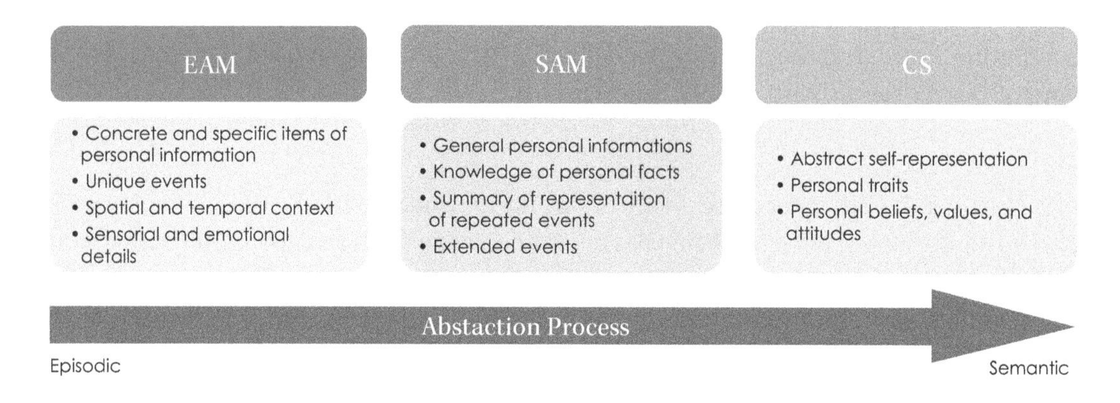

FIGURE 2.7. Types of Memory

Neurobiologically, the self or identity is both a reflection of the past through memory and a projection of the self into the future. The structure implicated in both is the vmPFC (Bonnici et al., 2012; Murayama et al., 2013). For our purposes in understanding the role of the brain in the representation of self, we look to Martinelli et al. (2013) review of the literature and subsequent conceptual scheme. As depicted in Figure 2.7, a sense of self can be understood in terms of three types of self-representations: episodic autobiographical memory (EAM), semantic autobiographical memory (SAM), and the conceptual self (CS). These move from concrete markers of self to more abstract ones, from event-based (episodic) to semantic (declarative or expressed).

Generally speaking, autobiographical memory refers to the memories related to oneself in context: experiences, relationships, and environments (Purves et al., 2018, as discussed in Luke, 2020. *Episodic autobiographical memory*, then, "consists of concrete and specific items of personal information that are closely related to unique autobiographical events situated in a specific time and place (Piolino et al., 2009; Tulving, 2002), which refer to the individual in relation to a specific episodic context" (Martinelli et al., 2013, p. 1516). This describes how we understand ourselves in relation to events in concrete terms. *Semantic autobiographical memory*, on the other hand, "contains semantic personal information, comprising general knowledge of personal facts ... but also general events encompassing both repeated and extended events" (p. 1516). SAM may be thought of as a sense of self requiring effort and attention, whereas EAM may be a more implicit understanding of self in relation to what Martinelli et al. describe as mental reenactments of personal events. The conceptual self is stored in semantic memory in the form of summaries of personal beliefs, values, and attitudes (Conway, 2005), self-knowledge of personality traits (Klein, 2010), and judgments on a number of categories of self-identity (Haslam et al., 2010) that represent our personal identity" (p. 1516).

EAM and SAM have been correlated with activation of limbic structures, the hippocampus, medial PFC, precuneus, and posterior cingulate cortex (PCC), among others (Martinelli, et al., 2013). One key difference is the activation in the hippocampus during EAM.

WHY THIS MATTERS IN WORKING WITH TEMEKA

In listening to Temeka's frustrations, it might be tempting to focus on stress management interventions and coping skills. However, this would inadequately address the cycle of stress she has fallen into with work identity issues at the center. Tuning in to her culture-bound narrative, it is apparent that not completing college and working at limited-growth jobs has added to her stress. Temeka does not sound as if she has a choice but to work these types of jobs, in part because of her many roles, but she also feels she made a bad decision regarding college when she became pregnant with her oldest child about 12 years ago. Luke (2018) offers a glimpse into the role of neuroscience and identity that fits with Temeka's situation:

> One of the implications of this process is the perception (and reality) of self-directed choice. For example, Murayama et al. (2013) demonstrated that self-directed task failure creates an almost positive feedback experience in the prefrontal cortex. In contrast, the reward-related structure (striatum) was conspicuously uninvolved in failure during self-directed tasks. The implications of Murayama's findings could indicate that, when individuals engage in a self-directed task in which they experience failure, this failure is seen (by the brain) as helpful information, rather than internalized as a negative reward.

Occupational Information and the Brain

Occupational information consists of knowledge about the world of work in terms of categories of work and specific job titles, along with the skills, knowledge, and interests needed to be successful and to find satisfaction. To know about these components of occupational information, one must be *exposed* to accurate information about these jobs and their requirements. One way to experience this is through *proximity*, which is the exposure to the work done by important others. It is not uncommon for work interests to develop based on the work of those around us. It is also a low-risk strategy for learning about work (but more on this in a moment). The second way is to seek out knowledge *directly*, through print and web-based searches, reaching out to others to learn about their work, and other forms of occupational information training and exposure. An important component of this information-seeking behavior involves motivation to obtain and potentially use this information. Based on what we have seen so far in this chapter, motivation to learn (or to engage in the precursor processes to learning) is related to how one views themselves.

Episodic prospection is the "ability to imagine future events or generate hypothetical scenarios" (Verfaellie et al., 2019, p. 160). It is part of the memory system that uses memory to formulate hypotheses about the self in the future. It is primarily regulated by a network, mediated by the prefrontal cortex. As we have previously seen, the prefrontal cortex is also involved in decision-making and self-knowledge, particularly self-referential thinking. It becomes active when a person is thinking about themselves relative to some goal or future event (Verfaellie et al., 2019). What this means is that, to some extent at least, motivation to seek occupational information today (or absorb it when shared in class or counseling) may be the relevance of this information to some future goal or version of oneself. In other words, simply delivering information to an individual regarding occupations may be of limited value if the person does not see themselves in that work in the future.

WHY THIS MATTERS IN WORKING WITH TEMEKA

Sometimes, in the process of pre-K–16 education, students are taught copious amounts of information, just in case. Just-in-case learning can evoke the "When am I ever going to need to know this or use?" response from children, adolescents, and emerging adults. Similarly, occupational information can come in like a flood, overwhelming individuals. More information about occupations is available now than ever, and with it comes confusion over how to make sense of it all. For clients like Temeka struggling with work-related issues, seeking additional occupational information may not seem worth it. A counselor's role includes delivering information when the client is both ready for it and able to handle it. For Temeka, additional occupational information in her current state may be overwhelming and easily dismissed as long as she stays in a fixed-identity state, as described above.

Decision-Making and the Brain

Decision-making, possibly the modern equivalent of Parsons's "true reasoning," is more than an abstract concept; it is the precursor to behavior (1909). The goal of career-focused counseling is to support clients and students to take meaningful action on their behalf as it relates to work-related issues. But this resultant behavior is more complex than it might appear on the surface. In fact, "behavior is not limited to motor actions but also includes perception, attention, emotion, memory, and more" (Purves et al., 2018, p. 726). This has implications for decision-making as well, as it is not a one-time cognitive act.

The process of how the brain makes decisions has eluded neuroscientists, philosophers, and psychologists alike. In its place are theories and models for making sense of the complexities of decision-making in the brain. Rather than survey these many models, we explore some of the neuroanatomy and physiology that give rise to the various components of decision-making, in general, and add these to our understanding of career decision-making, specifically. In fact, one of the primary ways of understanding the neurocircuitry of decision-making aids in more effective decision-making is the recognition of the network of networks involved—from reward processing to memory. The process of making decisions, as evidenced by these interconnected networks, highlights the challenges involved in making a decision.

We offer brief, simplified descriptions of some key structures, systems, and functions as a way to inform the process of decision-making. Much of the information in this section is drawn from the sixth edition of *Neuroscience* by Purves et al. (2018), who asserted that "behavior depends not just on sensory input, but on remembered information, goals, and prediction about what might happen" (p. 724).

Executive function in the brain, therefore, involves thinking, planning, and deciding. It is a type of control system that the authors liken to the thermostat in a home, where changes in the environment (e.g., cooling down of the air) require responses by the system (e.g., the heat goes on). Decision-making, then, depends upon multiple systems that include short-term memory, reward evaluation, conflict resolution, and response inhibition. Each of these components come together as a person makes a decision.

This is a lot of information to digest and perhaps even more challenging to make sense of and apply to counseling for work-related issues. Essentially, decision-making is a complex process that emerges from the multiple brain regions, structures, and networks, but which is primarily governed by the prefrontal cortex. Flexibility seems to be the key in making effective decisions, recruiting multiple structures and circuits to evaluate information and form value representations of changing information. This is in contrast to reflex-based behaviors, which are guided by much more primitive regions of the brain and are rooted in survival with the goal of not dying versus the future-oriented goal-directed response of flexibility. In fact, it has been argued that decision-making is a more emotional, visceral process that is rationalized after the fact. For example, a car is not simply a motor or a set of tires. It is a collection of parts and systems that work in synch to move the whole vehicle forward. If one part overheats (similar to emotional overwhelm) the vehicle breaks down. Likewise, decision-making takes coordinated effort in multiple brain systems, each requiring balance and communication with the other. What this means is advice like "just make a decision" is, quite obviously, easier said than done.

WHY THIS MATTERS IN WORKING WITH TEMEKA

In applying this to career-focused counseling with Temeka, we can see the complexity involved, noting that many clients and students may have been told or have told themselves that they need to "just make a decision." While at some level this is true—we must take meaningful action on our behalf—it is also true that it is often easier said than done. From a neurobiological perspective, decision-making involves much more than simple information or action. Instead, it involves memory, emotion, cognitive, context, reward and evaluation, and attention. Understanding these components can aid counselors and career professionals in breaking down decisions—and barriers to decisions—into their component parts to facilitate effective decision-making.

Work-Related Stress

McDonald and Hite (2016) noted that, "while [work–life balance] is frequently used, there appears to be less agreement as to what work–life balance really means" (p. 162). Balance is, in addition to being ill-defined, elusive and illusory for many workers (Kelliher et al., 2019). Balance for these individuals—those working many hours, multiple jobs, and managing multiple life roles—certainly does not mean balance in the sense of division into equal parts, as with a set of scales. Instead, balance may be more related to expectations for achieving balance, or finding pockets of time, energy, and opportunity to make time for self. It is in this context that counselors work with individuals who are experiencing work-related stress as well as life stress that affects work.

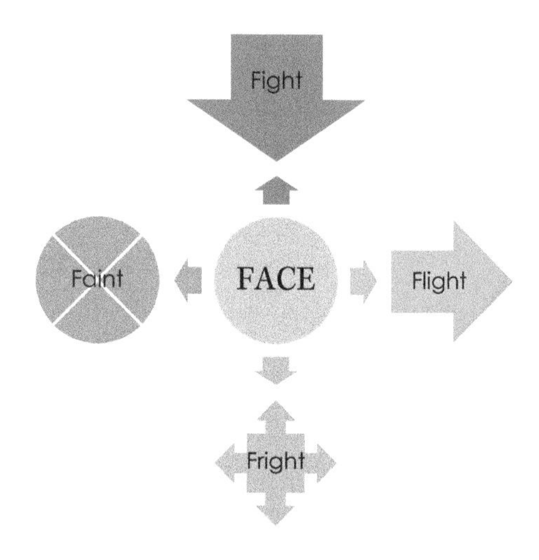

FIGURE 2.8. Types of Stress Responses

A lot has been written about stress (see the seminal work of Hans Selye) and work-related stressors, so our review here focuses on five types of stress responses, as shown in Figure 2.8, the relevance of neuroscience in understanding the stress response, and how this information can better inform counseling (Byrd & Luke, 2021). The following paragraph is paraphrased from Luke and Field (2017).

Stress is both *external* and *internal*. Stress can be an objective, observable phenomenon; it can be a subjective, internally experienced one as well. Stress perception and response can vary based on an individual's sense of self, and can be understood neurobiologically (Bruce et al., 2009). For instance, early trauma or nonnurturing environments can make individuals more susceptible to stress in the work environment by priming the brain's stress response. Individuals with stress-vulnerable brains can be limited in their ability to marshal their internal resources to cope with stress. At the same time, there is growing evidence that change and healing is a result of psychosocial interventions (Bruce et al). While stress and work-related stress have intra- and

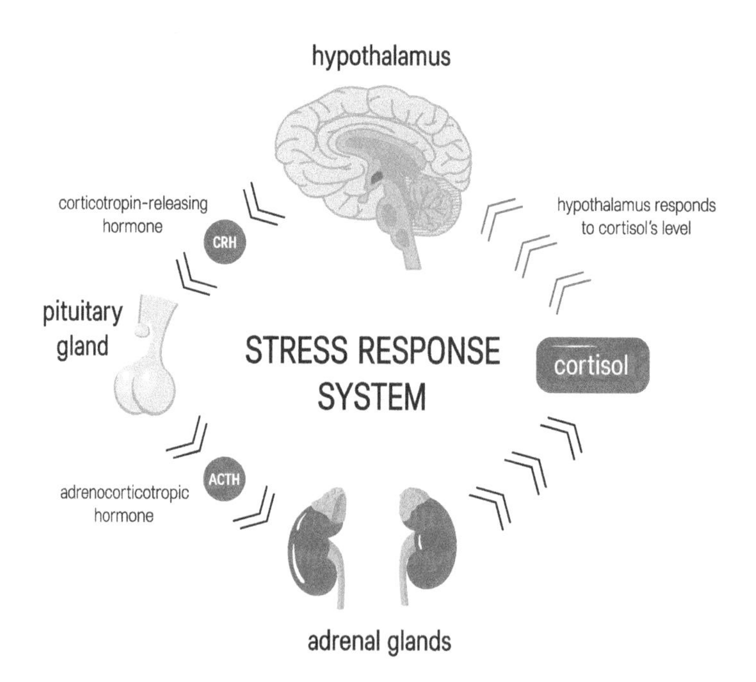

FIGURE 2.9. Stress Response System

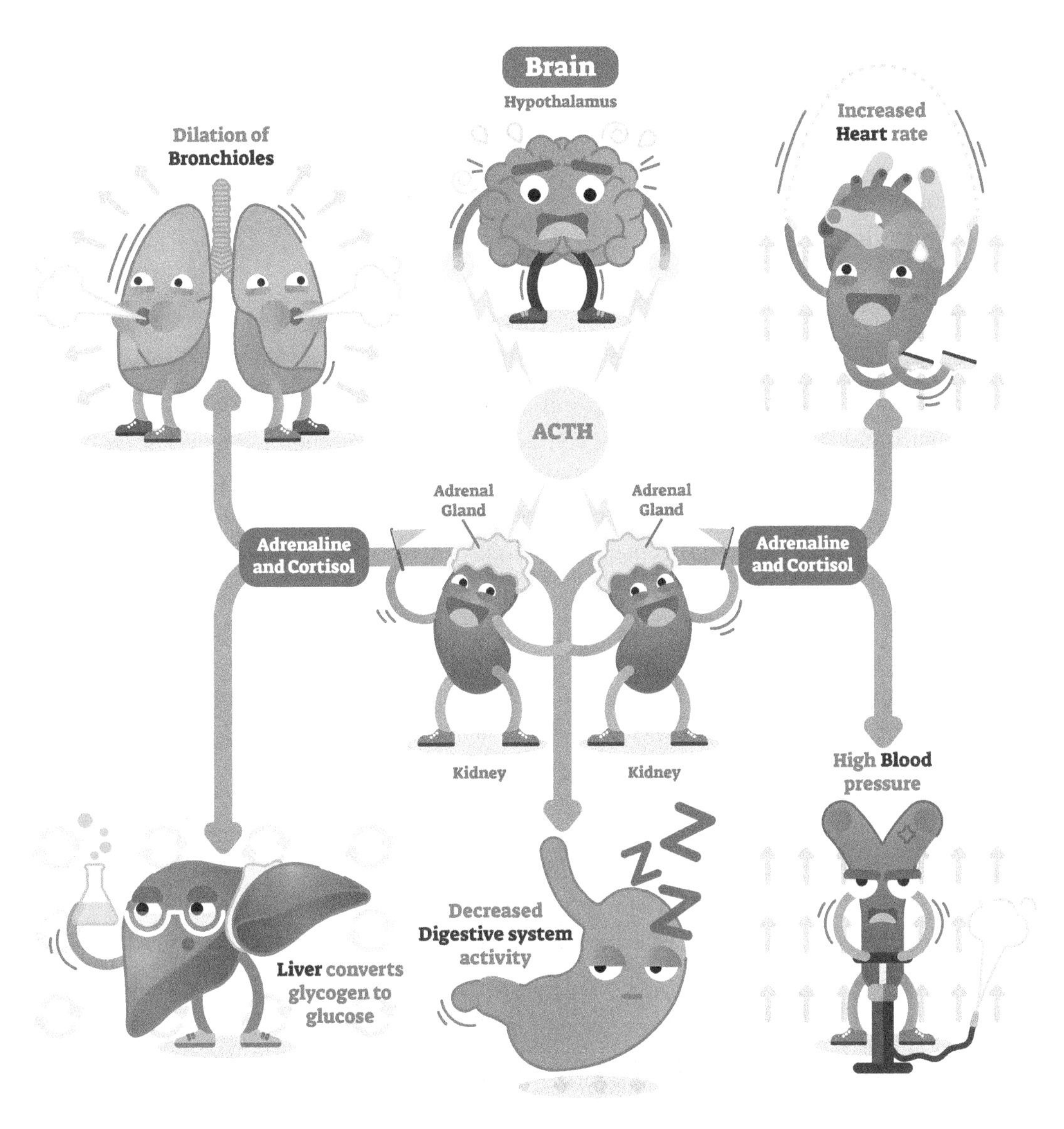

FIGURE 2.10. Effects of Stress

interpersonal features (Zunker, 2016), Fisher and Berkman (2015) found that both acute and chronic stress show plastic responses to counseling interventions.

WHY THIS MATTERS IN WORKING WITH TEMEKA

It is very important for counselors to understand the body's stress response system and how it affects an individual like Temeka's ability to perceive reality and to take in information. As she becomes stressed, her body's sympathetic nervous system takes over, resulting in panic behavior rather than rational, sound behavior. This is happening internally so it can be difficult to directly observe if the client is not forthcoming. There certainly are external indicators, of which counselors can become aware. For example, McDonald and Hite (2016) noted that work-related stress may show itself physiologically (e.g., via headaches, irritable bowel syndrome, high blood pressure, etc.); psychologically, (e.g., via anxiety and depression); and behaviorally (e.g., via substance use, tardiness, or missing work). That said, it is important to recognize the difficulty these individuals have in being present during the meeting. Luke and Field (2017) describe the internal stress response this way:

> The implications of the human stress response system and its limitations have ramifications for addressing work stress in career-focused counseling. It is important to note that the [stress mechanism in the brain] does not discriminate in terms of stress response between perception and "reality." For the response, it is all "real." Sensory input from the five senses is routed through the limbic region and namely the amygdala to determine if what is being perceived is similar in any meaningful way to stored material that has fear/anxiety salience. Once perceived as a threat (stress), [various parts of the brain are activated and] cortisol (as well as epinephrine and norepinephrine) is released in order to prepare the body for fight or flight, or to prepare to freeze when the system is utterly overwhelmed (LeDoux, 2003). This is an efficient system in terms of preparing the body to protect itself. It has, however, at least three specific characteristics which can serve as two-edged swords: it fires quickly, but returns to homeostasis slowly; it acts solely based on perception, regardless of reality; the long-term effects trigger the law of diminishing returns.

Neuroscience, Culture, and Development

Temeka's identity—both personal and vocational—is the product of her lived experience over time. For Temeka, (a) her social and cultural worlds that give rise to her life are preexistent and, as such, have a pervasive, implicit, and explicit impact on how and where she enters the world. Against this sociocultural backdrop lie (b) the genetic residue of previous generations, along with the in utero influences of mother's physical and emotional conditions that affect her development and even temperament. It is in this context that (c) Temeka's most significant initial relationship is formed: her relationship with her mother. Once outside the womb, she follows a relationally dependent course of growth and development. Even during the process of individuating, beginning at 18–30 months, the primary reference point was her mother. This key relationship contributes to and is affected by (d) her early environment, one that may be filled with majority risk or protective factors. Her early environment further shapes her neurobiological development, especially in the first few years of life, leaving an almost indelible neurobiological impression. Within the context of this early environment, Temeka had many (e) early-life experiences, which further shaped her brain and body. Likewise, the context (i.e., environment) in which these experiences occurred influenced the relative impact these experiences have on her development, both positive and negative. These experiences, occurring in specific environments, with her sociocultural and relational norms, fueled by her underlying neurobiology and overall health, affect Temeka's patterns of thoughts, feelings, and behaviors. These (f) thoughts are instrumental and reciprocal with (g) feelings, as they mutually influence one another and lead to (h) action or behavior. These behaviors are often the most visible and external indicators of all seven of the other processes, which also lead the way to effective treatment.

Take Away and Use Today

Neuroscience has attained great popularity and may be at risk for superficial applications. In this chapter we have tried to show rich dimensions of applications of neuroscience to career-focused counseling. This chapter covered a brief tour of the brain to orient readers, followed by discussions of the neurobiology underlying four key areas for counselors in exploring the role of work in people's lives. The chapter also included a discussion of eight dimensions of neuroscience-informed functioning as applied to work. We concluded with a walkthrough of this eight-factor meta-model of Temeka's case. The next step is to put this into practice. The following section provides a starting point.

As demonstrated in this chapter, individual work-related functioning begins with the sociocultural milieu and manifests through specific behaviors. To that end, we offer the application of two neuroscience-informed diagnostic and goal-focused questions, first described in (Byrd & Luke, 2021):

1. What is the work-related or personal *behavior* that causes you the most concern? If a camera recorded you during the height of the *behavior* of concern, what would it show?
2. If our time together in counseling is successful, how would you *behave* differently (what would you be doing more of or less of)? If a camera recorded you after the improvement, what would it show?

These questions assist clients and students to frame their concerns in terms that they can directly influence for developing goals that are directly under their influence. They may be uncertain, confused, or reluctant to try this at first, but gently return them back to the problem in terms of their behavior (without blame) and solutions in terms of their behavior.

References

Bear, M. F., Connors, B. W., & Paradiso, M. A. (2016). *Neuroscience: Exploring the brain*. Wolters Kluwer.

Bruce, J., Fisher, P. A., Pears, K. C., & Levine, S. (2009). Morning cortisol levels in preschool-aged foster children: Differential effects of maltreatment type. *Developmental Psychobiology, 51*, 14–23. https://doi.org/10.1002/dev.20333

Bonnici, H. M., Chadwick, M. J., Lutti, A., Hassabis, D., Weiskopf, N., & Maguire, E. A. (2012). Detecting representations of recent and remote autobiographical memories in vmPFC and hippocampus. *Journal of Neuroscience, 32*(47), 16982–16991. https://doi.org/10.1523/JNEUROSCI.2475-12.2012

Bruce, J., Fisher, P. A., Pears, K. C., & Levine, S. (2009). Morning cortisol levels in preschool-aged foster children: Differential effects of maltreatment type. *Developmental Psychobiology: The Journal of the International Society for Developmental Psychobiology, 51*(1), 14–23. https://doi.org/10.1002/dev.20333

Byrd, R., & Luke, C. (2021). *Counseling children and adolescents: Cultivating empathic connection.* Routledge.

Conway, M. A. (2005). Memory and the self. Journal of Memory and Language, 53, 594–628. https://doi.org/10.1016/j.jml.2005.08.005

Fisher, P. A., & Berkman, E. T. (2015). Designing interventions informed by scientific knowledge about effects of early adversity: A translational neuroscience agenda for next-generation addictions research. *Current Addiction Reports, 2*(4), 347–353. https://doi.org/10.1007/s40429-015-0071-x

Haslam, C., Jetten, J., Haslam, S. A., Pugliese, C., & Tonks, J. (2011). 'I remember therefore I am, and I am therefore I remember': Exploring the contributions of episodic and semantic self-knowledge to strength of identity. *British Journal of Psychology, 102*(2), 184–203. https://doi.org/10.1348/000712610X508091

Kelliher, C., Richardson, J., & Boiarintseva, G. (2019). All of work? All of life? Reconceptualising work–life balance for the 21st century. *Human Resource Management Journal, 29*(2), 97–112. https://doi.org/10.1111/1748-8583.12215

Klein, S. B., & Lax, M. L. (2010). The unanticipated resilience of trait self-knowledge in the face of neural damage. *Memory, 18*(8), 918–948. https://doi.org/10.1080/09658211.2010.524651

Luke, C. (2018). *Essentials of career-focused counseling: Integrating theory, practice, and neuroscience.* Cognella Academic Publishing.

Luke, C. (2020). *Neuroscience for counselors and therapists: Integrating the sciences of mind and brain* (2nd ed.). Cognella Academic Publishing.

Luke, C., & Field, T. A. (2017). Neuro-informed career-focused counseling. In T. A. Field, L. K. Jones, & L. A. Russell-Chapin, *Neurocounseling: Brain-based clinical approaches* (pp. 195–210). American Counseling Association.

McDonald, K., & Hite, L. (2016). *Career development: A human resource development perspective.* Routledge.

Martinelli, P., Sperduti, M., & Piolino, P. (2013). Neural substrates of the self-memory system: New insights from a meta-analysis. *Human Brain Mapping, 34*(7), 1515–1529.

Parsons, F. (1909). *Choosing a vocation.* National Career Development Association.

Piolino, P., Desgranges, B., & Eustache, F. (2009). Episodic autobiographical memories over the course of time: Cognitive, neuropsychological and neuroimaging findings. *Neuropsychologia, 47*(11), 2314–2329. https://doi.org/10.1016/j.neuropsychologia.2009.01.020

Purves, D., Augustine, G. J., Fitzpatrick, D., Hall, W. C., LaMantia, A. S., Mooney, R. D., Plat, M. L., & White, L. (Eds.). (2018). *Neuroscience.* Sinauer Associates.

Selye, H. (1955). Stress and disease. *Science, 122*(3171), 625–631. http://ezproxy.tntech.edu/login?url=https://www.jstor.org/stable/1749664

Super, D. E. (1990). A life-span, life-space approach to career development. In D. Brown & L. Brooks (Eds.), *Career choice and development: Applying contemporary approaches to practice* (2nd ed., pp. 197–261). Jossey-Bass.

Tulving, E. (2002). Episodic memory: From mind to brain. *Annual Review of Psychology, 53*(1), 1–25. https://doi.org/10.1146/annurev.psych.53.100901.135114

Verfaellie, M., Wank, A. A., Reid, A. G., Race, E., & Keane, M. M. (2019). Self-related processing and future thinking: Distinct contributions of ventromedial prefrontal cortex and the medial temporal lobes. *Cortex, 115*, 159–171. https://doi.org/10.1016/j.cortex.2019.01.028

Zunker, V. (2016). *Career counseling: A holistic approach* (6th ed.). Cengage Learning.

CREDITS

CHAPTER 3

Intersections of Career and Culture

CHAPTER GOALS

- Provide an understanding of the intersections between career and culture.
- Learn about theories that describe the impact of these intersections.
- Understand the impact of certain cultural identities on career development.

OPENING VIGNETTES

Peter is a married father with two small children. He is struggling with providing for his family, attending to his relationship, and finding time for his own wellness. In his first counseling session, Peter says his primary goals are to explore ways to reduce his stress related to financial and family concerns.

Zoe has been working as a plumber for over 20 years and really enjoys her job. Now that she is 50, and her children have grown, she is considering her options for the next steps in her life, both personal and career-related. Zoe does have some additional responsibilities, such as caring for her aging parents, but she feels now she is the right time to review her life goals and possibly make some changes.

Lucy is a high school student, who is trying to determine her plans after high school. While her dream is to become a computer scientist, her family is encouraging her to consider pursuing a career in education instead because it will be easier to have a family. Lucy knows she does not need to decide immediately, but she also feels a lot of pressure to choose a college that specializes in education rather than STEM careers.

Tyler is a middle school student, whose teacher has referred him to the school counselor because he is distracted in class and often fails to turn in assignments. During his first meeting with the counselor, Tyler says he plans to become a professional basketball player, so grades and paying attention in class don't really matter. He explains that his cousin is helping him train at the gym, and that is where his focus needs to be, so he can get on the varsity team next year.

Jacinta is pursuing an associate degree at her local community college. She has been talking with the counselor there about her social anxiety and fear of failure. She worries about whether she should stay in school or enter into the world of work full-time. Jacinta explains that she feels like an imposter most of the time and fears that "faking it until you make it" is no longer working as a coping strategy.

TAKE A MINUTE

What are your initial thoughts about each case? What questions do you have to help you better understand each client? How might additional demographic information or cultural variables impact your initial thoughts about each case?

REFLECTION ACTIVITIES AND QUESTIONS

1. Stop for a moment, and think about these words: power, privilege, equity, access. What comes to mind for you? How are these related to career and educational development, planning, and choice? If you are in class, turn to a partner, and share your reflections.
2. Now, think about how you chose your own career path? What led you to your decision to enter counseling or a related field? How did your own power, privilege, equity, and access impact your ability to enter this field?
3. Lastly, think about what you say to others (or others say to you) about how to choose a career? Do terms like meaning-making, interests, values, or personality match enter into these discussions? How might these be related to the ideas of power, privilege, equity, and access?

Introduction

It is hard to imagine, but counselors used to ignore the impact of culture on career development. Theories were one-size-fits-all, typically based on White, college-educated, males. When culture was noted, it was typically as an afterthought, rather than a central concern. Today, of course, we have recognized the error of our ways and now view the intersection of culture and career as a necessary component to helping our clients. In this chapter, we discuss how a culturally-sensitive lens helps us fully serve clients.

What stands out for you regarding your responses to the reflection questions? Early career development theories focused on understanding self, understanding careers, and finding positive matches between these (Hartung & Blustein, 2002). We now recognize the importance of context in career selection and instead consider careers from a postmodern perspective, where there is not a single reality that fits everyone (Savickas, 1993). We know that background context, such as socioeconomic status, gender, ethnicity, race, and parent education level, impact career development. We also recognize that systems, such as quality of education, family dynamics, neighborhood, and national- and global-issues, also impact career development.

Each of us develop in unique ways that directly and indirectly impact our access, power, and privilege related to career choices.

Ethics and Culture

The *ACA Code of Ethics* (2014) includes various components related to issues of diversity and social justice. The introduction includes a statement about honoring diversity and engaging in a social justice mission. Counselors are reminded about the need to be aware of personal values and how these should not be imposed on clients. The code offers statements about applying cultural context to the understanding of confidentiality and notes that counselors should be aware of differing views toward information disclosure and privacy. Additionally, the code highlights the importance of using caution when selecting assessments to ensure that the selected assessment is normed on populations similar to your client. Assessments should also be screened for potential bias and used only as one part of the counseling process (ACA, 2014). Lastly, the code describes the importance of nondiscrimination in work with diverse populations and recommends considering cultural identities during the diagnosis process. Counselors working with diverse clients must follow the *ACA Code of Ethics* to demonstrate cultural awareness and competency when counseling.

MSJCC and Cultural Humility

Although not developed specifically for career development and counseling, the *Multicultural and Social Justice Counseling Competencies* is quite relevant for this course. First published in 2016, the MSJCC (Ratts et al.) expanded upon the multicultural counseling competencies (MCC) by broadening the understanding of culture to include intersectionality and to focus more on social justice. Intersectionality refers to the understanding that cultural identities, such as race, gender, sexuality, and age, are not mutually exclusive but rather "reciprocally constructing phenomena that in turn shape complex social inequalities" (Collins, 2015, p. 2). Social justice refers to the actions that help empower clients through advocacy at the individual, local, and larger systemic levels (Crethar & Winterowd, 2012).

Although the development of the MSJCC is beyond the scope of this chapter (see Ratts et al., 2016), a basic overview can be helpful. The MSJCC uses four quadrants to consider the intersection of power and privilege for both clients and counselors. Within these quadrants, counselors consider their own self-awareness, client worldview, the counseling relationship, and social justice actions. Doing so helps the counselor become aware of potential biases that may negatively impact marginalized clients, while proactively encouraging advocacy at all systemic levels. Using the MSJCC helps all counselors create safe and affirming environments for their clients (Ratts et al., 2016).

Although not specifically included, the concept of cultural humility is embedded into the MSJCC. Cultural humility refers to a way of being that includes openness, collaboration, self-awareness, and understanding of the centrality and impact of cultural and social identities (Davis et al., 2018). Counselors demonstrating cultural humility work to create a comfortable space where discussions of culture can arise and seize opportunities to engage in discussions about the impact of culture on client issues (Watkins et al., 2019). When counselors demonstrate cultural humility, they send a message to clients that conversations on this topic are welcome.

Psychology of Working Theory

Blustein and colleagues (2008) introduced the concept of psychology of working (PWT) to broaden the perspective of career beyond simply an expression of interests and personal meaning. For most adults, work may be about survival rather than self-expression. However, many career theories focus on the privileged group that is able to choose a career path based on their personality, interests, and personal values (Blustein et al., 2008). PWT aligns well with the goals of the MSJCC in that it strives to create a more inclusive and equitable perspective on work and career (Blustein et al., 2019).

Although PWT can be used as a primary career counseling theory, this section describes how to use it as a framework for viewing career issues in general. Counselors can use the core assumptions from this theory to better understand the role of work in clients' lives, particularly in clients with less power and privilege. A core concept of PWT is the idea of decent work, or work that provides reasonable pay, safety and security, autonomy for workers and fair treatment (International Labour Organization [ILO], n.d.). Duffy et al. (2016) noted that decent work must also support the worker's own personal and family values, and ideally, decent work should include all of these aspects, but it is possible to only include some of the components.

Duffy et al. (2016) further recognized that cultural and social identities impact access to decent work, and this impact is further complicated by the intersections of various identities. According to PWT, marginalization may relate to gender, ethnicity, sexual orientation, disability, religion, physical appearance, or socioeconomic status (SES), among other factors (Duffy et al., 2020). In other words, someone who has several identities that are considered marginalized may struggle more to secure decent work than someone with identities with more privilege. For example, a Latina female who comes from a low socioeconomic background is challenged by the intersections of these various identities. The intersection of being female, having a background of low SES, and being Latina is more than the sum of the individual experiences and, rather, multiplies the impact that these combined identities have on career development.

Clients with less power and privilege may be impacted in multiple ways. They may perceive having less choice, or volition, in their career development (Duffy et al., 2016). They may also feel less control over and confidence in their work choices. PWT posits that counselors can help clients develop skills to combat the impact of less power and privilege. Theorists suggest that being proactive, developing a sense of critical consciousness, and increasing social support can increase work volition and sense of control (Duffy et al., 2016). These actions and beliefs increase a sense of agency when faced with the challenge of securing decent work. Clients can reflect on what they are able to control and where agency is present in their lives (Blustein et al., 2019). When clients identify whether work is helping them achieve the needs of survival, social connection, and/or self-determination, they can then take action to make changes (Blustein et al., 2019). For example, counselors may help clients identify if their work helps them pay for their basic needs, whether it helps them connect with others in a meaningful way, and whether they can find areas where they do have autonomy. Increased awareness of these needs being met may increase overall meaning-making and engagement for clients unable to access work that matches their personal interests.

Ecological Systems Theory

The other theory that is useful in considering the intersection of career and culture is Bronfenbrenner's ecological systems theory (Bronfenbrenner, 1979). This is a well-known theory of development that considers the intersections of various systems in which a person lives. Often visualized as a series of nested circles, the theory includes four different systems that interact with each other and with the individual. Briefly, the *microsystem* includes the direct contacts made between the individual and those in their immediate environment (Bronfenbrenner, 1979) and is shown in Figure 3.1. In childhood, these relationships might include family, school, childcare, and the local neighborhood. Specific to career could be how a child's school shares information about career development or how they make decisions about enrichment activities. Also in the microsystem is direct access to role models; students from some cultural identities may lack access to successful models that look like them or come from similar backgrounds. Next is the *mesosystem*, which includes the interactions between two microsystems, such as interactions between a child's school and their parents. Career and educational development are impacted by how schools communicate with families, such as messages given from teachers to caregivers about ability level or career opportunities.

Moving outward to the next circle is the *exosystem*. These are systems that do not directly involve the child but which still impact them. These might include a parent's workplace or family friends. The safety of the local neighborhood, for example, may be part of the exosystem. Students who grow up in high-crime areas are often negatively impacted by the stress caused by living in fear, which can impact their ability to focus on school and career (Cook et al., 2005). The last circle represents the *macrosystem*, which includes the influences of community and national values and customs. These are not typically influences that children have control over, but they may still directly impact them and include everything from socioeconomic status to ethnicity. For example, cultural stereotypes about race or gender may perpetuate further systemic oppression or lead to microaggressions. All four systems are impacted by the *chronosystem*, or transitions and changes over the course of a lifetime.

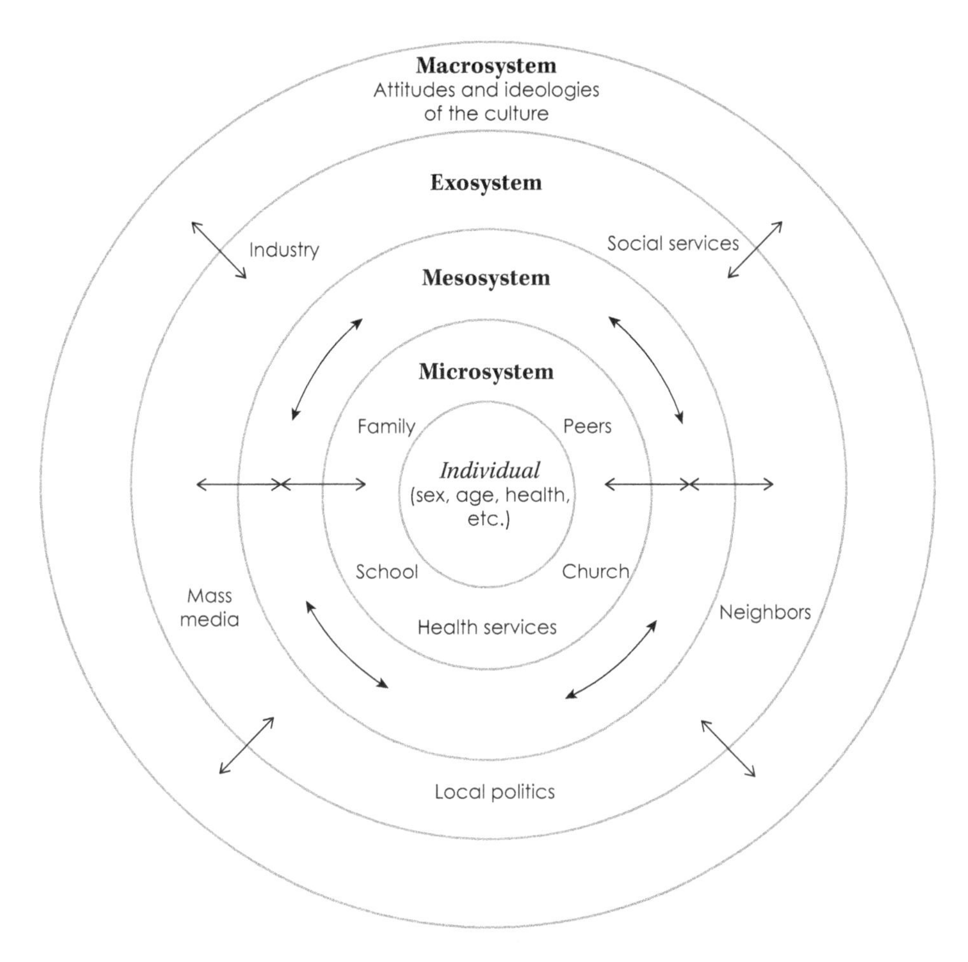

FIGURE 3.1. Bronfenbrenner's Ecological Model

Understanding the impact of systems on individual growth, development, and beliefs can be helpful for considering multicultural influences. Bronfenbrenner and Ceci (1994) proposed that systems impact each other, with more direct and ongoing interaction being more influential than limited exposure. They also highlighted the importance of context, or cultural and social identity, as particularly impactful on development. In other words, cultural and social background impact how we develop, and the systems in which we live and interact with also impact our development. Therefore, people cannot be understood without knowing about the context of their lives, and this context includes their many identities and cultural background.

Social Justice in Counseling

Discrimination impacts clients in a variety of ways. Research, as described below, demonstrates that discrimination can occur related to race, ethnicity, gender, gender identity, sexual orientation, ability status, or SES. Allen (2019) reviewed the research on workplace discrimination and its impact on physical and mental health. He found that discrimination impacted job opportunities, access, and overall treatment in the workplace. These experiences, then, increased overall stress, which negatively impacted physical and mental health (Allen, 2019). He also noted that people with multiple marginalized identities (e.g., African American, female, and low SES) were at even greater risk for discriminatory experiences that negatively affected health. The sections below describe some of the discrimination and challenges experienced by various cultural groups.

A Word about Race and Ethnicity

Race and ethnicity impact career development, access, and equity. For example, while the overall unemployment rate in the United States was 3.7% in 2019, it was 6.1% for African Americans and American Indians (Bureau of Labor Statistics [BLS], 2019). Earnings also differ by race and ethnicity. While 55% of Asian Americans and 41% of White/Caucasian Americans work in higher-paying managerial or professional occupations, only 32% of African Americans and 23% of Hispanics hold these positions. Overall, White and Asian workers earn higher wages than Black or Hispanic workers. Gender exacerbates these differences, with Asian men earning the most ($1,336), followed by Asian women ($1,025), White men ($1,036), White women ($840), Black men ($769), Hispanic men ($747), Black women ($704), and Hispanic women ($642) in weekly earnings (BLS, 2019).

In addition to wages, differences in education level exist by race and ethnicity. Over 90% of working adults age 25 and older who are White, African American, or Asian have at least a high school diploma, but only 76% of Hispanics have completed high school (BLS, 2019). Disparities increase with education level, as 65% of Asians, 41% of Whites, 32% of African Americans, and 22% of Hispanic adults have graduated from college.

Career aspirations are impacted by race and ethnicity. Native American adolescents had lower prestigious career aspirations and demonstrated interest in careers with lower educational requirements than those from other ethnicities (Howard et al., 2011). Students of color who do attend college are still impacted by their race and ethnicity. College students who perceive and experience racial discrimination barriers related to education and career are much more likely to drop out of college or lower their career and educational expectations, particularly for women of color (Li et al., 2021).

Of course, no one is just their ethnicity or race, so intersections between ethnicity and other cultural identities, such as gender, sexual orientation, ability, and others, further complicate our understanding of the impact of this particular identity. Flores et al. (2019) described the necessity of considering intersectionality when approaching career for people of color. They suggested that race and ethnicity should be considered within the context of the client's other identities to fully understand their levels of oppression, privilege, marginalization, and overall experience.

CASE VIGNETTE

Let's return to Jacinta's story that we first read about at the beginning of this chapter. What if you learned that Jacinta was biracial, having a Native American/Indigenous father and Latina mother? Would that shift your perspective on Jacinta's social anxiety or imposter syndrome? What might you want to know about Jacinta's racial and ethnic background as you continue your work together?

A Word About Gender and Gender Identity

The World Health Organization defines gender as "... the characteristics of women, men, girls, and boys that are socially constructed. This includes norms, behaviors, and roles associated with being a woman, man, girl, or boy ..." (WHO, 2021). Although gender and sex are intertwined, sex refers to biological characteristics only. Related to both of these, gender identity refers to a person's feeling of oneself as male, female, or something else (American Psychological Association [APA], 2012). Within these groups, those who identify as female, transgender, or a person whose gender identity does not match to their sex assigned at birth (APA, 2015), are more likely to experience work-related discrimination, although those who identify as male occasionally experience this as well.

So what do we know about discrimination and gender-related identities? Garriott et al. (2017) reviewed articles published between 2005 and 2015 that were focused on career and culture. Of the 1,013 articles they found, gender was the focus in 11%, but gender identity was only the focus in less than 1%. So while the field of career counseling research has explored the intersection of gender and career, gender identity has been minimally reviewed. Much of the research on gender focuses on how to increase the number of females in the science, technology, engineering, and medical (STEM) fields, which have typically employed mostly males (Garriott et al., 2017).

MALE AND FEMALE GENDER

Men and women have different experiences in the workplace. A wage gap still exists, with women earning 82 cents for every dollar earned by men (U.S. Census Bureau, 2019). When considering both gender and race, the picture is even more unbalanced. Compared to White males, Black females earn only 62 cents for every dollar, and Hispanic/Latino females earn only 54 cents. White women earn 79 cents for every dollar, and Asian women earn the most at 90 cents (U.S. Census Bureau, 2018). All of this translates into less annual earnings, with men earning an average of $57,456 and women earning an average of $47,299 (U.S. Census Bureau, 2019).

Women also experience gender discrimination in the workplace. A national survey found that compared to 22% of men, about 40% of women reported feeling discriminated against at work (Pew Research Center, 2021). Although only 6% of men noted feeling they were treated as less competent, 23% of women felt this way at work. Women also reported experiencing gender-related slights, receiving less support from upper management, and being passed over for promotions more frequently than men.

Work-related gender differences begin long before entering the workplace. For example, male college students demonstrate more interest in entering a STEM career at the start of high school, and this interest seems to be stable across the four years. However, the smaller percentage of females interested in a STEM career at the start of high school actually decreases before they enter college (Sadler et al., 2012). Overall, the strongest predictor of career interest for college students is their career interest in 9th grade, especially for boys. Therefore, fewer females enter college interested in STEM careers. Female middle and high school students aspire to careers with more financial prestige than male students, although students from lower SES households, regardless of gender, had lower career prestige aspirations (Howard et al., 2011). Girls in the same study also aspired to higher levels of education than did boys.

Of course, there are other factors that influence career choice. Although these are discussed more below, it is important to note that socioeconomic factors, ethnicity, sexual orientation, and ability level all also impact career choice for both girls and boys. Females typically perceive more barriers to career than men and anticipate discouragement against selecting a nontraditional career (Watts et al., 2015).

TRANSGENDER PEOPLE

A small literature base has focused on the experiences of transgender people in the workplace. Ciprikis et al. (2020) reviewed a national U.S. sample and found that adults who identified as transgender were less likely to be employed, less likely to graduate from college, earn less money, and are more likely to have health issues compared to cisgender adults. Overall, employed transgender adults are more likely to be low-income, regardless of the financial status of their family of origin. Clearly, workers who are transgender are likely to experience discrimination and lack of equity in the workplace.

A few specific studies are worth noting. In one, researchers interviewed a group of female-to-male transgender persons on their experiences with work-related discrimination (Dispenza et al., 2012). The participants reported a wide range of types of discrimination, including microaggressions, health care restrictions, workplace and government policy issues, and school-based discrimination. The impact of these layers of discrimination included high levels of anxiety and stress and development of coping skills to combat these stressors (Dispenza et al., 2012). A more recent study of transgender men and women found that after sex reassignment surgery, mental health, life satisfaction, and job satisfaction increased, with male-to-female transgender individuals experiencing higher job satisfaction than those identifying as female-to-male. This study is important because it demonstrates that sex reassignment surgery may be a vital component toward combating workplace issues for transgender individuals. Counselors likely need to inquire about where their clients are in the transition process and be aware of this connection.

CASE VIGNETTE

Lucy, the high school student from the start of the chapter, tells her school counselor she wants to be a computer science major, but her family feels that this is not an appropriate job for girls. They are pressuring her to become a teacher, so she can be around to raise a family. Her mother also says that Black girls don't become computer scientists, explaining "that is a White world with a load of hurt for those who don't fit in." How does this new information impact your understanding of Lucy's needs?

A Word about Sexual Orientation

People who identify as lesbian, gay, or bisexual (LGB) often report experiencing challenges related to career development. Approximately 5.4% of the U.S. population identifies as LGB (Gallup, 2021). The impact of sexual, or affectional, orientation on career development is complex. Perceptions of discrimination impacted levels of college adjustment, but social support appears to mitigate some of the negative impact of discrimination on career decision-making (Schmidt et al., 2011). In one study, the most frequent career-related barriers identified by working LGB women included career dissatisfaction, role conflict, and issues with confidence levels, while for men the top three issues were career dissatisfaction, lack of confidence, and challenges with decision-making. Differences exist between those who identify as gay, lesbian, or bisexual (Parnell et al., 2012). Those identifying as bisexual anticipate more career-related barriers than those who identify as gay or lesbian. Similarly, federal employees who identify as LGBT reported less perceived fairness, respect, and overall job satisfaction than their peers (Cech & Rothwell, 2020). Those who were also people of color reported even greater levels of work-related challenges.

One theory regarding the intersection of career and sexual orientation is the bottleneck effect (Hetherington, 1991), which suggests that it is difficult to engage in both sexual identity development and career development simultaneously. Since both types of identity development often occur during adolescence, the theory suggests that career development may be delayed as adolescents focus on understanding their sexual orientation. Schmidt and Nilsson (2006) tested this theory and found that adolescents with sexual identity conflict and low levels of social support struggled with their career development. In other words, as these students focused on understanding their sexual orientation, they spent less time focused on their career decision-making, thus, supporting the bottleneck theory.

LGB identity development also impacts career decision-making in college students. Again, stronger social support moderates this relationship, with those perceiving higher levels of support being more able to tackle career decisions (Jang et al., 2021). Winderman et al. (2018) found similar results, as students with higher perceived social support demonstrated more career decision-making preparedness. The evidence suggests social support can be important in helping LGB students navigate their career development and goals.

CASE VIGNETTE

Recall the case of Peter from the beginning of the chapter. He is a married father of two, who has financial and life balance concerns. Let's learn a bit more about him:

CMHC: Tell me more about your family.

Peter: Well, my husband, Aaron, stays home with our kids and works part-time on the weekends. Since I work during the week, we often don't see much of each other and have very little time just the two of us. Our kids are our world, which is great, but it can also be tough. And since I am the one bringing in most of our income, I constantly feel stressed about making ends meet.

CMHC: That does sound stressful. Can you tell me a bit more about your job and work life?

Peter: Well, I work for a mid-sized company that distributes electronics. My colleagues are all fine, I guess, but many of them don't know about Aaron. I talk about my kids, but it is just easier to leave out the fact that I am gay; we don't have work get-togethers very often, so it is pretty easy to avoid.

What are your thoughts now about Peter? Has your view of his situation changed as a result of this information?

A Word About Ability

No disability is the same, and neither does any disability have clear edges. For example, a person seeking counseling may have a congenital disability, something they were born with, that has shaped their identity, or in contrast, since they lived their whole life with it, they may have integrated their identity with disability. They may not even see their disability as a disability but more of a feature of themselves. On the other hand, others may have acquired their disability through injury or disease. This, too, affects how the individual experiences their disability and the modifications to their life that accompany the disability. For both groups, the disability can be visible or not, it can be mild to severe, and the person may be at any stage of acceptance and integration with their disability. Persons with disabilities tend to not seek sympathy and certainly not pity; instead, they want to be seen as fully human, capable of asking for help when needed and receiving that help. In fact, research shows that self-determination, not self- or others' pity, is more instrumental in the life and career success of persons with disabilities (Shogren et al., 2021; Wehmeyer et al., 2018).

The Americans with Disabilities Act (Department of Labor, 2017) prohibits discrimination against people with disabilities, including in the workplace. However, career disparities for people with disabilities still exist. Although 77% of adults without disabilities are employed, only 34% of those with disabilities have paid employment. The percentage of those employed varies by type of disability, with 53% of those with a hearing disability being employed, but only 44% of those with a visual disability, 28% of those with a cognitive disability, and 25% of people with an ambulatory disability being employed (American Community Survey [ACS], 2018). Annual earnings of people with disabilities who do work is also concerning. Adults with disabilities earn 66 cents for every dollar someone without a disability earns (U.S. Census Bureau, 2019).

Vocational rehabilitation programs (VR) are designed to help people with disabilities. Funded by the U.S. Department of Education through Rehabilitation Services Administration, these programs provide career and educational assistance for people with disabilities. Each state has their own vocational rehab program, and all are designed to help people with disabilities successfully enter into competitive employment. Not all people with disabilities are eligible for this program, however, and often, agencies have insufficient resources to serve all eligible clients; even among those served, not all maintain competitive employment (U.S. Department of Education, 2020). Lack of funding, staff turnover, and changes in federal legislation all impact VR services. Therefore, counselors cannot simply assume that VR will be the solution for all clients with disabilities.

Workers with disabilities are also more likely to experience discriminatory acts. In an exploration of discriminatory experiences reported to the U.S. Equal Employment Opportunity Commission over a 20-year period, researchers found that over 350,000 allegations were reported (Graham et al., 2018). Of these, people with physical impairments had the highest rates of allegations overall; those with mental health or addictions disabilities had the highest number of reports related to unfair termination and harassment, and those with hearing and vision impairments reported the highest rates of hiring and advancement discrimination. This study not only demonstrates the high levels of perceived discrimination for people with disabilities, but it also provides information suggesting that not all experiences are the same but rather are dependent on the type of disability.

CASE VIGNETTE

Remember the case of Zoe the plumber? During her counseling session, Zoe reveals she has been diagnosed with multiple sclerosis, which has affected her balance and made the left side of her body weak. The MS also affects her vision and ability to concentrate—plus, it just zaps her overall energy level. Zoe has been successful in building her plumbing business but now feels like she may not be able to continue with her job given her physical challenges. She feels depressed and is unsure what to do next; she had always assumed she would work until her mid-60s and needs to do so to support herself and help her parents, but she is unsure what to do at this point. How does this information change your view of Zoe and her career development needs?

A Word About SES

Socioeconomic status (SES) affects career development and access in multiple ways. Youth growing up in low-income households often experience less access to college-educated role models, information about the world of work, and enrichment activities, often leading to less academic attainment or entry into lower-paying careers. Adults who earn low wages continue to be negatively impacted; they may experience difficulties meeting basic needs and find it difficult to access higher-paying positions. According to PWT, social class status impacts access to decent work in two ways (Duffy et al., 2016). First, limited economic resources may increase the likelihood of access to high quality education and career development opportunities. Second, low SES likely reduces connections to those who may be helpful in the career development process.

According to the Bureau of Labor Statistics (2020), over 38 million people live in poverty. In 2020, households with four people were considered to be in poverty if they earned less than $26,695, although the specific amount varies slightly by state of residence (U.S. Census Bureau, 2021). Poverty impacts postsecondary education experiences, and these students often experience more emotional distress, challenges with identity development, and negative stereotyping and bias that can impact their career futures (Jury et al., 2017). In case there was any doubt, understanding the intersection of SES and career is vital.

CHILDREN AND ADOLESCENTS

As noted above, living in a low-income household impacts career development. SES appears to negatively impact beliefs about ability to successfully enter a career, particularly for students who are also marginalized in other ways, such as by race or ethnicity (Flores et al., 2016). Students who perceive themselves to be from a lower social class often demonstrate reduced educational aspirations and expectations (Eshelman & Rottinghaus, 2015). Relatedly, students from low-income families tend to aspire to careers with less income potential than students from families with higher incomes (Howard et al., 2011). This may be because parents from low-education backgrounds often feel uncertain about how to assist their students as they consider postsecondary education (Hallett & Griffin, 2015).

Many students from low-income families are prospective first-generation college students or those who would be the first in their family to attend college. These students often lack social capital or access to mentors and a professional network (Tate et al., 2015). Prospective first-generation college students also perceive more barriers to college-going and worry more about how to pay for college compared to their peers (Gibbons & Borders, 2010) and oftentimes decrease their college-going intentions as they move through high school (Gao & Eccles, 2020). Students from low-income families also may have financial or family obligations that negatively impact their postsecondary plans (Mitchall & Jaeger, 2018). These obligations may impact their academic experience by limiting their ability to visit colleges, volunteer, or engage in extracurricular activities.

ADULTS

Challenges for low-income students continue for those who enter college. They often enter college with less advanced math courses, fewer enrichment experiences, and lower aspirations for continuing their education (Hahs-Vaughn, 2004; Martinez et al., 2009). These students typically work while in college, which may continue to challenge their ability to be successful academically and in career preparation. Those who are successful in college often note the importance of family support during this time, particularly when their parents wanted them to attend college (Gofen, 2009). Often, these students discuss needing to compromise their career aspirations due to external factors to be successful (Packard & Babineau, 2009).

Adults who live in poverty experience a host of other challenges. Of adults living in poverty, seven million were characterized as working poor, meaning they worked full time or actively sought work but still lived in poverty. Women, African Americans, and Hispanics are most likely to be considered working poor, and being working poor is directly related to education level (BLS, 2020). These statistics mean that, although they are employed, the working poor are still struggling financially. Another challenge is the impact poverty has on mental health. Those living in poverty are likely to experience high stress levels but lack access to mental health services (Santiago et al., 2012). Stress can be exacerbated by unsafe living conditions, health issues, childcare concerns, and meeting basic needs such as food and shelter. SES also impacts beliefs about career options and opportunities. Although all workers want access to meaningful work, those from higher SES backgrounds appear to be better able to access this type of work, including being able to find higher prestige positions with higher salaries (Autin & Allan, 2020).

CASE VIGNETTE

At the start of the chapter, you were introduced to Tyler, the 8th grade student who wants to be a professional basketball player. His school counselor, Mr. Flanagan, knows Tyler fairly well because he worked with him when his father passed away two years ago. At that time, Tyler was a good student, who had dreams of attending the local college. Now, Tyler says that college is not an option because it is too costly, and he believes he can be drafted into the NBA right after high school, so grades are not important. His family is struggling financially, so earning money as soon as possible is critical. What are some additional components to helping Tyler now that you know more about his story?

Other Cultural Identities of Importance

It is impossible to fully explore the intersection of career and cultural identity in a single chapter, but it is important to note other cultural factors that impact career and educational development, planning, and decision-making. We will include four additional cultural factors that may be particularly relevant: religion, rurality, age, and immigration status.

RELIGION/SPIRITUALITY

Although recent polls suggest participation in formal religious activities has declined in recent years, the majority of Americans still have a religious affiliation (Gallup Poll, 2021). Most of our clients will either identify as *spiritual*, believing in inner ways of making meaning (Garner et al., 2017), or *religious*, following "organized beliefs common to a culture" (ASERVIC, n.d.). Spirituality and religion intersect with career in multiple ways. Some clients may view a career as a *calling*, meaning they feel compelled to serve others through a specific career path. A calling may emerge from a structured religious commitment or be linked to social justice pursuits and can result in satisfaction and connection or doubt and struggles (Hernandez et al., 2011). A strong religious background can also impact career development through value and core beliefs related to gender roles (Duffy, 2010). Religion can also lead to discrimination in the workplace, particularly for those with nonmajority belief systems, such as Judaism or Islam.

RURALITY

According to the U.S. Census (2017), nearly one-fifth of all Americans live in rural communities, making it likely that all counselors will encounter this group. Educational attainment is lower for those in rural areas, with only 28% of adults completing a two- or four-year degree compared to 41% in urban communities (USDA, 2017). People of color from rural areas have even lower rates of educational attainment, with only 17% of African American and 14% of Latinx Americans completing at least a two-year college degree. Generally, adults in rural communities earn less than their urban counterparts, regardless of degree status, and poverty rates are higher, particularly for youth (USDA, 2017). Rural communities also have other issues that may impact career opportunities. For example, people from rural communities are less likely to have reliable internet, more likely to have a disability, and more likely to regularly encounter infrastructure issues, such as deteriorating roads, lack of interstate access, and lack of public transportation (TRIP, 2020). Many of these issues are unique to rural communities.

AGE

People are staying in the workforce longer than in the past, with the average age of all workers being 42 in 2020 compared to 39.3 in 2000, and the percentage of workers over age 55 is growing every year (Toossi & Torpey, 2017). A large national study of older adults in the workforce found that just over half experienced some type of daily discrimination, with 34% reporting that the discrimination was related to their age (Foley & Lytle, 2015). This daily discrimination was found to have a strong, negative impact on overall work satisfaction for older adults, suggesting that bias against older workers can be quite harmful. With the move to delay retirement, career satisfaction among older adults becomes important. Retirement has also shifted from earlier versions, with options now including continuing to work during retirement to staying in their current job past the average age of retirement to entering an entirely new career later in life. In fact, a recent survey found that 64% of older adults (age 62+) were still working, and only 15.5% had fully retired (Boveda & Metz, 2016).

IMMIGRATION STATUS

Career development for people not born in the United States can present unique challenges. Challenges can exist with being able to access career and educational opportunities, engaging in meaningful and sustaining work, and fitting within the U.S. work context. Compared to workers born in the U.S., immigrant workers report lower levels of satisfaction with their income; English fluency and coworker support positively impact overall job satisfaction (Ko et al., 2015). Relatedly, acculturation to American belief systems, a strong ethnic identity, and minimal discrimination experiences lead to higher levels of job satisfaction for immigrant workers. While these characteristics all seem attainable, they can actually be quite challenging for those who were not born in the United States. For example, if someone resettles here due to refugee status, they likely have a plethora of challenges, including economic hardship, lack of English proficiency, and high stress levels (Massengale et al., 2020). They may also be entering communities without any local connections or social support systems, and they may even face overt discrimination or more subtle microaggressions (Leong & Tang, 2016). Immigration status can make career-related issues even more difficult.

Exploring Culture with Clients

As described in both the *ACA Code of Ethics* and the MSJCC, counselors must create a safe space for clients to describe their cultural identities and explore how these impact their current issues and goals. Day-Vines et al. (2020) introduced the multidimensional model of broaching behavior (MMBB) as a way of intentionally introducing and supporting discussions of culture. In this model, counselors attend to various components of broaching. First, they try to reduce the power differential that exists between counselor and client by using immediacy and acknowledging times when they may not fully understand a client's culture-related concerns. Termed cultural immediacy, the counselor initiates discussions related to multicultural identities and works to create a trusting and authentic counseling relationship (Day-Vines et al., 2020). Counselors are also tasked with broaching how societal oppression and discrimination has impacted diverse clients while acknowledging the intersections of multiple identities. This behavior is aligned with the MSJCC (Ratts et al., 2016). These actions occur parallel to counselors' knowledge and awareness of the impact of intersecting cultural identities on clients' lives.

One way to begin the broaching process is to use the Career-in-Culture Interview (CiCI; Ponterotto et al., 2000). The CiCI is a semi-structured interview that intentionally asks clients to consider the impact of their various identities on their career development. Questions range from the client as an individual (e.g., career goals, concerns, and occupational awareness) to their self-view (e.g., work experiences and work values) to the impact of culture, religion, family, and community (e.g., cultural background, spiritual background, and family and community influences) and, finally, to their perceptions of barriers and oppression (e.g., culturally related challenges and assets). The CiCI provides a somewhat structured method of introducing the importance of cultural context and its impact on career development and choice, while allowing the client to identify themes and patterns and ultimately decide what identities are most salient for them. Because it is semi-structured and qualitative, this assessment can be adapted to meet theoretical orientation or client needs.

Putting It All Together

Consider the case example below. At each question, stop and explore your thinking. How does each additional detail help you better understand Michael? How does the information shift your understanding?

Michael has a certificate degree in welding and currently works as a welder for a mid-sized construction company. Michael is uncertain about whether to stay in the field of welding and comes to you for help.

TAKE A MINUTE

What are your initial thoughts about Michael?

As you build rapport with Michael, you learn that Michael's salary is sufficient to cover all basic needs, such as housing, food, and general safety. You also learn that Michael has a long-term romantic partner named Lisa, and they have a young daughter named Chloe. Lisa works as the assistant office manager at the same construction company as Michael.

TAKE A MINUTE

How does this information shift your understanding of Michael?

As you continue to meet with Michael, you learn more. Michael has recently begun using the pronouns "they" and "them" and has asked their family and friends to use these pronouns. This is a change for everyone.

TAKE A MINUTE

How does this information shift your understanding of Michael?

Later, you learn more about Michael's work context. Michael enjoys welding and has received positive affirmations from their employer about their work. Michael notes they have been a welder for over 10 years, and they also like their coworkers and bosses. Michael says they are happy with Lisa and want to stay with her, but Lisa has expressed concerns about whether Michael can truly be happy with her given their new gender identity.

TAKE A MINUTE

How does this information shift your understanding of Michael?

Michael also reveals they are of Latin descent, and their family of origin does not understand Michael's gender identity at all. Michael describes their church, where Michael and Lisa are active members, as somewhat conservative and traditional, and many of their church members work for the same construction company. Finally, in your third session with Michael, they reveal a recent diagnosis of early arthritis and admit this is making it difficult to complete welding tasks efficiently. They are worried about all the factors going against their career as a welder and begin to quietly cry, stating that "welding has always been part of my identity. I love my job, but it feels like the world is against me continuing as a welder."

TAKE A MINUTE

How does intersectionality impact your understanding of Michael?

Take Away and Use Today

The intersection of career and culture is deep and complex. Understanding the unique barriers and challenges related to various cultural identities can help ensure that you serve your clients well. We urge you to utilize the psychology of working theory as a frame for this understanding or to consider how to connect Bronfenbrenner's work to your theoretical frame. Being intentional, open, and humble as you work with clients from various backgrounds is the ultimate goal.

References

Allen, E. (2019). Perceived discrimination and health: Paradigms and prospects. *Sociology Compass, 13*(8). https://doi.org/10.1111/soc4.12720

American Counseling Association. (2014). *2014 ACA code of ethics*. https://www.counseling.org/resources/aca-code-of-ethics.pdf

American Community Survey. (2018). *Employment ages 16–64 by disability type.* https://disabilitystatistics.org/reports/acs.cfm?statistic=2

American Psychological Association. (2012). Guidelines for Psychological Practice with Lesbian, Gay, and Bisexual Clients. *American Psychologist, 67*(1), 10–42. https://doi.org/10.1037/a0024659

American Psychological Association. (2015). Guidelines for psychological practice with transgender and gender nonconforming people. *American Psychologist, 70*(9), 832–864. https://doi.org/10.1037/a0039906

ASERVIC. (n.d.). A white paper. https://aservic.org/aservic-white-paper/

Autin, K. L., & Allan, B. A. (2020). Socioeconomic Privilege and meaningful work: A psychology of working perspective. *Journal of Career Assessment, 28*(2), 241–256. https://doi.org/10.1177/1069072719856307

Blustein, D. L., Kenna, A. C., Gill, N., & DeVoy, J. E. (2008). The psychology of working: A new framework for counseling practice and public policy. *The Career Development Quarterly, 56*(4), 294–308. https://doi.org/10.1002/j.2161-0045.2008.tb00095.x

Blustein, D. L., Kenny, M. E., Autin, K., & Duffy, R. (2019). The psychology of working in practice: A theory of change for a new era. *The Career Development Quarterly, 67*(3), 236–254. https://doi.org/10.1002/cdq.12193

Boveda, I., & Metz, A. J. (2016). Predicting end-of-career transitions for baby boomers nearing retirement age. *The Career Development Quarterly, 64*(2), 153–168. https://doi.org/10.1002/cdq.12048

Bronfenbrenner, U., & Ceci, S. J. (1994). Nature–nurture reconceptualized in developmental perspective: A bioecological model. *Psychological Review, 101*(4), 568–586. https://doi.org/10.1037/0033-295X.101.4.568

Bronfenbrenner, U. (1979). *The ecology of human development: Experiments by nature and design.* Harvard University Press.

Bureau of Labor Statistics. (2019). *Labor force characteristics by race and ethnicity, 2019.* https://www.bls.gov/opub/reports/race-and-ethnicity/2019/home.htm

Bureau of Labor Statistics. (2020). *A profile of the working poor.* https://www.bls.gov/opub/reports/working-poor/2018/home.htm

Cech, E. A., & Rothwell, W. R. (2020). LGBT workplace inequality in the federal workforce: Intersectional processes, organizational contexts, and turnover considerations. *Industrial & Labor Relations Review, 73*(1), 25–60. https://doi.org/10.1177/0019793919843508

Ciprikis, K., Cassells, D., & Berrill, J. (2020). Transgender labour market outcomes: Evidence from the United States. *Gender, Work, and Organization, 27*(6), 1378–1401. https://doi.org/10.1111/gwao.12501

Collins, P. H. (2015). Intersectionality's definitional dilemmas. *Annual Review of Sociology, 41*, 1–20. https://doi.org/10.1146/annurev-soc-073014-112142

Cook, E. P., Heppner, M. J., & O'Brien, K. M. (2005). Multicultural and gender influences in women's career development: An ecological perspective. *Journal of Multicultural Counseling and Development, 33*(3), 165–179. https://doi.org/10.1002/j.2161-1912.2005.tb00014.x

Crethar, H. C. & Winterowd, C. L. (2012). Values and social justice in counseling. *Counseling and Values, 57*(1), 3–9. https://doi.org/10.1002/j.2161-007X.2012.00001.x

Davis, D. E., DeBlaere, C., Owen, J., Hook, J. N., Rivera, D. P., Choe, E., Van Tongeren, D. R., Worthington, E. L., & Placeres, V. (2018). The multicultural orientation framework: A narrative review. *Psychotherapy, 55*(1), 89–100. https://doi.org/10.1037/pst0000160

Day-Vines, N. L., Cluxton-Keller, F., Agorsor, C., Gubara, S., & Otabil, N. A. A. (2020). The multidimensional model of broaching behavior. *Journal of Counseling and Development, 98*(1), 107–118. https://doi.org/10.1002/jcad.12304

Department of Labor. (2017). *Americans with disabilities act*. https://www.dol.gov/general/topic/disability/ada

Dispenza, F., Watson, L. B., Chung, Y. B., & Brack, G. (2012). Experience of career-related discrimination for female-to-male transgender persons: A qualitative study. *The Career Development Quarterly, 60*(1), 65–81. https://doi.org/10.1002/j.2161-0045.2012.00006.x

Duffy, R. D. (2010). Spirituality, religion, and work values. *Journal of Psychology and Theology, 38*(1), 52–61. https://doi.org/10.1177/009164711003800105

Duffy, R. D., Blustein, D. L., Diemer, M. A., & Autin, K. L. (2016). The psychology of working theory. *Journal of Counseling Psychology, 63*(2), 127–148. https://doi.org/10.1037/cou0000140

Eshelman, A. J., & Rottinghaus, P. J. (2015). Viewing adolescents' career futures through the lenses of socioeconomic status and social class. *The Career Development Quarterly, 63*(4), 320–332. https://doi.org/10.1002/cdq.12031

Flores, L. Y., Martinez, L. D., McGillen, G. G., & Milord, J. (2019). Something old and something new: Future directions in vocational research with people of color in the United States. *Journal of Career Assessment, 27*(2), 187–208. https://doi.org/10.1177/1069072718822461

Flores, L. Y., Navarro, R. L., & Ali, S. R. (2016. The state of SCCT research in relation to social class: Future directions. *Journal of Career Assessment, 25*(1), 6–23. https://doi.org/10.1177/1069072716658649

Foley, P. F. & Lytle, M. C. (2015). Social cognitive career theory, the theory of work adjustment, and work satisfaction of retirement-age adults. *Journal of Career Development, 42*(3), 199–214. https://doi.org/10.1177/0894845314553270

Gallup. (2021). What percentage of Americans are LGBT? https://news.gallup.com/poll/332522/percentage-americans-lgbt.aspx

Gao, Y. & Eccles, J. (2020). Who lower their aspirations? The development and protective factors of college-associated career aspirations in adolescence. *Journal of Vocational Behavior, 116*, 103–367. https://doi.org/10.1016/j.jvb.2019.103367

Garner, C. M., Webb, L. K., Chaffin, C., & Byars, A. (2017). The soul of supervision: Counselor spirituality. *Counseling and Values, 62*(1), 24–36. https://doi.org/10.1002/cvj.12047

Garriott, P. O., Faris, E., Frazier, J., Nisle, S., & Galluzzo, J. (2017). Multicultural and international research in four career development journals: An 11-year content analysis. *The Career Development Quarterly, 65*(4), 302–314. https://doi.org/10.1002/cdq.12109

Gibbons, M. M., & Borders, L. D. (2010). Prospective first-generation college students: A social–cognitive perspective. *The Career Development Quarterly, 58*(3), 194–208. https://doi.org/10.1002/j.2161-0045.2010.tb00186.x

Gofen, A. (2009). Family capital: How first-generation higher education students break the intergenerational cycle. *Family Relations: Interdisciplinary Journal of Applied Family Science, 58*(1), 104–120. https://doi.org/10.1111/j.1741-3729.2008.00538.x

Graham, K. M., McMahon, B. T., Kim, J. H., Simpson, P., & McMahon, M. C. (2018). Patterns of workplace discrimination across broad categories of disability. *Rehabilitation Psychology, 64*(2), 194–202. https://doi.org/10.1037/rep0000227

Hahs-Vaughn, D. (2004). The impact of parents' education level on college students: An analysis using the beginning post-secondary students longitudinal study 1990–92/94. *Journal of College Student Development, 45*(5), 483–500. https://doi.org/10.1353/csd.2004.0057

Hallett, R. E., & Griffen, J. (2015). Empowering parents in the college-planning process: An action-inquiry case study. *Journal of Education for Students Placed at Risk, 20*(1–2), 101–119. https://doi.org/10.1080/10824669.2014.984035

Hartung, P. J., & Blustein, D. L. (2002). Reason, intuition, and social justice: Elaborating on Parsons's career decision-making model. *Journal of Counseling and Development, 80*(1), 41–47. https://doi.org/10.1002/j.1556-6678.2002.tb00164.x

Hernandez, E. F., Foley, P. F., & Beitin, B. K. (2011). Hearing the call: A phenomenological study of religion in career choice. *Journal of Career Development, 38*(1), 62–88. https://doi.org/10.1177/0894845309358889

Hetherington, C. (1991). Life planning and career counseling with gay and lesbian students. In N. J. Evans (Ed.), *Beyond tolerance: Gays, lesbians, and bisexuals on campus* (pp. 131–145). American College Personnel Association.

Howard, K., Carlstrom, A. H., Katz, A. D., Chew, A. Y., Ray, G. C., Laine, L., & Caulum, D. (2011). Career aspirations of youth: Untangling race/ethnicity, SES, and gender. *Journal of Vocational Behavior, 79*(1), 98–109. https://doi.org/10.1016/j.jvb.2010.12.002

International Labour Organization. (n.d.). *Decent work.* https://www.ilo.org/global/topics/decent-work/lang-en/index.htm

Jang, H., Smith, C. K., & Duys, D. K. (2021). Correction to: LGB identity and career decision-making self-efficacy among sexual minority college students. *International Journal for Educational and Vocational Guidance, 21*(3), 717–717. https://doi.org/10.1007/s10775-021-09463-6

Jury, M., Smeding, A., Stephens, N. M., Nelson, J. E., Aelenei, C., & Darnon, C. (2017). The experience of low-SES students in higher education: Psychological barriers to success and interventions to reduce social-class inequality: Low-SES students in higher education. *Journal of Social Issues, 73*(1), 23–41. https://doi.org/10.1111/josi.12202

Ko, J., Frey, J. J., Osteen, P., & Ahn, H. (2015). Moderating effects of immigrant status on determinants of job satisfaction: Implications for occupational health. *Journal of Career Development, 42*(5), 396–411. https://doi.org/10.1177/0894845315572890

Leong, F. T. L., & Tang, M. (2016). Career barriers for Chinese immigrants in the United States. *The Career Development Quarterly, 64*(3), 259–271. https://doi.org/10.1002/cdq.12059

Li, X., Kim, Y. H., Keum, B. T. H., Wang, Y.-W., & Bishop, K. (2021). A broken pipeline: Effects of gender and racial/ethnic barriers on college students' educational aspiration–pursuit gap. *Journal of Career Development*, 89484532199419–. https://doi.org/10.1177/0894845321994196

Martinez, J. A., Sher, K. J., Krull, J. L., & Wood, P. K. (2009). Blue-collar scholars? Mediators and moderators of university attrition in first-generation college students. *Journal of College Student Development, 50*(1), 87–103. https://doi.org/10.1353/csd.0.0053

Massengale, M., Shebuski, K. M., Karaga, S., Choe, E., Hong, J., Hunter, T. L., & Dispenza, F. (2020). Psychology of working theory with refugee persons: Applications for career counseling. *Journal of Career Development, 47*(5), 592–605. https://doi.org/10.1177/0894845319832670

Mitchall, A. M., & Jaeger, A. J. (2018) Parental influences on low income, first-generation students' motivation on the path to college. *Journal of Higher Education, 89*(4), 582–609. https://doi.org/10.1080/00221546.2018.1437664

Ratts, M. J., Singh, A. A., Nassar-McMillan, S., Butler, K. S., & McCullogh, J. R. (2016). Multicultural and social justice counseling competencies: Guidelines for the counseling profession. *Journal of Multicultural Counseling and Development, 44*(1), 28–48. https://doi.org/10.1002/jmcd.12035

Packard, B. W., & Babineau, M. E. (2009). From drafter to engineer, doctor to nurse: An examination of career compromise as renegotiated by working-class adults over time. *Journal of Career Development, 35*(3), 207–227. https://doi.org/10.1177/0894845308327270

Parnell, M. K., Lease, S. H., & Green, M. L. (2012). Perceived career barriers for gay, lesbian, and bisexual individuals. *Journal of Career Development, 39*(3), 248–268. https://doi.org/10.1177/0894845310386730

Pew Research Center. (2021). Gender pay gap in U.S. held steady in 2020. https://www.pewresearch.org/fact-tank/2021/05/25/gender-pay-gap-facts/

Ponterotto, J. G., Rivera, L., & Sueyoshi, L. A. (2000). Effective techniques: The career-in-culture interview: A semi-structured protocol for the cross-cultural intake interview. *The Career Development Quarterly, 49*(1), 85–96. https://doi.org/10.1002/j.2161-0045.2000.tb00753.x

Sadler, P. M., Sonnert, G., Hazari, Z., & Tai, R. (2012). Stability and volatility of STEM career interest in high school: A gender study: Stability and volatility of STEM career choice. *Science Education, 96*(3), 411–427. https://doi.org/10.1002/sce.21007

Santiago, C. D., Kaltman, S., & Miranda, J. (2012). Poverty and mental health: How do low-income adults and children fare in psychotherapy? *Journal of Clinical Psychology: In Session, 69*(2), 115–126. https://doi.org/10.1002/jclp.21951

Savickas, M. L. (1993). Career counseling in the postmodern era. *Journal of Cognitive Psychotherapy, 7*(3), 205–215.

Schmidt, C. K., & Nilsson, J. E. (2006). The effects of simultaneous developmental processes: Factors relating to the career development of lesbian, gay, and bisexual youth. *The Career Development Quarterly, 55*(1), 22–37. https://doi.org/10.1002/j.2161-0045.2006.tb00002.x

Schmidt, C. K., Milers, J. R., & Welsh, A. C. (2011). Perceived discrimination and social support: The influences on career development and college adjustment of LGBT college students. *Journal of Career Development, 38*(4), 293–309. https://doi.org/10.1177/0894845310372615

Tate, K. A., Caperton, W., Kaiser, D., Pruitt, N. T., White, H., & Hall, E. (2015). An exploration of first-generation college students' career development beliefs and experiences. *Journal of Career Development*, 1–17. 10.1177/0894845314565025

Toossi, M., & Torpey, E. (2017). *Older workers: Labor force trends and career options.* U.S. Bureau of Labor Statistics.

TRIP. (2020). *Rural connections: Challenges and opportunities in America's heartland.*

U.S. Census Bureau (2018). *Personal income in 2018.* https://www.census.gov/data/tables/time-series/demo/income-poverty/cps-pinc/pinc-05.2018.html

U.S. Census Bureau. (2019). *Income and poverty in the United States, 2019.* https://www.census.gov/library/publications/2020/demo/p60-270.htm

U.S. Census Bureau. (2021). *Poverty thresholds.* https://www.census.gov/data/tables/time-series/demo/income-poverty/historical-poverty-thresholds.html

U.S. Department of Education, Office of Special Education and Rehabilitative Services. (2020). *The state vocational rehabilitation services program before and after enactment of the workforce innovation and opportunity act in 2014.*

Watkins, C. E., Hook, J. N., Owen, J., DeBlaere, C., Davis, D. E., & Van Tongeren, D. R. (2019). Multicultural orientation in psychotherapy supervision: Cultural humility, cultural comfort, and cultural opportunities. *American Journal of Psychotherapy, 72*(2) 38–46. https://doi.org/10.1176/appi.psychotherapy.20180040

Watts, L. L., Frame, M. C., Moffett, R. G., Van Hein, J. L., & Hein, M. (2015). The relationship between gender, perceived career barriers, and occupational aspirations. *Journal of Applied Social Psychology, 45*(1), 10–22. https://doi.org/10.1111/jasp.12271

Winderman, K., Martin, C. E., & Smith, N. G. (2018). Career indecision among LGB college students: The role of minority stress, perceived social support, and community affiliation. *Journal of Career Development, 45*(6), 536–550. https://doi.org/10.1177/0894845317722860

World Health Organization. (2021). Gender and health. https://www.who.int/health-topics/gender#tab=tab_1

CREDIT

PART II

Theory, Assessment, Resources in Career-Focused Counseling

A Word About Theory

Think back to the theories you learned in your introductory courses. When you were learning about the theories, your professor may have asked you to consider the ways in which you believe people learn, change, and grow. Perhaps, some of your peers mentioned that people change by trying out new behaviors and assessing the impact of these actions. Or maybe, some of your peers believed that insight into why we make the choices we do helped with personal growth. Others may have identified the need to change the way we think about our issues as the core to change. During these discussions, you hopefully began to realize that not all people view change and growth in the same way and that the various counseling theories you learned varied on the ways they helped people grow and learn. The same is true for career counseling theories—many exist, and they differ on their focus in helping people grow, change, and learn.

Theory is a lens through which we view a phenomenon. If you have ever used a camera that had filters or used the tools on your smartphone for altering a picture, you may intuitively understand this: the filter affects the perception of the image being viewed without changing the actual image. Nothing has changed about that which is observed, only the lens or filter through which it is viewed. Career counseling theories, or filters, are grounded in repeated study and lead to a set of connected principles that describe, explain, predict, and seek to control a phenomenon (i.e., the scientific method). In CFC, we seek to find lenses that focus our view of the career-related issues of our clients in order to more adequately describe them, explain them to the client, predict what may happen, and provide the client with a sense of control over what comes next. Often, our work in this area revolves around the decisions people make regarding their work or career (Luke, 2018).

We know that, for many of you, career counseling will not be the primary focus of your work with clients or students. You may envision yourself working as a middle school counselor, a substance abuse counselor, or a couples therapist. You may want to primarily work with emerging adults or people with significant and pervasive mental health concerns. You may see yourself working at a community college or local jail or domestic violence shelter. In all of these examples, most of your clients will either be planning for the world of work, engaging in the world of work, trying to reenter the world of work, or reducing their time spent in the world of work. Therefore, you need a frame or lens for how to help address career-focused issues that arise. You also need to understand how work impacts a person's life and how to help your clients consider that impact in their own lives.

These next chapters will provide an overview of several career counseling theories that may be helpful. Each view development and engagement differently—just like the many counseling theories you learned about in your other courses. Some focus on background influences, others focus on dysfunctional thinking or underlying feelings, and still others focus on systemic influences or personal behaviors. As you learned about these theories, you may have felt drawn to one or another because they matched your worldview perspective on how people learn, change, and grow. You chose one or more theories to use in your own work because they best helped you facilitate your counseling sessions and provide a frame of reference for your work with clients.

Career counseling theories can be used as a primary theoretical orientation for those who want to focus on career-related concerns. They can also serve as supplementary theories for all counselors. It is vital for counselors to understand how to address career-focused issues with their clients and to use empirically-supported interventions in their work. If you plan to be a career counselor, you will want to read through each chapter carefully and consider how well the theory matches your beliefs about how people grow and change.

For the many of you who do not plan to focus solely on career counseling, you will still need to understand these theories. As you read through the next several chapters, consider how each theory complements your primary theoretical orientation. Ask yourself the following questions:

- What is my primary theoretical orientation? Why am I drawn to this theory?
- Does the career counseling theory fit with my beliefs about how people learn and grow?
- Does the career counseling theory fit with my beliefs about the underlying focus needed for growth?
    - Does my primary counseling theoretical orientation focus on background, feelings, thoughts, behaviors, and/or systems?
    - Does this career counseling theory match or complement the focus of my primary approach?

Once you identify a theory that fits within your view of how people change and grow, then you can include it in your work with clients. Identifying a theory that is consistent with your beliefs will help you flow smoothly from theory to theory and intervention to intervention. Career is a critical part of your clients' lives and needs to be addressed. The theories that follow provide ways to do this work, but it is up to you to identify the theory that best fits how you engage with clients.

Career Theory	Theorist	Counseling Theory	Theorist
Life-span, life-space	Super	• Individual psychology • Brief psychodynamic	• Adler • Various
Person–environment	Holland	• Solution-focused • Reality	• De Shazer and Berg • Glasser and Wubbolding
Social cognitive career theory	Lent, Brown, and Hackett	• Social cognitive • Ecological • REBT • ACT	• Bandura • Bronfenbrenner • Ellis • Hayes

continued ...

Career Theory	Theorist	Counseling Theory	Theorist
Cognitive information processing	Peterson et al.	• Cognitive behavior therapy	• Beck
Narrative/career construction	Savickas	• Narrative • Feminist • Existential	• Epston and White • Various • Frankl and Yalom
Happenstance learning theory	Krumboltz	• Solution-focused • CBT • Motivational interviewing	• De Shaver and Berg • Beck • Miller and Rollnick

CHAPTER 4

A Primer on Assessment and Resources in CFC

CHAPTER GOALS

- Identify valid sources of information about career-focused topics.
- Understand the ways in which assessment can be used in career-focused counseling.
- Learn how to effectively include assessment in career-focused counseling.

REFLECTION ACTIVITIES AND QUESTIONS

1. Turn to a partner, and discuss your experience taking the SAT or ACT. Share whether you felt your scores, and the test itself, accurately reflected your ability to do well in college. Identify your specific feelings associated with taking the test; were they mostly positive or negative? Why do you think you felt that way?
2. Now think about your journey to selecting your college major. How did you make your choice? To whom did you turn for help? What got in the way of making the decision? What do you wish you had done differently or known prior to deciding?

Introduction

What comes to mind when you hear the word assessment? Do you have a positive, negative, or neutral reaction? Many counseling students dread the idea of an assessment, especially a formal one. They think of words such as impersonal, statistics, norms, and find these concepts to be alienating or unwelcoming. Others find comfort in assessment and think of words such as answers, explanations, and comparisons. Still others find themselves generally accepting of but not excited about assessment, recognizing both their value and limitations.

Many counseling students assume that career counseling is about using formal assessments to identify client traits and match these with possible careers. While this may be a component of career counseling today, it will likely not be a primary focus in your work unless you become a career counseling professional. Instead, you may need to use formal career instruments sparingly but may more often use informal assessments or just good old-fashioned counseling skills to help your clients. This chapter will help you understand what assessments are available and how you might use them to address specific client needs. Then, we will describe some strong online tools that can help with locating helpful career-related information.

Ethical Use of Assessments

As mentioned in previous chapters, the *ACA Code of Ethics* can be used to ensure appropriate practices in counseling. It includes information about ethical strategies when using assessments. Counselors using career-related assessments should only use measures that are valid and reliable and in which they have been trained in appropriate use. Counselors should not use assessments without proper training, and career-related decisions should not be solely based on test results but rather a holistic understanding of the client. Clients should be informed of the purpose of each assessment and understand how the assessment will be used in counseling. Assessments should be reviewed for cultural appropriateness and normed on groups similar to those of the specific client. Lastly, counselors should provide interpretation of all results and answer questions as needed (ACA, 2014).

Cultural and Developmental Appropriateness

Assessments need to be considered for their cultural and developmental appropriateness. Counselors can explore the norming groups for formal assessments to better understand if the assessment is appropriate for specific populations. The Association for Assessment and Research in Counseling (AARC) produced the Multicultural Assessment Standards (AARC, 2012) to help ensure that counselors engage in best practices when selecting culturally-sensitive assessments for use with clients. AARC states that counselors should understand how the assessment was developed, discover its past use with diverse populations, and understand the limits of assessments based on cultural sensitivity. Additionally, interpretation should be holistic, embed an understanding of cultural identities, be explained at an appropriate developmental level, and include systemic and environmental factors that impact the client.

Types of Assessments

Assessment can be either qualitative or quantitative in nature. In this section, we briefly describe some of the popular quantitative assessments used in career-related counseling. However, we also recognize that many of you will lack access to these assessments, as many have a cost associated with them. Therefore, we more deeply describe qualitative assessments that can be used free of charge. For a detailed review of career assessments, we encourage you to read *A Comprehensive Guide to Career Assessment* by Kevin B. Stoltz and Susan R. Barclay (2019).

TAKE A MINUTE

Before you read about many of the career-related assessments available to you, consider the role that the career domain of life plays in your life, especially compared to other areas. Because this text is first and foremost about counseling, it is important to first assess the life domains of our students or clients and how career is situated relative to others. Use the following link to see how you rate career and other domains on the wheel of life: https://wheeloflife.noomii.com/.

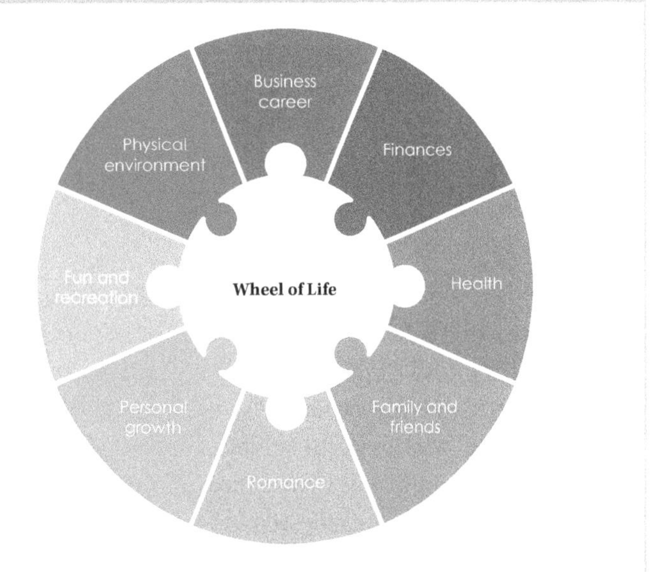

FIGURE 4.1. Wheel of Life

Career Interests

SELF-DIRECTED SEARCH

Developed by John Holland and based on his theory, the SDS was first created in 1970 and last revised in 2017. It assesses career interests and preferred work environments (Luke & Budesa, 2019). Anyone can purchase, take, and use the SDS without specialized training; in fact, no counselor is required, as its purpose is to be self-directed. It can be used for ages 11 and up and was normed on a group of nearly 2,000 people well-matched with the U.S. population (Sampson et al., 2020).

STRONG INTEREST INVENTORY

Also based on Holland's theory, the SII was first developed in 1927 and has undergone multiple revisions. It has the same purpose as the SDS: to understand career interests and preferred work environments. The SII was normed on over 2,000 adults representative of U.S. racial and ethnic demographics. It provides a RIASEC code, which helps clients understand their career-related interests and personality, followed by information on the compatibility of one's code to 260 different occupations. Counselors must be trained in assessment practices and on the Holland codes prior to using the SII. Details on interpreting the SII can be found in Chapter 6.

O*NET INTEREST PROFILER

Found on the O*NET website (see https://www.mynextmove.org/explore/ip), this is a free interest inventory designed for use with high school students and older. Based on Holland's theory, the survey has 60 questions about work activities that results in interest areas that can connect to various occupations on the O*NET website (described later in this chapter). The profiler is also available in Spanish (see https://www.miproximopaso.org/explore/ip).

Ability, Aptitude, Personality

ASVAB

The Armed Services Vocational Aptitude Battery (ASVAB) Career Exploration system was developed by the U.S. Department of Defense and is primarily used by military recruiters but useful for all high school and college students. This completely free assessment for grades 10+ measures aptitude for success in various career areas. It includes eight areas of aptitude, ranging from general science to electronics information to paragraph comprehension as well as an optional career interest inventory. Military recruiters will provide a free post-test interpretation if requested (ASVAB, 2020).

ACT

The American College Test (ACT) is a career and college readiness assessment often used for college entrance. It can also be used to assess baseline achievement for high school seniors. The ACT has four sections—English, reading, math, and science—and scores range from 1–36 for each section, with higher scores indicating higher levels of readiness. Test items are based on a national curriculum survey and are differentiated, so some are more difficult than others (ACT, 2020).

SAT

The Scholastic Aptitude Test (SAT) also serves as a career and college readiness test. Used mostly with high school students, it has two sections: math and evidence-based reading and writing. Scores range from 200–800 for each section, with a total score range of 400–1600. It was recently redesigned to include more relevant questions based in real-world situations (College Board, 2017).

MYERS–BRIGGS TYPE INDICATOR

The Myers–Briggs Type Indicator (MBTI) is a personality inventory that is often used in career counseling. Based on four preference continuums, the MBTI offers a total of 16 different personality types that can be aligned to various careers; career fit is based on the degree of match between a personality type and a work environment.

Career-Related Beliefs

CAREER DECISION SELF-EFFICACY SCALE

The Career Decision Self-Efficacy Scale (CDSE) was developed by Betz and Taylor in 1993 and most recently revised in 2012. Two forms exist: the full-scale version with 50 items and the short-form (SF) with 25 items. Both include five scales: self-appraisal, occupational information, goal selection, planning, and problem solving. The overall scale measures beliefs a person has about their ability to successfully complete career decision-making tasks. Counselors can use the results to better understand a client's decision-making confidence. The assessment may be purchased for use with clients (see www.mindgarden.com).

CAREER THOUGHTS INVENTORY

Developed by Sampson et al. (1999), the Career Thoughts Inventory (CTI) is a survey that helps identify people who might benefit from career counseling. It also helps in increased understanding of career needs. The CTI has three subscales—decision-making confusion, commitment anxiety, and external conflict—that combine to give a total score indicator of negative thinking related to career decision-making. Appropriate for clients ages 17+, it was normed and validated on a large group of culturally diverse adolescents and adults. Counselors must have graduate-level training and familiarity with the CTI and its underlying theoretical foundation prior to use.

MY VOCATIONAL SITUATION

This free assessment was first developed by Holland and colleagues in 1980 and has gone through several revisions. It helps with identifying challenges in career decision-making. The My Vocational Situation (MVS) test has three scales that measure vocational identity, occupational information, and career barriers. Counselors can use the assessment with middle schoolers though adults, and it was normed on a variety of ages and with people from diverse backgrounds.

Constructivist and Qualitative Assessments

CAREER CONSTRUCTION INTERVIEW

Described in detail in Chapter 9, the Career Construction Interview (CCI) was developed by Savickas and Hartung (2012) to help elicit narratives about meaning-making related to career development. While primarily used in career construction theory, it can be easily adapted as a helpful tool with many clients.

CAREER GENOGRAM

Many counselors use genograms to better understand multigenerational relationships, messages, and norms. A typical genogram includes a tree diagram of three family generations, with

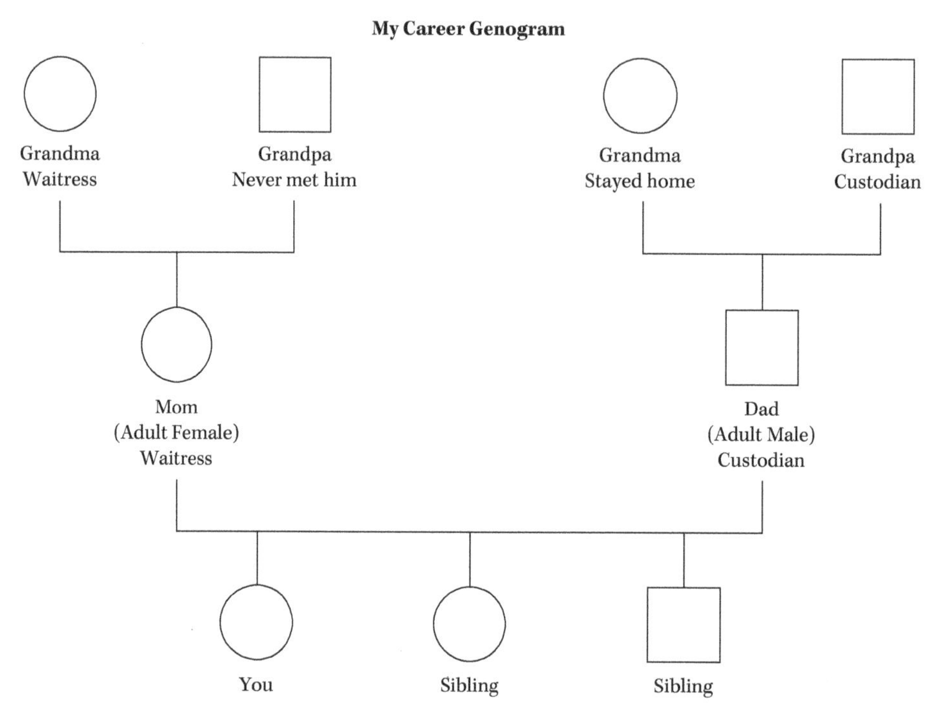

FIGURE 4.2. Sample Career Genogram

marriages, children, deaths, divorces, and relationship status all included. A career genogram still includes three family generations, but the focus is on careers held by family members and family influences on a client's career development (Bakshi & Satish, 2015). Questions about work values, beliefs about education, role stereotypes, and multigenerational career messages can help elicit stories about career beliefs. Given the strong influence of family of origin on career development (Whiston & Keller, 2004), career genograms can be helpful in providing a visual representation of this influence for clients. Awareness of these influences can help empower clients to make decisions about what messages they believe and which they want to reject.

Cleo is a fifth-grade student who you see every other week during your classroom guidance lessons. The focus of this month's lessons is career awareness and exploration, and you have asked all of your students to complete a simple career genogram before you visit their class. There are spaces for grandparents, parents or adult caregivers, and siblings, plus a space for up to three other important family members. For each, the students are asked to find out the career of the person and their education level. In class, you ask students to share one thing they learned from completing the genogram. Cleo says she learned that her family doesn't care about school and hates their jobs. After the guidance lesson, you meet with Cleo individually to talk about the activity. Cleo explains that only one family member graduated from high school, and everyone works either at a restaurant or cleans at the hospital. She further shares that no one cares what she does for a career and that she assumes she will just work at a restaurant too.

Reflection Questions

1. How was the career genogram helpful in learning about Cleo's understanding of work?
2. What might you do to help Cleo revise her negative understanding of career and jobs in her family?

CAREER LIFELINE

A lifeline also helps with understanding influences on career development, but its focus is on events and relationships connected to times of transition. Counselors ask clients to create a lifeline of their life, starting at birth and going through until present day. On the lifeline, clients add important experiences in their life that impacted them in some way (Fritz & Van Zyl, 2015). Clients do not need to focus on career-related issues, as meaning-making will occur regardless of the chosen experiences. Counselors ask clients to identify each event, note the important people associated with the event, and list the emotions experienced during the event. Typically, listed events include times of transition, change, stress, or excitement. They represent the important times in clients' lives, and through their stories about each event, counselors can help clients identify themes and meanings related to their current career issue.

The following is a sample lifeline: Todd is in required mental health counseling following his second time in rehab for addiction to painkillers. He must find employment as part of his rehab program but expresses uncertainty and fear related to working again. In the lifeline below, Todd identifies six events that have strongly impacted him, as shown in Figure 4.3.

Reflection Questions

1. What themes do you notice from Todd's lifeline? Consider his titles (in quotations) and feelings associated with each event.

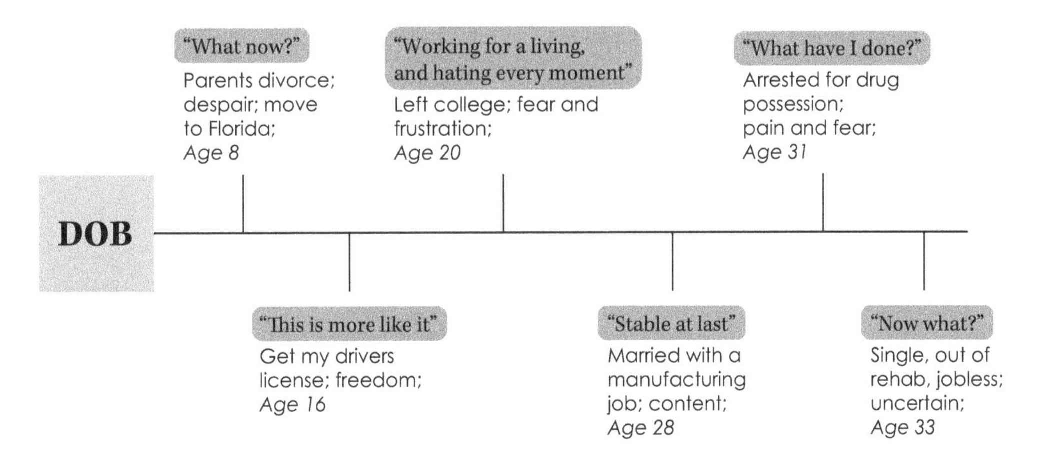

FIGURE 4.3. Lifeline

2. How might you identify the impact of cultural identities related to these events?
3. What are three ways you might help Todd process his feelings and thoughts regarding employment?

CAREER LIFE ROLE CIRCLES

Developed by Brott (2005), a life role circles assessment is an activity typically completed early in narrative career counseling, although it can be used with a variety of clients. Counselor and client discuss the concept of life roles or the various responsibilities we hold at different life stages, such as parent, child, partner, worker, friend, or volunteer. Brott (2005) suggested helping clients identify their various life roles and then having them draw circles representing both the time spent in each role and its perceived importance. The client then uses a second sheet of paper to redraw their life role circles to represent their future vision and hopes for these different roles. Counselors can use the two pictures to elicit stories about each role, the relationships between and across roles and role conflicts. Themes are then identified and underlying meanings are revisited and restructured to help clients become more satisfied with their involvement in these life roles (Brott, 2005).

Sample Life Role Circles

Candace is a student at the local community college. She attends school part-time and works full-time at two different jobs. She is considering leaving school because she feels she will never be able to successfully finish her business degree, as she finds school unwelcoming and very difficult. One of her employers has offered her a full-time position as an assistant manager, but she doesn't really enjoy the job, so she is uncertain about her next steps. She also feels that she never gets to just relax or do things for fun, and since she still lives at home, most of her free time is spent caring for her younger siblings. She completes the life role circles with the size of the circle representing the time she feels like she spends on each role (see Figure 4.4). When asked about placement of each circle, she says she wishes she could spend less time in the daughter role because it just feels like another job, and that the other roles are all connected to one another. Candace wishes she "could spend time with friends, like discovering myself, and not be so pressured to go, go, go and become an adult. I thought school would be fun, but it is really just another task in my day."

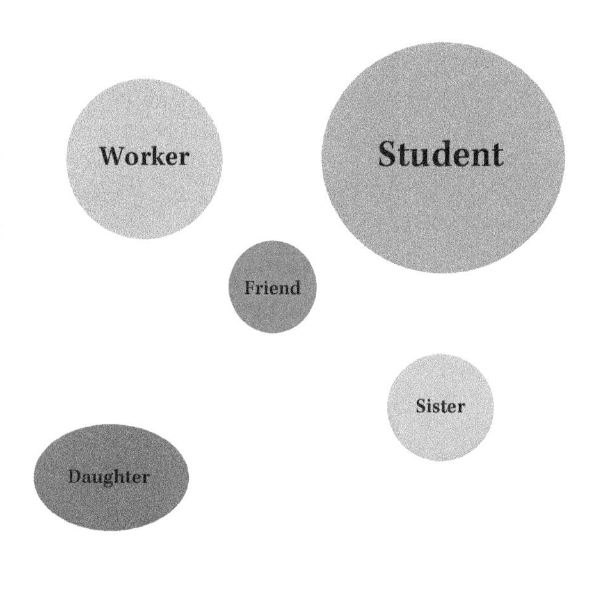

FIGURE 4.4. Life Role Circles

Reflection Questions

1. How do the circles help you in understanding Candace?
2. What other questions or probes do you have for Candace?
3. What has Candace revealed about her identities?

VALUES CARD SORT

Card sorts are often used in career counseling and can be purchased, designed by the counselor, or found online. These qualitative assessments are not standardized and are used to visually represent a client's views about their work-related values (Osborn & Bethell, 2009). Card sorts designed by counselors can be tailored to specific cultural or developmental groups if desired (Osborn & Bethell, 2009). In all cases, a packet of "cards" are given to the client and sorted into different piles, such as not at all important, somewhat important, and very important. A sample of values that can be used to create a values card sort can be found in Table 4.1.

Sample Values Card Sort

Abdul is a middle-aged father of four children, married to his high school girlfriend, Haruko. They live in a large, urban city that is culturally diverse and have a group of diverse friends. Now that their children are grown, Haruko has decided to return to her previous career in medical research and has been offered the opportunity to work at a prestigious company. However, the company headquarters are located in a small, rural community about 10 hours from where they live. Abdul wants to support his wife but is unsure about moving and knows it will require him to find new employment. He comes to counseling for help.

In the session, Abdul notes that he wants to continue his job in computer software design and acknowledges that there are some career opportunities near where they plan to move. He explains that he has worked at the same company for the past 15 years and does not know what he wants in a new organization. His counselor suggests a values card sort to identify characteristics of importance for Abdul, and he agrees. Abdul identifies these top values: community, creativity, intellectual stimulation, contribution, and challenge. Through discussion, Abdul shares that he wants a work environment where his skills will be recognized and valued and where people get along and support each other. He says these are the reasons he is sad to leave his current job, noting that he enjoys talking with his colleagues and feels appreciated by them. His counselor and he also discuss Abdul's concerns about leaving his diverse community and moving to a small town; together they research career opportunities that meet his values, while also offering a diverse workspace. Eventually, Abdul finds a job where he can work remotely part of the time and then travel several times a month to the company's main offices in a large, more diverse city. Counseling ends as Abdul and Haruko move to begin the next phase of their lives.

TABLE 4.1 LIST OF VALUES AND THEIR DEFINITIONS

Achievement	feelings of accomplishment
Advancement	opportunities to move up professionally
Adventure	new and exciting experiences
Altruism	helping others
Challenge	demand for the best use of your abilities
Collaboration	working with others
Community	kinship and unity at the workplace
Constancy	systematized job; duties clear and unchanging
Contribution	work essential to success of organization
Creativity	opportunities for innovation
Financial Stability	dependable income; pay does not fluctuate
Freedom	autonomy to develop own ideas and work independently
Friendship	job provides opportunities to make friends
Influence	persuasion of others
Intellectual stimulation	workplace provides scholarly challenges
Knowledge	opportunity for learning
Leadership	decision-making and management
Location	place of work is stable
Mobility	travel and opportunities to relocate
Personal Development	opportunities for growth as a person
Personal Time	job leaves time for pursuits outside of work
Popularity	to be well liked by others
Risk	possibility for taking chances
Security	job is not likely to be eliminated
Spirituality	job relates to spiritual beliefs; moral fulfillment
Status	importance in the organization; prestige
Time Freedom	flexible schedule
Variety	job involves numerous responsibilities; not same day to day
Wealth	financial reward

Accessing and Utilizing Career Information and Resources

Another valuable way to help clients with career-related concerns is through accessing online material. The internet is filled with career-related resources—some good and some less so. Identifying quality resources is vital for helping clients. But how do you find quality sources of information? One option is to review the website to better understand its merits and limitations. As you visit a career-related website, you can ask yourself the following questions:

1. Who is the website owner? What is their motivation for offering the information on the site?
2. What is the purpose of the site?
3. Who is the target audience, and what type of client might benefit from the site?
4. What career-related need does the website fill?
5. How is the overall visual appearance and ease of navigation? Can you easily find what you need?
6. How well does the site attend to cultural diversity? Does the site appear to value diverse people and worldviews?
7. What are the primary strengths and weaknesses of the site?

Answering these questions will help you decide if the site may be helpful in your work with clients. For example, some sites might work well for adult clients but be less helpful for younger clients. Or a site might look appealing but have multiple pop-up ads that negatively affect the ease of use. Also, some sites might be made specifically for specific cultural groups while others may be more general or generic.

Another option is to find sites that have been created by or reviewed by reliable sources. Below is a list of sites that were developed by reliable sources and offer quality career-focused information. Not all sites work for all types of clients, but within this list, you should be able to find a number of helpful resources.

1. Government websites: Websites ending in .gov are often quite helpful for career-related information.
   a. **www.studentaid.gov**: This website provides information about federal student aid. Information is available for students, parents, and counselors on how to access and understand federal loans and grants.
   b. **www.bls.gov**: The U.S. Bureau of Labor Statistics website offers a wealth of job-related information, including job statistics, economic reports, and pay and benefits information.
      i. **https://www.bls.gov/ooh/**: Within the BLS website is the *Occupational Outlook Handbook*. This site provides information about different occupations, such as work tasks, environment, preparation, pay, and outlook.
   c. **https://www.dol.gov/agencies/odep/topics**: The Office of Disability Employment Policy within the U.S. Department of Labor provides quality information about employment for people with disabilities.
   d. **https://www.usa.gov/**: This site provides a wealth of information on government services, making it a great resource for a wide range of topics. There are several sections specific to career development.

i. **https://www.usa.gov/jobs-and-unemployment**: This section of the USA.gov website offers information on government-related services related to jobs and unemployment. Especially helpful is the section on labor laws, retirement, and unemployment.
ii. **https://www.usa.gov/education**: In this section of USA.gov, you can find information about financial aid and attending college. Information on education benefits for service members and veterans and people with disabilities is also included.

e. **https://www.careeronestop.org/**: Career OneStop is sponsored by the U.S. Department of Labor and offers a comprehensive list of career exploration and job search tools. The site includes job exploration self-assessments, career information and videos, job preparation materials, and resources for diverse populations.
f. **https://nces.ed.gov/**: The National Center for Education Statistics serves as a federally-funded site for data related to educational programming and services.
g. **https://nces.ed.gov/collegenavigator/**: Included in this site is the College Navigator, a college search engine.
h. **https://www.apprenticeship.gov/career-seekers**: This site provides information on hands-on career training or apprenticeship in such areas as construction, welding, and animal care.
i. **https://nationalreentryresourcecenter.org/**: Funded and administered by the U.S. Department of Justice's Bureau of Justice Assistance (BJA), the National Reentry Resource Center (NRRC) is the nation's primary source of information and guidance in reentry.
j. **https://www.benefits.va.gov/vocrehab/**: Veterans may receive these services to help with job training, employment accommodations, resume development, and job seeking skills coaching.
k. **https://www.ssa.gov/work/**: A free and voluntary program that can help Social Security beneficiaries go to work, get a good job that may lead to a career, and become financially independent, all while they keep their Medicare or Medicaid. Individuals who receive Social Security benefits because of a disability and are ages 18 through 64 probably already qualify for the program.

2. **https://www.ncda.org/aws/NCDA/pt/sp/resources**: The National Career Development Association is a division of the American Counseling Association specializing in career counseling and education. The resources tab offers a list of websites reviewed by their technology committee. Topics include general information, special populations (including LGBTQ+, older workers, youth, veterans, and ex-offenders, and others), and job search.
3. Information on assessment-related websites
   a. **www.act.org**: In addition to test-prep information, the ACT website offers content on college and career planning, such as selecting a college, preparing for college fairs, and succeeding in high school.

   b. **www.collegeboard.org**: The home to the PSAT, SAT, and AP tests, College Board also offers information about planning for life after high school. The "Big Future" page (https://bigfuture.collegeboard.org/) includes a college search engine, a career finder, and various other sources for diverse students.
   c. **https://www.onetonline.org/**: Created in collaboration with the U.S. Department of Labor, O*Net provides information on occupations that can be searched via job name, interests, or job activities. O*Net also includes a page specifically for veterans.
4. Well-known career networking and search engine sites
   a. **www.monster.com**: Primarily a job-search engine for both employers and job seekers, Monster also has information about creating resumes and cover letters, preparing for job interviews, and selecting a job.
   b. **www.indeed.com**: Indeed helps connect job seekers with employers through its comprehensive search engine. Resources on job preparation are also available.
   c. **www.linkedin.com**: The goal of LinkedIn is to help create an online professional network. Members can grow their network by inviting other members to connect or by joining online groups with similar shared interests. Job postings and events are also available.
5. Other sites of interest
   a. **https://www.aarp.org/work/**: Focused on the unique needs of people over age 50, AARP offers helpful information on issues such as retirement planning, job reentry, ageism, and general job searching for older adults.
   b. **www.idealist.org/en/**: Idealist offers career-related resources for those interested in advancing dignity and equity in the workplace. Internships, volunteer options, jobs, organizations, and graduate school opportunities are easily searchable by location or interest area.
   c. **https://employdiversity.com**: Employ Diversity offers professionals with diverse identities helpful information about career development and employment. All services are tailored to be helpful for people from diverse backgrounds.
   d. **www.recruitmilitary.com**: Veterans and their families can use this site to find potential employers and educational resources.
   e. **https://careerwise.minnstate.edu/exoffenders/index.html**: Advice can be accessed from Minnesota State CAREERwise on assessing yourself, exploring careers, creating a plan & setting goals, expanding skills, finding a job, and managing a career.
   f. **https://askjan.org/index.cfm**: JAN's Searchable Online Accommodation Resource (SOAR) system is designed to let users explore various accommodation options for people with disabilities in work and educational settings
   g. **https://ccresourcecenter.org/state-restoration-profiles/50-state-comparison-comparison-of-criminal-records-in-licensing-and-employment/**: This project provides a 50-state comparison of criminal record in employment and licensing with links to analysis and legal citations.
   h. **https://goodjobsdata.org/**: A project from The Georgetown Center that provides a wealth of information about jobs that do not require a bachelor's degree.

Why It Matters

For counselors who do not specialize in career counseling, it may seem that knowing about assessments and online resources specifically for career-related issues is unnecessary. However, clients often bring up career concerns while talking about the issues in their lives. Rather than referring them to a career counselor, you can use the information in this and the next chapter to serve their needs. You may only need the information occasionally, but it is important to know how to find what you need when you need it.

Let's consider a few examples:

1. Carl is in counseling as part of his alternative sentencing plan; he must complete community service and counseling in order to avoid active jail time for attempted robbery. The judge has also required Carl to find full-time employment within six months.
2. Kelly is a 17-year old in foster care. She is part of your caseload and your work has mostly focused on her trauma history. Now, however, you have shifted to focus on her upcoming transition out of the foster care system and Kelly has expressed fear about what she will do without the state-provided resources.
3. Juan has recently received his honorable discharge from the Army after 10 years of service. He completed his associate's degree during his enlistment, and now needs to decide what he will do now that he is no longer active in the military.
4. Bailey is a student at the community college where you work. She has returned to school after three years of working full-time as a waitress and is hoping to find a more secure career path that will provide health insurance for her and her son, who has asthma.

In each of these cases, the client needs resources, support, and career-focused counseling. Review the assessments and websites listed in this chapter, and identify which ones might be helpful for each client. How might you use them if you were the counselor?

Take Away and Use Today

This chapter offers a wealth of resources designed to help counselors and clients find quality career-related information and assessments. It is not necessary to memorize all of the information, but you do need to be able to find information when clients ask for it. We recommend bookmarking this chapter and making it readily available when you provide counseling services. It will save you time in the long run.

References

ACT. (2020). *The ACT technical manual*. https://www.act.org/content/dam/act/unsecured/documents/ACT_Technical_Manual.pdf

Association for Assessment and Research in Counseling. (2012). *Standards for multicultural assessment* (4th ed.).

American Counseling Association. (2014). *2014 ACA Code of Ethics.* https://www.counseling.org/resources/aca-code-of-ethics.pdf

ASVAB. (2020). *ASVAB career exploration program overview.*

Bakshi, A. J., & Satish V. (2015). Qualitative career assessment using a genogram. In: M. McMahon & M. Watson (Eds.), *Career assessment.* SensePublishers. https://doi.org/10.1007/978-94-6300-034-5_8

Betz, N. E., & Taylor, K. M. (2012). *The career decision self-efficacy scale.* Mind Garden. https://www.mindgarden.com/79-career-decision-self-efficacy-scal

Brott, P. E. (2005). A constructivist look at life roles. *The Career Development Quarterly, 54*(2), 138–149. https://doi.org/10.1002/j.2161-0045.2005.tb00146.x

College Board. (2017). *SAT suite of assessment technical manua*l. https://collegereadiness.collegeboard.org/pdf/sat-suite-assessments-technical-manual.pdf

Fritz, E., Zyl, G.V. (2015). Lifelines. In: M. McMahon & M. Watson (Eds.), *Career Assessment.* SensePublishers. https://doi.org/10.1007/978-94-6300-034-5_10

Luke, C. & Budesa, Z. (2019). *The self-directed search.* In K. Stoltz and S. Barclay (eds.) A comprehensive guide to career assessment (7th ed., pp. 235–244). National Career Development Association.

Mi Próximo Paso. (n.d.). *Perfil de intereses O*NET en mi próximo paso.* https://www.miproximopaso.org/explore/ip

My Next Move. (n.d.). O*NET interest profiler at my next move. https://www.mynextmove.org/explore/ip

Osborn, D. S., & Bethell, D. S. (2009). Using card sorts in career assessment. *Career Planning and Adult Development Journal, 25*(4), 101.

Sampson, J. P., Peterson, G. W., Lenz, J. G., Reardon, R. C., & Saunders, D. E. (1999). *The use and development of the career thoughts inventory.* ERIC. https://eric.ed.gov/?id=ED447362

Sampson, J. P., Peterson, G. W., Lenz, J. G., Reardon, R. C., & Saunders, D. E. (2020). *The career thoughts inventory.* PAR. https://www.parinc.com/Products/Pkey/73

Savickas, M. L., & Hartung, P. J. (2012). The career construction interview. Vocopher. http://vocopher.com/

Stoltz, K. B., & Barclay, S. R. (Eds.). (2019). *A comprehensive guide to career assessment* (7th ed.). National Career Development Association.

Whiston, S. C. & Keller, B. K. (2004). The influences of the family of origin on career development: A review and analysis. *The Counseling Psychologist, 32*(4), 493–568. https://doi.org/10.1177/0011000004265660

CREDITS

Fig. 4.1: Adapted from source: https://coachcampus.com/resources/coaching-101/the-wheel-of-life/.

Fig. 4.1a: Copyright © 2013 Depositphotos/levente.

CHAPTER 5

Career-Focused Counseling Nuts and Bolts

Chad Luke, Anita Neuer-Colburn, and Melinda Gibbons

CHAPTER GOALS

- Develop skills for managing one's own career.
- Equip readers to help clients with job-seeking skills.
- Reflect on the relationship between career management and wellness/wellbeing.

OPENING VIGNETTES

LaKeisha and a Master's Degree in Counseling

LaKeisha is a counseling student entering her second year of her program. She is applying for an internship and must produce a copy of her résumé. The last time she drafted a resume was for a technical writing course in her undergraduate program and has not had to update it since—much less use it. The process has created some anxiety for her, as she wonders if it will be "good enough" to secure a place in internship at a desirable site. It has also activated her concerns over finding a job in the future and whether she has or will have sufficient experience to obtain a good job—one that is desirable and rewarding. She recalls the job search process when she graduated with her bachelor's degree, resulting in working for a year in a job that was low-paying and unsatisfying, even though it was somewhat related to her major. Up to this point, she has assumed, implicitly, that it will just work out. She decides to bring this up with her counselor at the campus clinic (personal counseling is an expectation of students in her counseling program).

Monte and Working with LaKeisha in a Campus Clinic

Monte is a licensed professional counselor with three years of professional counseling experience. Like many graduates, his counseling program included a required course in career development and counseling. Also, like many students, Monte was not particularly interested in taking the course, stating that he was interested in clinical mental health, not career counseling. Yet, as his experience has shown, a large percentage of clients he sees at the university counseling center have career-focused concerns that intertwine with other presenting concerns. In Monte's case, the center for career development is in the same building as the counseling center, so he regularly refers any career issues that crop up to that office. Recently, however, due to program and staffing changes, Monte has been asked by his supervisor to retain clients with explicit career-related concerns rather than referring them out. As Monte reviews his schedule for the week, he notes that his intake for Tuesday is LaKeisha, who is seeking resume and career help. Monte feels a sense of uncertainty about this appointment and is unsure where to begin.

REFLECTION ACTIVITIES AND QUESTIONS

- Thinking back on the first time or the most recent time you revised your resume, what were some of the thoughts and feelings you experienced?
- Where or how did you learn to write a résumé?
- How successful (or not) were you in the process?
- What information or insights do you wish you had at the time?

Introduction

Vocation and avocation are integral parts of life, so it is almost impossible for any clinical mental health or school counselor not to end up addressing some kind of career-related issue with every client and student they serve. One of the most daunting components of addressing work-related issues is the prospect of helping a client or student find a job. As discussed previously and throughout this book, we do not view career-focused counseling as simply job procurement but acknowledge that this topic is likely to arise with some clients. Despite training in career counseling, counselors and counselors-in-training may have limited experience and mentoring in their own career development and job search skills (Hodges & Connelly, 2010). This can unduly, if understandably, affect counselor decision-making in facilitating their client's or student's job search skills.

The purpose of this chapter is to describe the mechanics of job search skills as well as to explain the process of implementing job search skills. Regardless of your own approach or theoretical orientation to providing counseling to address career-focused concerns, you will need to be prepared to help your clients with basic job seeking skills. In this chapter, we will address strategies for assisting clients and students with job seeking skills and will also discuss skills for addressing your own career management. Throughout, we will highlight the connection between career management and mental health issues. Career-focused needs apply to you as a counselor as well as to the clients you will work with. When deciding about a career direction, looking for a job, wondering about making a change, or dealing with job loss, counselors will need to be attuned to their own and their clients' coping skills, self-efficacy, support systems, and propensity for depression or anxiety.

Before we get into the steps Monte might use to work with LaKeisha, we want to paint a picture for you of an oft-overlooked component of career-focused counseling. This chapter will not prepare you to become an expert on résumé writing or cover letter development, but it will help you understand how to work with clients who might need these skills. Helping clients with the job search process can be empowering and inspire hope. It can improve mood and negative self-image when done well. It can also introduce discussions of systemic oppression, networking challenges, stress-related concerns, or even prior trauma experiences. So rather than referring a client to a career counselor or just suggesting an online resume template, take the time to talk through their job search challenges, as this may be a window into underlying client concerns.

Returning to LaKeisha's actual presenting concern, she needs a resume. Monte is not an expert resume developer, any more than he is a personal trainer, and it is not necessary for him to try to become one. But that is OK because we argue that Monte does not need to be an expert on resumes to assist LaKeisha with hers. Here's why. First, there are innumerable resources online for writing a resume, so content is not the issue. In fact, we must ask ourselves: If the information is so readily available, why is LaKeisha seeking Monte's help with her résumé? This is the crux of career-focused counseling. It is not about being a "career expert" for career-related issues any more than treating depression in counseling requires a "depression expert." What is that, anyway? This understanding is fundamental to the work of counseling and career-focused counseling. Counselors often can see the path to health and wellness for their students or clients, but their role is to walk with them through the process, so they own the process for themselves.

Two preliminary issues are important to understanding before using the content in this chapter. The first is whether the struggle the student or client brings to you is the result of a skills deficit. Is LaKeisha struggling to write her résumé because she has not cultivated the skill of professional communication, of which résumé writing is one? When the counselor is certain that the issue is a skill-based deficit, then counseling can certainly move more quickly toward identifying resources and building the tools needed to complete tasks. More often, however, the issue is less about a skill, per se, and more about some cognitive, emotional, behavioral, or social barrier that limits the implementation of a skill or obtaining that skill. As a counseling student, is it likely that LaKeisha would not know how to write a resume or to find the resources needed to be able to write one? If it is not a skills deficit for her, then what is it? The answer begins to unfold in the opening vignette section. LaKeisha is anxious that what she puts on that résumé will be insufficient to allow her to secure a desirable internship site. This can lead to doubts about her career path and whether she is wasting time or money in a counseling program. If Monte had referred her to a career adviser for resume help, or if he had truncated the session by giving her resume advice, she may not have been able to receive the level of help she was seeking but struggled to ask for.

Unfortunately, there is precious little research or scholarly writing on the use of career-focused presenting concerns in the counseling literature. In our experience, career-focused concerns have led to some of the richest counseling experiences we have ever had. The challenge is to invest enough time and attention into creating several go-to resources for students or clients, while also accepting that career-focused counseling is real counseling and that jumping to referral or resources deprives both the student or client and the counselor of a meaningful interaction. The following sections are intended to support you in assembling your own nuts-and-bolts resources, while also guiding your thinking in how these features can be used therapeutically and not just informationally.

Our colleague, Kertesha Riley, worked in a college career center for many years and helped countless students with their job search process. She created the 3 Cs of Career Readiness: *career documents, creating connections, and communicating your value* (personal communication, 2021). Career documents include creating your résumé and cover letter; creating connections involves developing and utilizing your network; and communicating your value includes developing your elevator pitch, using social media informatively, and participating in the interview process.

Career Documents

RESUME WRITING

By far, one of the most daunting components of job or internship searching is writing a résumé. They are also an under-studied intervention in career-focused counseling, yet at the same time, they are one of the most useful tools in a counselor's toolbox. The purpose of a résumé is to get an interview and highlight your experience. Let's consider what actually goes on a résumé. Some of the standard information includes the following:

- **Contact information:** This includes your name, degrees (e.g., MS) or licensure, full or abbreviated address (city and state), your cell phone number, and your email address.
    - **Some helpful hints:** Make sure you use a professional sounding email address; Sailor4eva@gmail.com is not appropriate for the job search! Also, consider whether you want to include your preferred pronouns. Depending on your field, this may be appropriate here or on your cover letter.
- **Education:** Listed with the most recent degree first (whether earned or in process), include the name and location of each school, the degree earned, and the date of conferment. *Do not* include high school once you are in college.
    - **Some helpful hints:** Only include your GPA if you plan to include it for all of your degrees. Also, you may want to also include your major, minor, concentration, or special coursework, if relevant.
- **Experience:** This includes all relevant paid, volunteer, or internship work and should list your title, organization name and location, and dates held.
    - **Some helpful hints:** Highlight your knowledge and skills, use action verbs, and quantify your important accomplishments whenever possible. Also, there is no need to include standard activities (e.g., professional behaviors and basic oversight paperwork) in most situations.

- **Involvement or extracurricular activities:** These can include student organizations, community activities, professional memberships, or other activities related to your professional goals.
  - **Some helpful hints:** If you are pressed for space, you can leave out activities unrelated to your career path. You may have loved being in the cookie club, but if you are not planning to be a chef, you can probably leave it off!
- **Other possible sections:** Depending on your experience, you may have a section highlighting your honors and awards, publications and presentations, technical skills, language expertise, or other professional accomplishments.

To prepare for the job application process, clients should first make a list of the jobs (paid and unpaid) they've already had. Not every job application asks for all this information, but if a client presents at a prospective employer's location and doesn't have this information handy to provide, it could leave a negative impression on the hiring official. When completing application forms or writing resumes, always begin with the most recent job and work chronologically backward to the beginning. On job applications, fill in as many jobs as you are given space to include. On résumés, the general rule is to go back about 10 years or more if prior jobs are particularly relevant. When describing the jobs you had, use verbs to describe the actions you performed. If applying for a job for which you don't have prior experience, be sure to demonstrate the transferability of certain skills. Often, the process of drafting a résumé creates "noise." Several factors come into play when an individual approaches the resume writing process. Let's look a little closer at these in Monte's work with LaKeisha.

TRANSCRIPT EXCERPT

Monte: Hello. What brings you in today?

LaKeisha: Well, I'm in the mental health counseling program and beginning the search for internship sites. Apparently, I need a resume to accompany my application packet.

Monte: You don't seem overly thrilled about that component.

LaKeisha: I'm not! I haven't written a résumé in a long time and that was in undergrad. I'm not sure where to begin.

Monte: So maybe you'd like my help in finding where to begin?

LaKeisha: I guess. I mean, I downloaded a template from a website, so I think I know the basics. …

Monte: But you might be looking for more than what to put where on that document?

LaKeisha: Yeah, it makes me anxious to have to put my limited experience on one page.

Monte: Okay. It makes sense that you'd feel some anxiety if you feel your experience is limited.

LaKeisha: It seems like a lot comes down to what you have done, and I don't have a lot of counseling experience.

Monte: It does seem to be a bit of a catch-22: you need experience doing the thing you're trying to get experience in.

LaKeisha: Exactly. What if it's not good enough?

Monte: Almost sounds like, "What if I'm not good enough?"

LaKeisha: That's true. I mean, what if I've gotten this far in the program and I can't get an internship because I'm not meant for this profession?

Monte: Can you finish that thought? How would you respond to that "what if"?

LaKeisha: It would mean I've wasted time, energy, and money on this. Then, what would I do?

Monte: So it really does sound like your concerns extend beyond the resume; is that right?

LaKeisha: Definitely. And I'm the first in my family to go to college, so they just give me empty assurances that it will be OK.

Monte: It's hard to find support from folks who really understand what you're going through.

LaKeisha: Yes. They mean well, but what if I can't cut it?

Monte: You have some really big questions floating out there, LaKeisha; many which seem to have surfaced in preparation for internship. I do want to come back to that in a moment, but I wonder if we could return to the resume part?

LaKeisha: Sure. I still have to do one of those.

Monte: That's right. Okay. I'm curious to see if some of your concerns can be addressed through the resume writing process.

LaKeisha Smith
12345 Street Rd
City, State, Zip
555-1212
LaKiesha@email.com

Work Experience

• Babysitting
→ all through high school (2012-2015)

• Betty's Daycare (2015-2020)
→ Worked with children, watching and feeding

Education

• High School – ACME High School (May, 2015)

• College – University of College (2019)
→ Majored in Family Studies and Psychology

Practicum

• Youth Center for Troubled Teens
→ Watched the teens during staff lunches
→ Supervised recess
→ Sat in on family sessions

Volunteer

Worked for church's food pantry and clothing closet

Honors

Chi Sigma Iota Counseling Honors Society Member

FIGURE 5.1. LaKeisha's Résumé Draft

LaKeisha: Really? I'm game.

Monte: Thanks for taking a chance. Let's look at the draft you've brought in to start with.

TAKE A MINUTE

Take a look at LaKeisha's resume. What aspects has she done well? What parts of her resume could be improved? For example, has she used action verbs? Has she detailed her work experiences? Is she "selling" herself or selling herself short?

The process of writing a résumé can be both inspiring and motivating. Inspiring in that most people have done more than they give themselves credit for or undersell their history. For example, LaKeisha said she "supervised recess" during her practicum, but what really happened? What she actually did was engage the children in problem-solving and communication skills during free play. These two things are very different and can bolster her confidence in thinking about her experience. It can also provide motivation for her to increase her activity, so the next version of her résumé looks and feels stronger—like a better reflection of who she is. For example, currently she is a member of Chi Sigma Iota, but perhaps, she can take a more active role in the coming semester.

A word about experience: Young students or clients and career changers tend to do that same thing when writing their resume: apologize for their lack of experience. To paraphrase an ancient adage, don't let anyone look down on you for being young (or lack of experience). It has also been said that experience is something you get right after you need it. The "noise" created by a lack of experience can be a barrier to a successful job search. Rather than apologizing for a perceived or actual lack of experience, LaKeisha can focus on the quality of her experience and her goals for the future. She is also at an advantage in that she is a counseling student applying for an internship, and most internship sites will not expect counseling interns to have a significant amount of experience.

An easy activity to help LaKeisha might be to have her refer to her list of jobs and ask herself what she accomplished in that job, how she accomplished it (skills used), and what feedback she received from her supervisors about her performance. She can identify action verbs that represent these experiences. Monte can serve as a support for LaKeisha in helping her see the value in the part-time jobs or volunteer counseling positions she has held.

Another way to help her build a picture of success for her future is by drafting an ideal resume. An ideal résumé is a prospective activity in which the individual writes a standard résumé (a "today résumé") and then adds in experience they hope to have on a resume in 5–10 years. Many of us who write our résumé find ourselves wishing we had been more involved, taken a risk or two, and had generally accumulated certain types of experiences. The ideal resume exercise helps individuals project forward to the experiences they would like to one day document on their resume and then reverse engineer their career, working their way backwards to today. This pulls on both goal setting and motivation so that in five years, LaKeisha does not feel what she feels now about the quantity and quality of her experience. For instance, Monte might ask what certifications or recognitions LaKeisha would like to have in five years. She might identify being licensed as a professional counselor as well as having an active role in her state's counseling association. Working backward from those goals, the two of them can explore each of the preceding steps or conditions all the way back to today. Then, looking forward again, LaKeisha can identify one thing today, next week, next month, and next year to increase her chances of being able to list those things on her ideal résumé.

TAKE A MINUTE

Résumé and job scavenger hunt. Part of the mystique regarding career development revolves around limited access to and experience with careers and résumés in general. To address this, counselors can invite students and clients on a scavenger hunt. In this process, they will search and locate online five counseling-related (in Monte and LaKiesha's cases) résumés and job postings. These are résumés that resemble ones they would like to develop in the future. Likewise, they can be invited to find five job postings for counseling-related jobs, regardless of whether they feel qualified for them. In identifying these 10 total references, they can ask themselves the following questions in private or bring them back to the counselor:

- What struck me as I examined the sample résumés? Did I see experiences and qualifications that I could reasonably obtain, that I already possessed, or that I would like to possess in the future?
- In looking at job postings, did they include duties and responsibilities that I might actually want to do? When listing the qualifications, do they seem attainable—and in what timeframe?

The debrief includes a discussion about expectations versus reality as well as increased awareness regarding desire to do the work or gain the experiences and qualifications.

JOB APPLICATIONS

Job application forms ask for very specific information, but writers of résumés can be a bit more creative. This is important because the goal of a résumé is to present to a potential employer that you are worthy of being interviewed for an open position. Résumés should certainly include an accounting of your work history but should also demonstrate your ability to do the job for which you are applying—even if you haven't had prior experience. For example, let's suppose you are working with Deidra, helping her manage her job loss. In addition to helping her process her feelings of loss and helping bolster her stress management skills, you might conduct some career assessments with her to identify potential new career options. Let's suppose she decides she would like to pursue a job as a customer service representative. In this case, she could use her experiences having worked with a wide variety of people to demonstrate the requirement for a customer service job that one needs strong "people skills."

COVER LETTERS

If the purpose of a résumé is to get an interview, the purpose of the cover letter is to get the hiring official to look at the résumé. For this reason, it is important to use the language of the described job opening when composing a cover letter. Structurally, a cover letter has three parts: (a) the purpose for the cover letter, (b) the reason the hiring official should consider you for an interview, highlighting your specific qualifications, and (c) a clear request for an interview and follow up information. To prepare to write a cover letter, job seekers should be familiar with the actual job opening and should try to learn something about the organization to which they are applying, either by conducting internet research or by utilizing networking connections. In the opening of the cover letter, indicate the job you are applying for and where you saw the advertisement for the job or who referred you to the job. In the middle section, use the language of the job opening to describe your skills and abilities. Select an example from an experience you had on a previous job to demonstrate how you match the requirements for the job to which you are applying. In the final section, directly ask that the hiring official contact you for an interview.

Creating Connections

Once you decide the type of work you are looking for, you will need to find out where you can go to get a job like that. The places a person might go to find out about open jobs will vary based on the type of work they do or are qualified to do. For example, many professional associations host job boards or promote openings on their listservs. Additionally, certain community organizations might have local listings available. Many people utilize the internet for job searches, and some still utilize the good old fashioned newspaper. However, as basic as it seems, the best way to learn about job openings is to ask people. Ask everyone you know if they know any places that are hiring. Ask if they know someone else who might know.

The majority of recruiters, placement personnel, and employment gurus will tell you that networking is the number one way to find a job. When you connect yourself to the folks who need to know who you are, they remember you when someone in their network is needing to hire. And of course, the opposite is true. If you were an employer looking to hire, wouldn't you trust a referral from a friend over an applicant you'd never heard of before? Networking has become easier with the refinement of social media outlets. Additionally, users can cast a wider net when using internet sources for networking. As with any other online activity, you should be careful that the sites you are using are professional and trustworthy. At the same time, be sure to monitor your own social media presence, so if an employer wanted to look you up, you'd feel ok about what they discover.

A word about networking: Networking can have a negative connotation, as it can sometimes feel like getting to know people for the purpose of using them to get something you want. This is not what we are advocating; in fact, we prefer the term *professional relationship building*. First off, it is important to be able to build relationships with other professionals, and it requires skills and energy. You wouldn't try to build a relationship with just anyone, and you would not want to work just anywhere. This is why professional relationship building is both a skill and an art. Second, when you know you have something to offer, but no one else knows, they are missing the benefit of your skills. The only way for them to know is for you to tell them, and that is limited unless you know them. And this is the rub. Relationship building takes a lot of energy. It is far easier to post your résumé to dozens of job boards or other mass mailing strategies than to invest yourself in the process. This is part of the reason networking, or professional relationship building, is so valuable; it takes and shows investment.

Sometimes you may have to be strategic about putting yourself in the right place to have access to people who might be able to help you. For example, let's say you are a counseling student getting ready to graduate and pursue licensure in your state. Your first source of information might be the staff of the agency where you completed your internship. Or perhaps, there's a group of counselors that meet up monthly to talk about therapeutic issues and interventions; this would be a great group to join and nurture relationships, so when the time comes to ask if anyone's hiring, the people in the group will be familiar with you. Another great way to get in front of the right people is to volunteer for your state ACA or AMHCA branch. Volunteering gives you the chance to give back to the profession, the chance to get to know other counselors, exposure to potential clinical supervisors, and access to possible job openings that might otherwise not be made publicly known.

SECURING REFERENCES

In general, references are people from your network, who can attest to the strength of your work potential. References will generally fall into two categories: (a) previous supervisors and (b) people who can speak to your ability to do the job for which you are applying. Sometimes, you might need a reference to be available for a potential employer to contact, and other times, you may need a reference to write a letter for you. These variables are all dependent on the job and the employer. Be sure to secure permission from anyone you list as a reference, so they can prepare to receive inquiries about you. Choose your references wisely, and know that sometimes employers will try to learn information about you via their own informal networks. As with the ideal résumé, the relationship you build with your future references is not something that begins when you need the reference.

INFORMATIONAL INTERVIEWS

If the vast majority of jobs are obtained through someone the job seeker knows, what does a person do when they do not know many or any people in a field or location? They make connections. Informational interviewing is another great way to make connections and build up your network of people. To conduct an informational interview, first select a few organizations in the type of business you would like to work for and then locate a person who would know something about the type of job you would like to have. Access your existing network to see if you can get a referral to that person. When you make contact, indicate that you would like to talk with them for less than 15 minutes about your job search. Assure the person that you are not necessarily applying for a job there but that you are really just seeking information. When the time comes for the meeting, be sure to honor your initial promise not to keep them longer than 15 minutes. The questions you ask will depend on your own existing knowledge of the job, but some suggested questions might include:

1. Would you please review my résumé and offer some feedback?
2. What do you think are the greatest challenges associated with this type of work right now?
3. What do you think are the most important things that employers are looking for when hiring for this type of job?
4. Who do you know who might be able to help me more?

As you close the meeting, be sure to thank them for their time, and send a note or an email thanking them again. During your conversation, you may learn certain things that you are reminded of when conducting an informational interview with someone else. In this case, linking your contacts together shows them that you are not just looking for them to help you, but you are also interested in helping them.

Communicating Your Value

Assuming the resume and cover letter look good, clients will hopefully make it to the interview process. Interviewing is where we communicate our value and help the employer understand why the person they are interviewing should be hired. An *elevator pitch* can be a great start to the process. This is another name for a brief (less than one minute) introduction. The elevator pitch should include one's name, academic background or training, important work experiences, and relevant skills. It can be used to respond to, "Tell me about yourself" or to meet with those in your network.

TAKE A MINUTE

What is your elevator pitch? Try to draft a one-paragraph introduction that you could use with a potential employer. What would you highlight in less than a minute? What about for LaKeisha? What skills can she highlight? What qualifications would be important for potential internship site supervisors to know?

INTERVIEWING

Obviously, the purpose of the interview is, ultimately, to secure a job offer. One of the best ways to prepare for any interview is to understand as much as you can about the organization, the opening, and the person who will be interviewing you. This information is sometimes readily available and sometimes not, and this is another great reason for having a strong network in place and knowing how to conduct informational interviews. In preparing for the actual job interview, applicants should be ready for some rather predictable questions, including:

- Tell me about yourself.
- What you would do if ... (they fill in a likely situation that could occur on the job)?
- What are your strengths and weaknesses?
- Why do you want to work here?
- What would your last supervisor say about you?

Practicing strengths-based responses to these questions is a great way to prepare for an interview.

Monte can practice responses to these and other questions with LaKeisha and help her identify strengths-based answers that highlight her skills. She has a lot to offer a potential internship site, but her low confidence can get in the way, so Monte should help her prepare and teach her to catch when she falters or doubts herself. These skills, of course, will help LaKeisha beyond just with her internship search.

Be sure to be on time for the interview—maybe even just a few minutes early. Being too early is likely just as disruptive to the employer as being late, so no more than 5 minutes early. Look the interviewer in the eye (and in the camera if on a video interview). Remember to smile and be prepared to ask them some questions as well. Some suggested questions include:

- Tell me what this job would look like day to day.
- What is most challenging about this job from your perspective?
- What are the long-term goals for the department?
- Tell me about the hiring process in terms of what I might expect and when.

This information will help you sell yourself more effectively for the job and will also help you when following up after the interview. At the end of the interview, if they haven't already requested your references, share a document with them that includes the name, contact information, and identity (how they know you) of your references. After the interview, send a short note—usually an email—thanking the interviewer for their time. Highlight something from the interview you want them to remember about you or use the information from the questions you asked at the end to tell them something more about yourself you didn't share during the interview.

When negotiating salary and compensation, be prepared with industry standards. You will likely want a salary at or higher than your previous salary, and at the same time, you should consider from the employer's perspective what the going rate is for the job and for someone with your level of experience in the job. The employer may ask you in the interview about your desired compensation. If you've done your homework, you can respond with, "My understanding is that this job is in the *x* to *y* salary range. Is that correct?" The numbers you use for *x* and *y* should be well researched and should include what you think you are worth on the market. If your numbers are too low, you will be giving up possible pay, and if your numbers are too high you could lose the opportunity. Again, this is a great piece of information to run through your network.

PROVIDING CAREER-FOCUSED COUNSELING

Job searching can trigger concerns for both you and your clients. There is a certain vulnerability and potential for failure when it comes to finding and securing the right job. Maintaining perspective in job searching and career management is vital to mental wellness. Imagine now that LaKeisha is in her internship. Her first internship is in a school-based counseling program where she meets Jerome.

Jerome is a 16-year-old junior in high school who comes to talk with you following the college fair. He says he is uncertain about whether he wants to attend college or go straight to work. He has been working at a local restaurant, bussing tables, and he feels sure that he does not want to continue working "that kind of job" after he graduates. He reports that he would be the first in his family to go to college, and there is a lot of pressure for him to buck that trend. He enjoys electronics, but he does not have a sense of what kind of work he could do with that, especially while still in high school. He enjoyed the college fair, but it all seemed really overwhelming and made him feel like he might not "belong" in that environment.

Jerome is trying to navigate career choice with pressure from his family and lack of certainty about his own long-term goals. Putting on a developmental hat, this seems perfectly normal for a 16 year old. We can sense from this vignette that Jerome is carrying a fair amount of anxiety about this choice. He sounds stuck between doing the work he's been doing (which he doesn't like) and going to college (which he's not sure he really wants to do). Jerome would benefit from some assurance that there are always more than two choices available and that the goal is just to begin moving in a direction to allow him to investigate more. He might benefit from some career assessments and career exploration activities. He may benefit from learning about the local junior college and the potential for part-time studies that would still allow him to work and take his time in making more formal decisions. He could also benefit from reaching out into the community to learn more about what he might be able to do with his interest in electronics, whether it be a job or a possible apprenticeship. Finally, you may wish to work with Jerome in encouraging him to talk with his parents about his feelings regarding their expectations. Depending on the family, incorporating this support can strengthen family relationships and, thus, a support system.

During her second internship, LaKeisha is working in a community mental health agency. After working with Monte, she decided it would be important to get experience working with adults as well as children and adolescents.

Ben is in his mid-40s, seeking assistance in managing his mood. He reports feeling "down" much of the time, has lost interest in hobbies, and has grown distant from his family. Many evenings after coming home from work, he will leave after dinner to have "a couple of beers" in his "man cave." He said he is here (in counseling) because of family pressure to deal with the perceived distance. His intake form indicates that he makes an average salary in his middle management position. He wants to feel closer with his family (he has a wife of 10 years, a son, a daughter, and a stepson). As you wrap up the first session, Ben blurts out, "Oh and my wife made me promise to tell you that I really hate my job and that she thinks I need to make a change." He adds that he makes a decent living, is the primary breadwinner, and is, in fact, completely miserable in his job.

Ben is well beyond Jerome developmentally, yet he is dealing with very similar issues. As we read the vignette, we see symptoms of depression and isolation, and we learn at the end of the vignette that he is stuck between being miserable at his job and having the family responsibility of being the primary breadwinner. When counseling with Ben, you would want to first focus on the therapeutic alliance and help him know that you see how he's feeling stuck. Work to help him improve his positive coping skills. At the same time, help Ben understand what is happening in his life. Is it the work itself that makes him miserable? Is it the policies of his company? Or is it his relationship with his boss? Adults spend most of their waking hours involved in job-related tasks, so it is important to help clients get under the stress to pinpoint the actual source of the problem before trying to solve it.

Take Away and Use Today

As stated previously, working with students and clients on career- and work-related issues can be difficult on counselors because of the pressure we may feel to fix the problem. While it is not the role of a counselor to fix or problem-solve, having access to accurate resources can be of great benefit to students and clients. The information, tools, and resources in this chapter are intended to give counselors greater confidence in attending to their students and clients.

CHAPTER 6

Person–Environment Correspondence

CHAPTER GOALS

- Identify the implications and applications of Parsons's three-part model of career decision-making.
- Understand the implications and applications of trait and factor theory.
- Identify the implications and applications of Person–Environment Correspondence theory.

OPENING VIGNETTES

School-Based

Emma is a 15-year-old 9th grader seeing the school counselor, Amira, to set her high school schedule for the following fall. She is tearful as she describes feeling lost, even as the students around her seem to "know exactly what they want to do with their life." Realizing that Emma's concerns are more than just about her schedule, Amira invites Emma to join a career development group she is piloting for students in Emma's situation, using a trait and factor approach. Emma seems immediately relieved to sense that she is not alone after all and that there is a process for addressing her questions and concerns.

Agency-Based

Carl is a 40-something client who has been working with Dreama, a counselor at a community mental health agency for the past three months. Carl sought treatment following a referral from his job, where he is an assistant floor manager at a pharmaceutical packing plant. The referral was based on Carl's self-reported mood issues and difficulty concentrating at work. Dreama has focused their work toward Carl's goal of "feeling better" and being "happier at work" through the use solution-focused therapy, where they have been working to identify what is working for Carl in terms of his life and job, and what is not working. Progress has been slow, but Carl has been consistent in attending his appointments and "working" in session. During the 10th session, however, as they begin, Carl blurts out, "I hate my [expletive] job, and I don't want to spend another [expletive] minute trying to find the positives!" Dreama is taken aback a little, but realizes that the need to shift the focus of counseling to career, using a career-focused version of solution-focused counseling: person–environment fit.

REFLECTION ACTIVITIES AND QUESTIONS

- At what age did you become aware of the type of job or career that would be a good fit for you?
- Now, reflect on how you know, even now, that a career in the helping professions is a good fit for you? What evidence do you draw upon to support your decision?
- What do you know about yourself now in terms of fitting the profession that you wish you had known earlier? When and what do you wish you had known about yourself and the world of work?
- Lastly, what is your approach, in general, to matching what you know about yourself and behaviors and choices in your life?

Introduction

Have you ever held a job where you felt you just didn't fit? Were you able to do the work but did not feel satisfied? Like it was just a paycheck? How did that work out? Presumably, you are reading this in the context of being in a graduate counseling program and, perhaps, looking for a better fit. This chapter is all about fit.

In this chapter we discuss the theories associated with the father of career counseling, Frank Parsons. The material in this chapter describes theories that relate directly to his foundational model that matches the person with the work environment. This model, which has come to be known as trait and factor theory or person–environment fit (PE fit), has enjoyed high levels of influence and staying power and can be seen in the vast majority of contemporary career theory and practice. The purpose of this chapter is to briefly review the historical roots of these models but then move quickly to examine the most prominent modern versions of this model—those of Holland's theory of career choice and Dawis and Lofquist's theory of work adjustment (TWA), which is now known as person–environment correspondence (PEC). This chapter is an extension and elaboration of Luke's (2018) work. In it, we expect that readers will understand the basics of person–environment models as well as develop a deeper appreciation of the richness of self-understanding, world of work understanding, and the process of making meaningful connections between the two.

At the risk of oversimplifying the concept of person–environment fit, you might think of the models in this chapter like dating apps. When thinking of currently popular dating sites, the model is relatively similar: complete your profile, which includes a description of yourself in various dimensions and what you're looking for in a person or relationship. The app's algorithm searches for others' profiles to find correspondence. This correspondence is based on research that predicts which types of people and profiles are likely to get along well together. All that's left is to meet your match and find out if they are as good in person as they seemed online!

Theory Overview

The theories in this book and in this chapter in particular owe their beginning to Frank Parsons, even though his work can be seen throughout most career theories (Luke, 2018; Swanson & Fouad, 2015). Parsons was, above all, an activist, promoting vocational development for youth in the context of a rapidly changing work landscape driven by the industrial revolution. His legacy includes creation of the first centers of vocational guidance to assist youth in particular in finding work (Zytowski, 2001). Parsons ushered in a radical way of thinking that was a stark departure from the agricultural to industrial mindsets related to work. He challenged common wisdom by asserting vocation as a choice—not an inheritance wherein one must do the work their parents did. Of enduring significance, he developed a model in which youth could develop the skill of "true reasoning" to make meaningful connections between one's own characteristics and the characteristics of a job. His was the first career decision-making model, as before this, there was little choice—only behavior. To put it another way, career choice for some now seems like a birthright, the pendulum having swung to the opposite extreme in our modern culture. Parsons's work set the stage for what would become the leading applied career theory for many decades: Holland's theory of career choice (trait-and-factor model), which is a hallmark of trait and factor theories. Holland extended Parsons's work to create the theory of vocational choice, which has generated a truly massive number of studies.

Concepts

Trait-and-factor theories are deceptively complex, as a generation of researchers have discovered (see van Vianen, 2018 for a review and Kristof-Brown et al., 2005 for meta-analysis). We mentioned in Chapter 1 that Parsons's three-part model is deceptive in its simplicity, especially when viewed through a modern lens. Of course, it is important to know oneself and to gather information about occupations. Today, there are more resources available than ever before for learning about oneself and the world of work, but more information is not tantamount to more knowledge. As we explore this more closely in the next sections, it is helpful to review the components that Parsons described more than a century ago. Van Vianen (2018) summarized the three tenets of so-called "fit" models. First, the whole is greater than the sum of its parts, which is to say that fit between person and environment is more predictive of satisfaction than either of the person or environment characteristics alone. Second is the idea that matching the individual's characteristics with those of the work environment will lead to greater satisfaction for both the individual and the environment (work space), even if those characteristics are not "high." Third, lack of correspondence, or discrepancies between persona and environment, leads to dissatisfaction.

General Steps of All Trait and Factor Theories

Based on Parsons's original tripartite model, trait and factor approaches to career counseling were originally called the matching model (Briddick & Sensoy-Briddick, 2013). They involve measurement of *traits*, or personal characteristics, and *factors*, or what is needed for successful job performance, to identify *fit*, or the similarity between the person and the environment (Chartrand & Bertok, 1993). Regardless of the specific theory frame, all trait and factor approaches share the belief that people have a unique pattern of traits that can be measured and then matched to various occupations. The three-step process of these theories involves: (a) gaining self-understanding through assessment of various traits related to achievement, interests, values, or normal personality; (b) obtaining knowledge about the world of work to understand the specifics of different occupations; and (c) integrating traits and factors to identify potential satisfying matches (Chartrand, 1991). The shift from trait and factor to person–environment fit added the ideas that clients need to be actively involved in the assessment and interpretation process and that fit can be ongoing and reciprocal, where people change their environment while the environment also changes people (Chartrand, 1991). Both Holland's theory and TWA represent the concepts in person–environment fit.

THEORIST PROFILE: JOHN HOLLAND

It is important to recognize that Holland's work was not just focused on career decision-making but on career adjustment as well. A large volume of career development research focuses on high school and college students making their first career decisions, but Parsons and Holland's vision was broader, supporting initial choice, career adjustment, and career transitions. Holland offered the following to clarify this purpose:

> What personal and environmental characteristics lead to satisfying career decisions, involvement, and achievement, and what characteristics lead to indecision, dissatisfying decisions, or lack of accomplishment?
>
> What personal and environmental characteristics lead to stability or change in the kind and level of work a person performs over a lifetime?
>
> What are the most effective methods for providing assistance to people with career problems? (Holland, 1997, p. 1)
>
> To this end, Holland articulated four propositions that underpinned his work:
>
> a) in our culture, most persons can be categorized as a grouping of one to six personality types: **Realistic, Investigative, Artistic, Social, Enterprising, or Conventional;**
> b) there are six corresponding model environments: Realistic, Investigative, Artistic, Social, Enterprising, or Conventional;
> c) people search for environments that will let them exercise their skills and abilities, express their attitudes and values, and take on agreeable problems and roles; and
> d) behavior is determined by an interaction between personality and environment (Holland, 1997, pp. 4–5).

TABLE 6.1 HOLLAND PERSONALITY TYPES

Category	Personality Characteristics	Work Types
Realistic	Hands on	Mechanic, military
Investigative	Ideas	Scientist
Artistic	Creativity, flexibility	Musician, artist
Social	Helping others	Counselor, nurse
Enterprising	Leadership	Entrepreneur
Conventional	Order and structure	Accountant

The six categories of personality types are summarized in Table 6.1 along with their corresponding work environment characteristics.

The six categories of personality are not typically unidimensional, meaning that it is most common that an individual will have a two or three letter *Holland code*. There are 720 possible combinations, but there are certain patterns that have been identified in the literature (Nauta, 2020). This is best understood by a hexagon, though some have hypothesized a circle as more representative.

The six personality types are arranged clockwise, as shown in Figure 6.1, in order of their connection to one another. This is built on research highlighting the correlation of the types, though these have not been clearly verified in subsequent research. In general, adjacent letters or types are more closely associated with one another, while types across from one another on the hexagon are more weakly correlated. As we move clockwise around the hexagon, strong correlations are found. The *realistic* theme includes work that involves objects—not people. It includes working with tools, computers, machines, or physically, with one's body. The *investigative* theme involves using one's mind to solve problems—an enjoyment of puzzles and learning new information. Investigative occupations includes professors, scientists, and physicians. *Artistic* types prefer free-flowing environments and creative approaches to tasks, rather than highly structured work environments. Work related to the artistic themes includes music, art, and personal expression. The *social* theme, as the polar opposite of the realistic theme, involves working with people over objects. Work for this type includes counseling, ministry, and nursing. The *enterprising* theme involves roles in which one can use motivation and persuasion to lead others or sell items or services. Examples of enterprising work include sales, management, and performance-based work. The *conventional* theme involves a preference for structure, rules, and plans to solve problems. Jobs in this theme include accounting and support roles for management. Recalling that most people have a three-letter code, types tend to be made up of adjacent types. For instance, the most common Holland code for mental health counselors is SIA, or social, investigative, and artistic. These three are adjacent to one another, meaning more connection. This does not mean, of course, that a counselor-in-training who has a different Holland code could not be a counselor. It simply means that the majority of counselors have this code and are at least moderately satisfied in performing the work they do. They enjoy helping others (S) through understanding the human experience (I) using creativity (A).

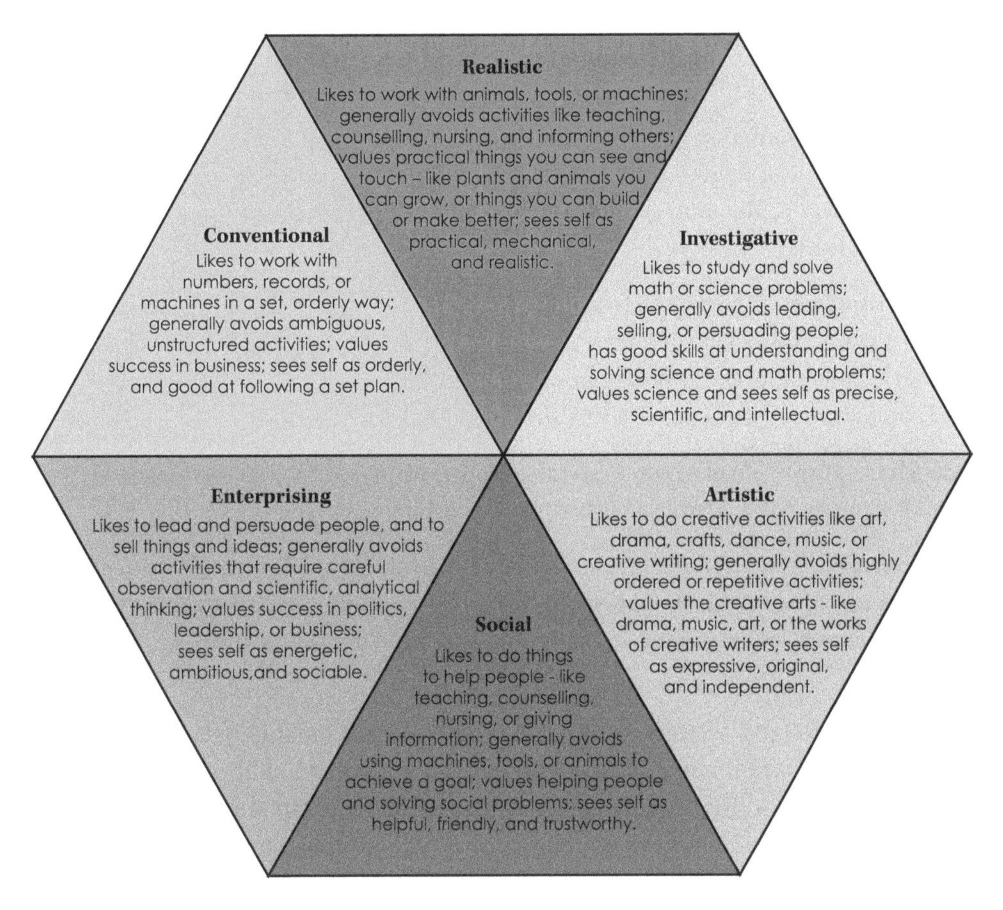

FIGURE 6.1. Holland Hexagon

Theory Essentials

Holland's theory includes several assumptions about the world of work and matching people to jobs. The choice of a vocation is an expression of personality; therefore, interest inventories are personality inventories. Vocational stereotypes have reliable and important psychological and sociological meanings. The members of a vocation have similar personalities and similar histories of personal development. Because people in a vocational group have similar personalities, they will respond to many situations and problems in similar ways, and they will create characteristic interpersonal environments. Vocational satisfaction, stability, and achievement depend on the congruence between one's personality and the environment in which one works (Luke, 2018, pp. 7–11).

To understand this more, Holland expressed several assumptions in the model:

Calculus—[r]efers to the hexagon structure, where distance between code types indicates interrelationships between type

Consistency—"the degree of relatedness between personality types or environmental models" and affect preference; adjacent types are more consistent

Congruence—matching personality and environment, where rewards match desires; and calculus—the degree of relationship of factors measured by distance on the hexagon graphic. The more similar the personality to the environment, the higher the congruence

Differentiation—"the degree to which a person or an environment is well defined"; in other words, the clarity of interests, which is needed for congruence. Ideally, clients should have some level of differentiation amongst their interests, so low differentiation indicates similar scores on all 6 RIASEC codes

Identity—"possession of a clear and stable picture of one's goals, interests, and talents"; higher identity levels relate to more differentiation and consistency

Environment—"when an environment or an organization has clear and integrated goals, tasks, and rewards that are stable over long time intervals"; clients need knowledge of the work environment to make career-related decisions. (1997, pp. 4–5).

To summarize, Holland systematically examined the relationship between individual differences (personality) and environment (work). The terms listed above indicate the ways counselors interpret RIASEC scores to better understand their clients. It is important to note that Holland's theory, like Parsons's before him, while simple, is not superficial. It was designed to be simple for counselors to explain to their clients so as not to overwhelm.

Strong Interest Inventory

The Strong Interest Inventory (SII) is a 291-item survey of interests and a commonly used assessment of interests based on the Holland codes. Respondents self-report items on a five-point Likert scale from "Strongly Dislike" to "Strongly Like" on prompts such as "making a speech" (CPP, 2004). The SII has been published and validated in multiple countries and languages and with diverse groups of people (Herk & Thompson, 2011). Responses are collated and compared with normative samples. These samples are matched with the occupations of those with a similar pattern of responses. The score report breaks down respondent results into several categories. The broadest category aligns with Holland's (1997) six types, which are called the general occupation themes.

The next level of specificity and focus on the SII is referred to as the basic interest scales. They represent a more detailed level of interest in that there are 30. They take the Holland (3-letter) codes from the six themes and identify the top five matches to occupations within those themes. For instance, for an individual with SIA, the basic interest scale might identify counseling and helping. The BIS answers questions like, "What are the fields individuals with my code go into?"

The occupational scales take the results one level deeper by identifying a list of top occupation matches that most closely match the individual's Holland code and profile from a list of 244. The occupational scales list specific jobs like mental health counselor or clergy. The 2012 update of the SII sought to balance gender expectancy in the results and expose respondents to their top job matches, regardless of historical gender norms. However, the SII is still based on the idea of binary gender and does not include a nonbinary option.

It is important to highlight here that the occupational scales do not predict what respondents will be good at; it is not an assessment of skill, ability, or capability. It merely takes respondents' scores and compares it with normative data to highlight the work that individuals in that group are employed in and share a similar SII profile. The normative group are those employed in a certain job and report at least moderate levels of satisfaction with the job. This provides a basis for comparison for respondents that there is room for believing that they too may find satisfaction in the work.

Next, in the SII score report is information on personal style scales. These five scales are work style, learning environment, leadership style, risk taking, and team orientation and are scored on a continuum. These scales provide information for reflection on how individuals approach the world of work. The report concludes with a profile summary, which presents a snapshot of the report.

Once clients or students complete the SII, they are given the option to use the information contained therein to explore a whole host of occupation options using their Holland code. For example, several vocational assessments include Holland codes (e. g., ASVAB, ACT), and there are many sites that include information based on Holland codes.

We say this throughout, but assessments like the SII are best used as conversation starters and idea generators. Many, if not most, clients and students will read into their results, viewing them as *prescriptive* rather than *descriptive*. An assessment like the SII or the MBTI (covered next) does not tell individuals who they are or which career path they should follow. It merely describes from their own input, clusters, or responses and provides leads for exploration and reflection. In fact, the conversation should begin before the individual takes the SII, though we recognize that, in many settings, career assessments are taken first, prior to an individual or group meeting. It is best to understand the individual's motivation for taking the assessment, listening for their goals or outcomes they expect from their results.

Myers–Briggs Type Indicator

In this section we offer an extended discussion of one specific assessment tool because of its clinical and practical utility. It offers a parsimonious look at some of the barriers students and clients face in finding school, career, and even relational satisfaction. The Myers–Briggs was developed by Isabel Myers following World War II (McCrae et al., 1989). It is based on the analytical psychology of Carl Jung (1921/1971). This personality assessment is intended to measure preferences in four domains of experience (Myers, 1980). It measures types, not traits or states, and has fairly strong test–retest reliability, according to a recent meta-analysis (Randall et al, 2017). It should be noted early on that reliability is distinct from validity, and there have long been questions regarding whether the MBTI actually measures what it purports to measure (McCrae & Costa, 1989). Jung's typology, from which the MBTI is derived, assumes that types and temperament are genetic; we are born with our temperament. Environmental and circumstantial factors certainly influence the expression of type, but at its core, type is hardwired. The MBTI has endured intense scrutiny and criticism because of its theoretical base and psychometric properties (King & Mason, 2020). However, it is hard to deny the practical and clinical utility of the MBTI. The applied features of the MBTI include its parsimonious explanation of person-environment fit, its ease of use, and practical steps.

In order to understand this better, Luke (2018) offers the following description of the four type dimensions:

- *Extraversion–Introversion*: This dimension identifies how individuals derive energy from their environments. Extraverts may prefer talking through ideas to understand them, whereas introverts may prefer to think quietly about their ideas and then talk about them.
    - Introverts are often criticized for being un- or antisocial.
    - Extraverts are often criticized for being superficial and talkative.

  Please note that this dimension is not "testing" social skills.
- *Sensing–Intuition*: This dimension identifies how individuals approach the world. Sensing individuals may prefer tangible information, such as that gained through their five senses. In contrast, intuition types may prefer experiencing the world through a sixth sense, or intuition.
    - Sensing types are often criticized as being too concrete or rigid.
    - Intuitive types are often criticized as having their head in the clouds.

  Please note that this dimension is not "testing" rigidity.
- *Thinking–Feeling*: This dimension identifies individual approaches to solving problems. Thinking types may prefer logic and rules in resolving conflict; whereas feeling types may prefer to consider relationships before rules.
    - Thinking types tend to be criticized as being cold and distant.
    - Feeling types are often criticized for being irrational and overly emotional.

  Please note that this dimension is not "testing" intelligence.
- *Judging–Perceiving*: This dimension identifies how individuals approach time. Judging types may prefer to have a clear plan while perceiving types may prefer spontaneity.
    - Judging types are often criticized for being rigid and inflexible in planning.
    - Perceiving types are often criticized for being irresponsible.

  Please note that this dimension is not "testing" one's tendency to be judgmental. (Luke, 2018)

Many clients and students struggle with their ability to make a career-related choice. It is similar to having anxiety and then being anxious about having anxiety. The MBTI moves clients and students away from pathologizing their confusion, indecision, or indecisiveness by pointing out their preferences instead. The MBTI can normalize their experience, leading to more productive conversation and exploration of options. For example, a person who scores high on introversion working in a loud, highly sociable work environment might criticize themselves (or be criticized by others) as not being a team player or being antisocial (colloquially, not clinically). However, they may simply be overstimulated in the environment and find it difficult to focus on their work or respond socially in ways the environment demands. Another use of the MBTI to normalize is a student or client with one type, like scoring high on feeling, but who grows in a home where thinking was the dominant preference. This individual may have grown to develop self-doubt regarding decision-making because they were "not logical enough." Counseling using the MBTI can help ease the burden that may have been carried for many years.

Luke presents an important caveat:

> The MBTI measures *preferences*, not skills or abilities, yet that is how they are often framed, particularly in relational conflict. The value of the MBTI in CFC is that it informs clients about how they may prefer to experience the work world and how they might approach particular tasks. Again, this information is descriptive, not prescriptive. There would rarely, if ever, be a job that introverts could not do; they just may not experience a particular job as energizing or rewarding, or they might approach an occupation that is counter to their type in unique and novel ways. (2018)

Person–Environment Correspondence (PEC)

Holland's work laid the foundation for "true reasoning" as applied first and foremost to decision-making and workforce entry. Dawis and Lofquist (1984) extended Parsons's work to decision-making within the work environment. The first name of their model, theory of work adjustment (TWA, 1976), highlighted the emphasis on what happens after a career decision has been made. Currently called person–environment correspondence (Lofquist & Dawis, 1991), the theory emphasizes the reciprocal impact that the person and (work) environment have on one another based on meeting the needs of each (Dawis, 2002).

PEC describes the person and the environment as each having requirements as well as capabilities (Dawis, 2002). In this way, the systems (person and work environment) use their respective capabilities to meet the needs (requirements) of the other. Dawis and Lofquist describe this as mutual responsiveness (1976). When this mutuality is successful, the person is said to be satisfied; that is, the environment meets their needs and requirements. *"Achieving satisfaction is the motivational force that powers the P-E interaction"* (Dawis, 2002, p. 433, emphasis in original). The goal, then, of PEC is to achieve *satisfaction*, wherein a person is able to meet the needs of the environment and to also have their needs met by the environment. This results in correspondence. When there is "dis-correspondence," on the other hand, the goal is to make adjustments in order to bring about or restore satisfaction. Once adjustment has been achieved, maintenance is established.

In PEC, four time-based styles work together to promote maintenance:

- *Flexibility* involves the ability (high or low) to tolerate dis-correspondence between personality factors and work environmental factors. Over time in an environment, correspondence increases as the person and environment adjust to one another, but flexibility is needed over this time to permit this to happen.
- *Activeness* describes an orientation in the individual and environment to actively bring about change in the other to increase correspondence and improve effectiveness and satisfaction.
- On the other hand, *reactiveness* is a style in which the person or environment seeks internal change to increase correspondence and subsequent satisfaction.
- *Celerity* (or perseverance), refers to the speed and duration of adjustment to increase correspondence.

To summarize, job satisfaction is an indicator of overall work adjustment and can be connected to various factors, such as coworker relationships, type of work, level of autonomy, ability to perform tasks, and work–life balance. Correspondence represents the match between worker needs and the work environment and is said to predict job satisfaction. The steps of TWA in counseling mirror the trait and factor approach; counselors begin by assessing abilities, values, work personality, and interest while also considering levels of satisfaction; they then review the requirements and conditions of various occupations; and finally, they help clients identify ways to increase match or fit (Chartrand, 1991).

In the next section, we describe sample interactions between Emma and her school counselor using a combination of Holland's theory and Parsons's three-step model. We then apply elements of person–environment correspondence to begin to address Carl's concerns.

EMMA IN SESSION

Emma is at a stage of her development wherein it is natural for her to doubt herself and to be ignorant of career options. She also feels alone in her struggle, due to both adolescent egocentrism (*I am the only one who feels this way*) and the difficulty in asking for help with career issues. A group experience is a great opportunity to challenge both areas. In this transcript, we explore how a school counselor might conduct a group following the administration of standard career assessments for high school freshmen.

During the first session, the counselor discusses confidentiality, group norms, and expectations and asks students to complete several career-related inventories to assess interests, personality, skills, and values. We join them in session two. For simplicity, we describe primarily Emma's interactions:

> SC: Welcome to our little group. I'm excited you all decided to come back. (SC uses a brief ice breaker to "warm up" the students.) Today I thought we would begin sharing your thoughts, concerns, hopes related to this group. Anyone can begin.

ST: I can go. I feel like I don't know where to begin, and I feel a lot of pressure to figure this out. Everyone is asking about college and career, and I just started high school. It's all overwhelming. The tests we took didn't seem to help—so many questions, and I felt lost.

(Several group members nod their heads in agreement and share similar experiences.)

SC: It does sound like it's a lot to take in and then the pressure to know what to do with it all feels like a burden. (Group members nod and sigh.) Can any of you think of a time when you had to make decisions this big? Like decisions about the rest of your life?

ST: Never. I had to decide about babysitting but nothing like this.

SC: It sounds like this is first for a lot of you. (ST nods.) It makes me wonder how you could feel anything but overwhelmed with the stakes being so high. I wonder if we could all agree together that this feels new, big, and uncertain. But then also acknowledge that all those who've gone before you have figured it out, so there must be a way through it.

ST: I guess I hadn't thought of it that way. How do we figure this out?

SC: Well, in this group, we'll take a look at the steps people can follow in learning about themselves, learning about work and career options and then how to put those things together and make decisions. But I'd like to add that we are not trying to get you to make a decision about the rest of your lives. This big scary decision that has us intimidated is really just a series of much smaller choices, and with each one is the opportunity to change and make a different decision. How does that sound?

ST: That doesn't sound so bad. I feel like everyone else wants me to make the big decision all at once.

SC: That's part of the work of our group: to be able to communicate with others in ways that don't result in you taking on their expectations. Let's begin with something a little simpler: Think of a person or people that you trust the most to both support you and to be honest with you. What words do they consistently use to describe you?

Self-knowledge beyond assessments by exploring how "wise ones" view them

ST: My gran always says I'm smart and I am creative. My friends tell me I'm pretty artistic.

SC: I sense something a little different in your energy when you recall those things, Emma.

ST: Yeah I feel embarrassed to say those things.

SC: Is there something else you're feeling?

Self-knowledge check to connect facts with feelings

ST: I feel kind of proud because I think of myself as a creative, artistic person. Those things kept coming up on my test results, too. But when my parents and family ask what I want to be, I can't tell them a specific job, and they tell me about going into business or science.

Exploring sources of occupational knowledge and evaluating their trustworthiness

SC: So we're back to finding ways of communicating to those we know and love about our interests. Let's practice a little. What do creative, artistic people do for a career?

(The group brainstorms. Instead of going off of our knowledge only, where can we go to get this kind of information?)

(The group describes asking family and friends, Google searches, and some remain silent.)

SC: (SC pulls up www.careeronestop.org.) Here we see the "arts" career cluster, along with information and videos about art-related careers. As we click on some of the job titles, we find information that answers the questions from even the most curious family members. What do you think about this kind of information and its role in helping you communicate your career interests?

ST: I wish I had this at the last family gathering! I can use some of it to help me decide how I could turn my interests into a career.

True reasoning or decision-making through experiential learning

SC: That's great. Let's take it a step further. Instead of looking at decision-making models, let's spend some time roleplaying how you would communicate with your family. Emma, would you like to select a partner to represent a person in your life that you struggle to communicate with about art-related careers?

TAKE A MINUTE

There is a riddle that asks, "How do you eat an elephant?" The answer is: one bite at a time. Consider for a moment how it was for you to make big life decisions, like your first job, first car, college, graduate school, and partner. You likely did not have a lot of experience in making that kind of decision since it was a first for you. In what ways did breaking down the decision into smaller, most digestible parts help in making that decision (or would have helped)? How might you lead the group above in breaking down career decisions "one bite at a time"?

CARL IN SESSION

Carl's situation and subsequent session outburst is an example of addressing a client's expressed need (generic work stress) through a solution-focused approach can uncover a more significant need. Carl has likely been unsatisfied in his work for some time, but the "symptoms" have only recently worsened and surfaced. Counseling with him will require making space for his emotional intensity while the counselor explores the long-term effects of career dissatisfaction.

MHC: Carl, I can feel your frustration. Would you say a little more about that?

CL: I've been trying to make this job work for a lot of years, and I'm realizing through these sessions that I am really just sick of it. I don't want to do it anymore ...

Sensing *dissatisfaction* and exploring further from PEC perspective

CMH: But ...

CL: But I feel an obligation to my family to make it work. I was raised to believe you take care of your family, keep a good job, and suck it up if it's bad.

MHC: "Suck it up"?

CL: You know, you live with all the [expletive] because you have to provide for your family.

MHC: Those are strong values. But something's not working?

CL: Yeah, I've been in a job I hate for so long, I can't enjoy anything, but I also feel like I can't leave.

MHC: And that's because of your values.

CL: Yes.

MHC: It feels like you cannot have it both ways: meet family obligations and have a job you enjoy.

CL: I hadn't thought of it that way, but yeah, I guess you're right. [Expletive].

Exploring *flexibility* from PEC perspective

MHC: Something about that affected you.

CL: Well, it never really occurred to me that I might be able to have both. At this point, it just feels like a fantasy.

MHC: Perhaps we could spend a little time exploring how it might be possible. (Carl nods in agreement.) Could you start by describing some of the basics of your work?

CL: Well, we have two shifts: 8 a.m.–8 p.m. and 8 p.m.–8 a.m. I supervise the 8 p.m.–8 a.m. shift.

MHC: So you work overnight?

CL: Yes, for many years now. And I'm responsible for my team meeting productivity.

MHC: What's that like for you?

Identifying areas of the work environment that require *reactiveness* because environment cannot change (roles and work shifts)

CL: I hate it. I have to always watch them to make sure no one's slacking.

MHC: What do you hate about it?

CL: I never wanted to be anybody's boss. I'm a live and let live kind of person. Having to push people to do their job so that we meet productivity makes me uncomfortable.

MHC: So, you're working overnight, pushing employees to perform. What else?

CL: Well, I also have to keep detailed records of our work and plan shift coverage and fill in when someone's out.

Further exploring *celerity*: persistence without *perseverance* to bring about correspondence

MHC: The face you're making while you describe that seems to indicate that you don't enjoy that part, either.

CL: Right.

MHC: What parts of the work have kept you there?

CL: I make a decent salary and can support my family.

MHC: I sense a "but" coming ...

CL: But I'm never home to enjoy them or when I am, I'm trying to catch up on sleep.

MHC: So the one positive also has a negative side as well. Anything else positive?

CL: I do enjoy working on a team, and I like leading—having goals and being strategic in meeting them.

MHC: So you appreciate working on a team, leading efforts to meet goals, and making a salary that supports your family?

CL: That's about it.

MHC: I have to say that you seem a little calmer now than when we started.

CL: It felt good to let out that frustration and it is helpful to be reminded of the things I enjoy. But I still hate it.

Opening to possibility of new work environment to create *correspondence*

MHC: You seem like you're stuck, but I can think of a lot of ways people who feel stuck like this can get unstuck. I wonder if you'd be open to exploring careers that include the things you like about your job but have fewer of the things you dislike?

CL: Yeah, that sounds good.

TAKE A MINUTE

As you reflect on Carl's situation, perhaps you can think of several things you love about your job or graduate school. Perhaps, you can also think of things you dislike or even hate about the job or school. What has been your process of discerning what you can live with and what would lead you to make a change? How might knowing this about yourself inform how you would work with a client like Carl?

Neuroscience, Culture, and Development

The self can be said to be located in memory and, more specifically, the autobiographical memory. This type of memory involves recollections about one's self in context. Declarative, episodic, and autobiographical memory serve to create a sense of self through recollection. This means that an individual's understanding of self, leading to self-knowledge, goes beyond what they think in the moment (interest inventories). Furthermore, memories of self that are recalled are context dependent, meaning that the current emotional and situational state of the individual affects recall and experience of the memory. This understanding of memory can assist counselors in helping clients explore their sense of self—both historically and currently. For example, a client in distress about making a career-related decision may have difficulty recalling interests, values, and skills, without tainting or coloring those experiences. This may come out in the form of forgetting successes altogether or, most commonly, minimizing successes. This often plays out when reviewing the individual's résumé, where their descriptions of their work are often dry and lack deeper reflection on their actual contributions to the job. These observations are not likely to be uncovered just by taking an interest inventory because, for one thing, that is not really their purpose but also because understanding an individual's experience of themselves through memory requires a skilled facilitator to work with their sense of self.

A second dimension of self can be understood in terms of development. One of the major barriers to living successfully for many clients and students is viewing themselves today in light of past characteristics or behaviors. For example, a five-year-old who is shouted at by parents for minor behaviors cannot comprehend any explanation for the parents' behavior except that it must be the child's fault. This sense of self forms around such instances, such that 20 years later they may find themselves in counseling for career-related issues because they are anxious in the work environment. It does not take long for a counselor to recognize that internalization of responsibility for others' behaviors, leading the client to feel unsatisfied and exhausted being at work. The self develops over time with moments of punctuated growth or setbacks through crises ("crisis" as used here is not the same as "trauma"). Since most growth occurs over time, it can be a challenge to recognize it—to see that, as an adult, we are no longer the five-year-old that feels responsible for any mistreatment we receive.

In thinking of identity, trait-and-factor models have a history of challenging perceived gender inequality. In fact, it was Strong who wrote as early as 1943:

> Before the advent of intelligence tests it was customary to view women as having intelligence inferior to that of men. Widespread use of these tests has demonstrated the fallacy of that view. But the fact that the two sexes obtain approximately equal scores in the tests does not mean that the character and quality of their intellectual processes is similar. They may have the same general capacity and at the same time use this capacity in different directions. (p. 216)

This was a call to the profession to recognize individual and group differences in terms of both interests and capabilities, leading to the significant findings of Betz and Hackett regarding the relationship between interest and abilities across gender lines. Women had similar abilities, they found, particularly in STEM fields, but lower interest in these areas. But this was not due to an actual disinterest as much as it was a belief in limited ability (based on internalized misogyny), which affects interests. To reiterate, research shows that low interest in an area may be reality to perceived inability, caused by social inequities. In practice, what this means is that a client or student who is a member of a marginalized or underrepresented group may score low in an area of interest, but this apparent lack of interest could be due to their sense of identity and what they are capable and permitted to do.

Take Away and Use Today

Trait and factor, person–environment fit, true reasoning, and work adjustment all share matching in common. These approaches to matching can appear simplistic to the untrained eye, but counselors and clients both know very well how complex this matching process can be. The first step in matching involves gathering pertinent information to match. This involves assessments that fit the theory used—in this case trait and factor—and, perhaps most importantly, guides clients in an appropriate interpretation of these assessments—what they say and do not say. The other pieces of information come from occupational resources that inform clients accurately about the world of work. These two categories of knowledge set the stage for the all-important matching step. This is where a well-trained counselor can assist clients in gathering the right information at the right time so as not to overwhelm the client. Once the information pieces begin to fall into place, counselors use their prodigious relational skills to facilitate the client's matching process, or true reasoning. This is the point at which counselors "sit" with clients in their anxiety about this often-ambiguous process. Next, they return to the Web and other informational resources to design next steps for the client, so they can take action. It's a sophisticated process that looks simple from a distance, which is why clients struggle to navigate it.

References

Briddick, W. C., & Sensoy-Briddick, H. (2013). Matching. In M. L. Savickas (Ed.), *Ten ideas that changed career development* (pp. 5–6). NCDA.

Chartrand, J. M. (1991). The evolution of trait-and-factor career counseling: A person x environment fit approach. *Journal of Counseling & Development, 69,* 518–524.

Chartrand, J. M., & Bertok, R. L. (1993). Current trait factor career assessment: A cognitive-interactional perspective. *Journal of Career Assessment, 1*(4), 323–340

Dawis, R. V. (2002). Person–environment–correspondence theory. *Career Choice and Development, 4,* 427–464.

Dawis, R. V., & Lofquist, L. H. (1976). Personality style and the process of work adjustment. *Journal of Counseling Psychology, 23*(1), 55–59. https://doi.org/10.1037/0022-0167.23.1.55

Dawis, R. V., & Lofquist, L. H. (1984). *A psychological theory of work adjustment.* University of Minnesota Press.

Herk, N. A., & Thompson, R. C. (2011). *International Technical Brief for the Strong Interest Inventory Assessment.* CPP, Inc.

Holland, J. L. (1997). Exploring careers with a typology: What we have learned and some new directions. *American Psychologist, 51,* 397–406.

Johnson, C.A, Weber, A.J., & Thompson, R.C. (2004). *Technical brief for the newly revised strong interest inventory assessment.* CPP, Inc.

Jung, C. G. (1971). *Psychological types (Collected works of C. G. Jung)* (Vol. 6, 3rd ed.). Princeton University Press.

King, S. P., & Mason, B. A. (2020). Myers–Briggs type indicator. In C. S. Nave & B. J. Carducci (Eds.), *The Wiley encyclopedia of personality and individual differences: Measurement and assessment*, 315–319. https://doi.org/10.1002/9781119547167.ch123

Lofquist, L. H., & Dawis, R. V. (1991). *Essentials of person–environment–correspondence counseling.* University of Minnesota Press.

Luke, C. (2018). *Career focused counseling: Integrating theory, research and neuroscience.*

McCrae, R. R., & Costa Jr, P. T. (1989). Reinterpreting the Myers–Briggs type indicator from the perspective of the five-factor model of personality. *Journal of personality, 57*(1), 17–40. https://doi.org/10.1111/j.1467-6494.1989.tb00759.x

Miller, W. R., & Rollnick, S. (2013). *Motivational interviewing: Helping people change.* Guilford Press.

Myers, I. B. (1980). *Gifts differing: Understanding personality type.* Davies–Black Publishing.

Randall, K., Isaacson, M., & Ciro, C. (2017). Validity and reliability of the Myers–Briggs Personality Type Indicator: A systematic review and meta-analysis. *Journal of Best Practices in Health Professions Diversity, 10*(1), 1–27.

Strong, E. K. (1943). *Vocational interests of men and women.* Stanford University Press.

Swanson, J. L., & Fouad, N. A. (2015). *Career theory and practice: Learning through case studies.* SAGE Publications.

Zytowski, D. G. (2001). Frank Parsons and the progressive movement. *The Career Development Quarterly, 50*(1), 57.

CREDIT

Fig. 6.1: Adapted from source: https://www.nhes.nh.gov/elmi/career/graphics/hexagon.gif.

CHAPTER 7

Career Development Theories

Super and Gottfredson

CHAPTER GOALS

- Understand the specific career development theories.
- Consider how career development occurs for clients.
- Apply these theories in work with diverse clients.

OPENING VIGNETTES

School-Based

Tara is a ninth grader in a rural high school. She is excited to start high school and believes she wants to be a nurse. Her family and teachers support this decision, and she knows her aunt, who is a pediatric nurse, is happy with the work she does. Because she is in honors math and science courses, one of her teachers asks Tara if she might ever consider being a doctor. Tara indicates that the doctors she knows are all men, and she questions her ability to handle such a difficult career. However, the question piques her curiosity, and Tara makes an appointment with her school counselor.

Agency-Based

Louis is a 32-year-old man who works as an assistant manager for a large clothing retailer. He has an associate's degree in business and has been working at the store for the past four years. He enjoys some aspects of the work, including interacting with customers and employees and enjoys the fast pace required in his position. However, he is generally dissatisfied with how he spends his time. Louis is the youngest of five children and lives in the basement apartment of his parents' home. To cover his rent, he does various chores around the house and takes his father to weekly physical therapy appointments. He recently broke up with his girlfriend of two years because they "wanted different things from life." He is seeking counseling because he feels depressed and lonely.

TAKE A MINUTE

What stands out to you about these? Where would you want to start? What are the immediate career-focused concerns you note?

REFLECTION ACTIVITIES AND QUESTIONS

1. Think back to when you were in elementary and middle school. What did you do for fun? What activities did you do that helped inform what you liked or disliked? Do you see any connections between these early activities and your current career path?
2. Most of us embody multiple roles at any given time. For example, you are a student, and this role likely takes up a lot of your time. What roles do you currently hold in your life? Think about the importance of each role; are some more important than others? If you could wave a magic wand, how would your various roles look?
3. What do you know about development theories? Perhaps you took a course in your undergraduate or graduate program, and perhaps, they discussed a number of different developmental theories (e.g., Piaget and Erikson's). What did these theories say about career development (my guess is not a lot)?

Introduction

Ah, development. It is so hard to believe that when research on career began, it was primarily viewed as a snapshot in time. In other words, a client needed career education or guidance and sought help. The helper provided information and activities designed to better understand current interests and goals. This information was put together to create a plan for occupational choice. Today, it would be almost inconceivable to not consider developmental level and stage as we explore career issues with clients.

Most career theories view career as a developmental process, beginning in childhood and constantly evolving throughout one's lifetime. Some of these theories are discussed elsewhere in this book, but two are specifically focused on career development and are therefore discussed here. As discussed in prior chapters, the earliest career theories saw career as a moment in time rather than a developmental process. Donald Super was one of the first theorists to propose a lifelong career perspective. Linda Gottfredson also focused her career theory on development but primarily on childhood through early adulthood. Both theories have informed our understanding of how career adapts and how career decisions are made across time.

Gottfredson's Theory of Circumscription and Compromise

Consider the following careers. For each career, identify whether it is a career typically for male-identifying people, mostly for female-identifying people, or for anyone. Then, identify its prestige level as *not at all prestigious*, *a little prestigious*, *somewhat prestigious*, *prestigious*, or *very prestigious*.

1. Accountant
2. Pro football player
3. Nuclear engineer
4. Actor
5. Surgeon
6. Preschool teacher
7. Postal worker
8. Pastry chef
9. Construction worker
10. Social worker

How did you make your decisions? Looking over your responses, what themes do you notice?

THEORY OVERVIEW

First proposed in 1981, Gottfredson's theory of circumscription and compromise focuses on the development of career aspirations and how career decisions are made. Gottfredson (1981) envisioned the theory as an extension to the understanding of career development offered by Super and Holland and wanted a more intentional inclusion of cultural factors that influence career. Even though the theory builds on the foundations offered by Super's theory, we are going to describe Gottfredon's ideas first, since she primarily focused on childhood and adolescence. We believe it is important to both acknowledge and condemn Gottfredson's perspectives on racial inequality and affirmative action. However, we also want to present her theory as one possible way to understand the impact of social factors on career decision-making. Gottfredson's theory has some empirical support and can be considered helpful in understanding the complexities regarding career interests and choices.

CONCEPTS

Gottfredson (1981) defined several key concepts related to her theory. First, *self-concept* is seen as a combination of how people view themselves as well as their understanding of their multiple identities, including gender, social class, and interests. Next, *occupational images* refer to beliefs someone has about a specific career. The image includes beliefs about the types of people in these jobs, including gender, prestige, and type of work being done. Career choice is ultimately made through a *zone of acceptable alternatives*, also called *social space*. This space includes the occupations that a person views as acceptable options based on their occupational images. Narrowing of the field of acceptable careers is called *circumscription*. Gottfredson believed that people consider whether an occupation is compatible with their self-concept, with those being more compatible being more highly valued. Beyond compatibility, people also consider the *accessibility* of entering the career field (Gottfredson, 1981). Therefore, *compromise* ultimately occurs in making final career decisions.

THEORY ESSENTIALS

According to the theory, people go through a series of stages of career development and choice.

- The first stage is *orientation to size and power* (ages 3–5 years). In this stage, children begin to identify adult roles and understand the concept of an occupation. Important concepts learned in this stage include little versus big and the idea of jobs. An example of this is when a child describes a career in terms of the tools used in that occupation. For example, a four-year old may say that a firefighter uses a ladder, hose, and firetruck to describe the job.
- The second stage is *orientation to sex roles* (ages 6–8 years). In this stage, children begin to realize that careers are tied to gender, with certain careers being for men and others for women. During this concrete stage, children learn to group jobs by sex type and gender. So a seven year old may say that home repair is a man's job—perhaps, because they have only seen male workers come to their home to fix their roof, air conditioning, or toilet.
- The third stage is *orientation to social valuation* (ages 9–13 years). In this stage, students become aware of how society values different careers. The socioeconomic prestige of various careers is particularly salient, as is the overall prestige attached to different jobs. For example, a sixth grade student may highlight the fame that comes with being a TikTok social influencer as a reason she wants that career for herself.
- The fourth and final stage is *orientation to the internal, unique self* (ages 14 and up). In this stage, adolescents become aware of their own interests and values and place these within their understanding of different careers. It is only here that the complexities of each individual enter into career choice. So a 15 year old may begin to recognize that he enjoys helping others, instructing, and being creative and use these as reasons to become a teacher.

Gottfredson (1981) believed that at each stage more and more occupations were removed from the *zone of acceptable careers*, often based on stereotypical beliefs about gender, prestige, and power. For example, a seven-year-old boy may decide that nursing is only for girls and, therefore, inappropriate as a career choice. A nine-year-old girl may believe that scientists are mostly men, so while they have social valuation, being a scientist is not a realistic career for girls. Views of careers also change over time. A boy may believe that a garbage collector is an acceptable occupation based on sex type, but as he grows older he may discard this occupation as not having a high enough level of social valuation.

Research on Gottfredon's theory gives some support to her ideas. In her earlier model, Gottfredson suggested that sex type would be the last belief about occupations that people were willing to compromise (Gottfredson, 1981), but she later suggested that this was only true when there was a high degree of compromise required. Blanchard and colleagues' research (2003) only partially supports these hypotheses, with both prestige and sex type being more highly valued than interests. In other words, people are willing to enter careers that do not match their interests more readily than enter careers that do not match their perceptions of prestige and sex type (Blanchard et al., 2003). Henderson et al. (1988), however, found that for children and young adolescents, career preferences were most influenced by sex typing and then by prestige. In their study, girls demonstrated more flexibility with sex typing than boys did, being open to less stereotyping of different occupations.

Gottfredson's theories about the impact of cultural identities on career also have some empirical support. Cochran et al. (2011) found that ability and parent socioeconomic status both impacted occupational aspirations, with adolescents from higher SES families and those with stronger abilities having to make less compromises in their final career selections. A longitudinal study of career aspirations demonstrated that as adolescents moved through high school, they shifted their career goals to be more aligned with their parents' expectations, which were aligned with their SES (Helwig, 2001). Compromises were, therefore, made based on family income level.

An important caveat to all of Gottfredson's ideas is the changing perspective on gender identity. When Gottfredson created her theory, gender was discussed solely in binary terms, with male and female being the only options and directly tied to sex at birth. Today, however, gender identity is considered more fluid and to be a choice made by individuals—not necessarily tied to biology. As Wada et al. (2019) pointed out, Gottfredson's theory relies on the idea of masculine and feminine careers, and its language may be inappropriate for use with gender nonconforming clients. They instead suggest considering how people choose or choose not to pursue gendered career paths. They acknowledge that many careers are still gendered in terms of power distribution, pay, status, and overall workforce demographics, and discussions about choices made to enter a career tied to a specific gender may be enlightening for all clients (Wada et al., 2019). In other words, discussions about how gender identity intersects with career choice can be powerful and important, but use of nonbinary language and acknowledgment of gender identity may be equally important.

WHY IT MATTERS

If you work with children or adolescents, it is likely that Gottfredson's theory will be important to understand. Students will be navigating their career development regardless of their reasons for visiting a counselor, and often, anxiety and stress about other life events will impact career-related beliefs. For example, children may feel afraid to make career decisions because they may not represent others' views of career. Or an adolescent may feel pressured by peers to select a career that is more financially lucrative than the one they really want to pursue. Understanding how career choice develops and how personal worldview impacts these choices is important for all counselors to understand.

For those of you planning to work with adults, you may wonder if understanding Gottfredson's theory is necessary. Consider the case of Joe, who seeks counseling because he is fighting with his partner Debbie. Debbie has indicated to Joe that he is unhappy with her career choice of police officer because he feels it is too dangerous and will be inappropriate when they have children. Joe says that Debbie has explained that the job is not just for men, and she makes a good living. Joe admits to feeling anxiety about Debbie's safety and concern about how they will care for their future children if she is a police officer. In this case, understanding how Joe developed his ideas about the appropriateness of different careers will help you gently challenge his beliefs in session.

In general, Gottfredson's theory is not used as a stand-alone counseling approach but rather as a way to understand early career development. In many ways, counselors can use Gottfredson's concepts similar to how they might use Erikson's theory of development. We now shift our attention to Donald Super and his theory of career development over the lifespan. As you read the next sections, be sure to consider how to embed Gottfredson's ideas into Super's life stages. The two together can provide a strong understanding of career development.

Super's Life-Span, Life-Space Theory of Career Development

THEORY OVERVIEW

Whereas Gottfredson's theory primarily focused on childhood and adolescence, Donald Super's theory offers a lifespan perspective of career development. Super (1954) proposed a need to study career development longitudinally and began the career pattern study to explore career over the lifetime. Super's research and subsequent theory led to a change in viewing career as a single choice to a process of choices over one's lifetime (Herr, 1997). A highlight of Super's theory was his willingness to constantly revise it as he learned more about career and better understood societal context. If you are interested, there is a fascinating article on the evolution of Super's theory (Salomone, 1996). Described below is the current version of the theory, with general descriptions about earlier perspectives.

THEORIST PROFILE

Donald Super began his career-focused work in the 1950s with his career pattern study (Salomone, 1996). In this longitudinal study, Super followed the career paths of a group of high school boys to understand how career developed over time (Lokan, 1996). He originally postulated that people have varied interests, abilities, and personalities and that these characteristics created a pattern that could be used to identify possible career paths. He also noted that vocational development occurred over the lifetime. In later iterations of his theory, Super moved away from his focus on a stage process that occurred in a linear fashion to one that was more dynamic and ever-changing, similar to the world of work. He ultimately helped create a range of career assessments and helped shift our understanding of career to include a developmental focus.

MAIN CONCEPTS

Super's theory is filled with constructs. *Life-space* refers to the many roles that people hold across their lifetime (Super, 1980). The life-space consists of nine major roles that are more or less salient at different times. These include: child, student, citizen, worker, homemaker, leisurite, spouse, parent, and pensioner. In the more recent iterations of this theory, Super focused on six primary roles, eliminating pensioner, spouse, and parent and combining the latter two with homemaker. These roles are represented on a *life–career rainbow* that helps visualize the importance of each role at different career stages. *Role salience* refers to the importance of a life role (Savickas, 2001), and in career counseling, work salience is the focus of life-space reviews. People typically embody multiple roles at any given time.

Five career stages constitute the *life-span* (Super, 1975). These stages were "borrowed" from psychologist Charlotte Buehler and revised over time to specifically focus on career development (Salomone, 1996). Super initially believed that people moved through the five life-span stages in a sequential order and even attached average ages to each stage. These ages have been largely eliminated now to account for the many different careers that people have over the course of their lives:

- **Growth:** Typically occurring in childhood but may be revisited later in life, the growth stage is characterized by development of abilities, interests, and values and identification of initial career interests. Super (1975) noted that relationships with important others strongly influence this developmental time. He also believed that early preferences were reflective of the emotional responses children have toward various careers, rather than based on aptitude or true interest.
- **Exploration:** Beginning in adolescence, exploration involves engaging in a variety of activities that help in learning about the world of work. Role models often impact goal development during this stage. During exploration, people try on various career possibilities, often moving from tentative interest to more sustained commitment (Super, 1975).
- **Establishment:** Beginning upon entry into the world of work, the establishment stage involves initial entry into the workforce. People in this stage are entering a specific career path and learning its intricacies. This stage is revisited every time a career shift is made.
- **Maintenance:** Typically occurring later in one's work life, maintenance involves keeping up with new work-related activities, engaging in advanced work, or revisiting work experiences. Maintenance stage workers may be learning new tasks related to their current career or advancing their work to create new opportunities.
- **Disengagement:** Sometimes referred to as decline, this stage typically occurs at or near retirement, when one leaves full-time employment. Work may become less central, or the type of work may change, but in either case, the pace of work often decelerates during this stage.

Super offered several additional definitions to better understand the cyclic nature of these stages. He revised his theory to include the concept of *recycling*, referring to the idea of returning to an earlier life-span stage because of changing careers or reconsidering choices (Smart & Peterson, 1997). He added the concept of recycling to better address the instability of the modern workforce and viewed the process as a positive one to enhance coping and adaptability (Smart & Peterson, 1997). Super also used the term *minicycle* to describe the brief returns to prior developmental stages as a result of recycling. Lastly, he used the term *maxicyle* to describe lifelong career development across the five stages (Super, 1980).

Another key concept in Super's theory is the idea of *career maturity*. This refers to a strong understanding of self that provides the readiness to make career decisions (Savickas, 1997). Super often used the word "planfulness" to refer to awareness of options and use of resources to learn about the world of work; planfulness is seen as a critical component of career maturity (Savickas, 1997). Importantly, Super shifted his idea of career maturity to *career adaptability*, referring to ability to cope with the constantly changing workplace and life roles people inhabit (Super et al., 1992). Adaptability later became the cornerstone to Savikas's career construction theory (see Chapter 9), but for Super's work, it helped establish a recognition that career was no longer linear.

MECHANISMS OF CHANGE

As indicated above, application of Super's theory involves understanding the life-stage and life-span for each client. Counselors help clients describe their career path from its early development to current state of being as well as encourage discussion of the salience of various life roles. Although Super promoted the use of formal assessments (as discussed in this chapter) to understand these in clients, most counselors using this theory today simply engage the client with basic counseling skills such as open-ended questions, reflections, and identification of themes.

To learn about life roles within a life-span context, for example, many counselors will have their clients complete a life career rainbow. Clients identify life roles (e.g., child, student, or worker) they have previously and currently hold and add them to a rainbow that represents the various life stages (i.e., growth through disengagement). This is important because each role carries with it different tasks and responsibilities and can aid clients in matching their own expectations with their current roles. Clients can make the rainbow arc for each role thicker or thinner based on the time spent or salience of each role. So a client who is currently a full-time worker and who cares for both their own children and their aging parents would have thicker arcs for worker, homemaker, and child—and, perhaps, thin arcs for student and leisurite. In comparison, a client who is a full-time student with no caretaker responsibilities might have thick arcs for student and citizen but thinner arcs for other life roles.

Super proposed the more formal Career-Developmental Career Assessment and Counseling (C-DAC) model to translate his developmental theory into an approach to career counseling (Super et al., 1992). The C-DAC model encourages the use of a variety of quantitative assessments designed to assess life-span, life-stage, work salience, interests, and work values. Designed for adolescents through adults, the C-DAC model suggests administering the following

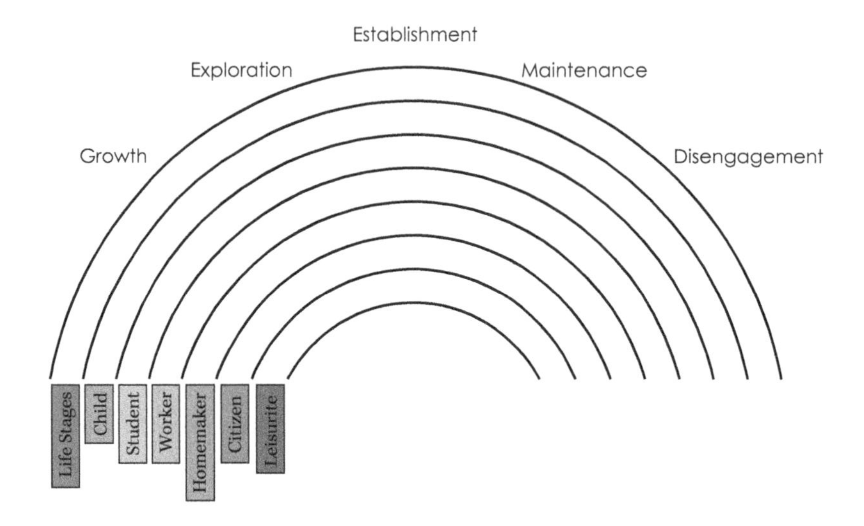

FIGURE 7.1. Life–career rainbow template. Shade each arc to depict the salience of each life role during each life stage.

assessments, all of which can be found for free on **http://vocopher.com/**. The site is intended for use with clients and students who register:

- Career Development Inventory (CDI; Super et al., 1988) or the Adult Career Concerns Inventory (ACCI; Super et al., 1988) to assess career readiness and adaptability
- Strong Interest Inventory (SII; Myers-Briggs Company, 2012) to assess for career interests
- The Values Scale (VS; Nevill & Super, 1989) to identify work-specific values
- The Salience Inventory (SI; Nevill & Super, 1986) to consider the importance of five life roles (student, worker, citizen, homemaker, and leisurite)

These assessments are all available free of charge on www.vocopher.com. However, many practitioners use a combination of formal assessments and general information gathering rather than using the full battery of surveys with clients. Clients may be put off by the sheer number of questions and different surveys, and the assessments themselves have not been normed for all cultural groups.

Whichever way the information is collected, the C-DAC model then involves sharing the results with clients and discussing how they fit into the client's view of career (Super et al., 1992). It is vital that discussions of career development stage and role salience are discussed in detail. Counselors can clarify these various constructs as needed and help the client understand how they are intertwined (Freeman, 1993). Counselors can then help by providing guidance on how to learn more about various careers and how these careers interact with client interests, values, and goals.

Super's theory has been partially supported by empirical evidence. Many researchers have expressed concerns about its usability in practice. For example, researchers have explored different ways to translate the theory into practice (e.g., Harrington & Harrington, 2002;

Hartung, 2002; Herr, 1997; Savickas, 1997), suggesting that while the theory is useful in providing an understanding of career development, it is less helpful with actual counseling processes. Super himself recognized the need for more connectivity of his many constructs and encouraged more work in this area (Freeman, 1993).

Theory in Session

SCHOOL-BASED TRANSCRIPT

School Counselor (SC): Hi, Tara. How are you today?

Tara (ST): I'm good. I wanted to talk about career plans. I always thought I wanted to be a nurse, but Mr. Roberts said my grades were good enough for me to consider becoming a doctor. So now I'm just confused. And with 10th grade registration coming up soon, I thought it might be good to talk about what I should do.

SC: I see. Well, you and I have spoken before about friendship stuff but never about career planning. It does seem like a good idea to have this conversation. Let me look up your schedule, so I can see what you are taking this year and how classes are going.

ST: Yeah, they are going really well. I have an A in honors biology and geometry, and high Bs in my other courses. I have always liked math and science and found them to be pretty easy, but I don't think I could ever be a doctor. Most of my family never even attended college, except for my one aunt who went to community college to become a nurse. Also, I want to be a mom someday, and that would be hard if I became a doctor.

The counselor is exploring role salience and life-stage.

SC: Yes, you are doing really well in your classes, and most of your teachers have recommended that you continue in honors coursework next year. I hear you talking about your interest in math and science and things that are important to you, such as having a family. What else is important to you or are you interested in?

ST: Well, I haven't really thought of any other careers besides nurse. You know that there are not a lot of different careers people go into around here; they work at the factory, own a shop, work in a restaurant, or do the other jobs such as teacher or lawyer. Most of the rest of my family works at the factory, and I know I don't want to do that, so seeing my aunt happy as a nurse made it seem like it would be a good fit. As far as things important to me, I don't know. I guess having friends, doing something that earns enough money, and doing something I don't hate are all important.

SC: So, Tara, you seem to have some knowledge about careers around here, but I wonder if you would benefit from learning more about your interests and values and careers that might match these? If so, I have a couple of short surveys that you can take. Would you be interested in these? And then we can discuss the results next week?

The counselor offers developmentally appropriate and free exploration activities.

ST: Okay. That sounds good.

The school counselor gives Tara an interest inventory and a values worksheet to complete in her office. Then, Tara reports back to class. The following conversation happens the next week:

SC: So how were the two surveys?

CL: They were fine. The career one had some jobs that I had never heard of before, like optometrist. But most of them I knew at least a little. The values checklist was easy. I just circled the 10 values that were most important to me.

ST: Great. So let's go over the results. It looks like you are most interested in careers that have math and science, like doctor, nurse, and pharmacist. You also seem interested in careers that allow you to be in charge, such as manager, engineer, and science teacher. And your most important values are challenge, opportunity to lead, solving problems, helping others, and collaboration. As you hear all of this, what stands out to you?

The counselor is helping to put together values, interests, and abilities for career self-concept.

ST: Hmmm ... I never thought about the importance of my values related to a career. It was always just something you did to pay the bills and I just hoped I wouldn't be miserable like my dad. I do like to have some say in what I do with my day and like to lead groups on projects and activities. I also like the fact that there are other science jobs besides doctor and nurse.

SC: It sounds like reviewing these assessments has helped open you up to new ideas about career choices. I think our next steps might be to find out more about some of the careers that looked interesting and also to make sure you are signed up for classes that will help you achieve your career goals. How does that sound?

The counselor is planning further counseling and reflection to put it all together.

ST: That would be great. I was worried about what to do next and not sure where to find more information, so I'm really glad you can help with that.

TAKE A MINUTE

How might you embed Gottfredson's concepts into work with Tara? What if Tara was uncomfortable with formal assessments; what might be some good alternatives to the more formal assessments used in the example?

AGENCY-BASED TRANSCRIPT

Mental health counselor (MHC): Louis, up until now, we have been talking about how your recent break up with your girlfriend and your challenges related to living at home have affected your overall feelings about yourself. Today, however, I heard you mention that your current job is also adding to your feelings of depression. Can you tell me more about this?

Louis (CL): Yes, definitely. I was a little afraid to bring this up because I know you are not a career counselor, but I have been thinking about whether to stay in my current job or even in my current career. I like my job okay, but it is not very exciting or challenging. I also feel like I don't really connect with my coworkers and wonder if that is related to my feeling lonely all the time.

MHC: Well, I think that career is directly related to how you feel and how all people feel. Most adults spend the majority of their time working, so it makes sense that work would impact how you feel.

The counselor is validating career role salience.

CL: Yeah, that's true. Even before I broke up with my ex, I was pretty unhappy at work. She said I just needed to deal with it, but looking back, I think I chose this job and a career in business, because it seemed like a path to support myself financially and there were lots of opportunities. Now, I wonder if what I am doing really fits for who I am and want to be.

MHC: Tell me a little more about how you chose your job and career.

CL: Um ... let's see. I graduated from high school and knew that four-year college was not for me. My grades were okay, but I had to stay home to help support my parents, and there was no university nearby that was affordable. But the local community college was there, and I could attend for almost nothing. So I enrolled part-time and worked full-time at a local convenience store. I had to pick a focus, sort of like a major, so I selected business. Not really sure why, but it sounded good at the time. It took three years for me to finish my associate degree, and then I got my first job at a clothing store in their management trainee program. I worked there for several years and was promoted to assistant manager. After that, I moved to my current position, where I'm still assistant manager, but at a much larger store, so I oversee a lot of employees.

MHC: Okay, I hear you saying that you did not really investigate a career path but rather followed your instincts?

The counselor is learning about Louis's investment in exploration.

CL: Kind of. I just didn't know what I wanted to do, but knew that I liked organizing, planning, and leading others. And those were the types of things that were in

Further learning of exploration activities.

the description of the business focus. I also wanted a career where, as a Black male, I would possibly find respect.

MHC: I see. So there was some intentionality in choosing your major. You thought about your personality and what you enjoyed and found a career option that offered these things. It seems you also wanted to work where your cultural identity would be accepted.

CL: Yeah, you are right. I just feel like I could have done more to really investigate careers to try and find a really good fit.

MHC: I think I can help with that. I have a few assessments that help people learn about their interests and values. I believe they are culturally respectful, but if you find them off-putting, please let me know. They might help you with identifying possible new careers. Also, I think it is important for us to talk about your life roles and how they intersect with your career. For example, you spend a lot of time caring for your aging parents, and I know that while you feel this is important, it is also a strain on your time. I'd like to start with a review of your life roles. Perhaps, we can make a list of your various roles and how much time you spend in each. We can also reflect on whether these time commitments reflect the value you place on each role. For example, you have previously talked about your volunteer activities, so that might be one role. Learning about these different roles might help give us some direction.

The counselor is helping to explore life roles.

CL: That makes sense. Since I have a lot on my plate, putting all of these activities on paper would be really helpful.

TAKE A MINUTE

What other life roles might be impacting Louis's career development and how might you address these with him? How are Gottfredson's ideas embedded into Louis's understanding of acceptable careers?

Neuroscience, Culture, and Development

Neuroscience underpins and underscores the nature of development. Luke and Redekop describe how this unfolds:

> One view of brain development is that brain regions developed as environmental needs required. The earliest of brain structures, the hindbrain, is focused on survival. It manages basic life functions such as regulating breathing and heart rate and includes

> an internal threat-detection system. Later, the limbic system developed to respond to a more social environment that contained rewards. Therefore, the early parts of the forebrain developed a reward-detection system. Most recently, the cerebral cortex developed to adapt to increasingly complex social environs, adding to the system a context-detection system.
>
> Therapy has been known to begin with interventions involving the most recently developed (in evolutionary terms) brain regions. In fact, cognitive behavior therapy and rational emotive behavior therapy are two of the main empirically supported treatments recognized by insurance companies and are often the most straightforward to measure for research purposes.
>
> These approaches posit that abstract reasoning, critical thinking and problem-solving skills are essential early on in counseling so that problem thoughts, feelings and behaviors can be brought into alignment with individual and social expectations (i.e., top-down processing). However, it has been increasingly demonstrated that assisting clients in managing their breathing and heart rate and engaging in other mindfulness-based interventions aids them in thinking about their problems more clearly (i.e., bottom-up processing). (2016, p. 16).

Career development theories such as those discussed in this chapter naturally attend to developmental level. They provide a sense of the typical career activities occurring for people across the lifespan, while also recognizing that career is not a linear path any longer. Unlike traditional development theories, career development theories today must acknowledge that stages will likely be revisited multiple times. Having a language to understand how career develops over time is vital to understanding how to best help clients. The activities related to career development differ by stage; for example, someone in exploration might need a values or interest inventory, but a person in maintenance might instead benefit from discussions about how to make their current career more exciting or challenging.

Attention to culture can be tricky with the theories discussed in this chapter. As mentioned earlier, these theories were developed when our understanding of cultural impact was quite different than today. Binary language, gendered career beliefs, and a focus on college-education might limit some of the utility of these approaches. However, applying a cultural lens can be helpful in adapting these theories to still be relevant. For example, using the concept of adaptability rather than maturity can better reflect the uncertainty of career paths for most people. Also, understanding that career may be paid or unpaid can extend the theory's relevance to those whose work involves volunteering or caring for loved ones.

These theories can be made more culturally sensitive in other ways as well. An easy adaptation is to recognize that the values included in some career values scales, including the one used in the C-DAC model, may not represent the values of all cultural groups. An easy alternative is to use a broader values card sort of larger values list, where values can be discussed more personally rather than being compared to a norm group. Another is to acknowledge that some of the activities found across the stages may only represent westernized points of view, as they tend to be focused on individualism and external success. Lastly, counselors using these approaches need to overtly acknowledge the systemic oppression that likely impedes career development for marginalized groups and offer open discussions about these topics in counseling.

Take Away and Use Today

Recognizing that career development occurs over a lifetime helps remind us that career-focused counseling is about more than just finding a job or major. It is about understanding how various life roles are impacted by career development tasks and how career development tasks impact our lives. This reminder helps ensure that, as counselors, we always inquire about career development and consider how career activities may be impacting the lives of our clients.

References

Blanchard, C. A., & Lichtenberg, J. W. (2003). Compromise in career decision making: A test of Gottfredson's theory. *Journal of Vocational Behavior, 62*(2), 250–271. https://doi.org/10.1016/S0001-8791(02)00026-X

Cochran, D. B., Wang, E. W., Stevenson, S. J., Johnson, L. E., & Crews, C. (2011). Adolescent occupational aspiration: Test of Gottfredson's theory of circumscription and compromise. *Career Development Quarterly, 59*, 412–427.

Freeman, S. C. (1993). Donald Super: A perspective on career development. *Journal of Career Development, 19*(4), 255–264. https://doi.org/10.1007/BF01354628

Gottfredson, L. (1981). Circumscription and compromise: A developmental theory of occupational aspirations. *Journal of Counseling Psychology, 28*(6), 545–579. https://doi.org/10.1037/0022-0167.28.6.545

Harrington, T., & Harrington, J. (2002). The ability explorer: Translating super's ability-related theory propositions into practice. *The Career Development Quarterly, 50*(4), 350–358. https://doi.org/10.1002/j.2161-0045.2002.tb00583.x

Hartung, P. J. (2002). Cultural context in career theory and practice: Role salience and values. *The Career Development Quarterly, 51*(1), 12–25. https://doi.org/10.1002/j.2161-0045.2002.tb00588.x

Helwig, A. A. (2001). A test of Gottfredson's theory using a ten-year longitudinal study. *Journal of Career Development, 28*(2), 77–95. https://doi.org/10.1023/A:1012578625948

Henderson, S., Hesketh, B., & Tuffin, K. (1988). A test of Gottfredson's theory of circumscription. *Journal of Vocational Behavior, 32*(1), 37–48. https://doi.org/10.1016/0001-8791(88)90004-8

Herr, E. L. (1997). Super's life-span, life-space approach and its outlook for refinement. *The Career Development Quarterly, 45*(3), 238–246. https://doi.org/10.1002/j.2161-0045.1997.tb00468.x

Lokan, J. (1996). Remembering the life and work of Donald Super (1910–1994). *Australian Journal of Career Development, 5*(2), 3–6. https://doi.org/10.1177/103841629600500202

Myers-Briggs Company (2012). *Strong Interest Inventory Manual (with supplement).*

Nevill, D. D., & Super, D. E. (1986). *Manual for the Salience Inventory.* Palo Alto: Consulting Psychologists Press.

Nevill, D. D., & Super, D. E. (1989). *Manual for the Values Scale.* Palo Alto: Consulting Psychologists Press.

Salomone, P. R. (1996). Tracing Super's theory of vocational development: A 40-year retrospective. *Journal of Career Development, 22*(3), 167–184. https://doi.org/10.1177/089484539602200301

Savickas, M. L. (1997). Career adaptability: An integrative construct for life-span, life-space theory. *The Career Development Quarterly, 45(*3), 247–259. https://doi.org/10.1002/j.2161-0045.1997.tb00469.x

Savickas, M. L. (2001). A developmental perspective on vocational behaviour: Career patterns, salience, and themes. *International Journal for Educational and Vocational Guidance, 1*(1), 49–57. https://doi.org/10.1023/A:1016916713523

Smart, R., & Peterson, C. (1997). Super's career stages and the decision to change careers. *Journal of Vocational Behavior, 51*(3), 358–374. https://doi.org/10.1006/jvbe.1996.1544

Super, D. E. (1954). Career patterns as a basis for vocational counseling. *Journal of Counseling Psychology, 1*(1), 12–20. https://doi.org/10.1037/h0061989

Super, D. E. (1975). Career education and career guidance for the life span and for life roles. *Journal of Career Development, 2*(2), 27–42. https://doi.org/10.1177/089484537500200204

Super, D. E. (1980). A life-span, life-space approach to career development. *Journal of Vocational Behavior, 16*, 282–298.

Super, D. E., Osborne, L., Walsh, D. J., Brown, S. D., & Niles, S. G. (1992). Developmental career assessment and counseling: The C-DAC model. *Journal of Counseling & Development, 71*, 74–80.

Super, D. E., Thompson, A. S., Lindeman, R. H., Jordaan, J. P., & Myers, R. A. (1988). *Manual for the Adult Career Concerns Inventory and the Career Development Inventory.* Palo Alto: Consulting Psychologists Press.

Wada, K., McGroarty, E. J., Tomaro, J., & Amundsen-Dainow, E. (2019). Affirmative career counselling with transgender and gender nonconforming clients: A social justice perspective orientation. *Canadian Journal of Counselling and Psychotherapy, 53*(3), 255.

CHAPTER 8

Social Cognitive Career Theory

CHAPTER GOALS

- Understand social cognitive career theory.
- Learn how to assess for social cognitive variables during counseling sessions.
- Apply SCCT to your work with clients and students.

OPENING VIGNETTES

School-Based

Lanie is a junior in high school, and her mother has been pressuring her to decide which colleges she wants to visit to plan for life after graduation. Lanie does well in school but often feels disconnected from class discussions and worries she is not smart enough to attend college. In addition, she is unsure she really wants to continue her formal education and has been thinking about cosmetology school. However, her mother is a college graduate and expects her to graduate from a four-year college and enter a "respectable, professional career"; Lanie is fairly certain that being a hairdresser would not be acceptable.

Agency-Based

John is a 28-year-old male, who is considering next steps in his career. John graduated from high school and works at a convenience store, starting as a cashier and now serving as an assistant manager. He is married to Laura, and they have a two-year-old son and another child on the way. Laura wants John to take courses at the local community college, so he can eventually move into a higher paying position in a business-related field. John likes the hours at his current job, feels he is well suited to the work, and is unsure about how successful he would be in a formal college setting. He remembers high school being difficult and isolating, and he often felt that his teachers had low expectations of him. He enjoys feeling a sense of worth in his current job and appreciates that his boss treats him well.

TAKE A MINUTE

What stands out to you about these? Where would you want to start? What are the immediate career-focused concerns you note?

REFLECTION ACTIVITIES AND QUESTIONS

1. As you were growing up, how did you develop your beliefs about what activities you were successful in and what activities you were less successful in?
2. What were some things that got in the way of, or made it harder to achieve, your educational or career plans and goals? What are some of your cultural identities and background characteristics that contributed to your career development?
3. Talk to a friend or family member who has been in a career for at least a few years. Ask about how they made their career choice, what helped and hindered their career path, and how their beliefs about their own abilities impacted their path. What did you learn about them from their answers?

Introduction

The last two theory chapters described some of the earlier theories of career counseling and development. With this chapter, we begin to explore more modern career theories that intentionally include cultural influences and overtly acknowledge the constantly changing world of work. Of these, social cognitive career theory (SCCT; Lent et al., 1994) has become the most researched career-focused theory existing today.

Theory Overview

Social cognitive career theory (SCCT) was developed by Robert Lent, Steven Brown, and Gail Hackett in 1994. The theory is based on Bandura's social learning theory and Hackett's work with Nancy Betz on the impact of self-efficacy beliefs on career development (Multon et al., 1991). SCCT focuses on the triadic relationship between self-efficacy, outcome expectations, and goals and how these are impacted by cultural background, perceived barriers, and supports to influence career and educational interests and actions (Lent et al., 1994). As shown in Figure 8.1, SCCT describes a multifaceted view of career development.

THEORY ESSENTIALS

Like most theories, SCCT includes multiple constructs that interact with one another. *Self-efficacy* (SE) refers to beliefs about one's ability to complete tasks related to specific activities

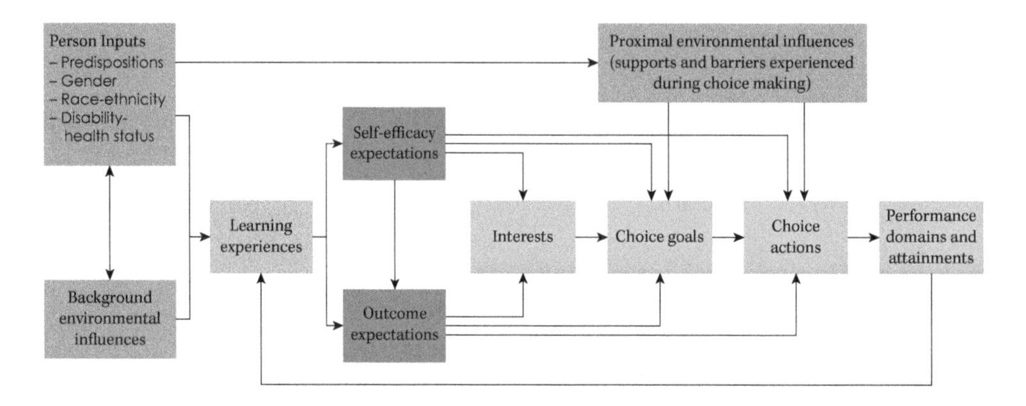

FIGURE 8.1. Social Cognitive Career Theory

(Lent et al., 1994). For example, if someone believes they have the skills, experience, and training needed to successfully engage in a tennis match, they can be said to have high tennis playing self-efficacy. On the other hand, if someone has never played tennis or believes they lack understanding of how the game is played, they would likely demonstrate low tennis self-efficacy. Because it is task specific, people can hold both strong self-efficacy beliefs related to some tasks and weak self-efficacy beliefs related to other activities (Brown et al., 2008). Specific to career and educational tasks, SCCT posits that self-efficacy beliefs directly impact interests. Typically, SCCT researchers consider self-efficacy related to career, career decision-making, education, and college-going when exploring career development (Lent et al., 1994).

SCCT posits that self-efficacy beliefs are developed through four general types of influences: personal performance accomplishments, vicarious learning, social persuasion, and physiological and affective states (Lent et al., 1994). Pulled directly from Bandura's (1986) work, these sources each impact overall self-efficacy beliefs. *Personal performance* refers to actual outcomes of an action and the relative failure to mastery level of this action. For example, earning a high grade on a math test will likely increase one's beliefs about the ability to do well in math. *Vicarious learning* is based on the observations of important others and one's reaction to these observations. When we see someone receiving praise or finding success after an activity, we are more likely to find value in that activity. *Social persuasion* refers to the messages received from influential others. So if a role model, such as an important teacher, gives you positive feedback after an action, this will likely positively impact your self-efficacy beliefs about this activity. Finally, *physiological and affective states* are the psychological and physical feelings associated with specific actions. For example, completing an activity while feeling stressed and depressed is going to negatively impact self-efficacy beliefs related to that activity—even if the feelings were not focused on the activity itself.

Outcome expectations (OE) refer to the if–then analysis related to engaging in a specific task (Lent et al., 1994). These expectations are typically based on the value one allots to a behavior. For example, a client who believes that attending college will lead to a better paying job, more career options, and overall success likely finds high value in college-going and has strong outcome expectations related to this activity. Alternatively, a client who believes that attending college may lead to more career options but will likely also increase financial debt and will not be very helpful overall has less strong outcome expectations for further schooling. Outcome expectations are directly influenced by self-efficacy beliefs and, in turn, directly impact interests (Byars-Winston & Fouad, 2008).

Goals are considered the motivators of behavior. They are the hopes and plans people have related to education and career options. Goals can help direct behaviors, increase motivation, and provide direction for people (Lent et al., 1994). They are not static and are directly impacted by interests and intentions and indirectly affected by self-efficacy and outcome expectation beliefs. They are also impacted by perceived barriers and supports (Lent et al., 1994). For example, a client that strongly desires to be a physician may use that desire to help motivate them during difficult science courses and help them recognize the importance of doing well. Alternatively, there are times when goals are not enough to motivate people; they may want something but question their ability to achieve a goal (self-efficacy) to the point where they abandon their plan.

Contextual factors are perceived barriers and supports that directly impact self-efficacy beliefs and may also impact interests, goals, and actions (Lent et al., 2000). They are the beliefs people hold related to structural, environmental, and social aspects that either encourage or hinder career and educational development. Common perceived *barriers* may include challenging family influences, lack of role models, lack of resources or concrete information, financial concerns, lack of preparation, indecision, or discrimination (Flores et al., 2017; McWhirter, 1997). Perceived *supports* can be relational, such as family, friends, and peers; content-based, such as knowing basic information and having access to information; and environmental, such as school or community responsiveness and opportunities (Lent et al., 2000). Barriers and supports moderate, or impact, interests, so interests tend to be higher when people perceive few barriers and many supports (Lent et al., 2000). A lack of perceived support can reduce self-efficacy and interest.

Background affordances and person inputs are often related to contextual factors but are not proximal but, rather, something you are born into or are introduced in childhood. Person inputs refer to what you are born with, such as sex, ethnicity, ability status, health, and innate talents. Background affordances, on the other hand, are contextual and environmental influences, such as socioeconomic status, parent education level, and local conditions that impact your learning experiences (Flores et al., 2017; Lent et al., 1994). Although it is possible to change these (e.g., receive medical care for a health issue), they still typically impact early learning experiences, thereby indirectly influencing self-efficacy beliefs and outcome expectations. Background affordances and person inputs directly connect to social justice and identity influences by overtly acknowledging the impact of culture on career development.

MECHANISMS OF CHANGE

According to SCCT, career interests and goals develop based on how exposure to various activities and messages received from important others are impacted by person inputs and background affordances (Lent et al., 1994). Self-efficacy and outcome expectations develop based on how a person categorizes their various experiences, and these beliefs are impacted based on perceived barriers and supports. All of these influence interests, goals, and actions. Therefore, the goals for counseling are to help clients increase career and educational self-efficacy beliefs, reduce or navigate barriers, and increase supports. Ideally, these changes will lead to more direct connections between self-efficacy beliefs, outcome expectations, and goals.

MODELS OF CAREER DEVELOPMENT

Lent et al. (1994) suggested that the SCCT model can be used to describe how *career interests develop*, how *career choices are made*, and how *career performance is explained*. In the interest model, direct and vicarious exposure during childhood and adolescence helps develop career interests. Cultural background (environmental influences) and person inputs directly impact these experiences, which, in turn, directly impact self-efficacy and outcome expectations. Over time, people create beliefs about their ability to successfully engage in various activities (self-efficacy) and typically become more interested in activities where they experience stronger self-efficacy beliefs. These ongoing experiences also impact outcome expectations as people attach value to different potential actions. These interests may also be moderated by perceived barriers and supports. Overall, interests tend to be greater for activities where people feel competency and value the possible outcomes.

In the choice model, the same constructs as above influence career and academic choices (versus interests). Choice goals are strongly impacted by background characteristics, proximal influences (barriers and supports), self-efficacy beliefs, and outcome expectations. As they all either directly or indirectly influence interests, the developed interests then directly impact choice goals (Sheu et al., 2010). However, perceived barriers or supports may mitigate the link between interests and choice goals (Lent et al., 1999). For example, a person may be interested in attending college to become a biologist, but financial constraints and family responsibilities may hinder that option. In these events, interests may be compromised and instead choices may be based on what feels possible in the moment. People with strong support systems are more likely to be able to directly link interests to choice goals.

Lastly, the performance model focuses on success in career and education and the level of persistence when barriers exist. Again, emphasizing the relationships between the primary constructs in SCCT, the performance model also adds in ability (Brown et al., 2011). A person's actual aptitude for a given task, along with their motivation to complete the task, affects performance of the task. In this model, self-efficacy and outcome expectations are impacted by ability, and all three are impacted by background environment and perceived barriers and supports (Brown et al., 2008). It is important to note that, even with extremely high self-efficacy beliefs, people without the actual ability to complete a task will likely have lower levels of performance. In other words, self-efficacy beliefs are not the same as ability.

SCCT IN ACTION

SCCT lends itself well to counseling practice. To start, counselors should build rapport with their client. As rapport is being created, the counselor can engage in discussions designed to learn about career and academic self-efficacy beliefs, outcome expectations, interests, and goals. In addition, the counselor should consider cultural context; for example, asking about a client's background or how beliefs developed can be helpful. Throughout, the counselor can inquire about perceived barriers and sources of support. In this first part of counseling, the counselor is using the theory constructs to develop a thorough understanding of the client's experiences and how beliefs developed.

In the second stage of counseling using SCCT, the counselor introduces new learning experiences that are designed to increase self-efficacy beliefs and outcome expectations, increase supports, decrease or navigate perceived barriers, and strengthen or clarify interests and goals. Depending on the client's overall career development, these activities may differ, but all are focused on identifying new learning experiences to shift beliefs, while still considering cultural and environmental context. Examples of new learning experiences include:

- For increasing self-efficacy and outcome expectations:
  - Activities that increase experience, such as learning career-specific skills. A client might learn how to search for jobs using an online platform or develop a résumé.
  - Activities that increase knowledge, such as learning about postsecondary options or career entry requirements. Students might explore different types of educational options available after high school or learn about the minimum schooling needed for a specific career.
  - Activities for vicarious learning, such as introduction of culturally similar role models in careers of interest. Clients might be introduced to those in their community who are working in careers of interest or be offered the opportunity to job shadow.
  - Discussion about the perceived value of various options, such as why furthering one's education might be useful. Students might be asked to reflect on what they believe might happen if they pursued a specific postsecondary degree or asked what they might feel if they changed majors.
- For clarifying interests and goals:
  - Activities to increase career awareness, such as job shadowing or informational interviews. Clients might meet with prospective employers at a job fair or watch online videos of people talking about their career (available in the *Occupational Outlook Handbook*).
  - Exploration of Holland codes and review of potential careers on O*Net. Students might complete a short career interest assessment and use the results to identify matching careers.
  - Discussion about how current interests link to future career opportunities. Clients might share why a career is of interest and how it relates to what they do for fun.
- For increasing supports:
  - Conversations with those from similar backgrounds about how they entered into their field of interest. Students might be paired with faculty from similar backgrounds to talk about how they navigated their career path.

  - Identification of ways to increase client networks and how to use these to navigate career activities. Clients might be asked to find new clubs or organizations to join and then use these to meet new people in careers similar to those of interest to them.
  - Increasing understanding of career and educational information to be used in decision-making. Students and their families might participate in a workshop on the various options after high school and how to select the best options.
- For decreasing or navigating barriers:
  - Open discussion about how to address microaggressions in the workplace. Clients might roleplay how to advocate for themselves when experiencing discrimination.
  - Exploration of scholarships, grants, and other ways to pay for education. Students might be given financial aid and scholarship information and encouraged to share it with their adult caregivers.
  - Acknowledgment of the reality of potential barriers and creation of possible ways to combat them.

In the final stage, clients may enact steps towards their existing goals or adapt and develop new goals. Based on new learning experiences, clients will hopefully have increased self-efficacy beliefs and outcome expectations, revised perspectives on perceived barriers and supports, and clarified overall goals and intentions.

SCHOOL COUNSELING VIGNETTE

Lanie has sought help from her school counselor Ms. Baxter. She has met with Ms. Baxter a few times in the past, mostly to discuss class changes. During their first meeting, Lanie explains that she is supposed to start selecting colleges:

> Lanie (ST): So my mom wants me to make a list of colleges that I want to visit, but I don't know where to start.
>
> Ms. Baxter (SC): It sounds like you are struggling with planning for life after high school.
>
> ST: Yeah. When I think about college, I feel kinda worried. It doesn't really fit with how I see myself.

Understanding self-efficacy, outcome expectations, barriers, and supports

> SC: Help me understand these feelings a bit more. Is it that you are worried about succeeding in college or that you are unsure if you want to attend college or something else?

College-going self-efficacy information

> ST: Well, you know how I asked you last year about the cosmetology class here? And then I said I changed my mind and decided to take computer applications instead?

(B nods). Well, I really wanted to take the other course, but my mom said I couldn't, and that I should take a class that might help me prepare for college. But, I'm not sure I'm the college type, ya know?

SC: Imagine if you do go to a four-year college. What do you think would happen? What would be the result?

ST: I feel confident that I could do college-level work, but I don't think I would find the work meaningful or related to any future career goals. It sort of seems like a waste of time.

College outcome expectations information

As Lanie and Ms. Baxter continue to talk, Lanie reveals that she would like a hands-on career that involves being social and creative, linking these desires to becoming a hairdresser. She also shares her belief that she might not fit in with other hair stylists because she comes from a family of high academic achievers. In their second session, Ms. Baxter tries to learn more about perceived barriers and supports:

SC: We have talked about your mom a lot and how she likely won't support your interest in cosmetology school. Can you tell me about other things that might get in the way of your career choice process?

ST: Yeah. I don't really know much about cosmetology school—like, what are good programs? How long do they take? What happens in them? So it's hard to know if I would actually like a program because I don't even know where to start. Also, I don't know anyone in that career other than my own hairdresser, and he is older and probably doesn't know much about training available today.

Perceived barriers of lack of information and lack of role models

SC: OK, and what about supports in place related to career decision-making? Who or what is helping you along the way?

ST: Well, talking with you is helpful. Also, my older sister always says I should follow my passion and stand up for myself, especially with my mom. And the cosmetology class could be helpful if I was allowed to take it.

Perceived supports

As Ms. Baxter and Lanie continue, they discuss steps Lanie can take to address some of her perceived barriers.

SC: I wonder if it might be helpful to learn more about local cosmetology programs.

New learning experience

ST: That would be great. Can you give me some websites to explore or at least point me in the right direction?

SC: Definitely. Also, I know you want to talk with your mom about how you feel about attending college. Would it be helpful to roleplay that in here first so you can practice what you might say?

ST: I'd like that. It will feel a little weird to pretend you are my mom, but I definitely want to at least list out my talking points.

TAKE A MINUTE

What other ways might Ms. Baxter help Lanie increase supports? How might cultural identities impact perceptions of perceived barriers for Lanie?

AGENCY VIGNETTE

John decides to seek counseling from a local community agency that his aunt used in the past. John begins counseling with Zachary, a White, middle-aged counselor. John, who is Latino, is hesitant at first because he wonders if Zachary can understand him, given how different their cultural identities seem to be. As they build rapport, however, Zachary takes time to acknowledge their similarities and differences and intentionally inquires about John's cultural background.

John (CL): So I grew up mostly with my mom and younger brothers. We had enough money but never a lot. My mom worked two jobs to make sure we had what we needed to survive, and she always hoped that my brothers and I would go to some kind of college so we could make a better salary than she did. But school was never my thing. There were very few Latino teachers and not a lot of support for the students of color at the school. It was like they expected us to graduate but then just go straight into work.

Background affordances and perceived barriers

Zachary (CMH): I hear you saying that your mom supported the idea of attending college, but the adults in your school didn't really add to that support and instead had very different expectations for you. It also sounds like being Latino was impactful related to your academic development.

CL: Yeah. None of my close friends had parents who went to college. The teachers didn't push us to consider college. My mom really wanted it, but since she didn't attend college herself, she encouraged us to get the information about applying from school, which obviously didn't happen.

Perceived barrier of lack of role models

CMH: So it was hard for you to imagine yourself as a college student because you didn't see others like you in college.

CL: Exactly. Plus, I wanted to start earning a living and not getting into debt. It seemed like that college would just lead to lack of money, and I needed to help my mom support my brothers, so earning an income was important. I get why my wife, Laura, is pushing me to return to school and I appreciate her belief that I can succeed there. I guess I'm a little hesitant to actually commit to something like this, where I might not be successful. In my job, I know I am good at what I do.

Outcome expectations and college self-efficacy beliefs

In session two, Zachary asks John what he wants from a career, so he can better understand his interests and goals.

CL: That's a good question. I haven't really thought much about what I want from a career. I like what I do now, so I guess I want to keep doing something like that. I like being an assistant manager, where I have some responsibility and decision-making choices, but not too much pressure. I enjoy talking with customers. I would like a better salary and healthcare benefits, especially with a second baby on the way. I don't want to move because we grew up here and our families are here.

CMH: Okay, this is really helpful. You know some of the values that are important to you but seem unsure about careers that match these interests and values. Is that correct? (John nods.) I wonder if you might consider completing a card sort with me. This is an activity where you review notecards with different careers listed on them and sort them into piles of interested, might be interested, and not interested. Then, we can talk about how you came to these decisions.

John agrees to the card sort and they complete it in session.

New learning experience

CMH: I noticed that most of the jobs you put in the not interested category involve science or math.

CL: Yeah, I really don't like anything to do with healthcare or science or lots of math. I can't see myself doing anything like that, and I don't think that is where my strengths are.

CMH: And many of the careers in the interested category are related to business and sales.

CL: Well, that is what I've been doing since high school and what I am good at. However, I also liked some of the other careers, like working at a hotel or being a restaurant manager. They are things I had never considered but think could be good fits. I don't know that I need more school for these; maybe I could just rely on my years of work experience instead.

As they continue to discuss career options, Zachary encourages John to talk with Laura about these new possibilities. When John returns for his next session, he explains that Laura will support his choices and is just excited he is trying to figure out what he wants from a job.

TAKE A MINUTE

What other learning experiences might help John as he continues on his career journey? What cultural and developmental aspects have not been included thus far in counseling with John?

Neuroscience, Culture, and Development

Culture and development are central to SCCT. Seen as a developmental approach to career, SCCT posits that background characteristics impact learning experiences, which, in turn, impact beliefs about career and educational pathways and goals. In more recent years, Lent and Brown (2019) have expanded SCCT models to describe career self-management and career satisfaction over the lifespan. Related to satisfaction, the core SCCT constructs (e.g., self-efficacy, outcome expectations, and goals) help predict work and life satisfaction. Positive feelings about work and life can motivate work persistence and help buffer perceived barriers. Career self-management focuses on how people consider career-related choices over the lifespan. These choices might range from initial career options to retirement, and the model still highlights the main SCCT constructs but shifts from simply actions and outcomes to how decisions are actually made (Lent & Brown, 2019). These extensions of the original models help ease the use of SCCT with clients of all ages.

Built into this framework is the importance of culture. In SCCT, all learning experiences are directly impacted by cultural identities and sociocultural factors. These characteristics make it easier to use SCCT with diverse clients. Additionally, SCCT research highlights its applicability with many different cultural groups and identities. These range from studies related to social class (Flores et al., 2017), people of color (Fouad & Santanta, 2017), international clients (Sheu & Bordon, 2017), and parent education level (Gibbons & Borders, 2010), among others. In general, the SCCT model demonstrates strong validity in predicting career development for diverse populations (Luke, 2018).

One of the features of SCCT is that, from a neuroscience perspective, it addresses both top-down processing and bottom-up processing. In this view, conscious, cognitive processes occupy a superordinate position in making decisions. Top-down processes include using the executive function of the prefrontal cortex to subordinate emotion and bodily processes (like respiration and heart rate). For example, exploration of self-efficacy beliefs, outcome expectancy, and setting effective goals provide mechanisms for regulating emotion. This will be familiar to students of counseling theory, particularly CBT, rational emotive behavior therapy (REBT), and reality therapy. These processes are particularly effective in executing predictable, "invariant" steps or tasks (Badenoch, 2008). Therefore, to harness the full power of top-down processing, models such as SCCT analyze and articulate sequential processes in career decision-making. The risk in this model is accounting for unpredictable experiences that can derail the process. In anticipation of these events, SCCT identifies safeguards (e.g., supports) in thinking and behaving that can inoculate the individual from such experiences.

In addition to top-down approaches, bottom-up processing can assist in unblocking cognitive evaluation processes. Bottom-up processes include using the body to manage emotions and cognitions. For example, taking a walk, breathing exercises, meditation, and similar exercises can aid in slowing down the sympathetic nervous system by activating the parasympathetic nervous system. Regarding Bandura's fourth mode of building self-efficacy, physiological arousal, it is important for counselors to assist clients in managing their thoughts and feelings about the process of career-related decisions. In particular, clients can benefit from learning techniques to manage their breathing and heart rate, as fast-paced breathing and high heart rate can indicate anxiety or fear, negatively impacting self-efficacy. Guided imagery and progressive muscle relaxation are two such techniques.

Taken together, these influences offer not only explanations of beliefs and behaviors but a way forward in terms of intervention. Counselors can leverage these to intervene in numerous ways with clients, from relaxation exercises (to address physiological arousal) to reflection exercises focusing on past success (personal mastery). This expands the intervention repertoire of counselors and instills hope for change in clients in regard to career-related issues.

Take Away and Use Today

SCCT suggests that self-efficacy beliefs, outcome expectations, and goals help determine career interests, goals, and actions. As we help our clients navigate their career paths, remember that new learning experiences designed to reduce barriers and increase supports can help clients increase their agency and efficacy in this complex process.

References

Badenoch, B. (2008). *Being a brain-wise therapist*. Norton.

Bandura, A. (1986). The explanatory and predictive scope of self-efficacy theory. *Journal of Social and Clinical Psychology, 4*(3) 359–373. https://doi.org/10.1521/jscp.1986.4.3.359

Brown, S. D., Lent, R. W., Telander, K., & Tramayne, S. (2011). Social cognitive career theory, conscientiousness, and work performance: A meta-analytic path analysis. *Journal of Vocational Behavior, 79,* 81–90. https://doi.org/10.1016/j.jvb.2010.11.009

Brown, S. D., Tramayne, S., Hoxha, D., Telander, K., Fan, X., & Lent, R. W. (2008). Social cognitive predictors of college students' academic performance and persistence: A meta-analytic path analysis. *Journal of Vocational Behavior, 72*, 298–308. https://doi.org/10.1016/j.jvb.2007.09.003

Byars-Winston, A. M., & Fouad, N. A. (2008). Math and science social cognitive variables in college students: Contributions of contextual factors in predicting goals. *Journal of Career Assessment, 16*(4), 425–440. https://doi.org/10.1177/1069072708318901

Flores, L. Y., Navarro, R. L., & Ali, S. R. (2017). The state of SCCT research in relation to social class: Future directions. *Journal of Career Assessment, 25*(1), 6–23. https://doi.org/10.1177/1069072716658649

Fouad, N. A., & Santana, M. C. (2017). SCCT and underrepresented populations in STEM fields: Moving the needle. *Journal of Career Assessment, 27*, 24–39.

Gibbons, M. M., & Borders, L. D. (2010). Prospective first-generation college students: A social-cognitive perspective. *Career Development Quarterly, 58*(3), 194–208. https://doi.org/10.1002/j.2161-0045.2010.tb00186.x

Lent, R. W., & Brown, S. D. (2019). Social cognitive career theory at 25: Progress in studying the domain satisfaction and career self-management models. *Journal of Career Assessment, 27*(4), 563–578. https://doi.org/10.1177/1069072719852736

Lent, R. W., Brown, S. D., & Hackett, G. (1994). Toward a unifying social cognitive theory of career and academic interest, choice, and performance. *Journal of vocational behavior, 45*(1), 79–122. https://doi.org/10.1006/jvbe.1994.1027

Lent, R. W., Brown, S. D., & Hackett, G. (2000). Contextual supports and barriers to career choice: A social cognitive analysis. *Journal of Counseling Psychology, 47*(1), 36–49. https://doi.org/10.1037//0022-0167.47.1.36

Lent, R. W., Hackett, G., & Brown, S. D. (1999). A social cognitive view of school-to-work transition. *Career Development Quarterly, 47*, 297–311.

Luke, C. (2018). *Career focused counseling: Integrating theory, research and neuroscience.*

McWhirter, E. H. (1997). Perceived barriers to education and career: Ethnic and gender differences. *Journal of Vocational Behavior, 50*, 124–140.

Multon, K. D., Brown, S. D., & Lent, R. W. (1991). Relation to self-efficacy beliefs to academic outcomes: A meta-analytic investigation. *Journal of Counseling Psychology, 38*(1), 30–38.

Sheu, H., & Bordon, J. J. (2017). SCCT research in the international context: Empirical evidence, future directions, and practical implications. *Journal of Career Assessment, 27*, 58–74.

Sheu, H. B., Lent, R. W., Brown, S. D., Miller, M. J., Hennessy, K. D., & Duffy, R. D. (2010). Testing the choice model of social cognitive career theory across Holland themes: A meta-analytic path analysis. *Journal of Vocational Behavior, 76*, 252–264. https://doi.org/10.1016/j.jvb.2009.10.015

CREDIT

CHAPTER 9

Narrative, Career Construction Theory, & Life Design

CHAPTER GOALS

- Understand the concepts associated with narrative career counseling and career construction theory.
- Learn to apply these concepts to work with clients.
- Consider how meaning making of life events can help clients with career-related concerns.

OPENING VIGNETTES

School-Based

As part of his high school classroom guidance curriculum, Jack wants to engage students in career exploration. However, he has decided against just presenting information about career and college and is searching for a more interactive way to engage students. Jack wants students to reflect on what they know, what they want to know, and how they might use their strengths to get what they want.

Agency-Based

Rita is a mental health counselor who has been working with Mark as he deals with the aftermath of coming out as gay to his parents and friends. Rita and Mark have focused their sessions on developing coping skills to address his family's resistance to his sexual orientation and processing what changes he wants to make in his life. In today's session, Mark mentions that he wants to come out at work as well but is unsure about the repercussions of doing so. He works at a nonprofit organization that helps provide for the basic needs of domestic violence survivors.

TAKE A MINUTE

What stands out to you about these? Where would you want to start? What are the immediate career-focused concerns you note?

REFLECTION ACTIVITIES AND QUESTIONS

1. Who were your role models growing up? What characteristics stood out to you that you admired?
2. The counseling profession includes a strengths-based approach. How do you help your clients build on their strengths to help address their concerns?

Introduction

Renowned author Alice Munro wrote, "A story is not like a road to follow ... it's more like a house. You go inside and stay there for a while, wandering back and forth and settling where you like and discovering how the room and corridors relate to each other, how the world outside is altered by being viewed from these windows. And you, the visitor, the reader, are altered as well by being in their enclosed space, whether it is ample and easy or full of crooked turns, or sparsely or opulently furnished. You can go back again and again, and the house, the story, always contains more than you saw the last time. It also has a sturdy sense of itself of being built out of its own necessity, not just to shelter or beguile you" (1996). As you read this quote, what stood out to you?

The narrative approach to career counseling was introduced to offer a more complex and layered approach to understanding career development. Narrative career theorists recognize that the route from start to end of a career is no longer linear but rather full of twists and turns and often includes multiple reimaginings of one's career over the course of a lifetime. The concept of narrative involves both the process of constructing stories and the meaning-making to understand these stories (Bujold, 2004). The plot of each story is important, but the underlying meaning across the stories helps uncover the way that people understand the world around them.

Constructivism refers to the idea that "each individual mentally constructs the world of experience through cognitive processes" (Young & Collin, 2004, p. 375). These beliefs are developed through interactions with others and the meaning people attach to these experiences. In narrative career counseling, counselors elicit stories from clients to discern these underlying beliefs, gaining insight into how they interpret the events around them (Bujold, 2004). Narratives and their underlying meanings change over time, depending on the current context of people's lives, so this approach naturally accounts for the instability and constant adjustment related to career over time. Ultimately, narrative approaches are founded on the belief that clients typically know what they must do to address their concerns, and that the answer lies within the client (Bujold, 2004; Savickas, 2011b).

Theory Overview

There is not a single theory of narrative career counseling but rather a collection of theories that are constructivist in nature. All of these theories utilize a similar structure of eliciting stories, uncovering underlying meaning, challenging assumptions to consider alternate meanings, and reconstructing career concerns with these new meanings in place. Narrative career theories include the assumption that meaning is not static but rather constantly evolving and shifting as new experiences occur (Young & Collin, 2004).

Savickas (2000) noted that a revision of career theories was needed because of the changes in the world of work. Early in the 20th century, people moved from mostly rural and farm-based jobs to urban centers, where new careers proliferated. Throughout this time, careers were primarily pathways, or linear structures, where employees "climbed the ladder" at one company (Savickas, 2000). In modern times, the world of work has undergone more changes. We now live in a global society, businesses have eliminated many middle management positions, and people are likely to not only change jobs and employers, but shift to new careers entirely. As a result, narrative career theorists believe that theories describing career development as linear and career choice as set are no longer sufficient (Savickas, 2000). Therefore, career construction theory and other narrative theories promote adaptability and meaning-making *in addition to* the traditional career concepts of matching traits and factors. Covering all of these theories is beyond the scope of this chapter and likely beyond your interest. Therefore, we focus on *career construction theory* (CCT) developed by Mark Savickas but also note other ways to elicit stories beyond the one used in this approach.

CONCEPTS

CCT is a multistage approach to career counseling. It is situated within the *life design paradigm*, a belief that career development occurs within the context of shifting perspectives (Savickas, 2012). Life design assumes the following:

- Current life context is more important than understanding personal traits and characteristics.
- People will change jobs and careers frequently, so people need ways to cope during these times of change.
- Counseling should focus on a more holistic view of the constantly changing world of career.
- People create unique narratives that represent their current view of reality and worldview.

Resulting from these assumptions are the beliefs that career construction is a life-long process that impacts all aspects of one's life and that context, as understood by the individual's worldview perspective, is the most important part of the person to understand (Savickas et al., 2009). Counselors help clients increase *adaptability* by examining and revising their life narratives. Career adaptability refers to the ability to cope with the constantly changing world of work and the ability to use their internal and external resources to do so (Savickas & Porfeli, 2012). Adaptability is demonstrated via concern, control, curiosity, and confidence, referred to by Savickas and colleagues (2009) as the 4 Cs. Concern relates to the ability to plan for the future, control refers to a belief of having ownership of that future, curiosity is the engagement in exploration, and confidence represents a feeling that choices and goals are possible.

CCT counseling involves a five stage process. First is *construction*, where counselors help clients share their experiences through *micronarratives*, or short stories (Savickas, 2012). Stories are told from three different perspectives, and it is part of the counselor's job to listen for each of these as clients share their micronarratives (Savickas, 2011a). First is the viewpoint of *actor*, in which the client discusses traits, interests, and general characteristics. RIASEC codes are great examples of the actor narrative. Next, clients share the view of *agent*, which involves goals and the actions taken to achieve those goals. Stories about goals set and the supports and obstacles related to goal attainment exemplify the agent narrative. Lastly, clients talk about self as *author*. They describe their unique identities and how they have combined actions and agency to enact their unique selves. A goal of career construction counseling is to help clients enact their self-authorship, helping them take ownership of their future. Clients demonstrate adaptability and agency when they view themselves as authors of their own future.

In traditional CCT, counselors use the *Career Construction Interview* (CCI; Savickas & Hartung, 2012) to elicit information. In this interview, counselors ask a series of questions in a specific order. Table 9.1 shares these questions, their purpose, tips for best practices, and interpretation purpose. During the CCI, Savickas (2015) encourages counselors to take notes to best capture the client's actual words, particularly repeated words and feelings.

TABLE 9.1 CAREER CONSTRUCTION INTERVIEW

CCI question	Purpose	Tips	Interpretation purpose
How can I be useful to you as you construct your career?	• Client ownership of session • Goal construction	• Use the response to frame goals for counseling • Focus on feelings. • Probe for additional details, as needed.	• Frames the focus of counseling; provides a goal or outcome to pursue.
Who did you admire when you were growing up? These can be real people or make-believe characters such as superheroes or book characters. Tell me about what you admired about them (elicit three total)	• Identify adjectives that describe the client's way of being or ways they desire to be. • Understand ways of being or becoming. • Build on this in later stages.	• Attend to adjectives related to ways of being. • Probe for details, as needed. • Request that clients move beyond parents or adult caregivers.	• I am/I am becoming ... —characteristics the client values and wants to build.
Do you read any magazines, watch any TV shows, or visit any websites regularly? Which ones? What do you like about these? (Elicit at least three.)	• Identify environment and activities of interest. • Understand career-related interest.	• Inquire about why they are drawn to each. • For magazines and websites, ask what they read first. • Focus on interests.	• I like being places where people do activities such as ....

(*Continued*)

TABLE 9.1 CAREER CONSTRUCTION INTERVIEW *(Continued)*

CCI question	Purpose	Tips	Interpretation purpose
What is currently your favorite book or movie? Tell me the story.	• Learn about scripts the client may be using to attain goals. • Understand strategies used or not used by the client.	• Emphasize wanting their current favorite, rather than a childhood favorite, to best connect to current issues. • Be sure not to use your own understanding of the story but rather focus on the client's narrative description.	• A possible solution to my problem is … . • Clients often have solutions to their problems already and just need these identified.
Tell me your favorite saying or motto. If you don't have a favorite, tell me one that comes to mind now.	• Understand advice the client gives to themselves. • Learn what the client may repeat to themself as a mantra or way of being.	• If they struggle with this, ask them to make up a saying. • Consider asking for a tattoo meaning if they still struggle.	• I will be most happy and successful when I follow this advice. • Another possible solution to current issue is … .
What are your earliest recollections? I am interested in hearing three stories about things you recall happening to you when you were three to six years old. Follow-up: What would you title or headline your memory? What feelings arise from your memory?	• Understand how the client views the current issue within their worldview. • Identify underlying feelings associated with current issue.	• Ensure that the recollection is their own memory, rather than a family story told to them. • Ask them to share only what they actually remember. • Ask for specifics for each memory.	• I am concerned about … . • What is getting in the way of achieving your goal?

Note. Adapted from Savickas (2012, 2015) and Savickas and Hartung (2012).

Other qualitative assessments can be used to elicit micronarratives. The goals in using these techniques are the same as for the CCI: to help the client tell stories that uncover underlying meaning-making and worldview beliefs that may be causing distress and prohibiting clients from achieving their goals (Whiston & Rahardja, 2005). These are described in more detail in chapter 5 but include the following:

- **Career genogram:** Used to understand the impact of family of origin on client career development, career genograms can help uncover job themes, cultural career stereotypes, and important career values (Bakshi & Satish, 2015).

- **Career lifeline:** Used to identify themes of meaning and action during times of transition, career lifelines elicit stories about major life events and the meanings attached to them (Fritz & Van Zyl, 2015).
- **Life role circles:** Used to understand interactions between various life roles, the life role circles activity help clients consider role importance, time spent in each role, and potential role conflicts (Brott, 2005).

For each of these, the counselor uses reflection, probing, and active listening skills to help clients share their micronarratives in the construction stage and then provide a tentative interpretation of underlying meanings in deconstruction.

After completing the CCI, the *deconstruction* stage begins (Savickas, 2012). Counselors carefully review the client's responses (stories) and gently offer ideas about potential dominant themes. They may discuss possible alternative views or meanings or cautiously challenge existing meanings. For example, perhaps a client comes to counseling with concerns about whether to take a new job. They worry about disappointing friends and family and believe that their family responsibilities prohibit their ability to consider their own wants and needs. The client shares a series of micronarratives where they feel a lack of agency in their career decisions. They may share early recollections of times when others made decisions for them or where a choice was criticized by others. They may discuss role models who demonstrate bravery or steadfastness when others disapprove of them. For this client, the counselor may gently point out that this discrepancy—that the client feels unable to make their own decisions, but they admire those who do this—and then use this idea to aid in reconsidering the current issue. During deconstruction, counselors open perspectives by examining narratives and encouraging their clients to consider stories with multiple meanings (Savickas et al., 2009).

Reconstruction is the third stage in the CCT process, and it flows naturally from the deconstruction process. In reconstruction, client and counselor work to identify new meanings to better achieve goals. The current theme or meaning assigned to events is reconsidered and reworked to one that offers a new perspective in which the client has increased agency and control (Savickas, 2012). In the above example, perhaps the client recognizes their desire to have a say in their career choices but also wants to support the needs of important family members. The counselor and client may work together to create a new theme that includes both the client's voice and the needs of valued others. This small shift can help the client see their situation from a new and more positive perspective.

Fourth, in *co-construction*, the client takes this new meaning and places it into the current issue. Typically, the client takes the lead in revising their narrative to be more accurate, holistic, and rich (Savickas, 2012). The counselor then helps the client extend this new narrative into the future by encouraging elaboration, flexibility, and curiosity. Prior tendencies are gently challenged and overcome as needed. Once the new narrative takes hold, the final stage of *action* begins. Clients engage in new activities based on their revised meanings to successfully address their presenting issues (Savickas, 2012). Next steps are actively identified and pursued.

MECHANISMS OF CHANGE

CCT counselors use a variety of skills to help their clients (Savickas, 2015). First, they strive to create an *egalitarian relationship* in counseling, in which the client is the expert of their own life, and the counselor is the expert on eliciting and interpreting stories. To accomplish this, CCT counselors build trust with their clients. CCT counselors also actively engage in *reflection* of feeling, meaning, and content to help clients increase their self-awareness of their own meaning-making and assumptions. Lastly, CCT counselors *tentatively interpret* client stories to help clients be intentional about how to shift their views and take control over their career decisions (Savickas, 2015). Ultimately, change occurs when clients buy in to the revised and reenvisioned meanings and actively use these to achieve their current goals.

Counselors using this approach believe that clients can make adjustments that allow them to take control over their lives (Rudolph et al., 2019). This focus on adaptability is central to CCT, and the narrative perspective helps clients uncover underlying meanings, so revisions can be made. Counselors strive to help clients be the authors of their own lives as a way to move toward action (Savickas, 2012). As needed, CCT counselors may offer career guidance or education to supplement storytelling, but the goal is always to help clients design their lives and construct their careers.

Theory in Session

SCHOOL-BASED TRANSCRIPT

Jack (SC) finds the *My Career Story* (MCS; Savickas & Hartung, 2012) workbook online and remembers from his graduate-level career counseling course that it can be used with students to help them tell and retell their career stories to gain understanding about how to approach their next steps. As a result, he designs a three part classroom guidance lesson for 10th graders based on this workbook.

Part 1 of the lesson is as follows:

> SC: So everyone should have a copy of the workbook on their computer. Today is a lot of individual writing and reflecting, but the next two meetings will be much more interactive. We are going to start on writing a short story about a concern you have about your career and educational planning and your goals for exploring this concern. Next, you will make a list of all the careers you have considered now and in the past. Third, you will see a series of questions about people you admire, TV shows or websites you like, your favorite movie or book, and your favorite saying. Answer each of these to the best of your ability. Let me know what questions you have.

Process of creating micronarratives

Part 2 of the lesson is as follows:

SC: As you remember, last week we completed a series of questions in the *MCS* workbook. Today, we are going to start figuring out what these all mean. Look at the words you used and write down the adjectives you used, words that were similar to one another, things the people you admire have in common, and significant phrases. These words and phrases describe you! Now, work with a partner to write two to three sentences about who you are.

Beginning deconstruction

SC: Now that you have created these sentences with your partner, it is time to share them with the class. Who would like to share?

Lacey: I will. My sentences say: I am strong-willed, independent, and funny. I like to take charge in situations and care about helping others.

Helping through reflection of feeling

SC: That is great, Lacey. How did it feel to write this?

Lacey: It was actually really nice. I don't always feel independent, but it is true that I try to be when I can.

SC: That is a good point. Some of the words we use in our sentences are characteristics we want to develop or gain. Who wants to share next?

Jack leads the class through the rest of Part 2, having them work in pairs to identify career interests, self-advice, and, ultimately, a success formula.

Part 3 of the lesson is as follows:

SC: Hi, all. Today, we are finishing our *MCS* workbooks and taking our success formula and self-advice statement to help address our career goals. Remember, your success formula is: I will be most successful when I am able to be ______, in places where people ______, so that I can ______. Your self-advice is the motto you identified earlier. Now, go back to the essay you wrote on day one about your career or educational concern. Use your formula and motto to answer how to address this concern.

Reconstruction to co-construction

SC: OK, thanks everyone for sharing your answers. They were really great and very creative. Our last step is to revisit careers of interest. Now that you understand yourself better, you may want to explore new careers. To do this, we are going to use O*NET (https://www.onetonline.org/), which is a great online resource for exploring careers.

Taking action

TAKE A MINUTE

How did Jack use the ideas of career construction within the framework of classroom guidance? How might school context, such as SES or the percentage of students entering college, impact how this approach might be used with students? Let's consider how Jack might work with a student who still has questions after the class activities. How might Jack increase adaptability with an individual high school student?

AGENCY-BASED TRANSCRIPT

Rita (CMH): So, Mark. Tell me more about your career concerns.

Mark (CL): Well, I originally chose my job because I want to work for an organization that helps people. I am just their business manager, but I like to think that I am helping them in some indirect way. Now that I have come out to my family and friends, though, I am thinking about trying to come out at work, too. But the shelter is associated with a church, and I worry that I might be asked to leave or to keep my sexual orientation quiet, especially around our funders and board of directors. I love my job, but I just don't know if they will like me this way.

CMH: Okay. It sounds like something worth exploring together. Would you be willing to work through an assessment with me? It is just a series of questions designed to help us both better understand what is happening for you and maybe identify a possible solution.

CL: Sure. I think it would be helpful.

Rita works with Mark to complete the CCI. Mark identifies his current concern as wondering if he should come out at work or whether he should seek a job someplace more accepting. His role models include his fourth-grade teacher, who was accepting, funny, warm, and cared about everyone; Kurt Hummel from the TV show *Glee*, who was an out gay high school student who was funny, open, and secure with himself; and a cousin, who was the first person Mark disclosed his sexual orientation to, and his reaction was accepting, understanding, and affirming. Next, Mark shared that his favorite TV shows and websites were CNN because he liked the financial and international reporting; *Grey's Anatomy* because all kinds of people were represented on the show, and they all tried to help people; and *Forbes* because it discussed businesses and how they were successful. His favorite book was the first Harry Potter novel, which he described as, "a kid without a home and whom no one wanted, who found out that he had people who cared about him and accepted him for who he was." Mark's favorite motto was: Do unto others as you would have them do. Lastly, his three earliest recollections were:

1. "I was about four and with my older brother. I wanted to go walking in the woods, but he wanted to hang out with his friend. I asked him over and over if the three of us could

go to the woods and play, and he just said, 'No, go by yourself. I'm busy now.'" Mark titled this memory "Sadness on a Beautiful Day."

2. "I guess I was about 5 or 6. I was at school, and we were assigned to small groups to do some type of project; I don't remember what it was. Anyhow, I was with two other kids and I suggested we make a drawing, but the other two wanted to write a short story. So I went along and wrote the story with them." This memory was titled "Sometimes You Have to Go With What the Group Wants."
3. "I was young, not sure what age, and with my mom, dad, and brother. We were driving to my grandmother's house, and I was looking out the window at the passing trees, and my mother said, 'Mark, did you hear what I just said? You are always daydreaming and never listening.' She then repeated what she had asked, and I answered and then went back to looking out the window." Mark titled this recollection "Looking for Something More but Being Called Out."

Deconstruction

Rita and Mark worked together to identify themes across his micronarratives. Mark immediately noticed commonalities between his role models and his repeated themes of openness, acceptance, warmth, and caring. As they spoke, Rita gently mentioned that Mark seems to want to be himself but believes he won't be accepted by others. She added that a theme seemed to be that Mark believes he cannot trust others to accept him as he is.

Co-construction

Mark became silent for a long moment and then began to cry. He admitted that he feared sharing his true self with others, particularly in the workplace, because he did not want to lose their respect and friendship. As Rita challenged these beliefs, Mark realized he was just adding another layer of himself but that his coworkers already appreciated and respected him.

Action

Mark identified those at work whom he thought would be the most open to his sexual orientation and decided to share the information with them. The next week, Mark told Rita that both his colleagues responded with acceptance and genuine care and indicated that they appreciated Mark's willingness to be honest with them.

TAKE A MINUTE

How might community type (e.g., rural or urban) impact Rita's work with Mark? What are some ways that Mark is struggling with sharing his true self? How might these struggles be related to his understanding of characteristics he might want to build (related to "I am becoming")?

Neuroscience, Culture, and Development

In this section, we include a passage from Luke (2018) on the process of meaning-making and its relevance to career-focused counseling. The brain is a meaning-making system, finding patterns and making meaning, rather than finding meaning itself. This is important to counselors' work as the reality a client or student constructs is the reality they live by.

> The brain makes meaning by drawing on past experiences (stored in memory systems), environmental conditions, and relationships. Meaning, in this way, is very much constructed in such a way that each individual's perception of experiences, environments, and relationships are highly phenomenological. This means that any individual can create a reality all their own, whether in the world of work or the world in general. It will be immediately obvious that these models are not suggesting that one can create their own reality about gravity, making it appear or disappear. However—and this is key—they can construct their own reality about what gravity means for their ability to function in the world. In counseling and in teaching counseling, I often use the example of the training of circus elephant to remain where their trainers want them. Early in their lives, baby elephants have a shackle placed around their ankle attached to a stake in the ground. At this tender age and size, they experience the limit and cease pulling against it. As they grow, as the narrative goes, the shackle can remain without being tethered to anything (not that it would do any good anyway, given the size and power of the animal). The adult elephant has crafted a narrative—a view of reality—that restricts its behavior. The brain arranges itself in ways that internalize these views in order to in-crease efficiency (no need to waste time and energy pulling against something immovable, especially when that energy could be directed toward finding food). Likewise, clients enter CFC possessing learning experiences that have shaped their views of reality. Counseling offers a context and process that permits challenging these realities through brain change, called neuroplasticity. (Luke, 2018)

Culture is naturally embedded into narrative career counseling. Meaning-making is based on a person's worldview, which, of course, is based on their environmental, systemic, and cultural context. Therefore, the stories clients tell represent their ways of knowing and being. Del Corso and Rehfuss (2011) noted that cultural scripts often help clients understand their world. Cultural scripts are models that represent characters from various cultural groups. They may be from popular novels, social media stars, oral storytelling, or current TV shows, but they serve to influence and impact the ways clients see the world and themselves (Del Corso & Rehfuss, 2011).

Some authors suggest using a career construction or narrative career counseling approach with diverse clients. The approach has been touted as particularly relevant for underprepared college students (Hughes et al., 2013), recently divorced homemakers (Locke & Gibbons, 2008), African refugees (Pierce & Gibbons, 2012), and people with disabilities (Santilli et al., 2018).

Given the view that meaning making is directly connected to culture, the theory's application to diverse individuals makes good sense.

Development is also addressed in this theoretical approach, although less so than in some of the other theories we have explored. The CCI and other qualitative assessments naturally reflect a client's developmental level, but career construction is not a theory of development; it is a theory of how we make meaning in the moment. Meaning-making changes over time, so the stories that seem relevant to someone today may be unimportant or less important five years from now. One article described the lifelong construction of identity as "The environment informs the self, which interacts with the environment, which in turn impacts the self. The interplay, between the two, like a needle and thread, weave one's identity over time" (Del Corso & Rehfuss, 2011, p. 336). The point is the idea of a *life* story—not a moment-in-time story. So the story changes as we change, but our current story represents our life up until the present moment. Researchers have found that the theory works well with a variety of age groups. Fasbender et al. (2019) applied the approach with workers ages 50+, while Santilli et al. (2019) noted it worked well with early adolescents. These studies and others offer evidence that career construction theory is useful with most clients.

Take Away and Use Today

Narrative career theories, such as career construction theory, focus on understanding how clients make meaning of their life experiences and how counselors can help these clients reauthor these meanings to create more satisfying lives. Qualitative assessments, such as the CCI, lifeline, or career genogram, help clients tell their micronarratives, so they can reflect on their overall experiences. In this way, counselors help clients construct a life they want through empowerment and a shared journey.

References

Bakshi, A. J., & Satish, V. (2015). Qualitative career assessment using a genogram. In *Career assessment* (pp. 69–80). SensePublishers. https://doi.org/10.1007/978-94-6300-034-5_8

Brott, P. E. (2005). A constructivist look at life roles. *The Career Development Quarterly, 54*(2), 138–149. https://doi.org/10.1002/j.2161-0045.2005.tb00146.x

Bujold, C. (2004). Constructing career through narrative. *Journal of Vocational Behavior, 64*(3), 470–484. https://doi.org/10.1016/j.jvb.2003.12.010

Del Corso, J., & Rehfuss, M. C. (2011). The role of narrative in career construction theory. *Journal of Vocational Behavior, 79*, 334–339. https://doi.org/10.1016/j.jvb.2011.04.003

Fasbender, U., Wohrmann, A., M., Wang, M., & Klehe, U. C. (2019). Is the future still open? The mediating role of occupational future time perspective in the effects of career adaptability and aging experience on late career planning. *Journal of Vocational Behavior, 111*, 24–38. https://doi.org/10.1016/j.jvb.2018.10.006

Fritz, E., & Zyl, G. V. (2015). Lifelines: A visual exploration of the past in order to guide the journey into the future. In *Career assessment* (pp. 89–96). SensePublishers. https://doi.org/10.1007/978-94-6300-034-5_10

Hughes, A. N., Gibbons, M. M., & Mynatt, B. (2013). Using narrative career counseling with the underprepared college student. *Career Development Quarterly, 61*, 40–49. https://doi.org/10.1002/j.2161-0045.2013.00034.x

Locke, W. S., & Gibbons, M. M. (2008). On her own again: The use of narrative therapy in career counseling with displaced new traditionalists. *The Family Journal, 16*(2), 132–138.

Munro, A. (1996). *Selected stories*. Knopf.

Pierce, L. M., & Gibbons, M. M. (2012). An ever-changing meaning: A career constructivist application to working with African refugees. *The Journal of Humanistic Counseling, 51*(1), 114–127.

Rudolph, C. W., Zacher, H., & Hirschi, A. (2019). Empirical developments in career construction theory. *Journal of Vocational Behavior, 111*, 1–6. https://doi.org/10.1016/j.jvb.2018.12.003

Santilli, S., Nota, L., Ginerva, M. C., & Soresi, S. (2018). Career adaptability, hope, and life satisfaction in workers with intellectual disability. *Journal of Vocational Behavior, 85*(1), 67–74. https://doi.org/10.1016/j.jvb.2014.02.011

Santilli, S., Nota, L., & Hartung, P. (2019). Efficacy of a group career construction intervention with early adolescent youth. *Journal of Vocational Behavior, 111*, 49–58. https://doi.org/10.1016/j.jvb.2018.06.007

Savickas, M. L. (2000). Renovating the psychology of careers for the twenty-first century. In A. Collin & R. Young (Eds.), *The future of career* (pp. 53–68). Cambridge University Press.

Savickas, M. L. (2011a). Constructing careers: Actor, agent, and author. *Journal of Employment Counseling, 48*(4), 179–181. https://doi.org/10.1002/j.2161-1920.2011.tb01109.x

Savickas, M. L. (2011b). The self in vocational psychology: Object, subject, and project. In P. J. Hartung, & L. M. Subich (Eds.), *Developing self in work and career: Concepts, cases, and contexts* (pp. 17–33). American Psychological Association.

Savickas, M. L. (2012). Life design: A paradigm for career intervention in the 21st century. *Journal of Counseling and Development, 90*(1), 13–19. https://doi.org/10.1111/j.1556-6676.2012.00002.x

Savickas, M. L. (2015). *The life-design manual*.

Savickas, M. L., & Hartung, P. (2012). *My career story: An autobiographical workbook for life-career success*. Vocopher. http://vocopher.com/

Savickas, M. L., Nota, L., Rossier, J., Dauwalder, J.-P., Duarte, M. E., Guichard, J., Soresi, S., Van Esbroeck, R., & van Vianen, A. E. (2009). Life designing: A paradigm for career construction in the 21st century. *Journal of Vocational Behavior, 75*(3), 239–250. https://doi.org/10.1016/j.jvb.2009.04.004

Savickas, M. L., & Porfeli, E. J. (2012). Career adapt–abilities scale: Construction, reliability, and measurement equivalence across 13 countries. *Journal of Vocational Behavior, 80*, 661–673. https://doi.org/10.1016/j.jvb.2012.01.011

Whiston, S. C. & Rahardja, D. (2005). Qualitative career assessment: An overview and analysis. *Journal of Career Assessment, 13*(4), 371–380. https://doi.org/10.1177/1069072705277910

Young, R. A., & Collin, A. (2004). Introduction: Constructivism and social constructionism in the career field. *Journal of Vocational Behavior, 64*(3), 373–388. https://doi.org/10.1016/j.jvb.2003.12.005

CHAPTER 10

Specialty Theories

CIP and Happenstance Learning Theory

Chad Luke, Seth Hayden, and Melinda Gibbons

CHAPTER GOALS

- Identify the components of cognitive information processing and happenstance learning theory.
- Apply these theories to students and clients in career-focused counseling.
- Understand the relationship between chance and planfulness.

OPENING VIGNETTES

School-Based (HLT)

Kiki is a 17-year-old student in an urban high school, seeking support from her school counselor for stress and career uncertainty. Kiki is a rising senior, who has struggled to identify a career path that makes sense to her. She states that she feels a lot of pressure to attend college or to select a vocational track in her senior year but feels really unsure about what she wants. Her confusion and ambivalence have disrupted her sleep and appetite. She feels stuck.

Agency-Based (CIP)

Ahmed is a 32-year-old construction worker, who is interested in changing careers, as recent circumstances, such as his physical health, have made it difficult for him to meet the physical demands of his profession. He is interested in specializing in a specific trade, such as welding, but wonders if this might be related to his familiarity with construction and industrial-oriented vocations as opposed to truly desiring this type of work. He indicates wanting to consider a broad range of options, but he is uncertain of how to navigate this process. He is married with young children, which, along with financial considerations, has contributed to a high-level of anxiety in making this decision.

REFLECTION ACTIVITIES AND QUESTIONS

1. In thinking about your own career journey, how did your thoughts about yourself and the world of work affect the career course your life has taken?

2. What role did emotion play in helping you "solve" the problem of choosing work?
3. What role did curiosity play in your exploration of the world of work?
4. Was it "safe" for you to take risks and try new things, or did you find yourself searching for the safe path?

Introduction

When was the last time you let your curiosity run wild? A time when instead of focusing on what you thought you could or could not do, you reflected on what you longed to do and followed your energy? How about a time you took action based on your interests or values without knowing how it would turn out? There are now countless stories of individuals who did just that: followed their energy and took a "risk" to do what mattered to them, even when they did not know how it would turn out.

Career theory, like other theories of human development, has continued to evolve as new research and practices have expanded. While postmodern thought is not new, its application to counseling and career development has continued to generate scholarly interests. In particular, as the nature of work has changed dramatically in the face of technological advances and globalization, career models that emphasize adjustment to change have received increased attention. This chapter addresses two such approaches to understanding career development in the modern world: cognitive information processing and happenstance learning theories.

Super (1980) described vocational identity as the projection of one's identity onto the world of work; postmodern and constructivist models describe reality as the projection of oneself onto the world. Reality is created as the individual experiences events and interprets them. As such, reality can shift and be recreated in ways that increase one's ability to function effectively. The same applies to career development (Luke, 2018).

The human brain tends to be naïve: It will believe anything you tell it (Luke, 2016). Much of career-related uncertainty relates to one's ability to manage career thoughts and emotions in ways that promote their success. Exerting cognitive and behavioral control over fear and unhelpful cognitions is vital in moving one's life in a desired direction. This comes through using the mind to tell the brain the "right" things. In this chapter we explore two distinct but related career development theories and their systems of understanding career issues. First, we explore cognitive information processing (CIP) of career decision-making. Then, we shift focus to happenstance learning theory (HLT).

Cognitive Information Processing Theory

Cognitive information processing theory is a career theory with a focus on the domains and processes associated with effective career decision-making and problem solving (Sampson et al., 2004, 2020). The primary tenets of this approach are (a) career choices engage our emotions (affect), thoughts, (cognition), and actions (behavior), as these elements are viewed as integrated and inseparable in a career choice; (b) effective career choices involve both knowledge (the content of choice or what we need to know) and a process for thinking about the pertinent knowledge (the process of choice or what we need to do); (c) knowledge of ourselves and the world we live in is constantly evolving and interacting—as we learn from lived experiences, we organize our knowledge in more complex ways; and (d) career problem-solving and decision-making are skills in which learning and practice improves our ability to make choices. Career resources and services are designed to help us think about and organize our knowledge by sorting through available information and then using the most relevant information in making choices while also learning and practicing information processing skills needed for effective career decision-making (Sampson et al., 2004, 2020).

This approach is designed to enhance agency by empowering the client via learning of the approach, which can then be implemented in future career decisions (Sampson et al., 2004, 2020; Hayden & Osborn, 2020). The adage of teaching someone how to fish as opposed to giving them fish speaks to a philosophical underpinning of CIP approach. The components inform the process of addressing a career concern in a manner that enables the client or student to enhance awareness of themselves, options, decision-making strategies, and cognitions.

Two important features of this approach are the knowledge and process domains of CIP. The *domains of knowledge* (i.e., self, options, decision-making, and executive processing) coupled with elements of a process (i.e., CASVE; communication, analysis, synthesis, valuing, and execution) form a framework in which to navigate a career concern. In reference to the learning dimension of this approach, the theory is openly shared with those receiving services and a modified versions outlining these domains with more accessible language is provided to the client (see Sampson et al., 2020).

Within these domains, executive processing composed of *meta-cognitions* (i.e., self-talk, self-awareness, monitoring, and control) has been found to influence aspects of career development (Bullock-Yowell et al., 2011; Bullock-Yowell et al., 2015; Chason et al., 2013; Hayden & Osborn, 2020). Assessing and addressing problematic negative career thoughts is essential for effective career decision-making and problem-solving. Adapting interventions to the specific needs of this population is a hallmark of this approach. Right-sizing the amount of support via the needs of the client or student ensures that clients received the appropriate amount of support. The conceptualization of readiness informs the structure of support.

Within CIP, readiness for career decision-making concerns the *capability* of individuals to make informed and careful choices in light of the complexity of the family, social, economic, and organizational factors that impact their choices (Sampson et al., 2000). Individuals with a high level of capability can fully engage all aspects of the pyramid of information processing domains, while individuals with low capability need support to engage in the learning necessary to explore and choose among options. *Complexity* concerns external factors that make it more or less challenging to solve problems and make decisions, including aspects of family, society, economy, and organization for those who are employed (Sampson et al., 2000). The amount of support is determined by the degree of readiness by assessing the combination of two components (i.e., capability and complexity). Ranging from individual case management (i.e., prolonged counseling support or high complexity, low capability) to self-help services, this multimodal service delivery offers flexibility based on readiness (Sampson, 2008).

In terms of interventions, there are specific strategies that can be employed to address both the knowledge and process domains. To track progress towards goals, an individual learning plan (Peterson et al., 1991; Sampson, et al., 2020) is collaboratively developed in which goals and associated activities are identified and prioritized. In relation to the CASVE cycle, the "Guide to Good Decision Making" (see https://career.fsu.edu/tech-center/resources/service-delivery-handouts), the Career Thoughts Inventory (CTI; Sampson et al., 1996a) and associated workbook (Sampson et al., 1996b), the "Decision Space Worksheet" (Peterson et al., 2016), the Career State Inventory (Leierer et al., 2017), and various information guides offer a means through which to effectively engage in career decision making. CIP is also closely tied to Holland's theory (1959, 1997) in relation to identification of interests and associated occupations aligned with self and options knowledge domains. Additional theories that focus on various components of CIP can be integrated to inform various phases of navigating a career concern.

MECHANISM OF CHANGE

CIP's roots in cognitive behavioral therapy influences the focus on cognitions within the helping process. A primary consideration is identifying and modifying negative career thoughts due to their substantially impact on career development (e.g., Bullock-Yowell, et al., 2013, 2015; Chason et al., 2013; Hayden & Osborn, 2020). When cognitions are identified via the CTI, cognitive reframing is enacted to develop more functional cognitions, which will propel, as opposed to inhibit, the attainment of career goals. Emotions have also been found to influence dimensions of career development (e.g., Hayden & Osborn, 2020). Assessing and addressing affective and cognitive dimensions of career development is an essential task within this approach.

This requires a comprehensive and expansive focus on the part of the counselor on internal and external factors relevant to a career concern. This positions career as a central feature of counseling, requiring the counselor, regardless of presenting concern, population, or setting, to be adept at integrating career and mental health support. In addition, CIP is a learning engagement, with the counselor and client or student collaboratively examining the career decision. The approach is openly discussed and continually revisited based on the circumstances of the concern. Generalizing the approach to future concerns and decisions also characterized a CIP-informed engagement.

AHMED IN SESSION

MHC: Hey Ahmed. What would you like to focus on today?

CL: Well, we discussed last time about all the things that are influencing my decision to change jobs. I spoke with my wife and she is pretty anxious about this. It's kind of freaking me out.

TABLE 10.1 CIP INTERVENTIONS

CIP Element	Interventions and Strategies
Self-Knowledge	• Standardized career assessments • Nonstandardized career assessments • Qualitative career assessments (McMahon & Patton, 2017), such as story crafting (McMahon & Watson, 2012) and *My Career Story* (Savickas & Hartung, 2012) • Computer-assisted career guidance programs • Constructivist resume (Scholl & Cascone, 2011) • Experiential activities, such as volunteering or shadowing • Discussion of key elements of self (e.g. interests, values, skills, strengths, etc.) and identities (e.g., gender, culture, race, ethnicity, religion, sexual orientation, etc.) and how these intersect
Options-Knowledge	• Occupational databases, such as O*NET and the *Occupational Outlook Handbook* • Job databases, such as Glassdoor, that detail occupational expectations • Informational interviews with people in jobs of interest • Company websites and social media accounts • Resources that describe educational and training options, including short-term online training • Professional associations • Social networks • Identifying job options related to self-knowledge
Decision-Making/CASVE Cycle	• Use of decision-making guides (e.g. "Guide to Good Decision Making"; Sampson et al., 1992) • Discussion of important individuals who influence one's career decision
Executive Processing	• Identifying, challenging, and altering negative self-talk with instruments, such as the Career Thoughts Inventory (Sampson et al., 1996a) or the *Career Thoughts Workbook* (Sampson et al., 1996b) • Attentiveness to the emotional aspect of the career concern • Cocreate individual action plans to help manage the process (Sampson et al., 2004)
Career Readiness	• Discussion of capability components, including internal factors, such as motivation, honest exploration, assuming personal responsibility, and awareness of how thoughts and feelings impact decision-making • Discussion of complexity components, including external factors, such as family, economy, and other social pressures, that weigh on a person's decision-making process • Exploration of issues impacting a person's career readiness through measures such as the Career Thoughts Inventory (Sampson et al., 1996a) and the *Decision Space Worksheet* (Peterson et al., 2016) • Determine which level of support (i.e., self-help, brief-assisted, or individual-case managed) would be most appropriate given the client's readiness

Note. From Hayden et al., 2021, p. 8.

MHC: Sounds like there is a lot that is being impacted by your consideration of different options based on a need to change jobs due to the physical demands of construction.

CL: Yeah. Part of me thinks it would just be easier to keep doing what I'm doing, but I just can't.

MHC: Sounds like this is really difficult for you right now. Ahmed, we talked last time about the impact of our thoughts and feelings on decisions and the results from your CTI, which assesses negative thoughts. External conflict and decision-making confusion were indicated in the test.

Self-knowledge

CL: That's right. Guess the family stuff is probably a big consideration for me right now. Also not sure how to make this decision. Seems like a really big change to make.

MHC: I agree. It is a lot to consider. With this in mind, I am wondering how you are feeling about things overall.

CL: I am pretty anxious to be honest. I have a family and have been working this job for a long time. Really wish I could keep going, but it's not possible. Part of me is excited about thinking about other jobs and I just don't know how to move forward.

MHC: So on one hand you are anxious as you are comfortable with what you are doing while also being slightly curious about other occupations.

CL: Yep. So what now?

MHC: Well, I think looking at items on the CTI you endorsed to see if we can deal with some of the thoughts and feelings you are experiencing. In addition, it seems it would be useful to step away from specific jobs and explore some of your interests, values, and skills and see what occupations may align with them. What do you think?

Self-knowledge

CL: Sure. Seems like a good way to go.

MHC: The career thoughts inventory workbook is something related to the assessment you completed. It allows us to consider some of the specific thoughts you are having related to your decision and modify them so that they do not get in the way of moving forward. Remember we discussed the pyramid and the cycle. Well, doing this work will allow us to better understand self and options knowledge. This will also enable us to consider your decision making process as it seems you are uncertain of how to move forward.

CL: Hm. Makes sense.

MHC: Okay. With that in mind, you endorsed, "I can't trust that my career decisions will turn out well for me."

Decision-making

CL: Yeah. I have never really had to make a decision like this as it was always obvious I was going to do this job.

MHC: So you are not confident based on not having made this type of decision before.

CL: Correct. I mean ... it's a big deal!

MHC: I agree. That being said, I wonder about other decisions you have made in your life in which you felt went well.

CL: Well, I did leave my first employer when my buddy offered me a similar job for more money. We had to move so I did have to think about my family. That being said, the money was a lot better, so that made it easier.

Executive Processing

MHC: Still, you had to navigate various things to decide between staying at your job or taking another one. How did you feel about your decision?

CL: Really good. Making more money, working with someone I know, and our family likes our new town. Overall, I think it went well.

MHC: Interesting. So it appears you have an example of a decision in which you were satisfied with what happened.

CL: Yes. I guess you could say that.

MHC: So, let's see if we can change the thought of, "I can't trust that my career decisions will turn out well for me" to something more accurate and functional.

CL: Okay. How do we do that?

MHC: Well, it is important that it uses your language as it is your thought. We can certainly work together with the language, and it is important you feel the new thought is yours.

CL: Okay. How about, "There have been times when I was able to make a career choice that worked out for me"?

Career Readiness

MHC: If you feel this represents your thoughts, this will work for sure. We can always change it if needed. Again, I think this is a great start. Now, let's try this out between now and the next time we meet meaning when you sense the old belief coming into your mind, you restate the new belief. How does that sound?

CL: I can give it a try.

MHC: Great. Now, let's look at some of your interests and how they may align with options.

CL: Okay.

MHC: Tell me about things you get energy from doing such as hobbies.

TAKE A MINUTE

Take a minute to reflect on your own decision-making process for college and career choices. Which of the three areas of the CTI best reflect the process: commitment anxiety, decision-making confusion, and external conflict. How would knowing about these three types of challenges have normalized any concerns you had?

Happenstance Learning Theory

John Krumboltz parlayed his 40-plus years of theory development into its current iteration, called happenstance learning theory (HLT; 2009). He spent many years refining models of career development based on social learning theory (Krumboltz et al., 1976, 1988; Krumboltz et al., 1994). His focus has been on the way individuals learn and how this learning influences behavior. In HLT, he makes a somewhat radical departure from traditional approaches, like trait and factor, and provides a rare exception to Parsons's (1909) tripartite model. For Krumboltz, HLT is a humility-based learning model that posits that the field gives too much credence to intentionality in career decision-making. Instead, he advocates for intentionality in learning from each step on the job path, recognizing that, more times than not, careers develop serendipitously (1998; Krumboltz & Levin, 2010), despite our intentions, not necessarily because of them (Luke, 2018).

MAJOR CONSTRUCTS

The core to HLT is the idea of *planned happenstance*. *Happenstance* refers to events that occur by chance (Vecchio, 2013). Krumboltz argued for the need to build the skill of planned happenstance, or creating circumstances where we can take advantage of these unplanned events and turn them into opportunities (Krumboltz, 2009). He proposed that creating these opportunities required three steps: taking actions prior to an event to make yourself available to experience it; being alert to the opportunity when it arises; and engaging in action-based activities to benefit from the event (Krumboltz, 2009).

A story I (Melinda) often share with my students is about a time soon after college. I was working as a waitress and was dissatisfied and wanting a change. I mentioned my unhappiness to the bartender at my restaurant; she was speaking to a customer soon after, and he was discussing his need for a new employee at his organization. The bartender called me over and introduced us. Two weeks later, I had a job interview and, soon after, a new position. This story demonstrates the three steps described by Krumboltz: I let others know I was job seeking, I took advantage of the opportunity to talk with a potential employer when it arose, and I followed up with actions that resulted in a new job.

HLT proposed that people learn to behave the way they do based on complex and ongoing interactions with their environment. Krumboltz (2009) acknowledged that genetics, or conditions we inherit from birth, do play a role in our learning process. Observations of others and outcomes of our own actions also contribute to learning experiences. Our proximal environment (e.g., family, peers, and school settings) also impact our learning and ways of being. Lastly, the imperfect world, or issues related to social justice, influence our power and privilege related to access.

Krumboltz describes four key assumptions from his model that indicate an active role for clients in learning and behaving (2009, p. 141–144). First, *the goal of career counseling is to help clients be able to engage in activities that produce increased satisfaction.* For Krumboltz, career counseling is about assisting clients in life transitions—not choosing a career. "Naming a future occupation is amazingly simple and can easily be faked. When asked about a future occupational goal, children can easily please their parents by naming some high prestige occupation" (2009, p. 142). He further notes what career counselors have long known to be true: that CFC can seem as simple as choosing an occupation, when this understanding of our work is simplistic and reductive.

Second, *assessments are meant to increase learning about self.* Krumboltz maintains that career-related assessments are meant to spark conversations and stimulate further learning—not attempt to make a match between a person and work. An example of this perspective is the career beliefs inventory (Krumboltz, 1992), in which attitudes and beliefs about career development are assessed—not interests, skills, or values.

Third, *clients learn new ways to create helpful unplanned events.* As noted above, a primary goal of HLT is to help clients learn to take action to create planned happenstance. Krumboltz (2009) cautioned against high risk-taking but encouraged actions that might not ultimately lead to success, noting that all actions provide learning opportunities.

Fourth, *a successful counseling outcome in HLT is demonstrated by what the client takes actions outside of session.* The most important outcome is not what happens in session but, rather, what the client does after they leave the counseling office. These can be simple actions or quite complex, and any stated actionable goals should be reviewed at the start of the following session. In HLT, these are referred to as *action steps*—activities the client engages in that will ultimately lead to a more satisfactory outcome.

HLT IN ACTION

Clients facing career-related issues are adept at transferring their anxiety about work onto their counselors, most often unwittingly. Perhaps, it is because the need for work is embedded in our collective unconscious as a means of proving our worth. Regardless, when counselors take ownership of and responsibility for finding clients jobs, they almost invariably will resist engaging in CFC. However, HLT offers a useful reframe of the role of counselors in this process. The first is to hand ownership back to the client by redefining the purpose of counseling. The counselor is not present in the relationship to help the client find a job or make a career choice. Instead, the role of the counselor is to increase client learning and motivate the client to take some action or actions. This is a completely different process from the former, and it leads to different outcomes. Success is not job-based; it is process-based. If this sounds conspicuously like "regular" counseling, that's because it is! Counselors are process experts who facilitate client learning and action, at least according to social learning theory (Krumboltz, 1975, 1979, 1988, 1994).

In the HLT, Krumboltz suggests four key propositions, described earlier in this chapter; one of which has vast implications for career assessment. As noted throughout this section, postmodern assessment is best used to create learning opportunities—not to deliver information and answers (2009). In HLT, career optimism (assuming new options are possible), tolerance of uncertainty (viewing the unknown not as a threat but as potential opportunity), and opportunity recognition (watching with expectation, a kind of active waiting) are key to navigating the career process. Marshall and Bennett (2020) framed these in terms of mindset and HLT in college.

TABLE 10.2 SPECIFIC HLT GOALS AND MINDSET REFRAMING SUGGESTIONS

HLT Goals	Fixed Mindset	Growth Mindset	HLT and Mindset Interventions
Orient Expectations	"There are majors and careers I can and cannot do; they will not change."	"Economics, politics, culture, and technology impact and create new careers—I will keep developing"	Myth busting
Understand Self	"If I fail this test, I fail this major; I am a failure"	"I can succeed and fail at different things, which gives me opportunities to reevaluate my goals, and create new ones."	Assessments
Make Decisions	"I must choose what I will do for the rest of my life. If I choose wrong I will be unhappy."	"There will be different career opportunities; they can be beneficial in different ways depending on my goals."	Goals setting and decision making
Real World Application	"What if I talk to someone in the field and they tell me I cannot make it or I try it and it is not what I thought it was. It's too much of a risk."	"If I try something and do not like it, I gain more insight into not only the work, but also myself and what I am interested in."	Informational interview or job shadowing
Happenstance	"If the interview does not go as planned, I will have no other alternative."	"Any opportunity is a networking opportunity I can use for more growth."	Internship

Note. From Marshall & Bennett, 2020.

HLT offers ideas counselors can use to apply these concepts with their clients (Krumboltz, 2009). Counselors should help clients understand the concept of planned happenstance and that unplanned events occur all the time but we can learn to create opportunities from them. All counseling should also be framed from the clients' perspective of what would make their lives more satisfying. Past actions can be revisited in session to help clients understand their experiences with unplanned events and how they successfully took advantage of opportunities. Clients can be coached to create situations that might offer chances for unplanned events and practice how they can take advantage of these. Counselors can also help clients by combatting dysfunctional beliefs that get in the way of engaging in planned happenstance (Krumboltz, 2009; Krumboltz et al., 2013). Let's consider how this might look in session with Kiki.

KIKI IN SESSION

SC: Thanks for stopping by, Kiki. I didn't see you at the college fair last week and wanted to check to see how things are going.

ST: Yeah, I know we talked about going, but I just wasn't up for it.

SC: You weren't? Can you say more about that?

Exploring expectations

ST: Everybody seems obsessed with me going to college, but what if it's not for me?

SC: What makes you think it's not for you?

ST: I don't know. It just seems overwhelming. What if I try it and fail? I'll look like a fool.

SC: You sound like you're wondering if you can be successful in college?

ST: Yeah, it's not like high school. My writing is not the best, so even if I did get in; I likely won't pass the first term.

Understanding self

SC: That helps me understand a little more. If you struggle in this one area, it's logical to think you'll struggle even more in college.

ST: Yeah, it's so much pressure.

SC: So, assuming you tried and got into college and then it didn't work out because you didn't enjoy it or the work was too hard, then what?

Making decisions

ST: That sounds terrible!

SC: I hear you. But what would actually happen?

ST: I guess I'd leave and get a job.

SC: Okay. What job would you like to get? Any job you can think of that you'd love to have.

ST: You're going to laugh at me, but I really like math and am pretty good at it. But I don't know of any "mathy" jobs.

SC: That's cool that you like math and that you know it. If you wanted to find math jobs, how may you find that out?

ST: I guess I could use the websites you showed us when you met with our class.

SC: That's great—thank you for remembering that! What else?

ST: I heard that you can work with money or budgets or something. My friend's dad is a CPA, but I'm not sure what that even is.

SC: How do you think he'd respond if you asked to meet with him to talk about it?

Real world application

ST: That would be really weird.

SC: I can see that. Do you think he would know someone he works with that you could talk with to make it less weird?

ST: I think so. I would just go up to someone and talk to them?

SC: Well, I have a little handout here that described the process. We call it informational interviewing. You can probably thing of a few questions you'd like to ask him.

ST: Yeah, like, do you have to go to college to do that job!

SC: And if he says yes, then what?

ST: Well, if it was something I was interested in and something I could do, it might not be so bad, I guess. I just thought you had to be good at everything to go to college.

SC: You'll certainly learn a lot about a lot of things, some of which will be more interesting than other things.

ST: I can see how it might be worth checking into.

Neuroscience, Culture, and Development

The brain makes meaning by drawing on past experiences (stored in memory systems), environmental conditions, and relationships. Meaning, in this way, is very much constructed in such a way that each individual's perception of experiences, environments, and relationships are highly phenomenological. This means that any individual can create a reality all their own, whether in the world of work or the world in general. It will be immediately obvious that these models are not suggesting that one can create their own reality about gravity, making it appear or disappear. However—and this is key—they can construct their own reality about what gravity means for their ability to function in the world. In counseling and in teaching counseling, I often use the example of the training of circus elephants to remain where their trainers want them. Early in their lives, baby elephants have a shackle placed around their ankle attached to a stake in the ground. At this tender age and size, they experience the limit and cease pulling against it. As they grow, as the narrative goes, the shackle can remain without being tethered to anything (not that it would do any good anyway, given the size and power of the animal). The adult elephant has crafted a narrative—a view of reality—that restricts its behavior. The brain arranges itself in ways that internalize these views in order to increase efficiency (i.e., there is no need to waste time and energy pulling against something immovable, especially when that energy could be directed toward finding food). Likewise, clients enter CFC possessing learning experiences that have shaped their views of reality. Counseling offers a context and process that permits challenging these realities through brain change, called neuroplasticity.

Take Away and Use Today

Postmodern and emergent approaches to CFC harness the power of curiosity, optimism, risk-taking, flexibility, and persistence (Mitchell et al., 1999). These approaches view indecision as opportunities. They seek better career-related questions rather than answers. Clients are free to explore how learning experiences from their environment have informed the ways in which they view themselves in the present and how the current view of the self impacts their decisions for the future. Clients are seen as the drivers of their narrative—both in how they interpret the past and how they construct their career futures (Luke, 2018).

References

Bullock-Yowell, E., Andrews, L., & Buzzetta, M. E. (2011). Explaining career decision-making self-efficacy: Personality, cognitions, and cultural mistrust. *Career Development Quarterly, 59*, 400–411.

Bullock-Yowell, E., Reed, C. A., Mohn, R., Galles, J., Peterson, G. P., & Reardon, R. C. (2015). Neuroticism, negative thinking, and coping with respect to career decision state. *Career Development Quarterly, 63*, 333–347. https://doi.org/10.1002/cdq.12032

Chason, A. K., Bullock-Yowell, E., Sampson, J. P., Lenz, J. G., & Reardon, R. C. (2013). Relationships among career thoughts, career interests, and career decision state. *Canadian Journal of Career Development, 12*(1), 39–47.

Hayden, S. C., & Osborn, D. S. (2020). Impact of worry on career thoughts, career decision state, and cognitive information processing skills. *Journal of Employment Counseling, 57*(4), 163–177.

Hayden, S. C., Osborn, D. S., Peace, C., & Lange, R. (2021). Enhancing agency in career development via cognitive information processing theory. *British Journal of Guidance & Counselling*, 1–12.

Holland, J. L. (1959). A theory of vocational choice. *Journal of Counseling Psychology, 6, 35.*

Holland, J. L. (1997). *Making vocational choices: A theory of vocational personalities and work environments*. Psychological Assessment Resources.

Krumboltz, T. D. (1988). *Career beliefs inventory*. Consulting Psychologists Press.

Krumboltz, J. D. (2009). The happenstance learning theory. *Journal of Career Assessment, 17*(2), 135–154.

Krumboltz, J. D. (2015). Practical career counseling applications of the happenstance learning theory. In P. J. Hartung, M. L. Savickas, & B. W. Walsh (Eds.), *APA handbook of career intervention, Volume 2: Applications* (pp. 283–292). American Psychological Association.

Krumboltz, J. D., Fuqua, D. R., Newman, J. L., & Walsh, W. B. (1994). The career beliefs inventory—Comment/reply. *Journal of Counseling and Development: JCD, 72*(4), 424.

Krumboltz, J. D., Foley, P. F., & Cotter, E. W. (2013). Applying the happenstance learning theory to involuntary career transitions. *Career Development Quarterly, 61*, 15–26. https://doi.org/10.1002/j.2161-0045.2013.00032.x

Krumboltz, J. D., & Levin, A. S. (2010). *Luck is no accident: Making the most of happenstance in your life and career* (2nd ed.). Impact Publishers.

Krumboltz, J. D., Mitchell, A. M., & Jones, G. B. (1976). A social learning theory of career selection. *The counseling psychologist 6*(1), 71–81.

Leierer, S., Peterson, G., & Reardon, R. (2017). The career state inventory (CSI) as intentional assessment. *Career Planning & Adult Development Journal, 33*(4).

Luke, C. (2018). *Career focused counseling: Integrating theory, research and neuroscience.*

Luke, C., & Redekop, F. (2016). Supervision of co-occurring career and mental health concerns: Application of an integrated approach. *Career Planning and Adult Development Journal, 32*(1), 130.

Mitchell, K. E., Levin, S., & Krumboltz, J. D. (1999). Planned happenstance: Constructing unexpected career opportunities. *Journal of Counseling & Development, 77*(2), 115–124.

Parsons, F. (1909). *Choosing a vocation*. Houghton Mifflin.

Peterson, G., Lenz, J., & Osborn, D. (2016). *Decision space worksheet (DSW) activity manual*. Florida State University Center for the Study of Technology in Counseling and Career Development.

Peterson, G. W., Sampson, J. P., & Reardon, R. C. (1991). *Career development and services: A cognitive approach*. Brooks/Cole.

Sampson, J. P., Osborn, D. S., Bullock-Yowell, E., Lenz, J. G., Peterson, G. W., Reardon, R. C., V. C. Dozier, S. J. Leierer, S. C. W. Hayden, & Saunders, D. E. (2020). Introduction to cognitive information processing theory, research, and practice. DigiNole. http://purl.flvc.org/fsu/fd/FSU_libsubv1_scholarship_submission_1593091156_c171f50a

Sampson, J. P., Jr., Peterson, G. W., Lenz, J. G., Reardon, R. C., & Saunders, D. E. (1996a). *Career thoughts inventory*. Psychological Assessment Resources.

Sampson Jr., J. P., Peterson, G. W., Lenz, J. G., Reardon, R. C., & Saunders, D. E. (1996b). *Improving your career thoughts: A workbook for the Career Thoughts Inventory*. Psychological Assessment Resources.

Sampson, J. P., Jr., Peterson, G. W., Reardon, R. C., & Lenz, J. G. (2000). Using readiness assessment to improve career services: A cognitive information processing approach. *The Career Development Quarterly, 49*, 146–174. https://doi.org/10.1002/j.2161-0045.2000.tb00556.x

Sampson, J. P., Reardon, R. C., Peterson, G. W., & Lenz, J. G. (2004). *Career counseling and services: A cognitive information processing approach.* Thomson/Brooks/Cole.

Super, D. E. (1980). A life-span, life-space approach to career development. *Journal of Vocational Behavior, 16*(3), 282–298.

Vecchio, C. A. (2013). Happenstance. In M. L. Savickas (Ed.), *Ten ideas that changed career development* (p. 12). NCDA.

PART III

Career-Focused Counseling Across Counseling Settings

CHAPTER 11

Career-Focused Counseling for K–12 Students

Melinda Gibbons, Haley Ault, and Chad Luke

CHAPTER GOALS

- Understand the career developmental goals for elementary, middle, and high school students.
- Learn about various activities that can be completed with K–12 students and their families.
- Consider how to provide career and college readiness programming that is equitable and accessible for all students.

REFLECTION ACTIVITIES AND QUESTIONS

Think back to when you were a child, maybe three to six years old. What did you dream of becoming when you grew up? Did you want to be famous? Did you want to have magical powers? Now, think about the first time you identified a specific career you wanted when you grew up. Was it a counselor or other professional helper? Or something completely unrelated to your current career path? Who and what have influenced your career goals? Now think back to 11th and 12th grade. When did you know you were ready for career and college? What led you to feeling ready? Did you know what career you wanted?

Introduction

This is the story of my (Melinda) own career development. The earliest memories I have related to career are about wanting to be Wonder Woman. I was a child in the 1970s, and Lynda Carter was the star of *Wonder Woman* on TV. I wanted to be her, so I spent hours in my backyard with aluminum foil bracelets on and twirling to try to become Wonder Woman. I was also very enamored with the idea of becoming a Charlie's Angel, another 1970s TV show. Both of these shows had role models of strong women, who were smart, beautiful, and helped others. As an insecure young girl who did well in school, these models appealed to me.

During this time, my parents went through a messy divorce, and I decided I would become a doctor—either a pediatrician or psychiatrist. I wanted to help children who were sick or hurting. I kept this plan through high school, even as I disliked my science classes. After taking a psychology class in high school, I added psychologist to my list of possible careers, although physician was still at the top. It was not until freshman year in college that I dropped the dream of becoming a medical doctor, mostly because I was failing my introduction to chemistry course and realized I did not really enjoy the physical sciences. From that point forward, I knew I wanted to work with youth in a mental health field.

What themes do you see from my story? How did I figure out what I wanted to be? What influenced my decision?

Career development is a journey that begins in early childhood. As described in the theory chapters, readiness is not an activity solely for adolescents and emerging adults but, rather, a complex construct that involves understanding self, the world of work, and how to be adaptable in a constantly changing world. Early career theorists, such as Super, Ginzberg, and Roe, believed that career development occurred in a sequential manner with somewhat predictable steps, similar to general theories of human development, such as Erikson's (Osipow, 1968). Most focused on a single career choice made in early adulthood and followed throughout a lifetime. These theories offered a list of events that needed to occur in childhood and adolescence to help ensure career decision-making success. We now understand that career development continues well past adolescence and begins very early in childhood. In this chapter, we discuss the early aspects of career development and offer ideas on how to maximize career-focused counseling for students across K–12 settings.

The idea that career development begins in early childhood is not a new one, but it is an under-researched topic. Magnuson and Starr (2000) promoted the idea that career planning begins in infancy, equating a child's play habits and overall preferences with the origins of early career development. They suggested that career development is constantly shifting based on our experiences and as children come to understand themselves and the world of work.

TAKE A MINUTE

Consider the following examples:

- Five-year-old Josiah's favorite activities are creating lemonade stands, building LEGO houses, and making paper airplanes (with a lot of help from his older brother).
- Seven-year-old Myia's favorite toys are her doctor kit and "lesson planning" book. She loves to play school and vet hospital with her stuffed animals.
- Eight-year-old Parker enjoys playing outdoors, building forts, searching for buried treasure, and tossing the football with his friends.

Think back to the chapter on Holland codes; what codes do you see represented in Josiah, Myia, and Parker's play? How are they similar to or different from each other? What careers might appeal to them based on these early interests?

Child and Youth Development

Consider some of the theories found in a recent textbook on child and adolescent development (Anthis, 2021). Piaget's theory of cognitive development suggests that children develop increasingly more complex thought processes as they grow. Even in infancy and early childhood, children develop goal-directed behaviors and the ability to understand multiple ideas at once. Erikson's theory suggests that by the time children enter school, they have already moved through the first two stages of development: learning about trust and autonomy. Before formal learning has even begun, children have started exploring levels of self-sufficiency and security outside the home. Vygotsky's theory also focuses on early development, suggesting that social interactions influence learning and that language development impacts cognitive development (Anthis, 2021). These well-known theories indicate that learning occurs early on, and this early development impacts views over the lifetime. It makes sense, then, that career-focused learning occurs during these early stages as well.

Elementary School

The developmental theories describe continued growth throughout childhood, adolescence, and into adulthood. For elementary-aged children, we can assume that they embrace curiosity, seek information, watch others, and learn from both their own and others' experiences (Magnuson & Starr, 2000). They learn about societal views of careers, identify role models, and evaluate their own capacity for different tasks. To positively impact career development in early and middle childhood, counselors can encourage positive interactions with the world of work (Magnuson & Starr, 2000). Elementary school children need *career awareness* activities, where options are opened and supported by significant others.

Remember the activities Super (1975) suggested in his growth stage: interactions with environment and important others, development of interests and perceived abilities, and understanding of cultural norms and values related to work. These are activities related to career awareness. To these, Hartung et al. (2008) added career adaptability. As students engage in activities, they envision themselves in various roles and assess their capacity for success in each. Children also develop the ability to cope with an ever-changing world, based on their levels of autonomy, self-reliance, and beliefs about their abilities. Hartung et al. (2008) noted that children can be provided experiences to foster optimum, control, curiosity, and confidence to help with later career adaptability. Attending to the issues raised in Gottfredson's theory is also important. Beginning with elementary school and continuing through to graduation, students need to unpack sex-typed career messages. Depicting culturally and gender diverse models of workers can be especially impactful.

TAKE A MINUTE

Let's return to Myia from the earlier vignette. In school, she enjoys her science and English classes and often serves as a support for students struggling with those subjects. Her teacher notices this and mentions that Myia would be a great teacher herself one day. Myia tells her grandfather about her teacher's comments, and he says she is "destined to be a great doctor one day, not a teacher."

- What messages is Myia receiving from her important others about the world of work?
- How are these various interactions influencing her career development?

Middle School

As children move into middle school, they become ready for *career exploration* activities. Described by Marcia (1993), adolescence is a critical time for identity development. Many students actively experiment with new roles and explore the many options of how to express themselves. This is especially true as they continue to learn about themselves and the world of work. Exploration activities involve understanding how to navigate the world of work in general and investigating specific careers of interest. Early college exploration experiences, such as campus tours and career speakers, may take place, and students may begin to envision their future selves.

Additionally, Harter (1999) noted that lower self-esteem during this time period can be addressed by activities that highlight students' areas of competence and develop emotional literacy skills, such as self-awareness, self-confidence, and self-regulation. Career exploration activities might involve students exploring their own interests, values, beliefs, and abilities and understanding how these connect to possible future careers. Students can focus on their strengths and explore careers that build on these characteristics. Middle school is an ideal time to discuss learning styles and how they connect to the world of work; then, students may explore how careers link to their styles of engagement. Students might also engage in initial volunteering and part-time work opportunities. It can be especially important to reinforce how these early opportunities connect to future career interests.

TAKE A MINUTE

Let's imagine that Josiah, our lemonade stand lover from above, is now in middle school. He continues to be creative but has been encouraged by others to consider how to make money from his ideas. His family struggles financially, so there is constant stress about meeting basic needs. He is told that the time for purely creative activities is over. He begins to consider sales or being a business owner because these still tie to activities he enjoys, but he hears from others that these careers can be lucrative as well.

- What activities might help Josiah explore his new career interests and how they match or mismatch with his personality?
- How might you address any issues of self-esteem?

High School

In high school, students can begin *tentative career decision-making*, where they select a tentative career path, choose courses needed to prepare for it, and identify possible next steps after graduation. At this stage, adolescents develop more abstract thought and can start to envision themselves in a more realistic future than ever before. Students can be guided through activities where they imagine what they want their life to look like in the future and identify the tasks they need to complete to accomplish their goals and objectives.

High school students also continue to form their sense of self through identity formation (Marcia, 1993). They may start to commit to goals, values, and aspirations aligned with their renewed sense of self. Simultaneously, high school students might begin to show more independence from their parents and caregivers, motivating them to establish more clearly defined post-graduation goals. As they continue to learn about themselves, counselors can use a basic decision-making model to assist students with specifying their goals. This process would include helping students identify that a choice needs to be made, examining what they know about themselves, reviewing and prioritizing their options, and outlining an action plan for one of these options. For students to make informed decisions, they must be provided concrete information on options for postsecondary education, sources of funding, and academic and/or technical requirements.

TAKE A MINUTE

Parker, from the earlier vignette, is now a high school junior. He has talked for years about becoming a college football star and was being noticed by recruiters until he tore his rotator cuff and was told he could no longer play competitively. He is now despondent and confused about next steps. He worries about being able to get into a good college without the support of football and expresses doubt that any other career would be of interest.

- How can you help Parker develop a renewed sense of self?
- How might you help him make tentative plans for the future?

Career and College Readiness

Most people reading this book are planning for life as a professional counselor. To achieve this goal, you likely completed high school, entered and completed your undergraduate degree, and are now seeking or actively pursuing a graduate degree. These activities took many years to complete and required many decisions along the way. You needed to be *career and college ready* to be successful in these tasks.

A BRIEF HISTORY LESSON

The first legislation regarding the rights of K–12 students and their education was the Elementary and Secondary Education Act (ESEA, 1965). This civil rights act provided funding to school districts to better serve low-income and specific education students, including funding for textbooks and scholarships. It also provided state funding to improve the quality of education. In 2002, Congress enacted the No Child Left Behind Act (NCLB), which increased accountability requirements for states and districts. NCLB and its revisions helped identify achievement gaps and engaged states in a quest to offer more equitable educational opportunities.

In 2015, President Obama signed the Every Student Succeeds Act (ESSA) into law to replace NCLB. ESSA was built on prior successes by requiring high academic standards to prepare all students for career and college. Local, state, and federal support is provided to grow local programs, share school-based outcomes, expand preschool options, and offer accountability standards for low-performing schools. As part of ESSA, all states were required to define career and college readiness and describe how they were promoting it for all students. Although state definitions vary for this term, in most cases career and college readiness is related to this definition: attainment of "the knowledge, skills, and dispositions needed to succeed in credit-bearing (non-remedial) postsecondary coursework or a workforce training program in order to earn the credentials necessary to qualify for a meaningful career aligned to his or her goals and offering a competitive salary" (National Forum on Education Statistics [NFES], 2015, p. vi).

These legislative acts were all proposed to help increase equity and success for all students as they move toward career and college. The rates for college-going differ dramatically by demographic group. Overall, approximately 41% of all 18–24 year olds enter into a two- or four-year college (NCES, 2021). As you can see from the data below, graduation and college-going rates differ by race, ethnicity, and sex:

TABLE 11.1 ENROLLMENT AND COLLEGE GRADUATE RATES DIFFER BY DEMOGRAPHIC

College enrollment rates (two- or four-year):	College graduation rates (four-year)
Overall college enrollment rates for 18-24 year olds (2019): 41% • Asian: 62% • White: 41% • Black: 37% • Hispanic 36% • American Indian/Alaska Native: 24% • Female: 57% • Male: 43% *Note. Adapted from NCES, 2021.*	Overall 6 year graduation rate: 63% • 62% public university • 68% private non-profit • 26% private for-profit • 66% females • 60% males • 64.4% White • 39.8% Black • 55% Hispanic • 74.1% Asian *Note. Adapted from U.S. Department of Education, 2021; NCES, 2021.*

Numerous researchers have explored how to help students become career and college ready. For example, the National Office for School Counselor Advocacy highlights eight components of career and college readiness counseling, and many of which begin in elementary school (College Board, 2010). The American School Counselor Association (ASCA) promotes the use of their *Student Standards: Mindsets and Behaviors for Student Success* (ASCA, 2021). Related to career and college readiness, the standards include six overarching belief systems and behaviors related to learning strategies, self-management, and social skills. The College Board also promotes career and college readiness strategies through their *Research Foundations: Empirical Foundations for College and Career Readiness* (2014). They promote activities such as proactively addressing academic gaps, creating a college-going culture, and offering advanced coursework to promote success for all students.

According to most of these standards, school counselors should help students gain awareness, knowledge, and skills related to career and college readiness, and both schoolwide and student-level data should be reviewed to best attend to issues of equity and access. In other words, it is not enough to consider only district- or state-level performance; counselors must also contemplate how students in their own schools are doing and how achievement differs by cultural or social identities, such as gender, income level, ethnicity, or special education status. The table below combines various components of career and college readiness and offers some ideas for addressing them at each school level. Some of the activities are described in detail below as well.

Self-Exploration

ELEMENTARY SCHOOL

Self-exploration at the elementary school level consists of students beginning to understand themselves as a unique and worthy person. They begin to identify early interests through

TABLE 11.2 COMPONENTS OF CAREER DEVELOPMENT

Component of Career Development	Elementary School: Awareness	Middle School: Exploration	High School: Tentative Decision-Making
Self-Exploration	• Uniqueness collage • Recognizing identities (i.e., sister, helper, friend, or singer) • My likes and dislikes • Sand tray	• Interest inventories • Skills/aptitude assessments • Values card sort • Career coat of arms • Future self-portrait	• Identifying and discussing strengths • Locus of control • Professional first impressions • Dismantling barriers to success
Transferable Skills	• Listening skills • Working as a team • Respectful workplace relationships • Early leadership skills • Responsibility	• Oral communication skills • Diversity and discrimination in the workplace	• Written communication skills • Job-seeking skills • Advanced leadership skills • Long-term goal setting

(Continued)

TABLE 11.2 COMPONENTS OF CAREER DEVELOPMENT *(Continued)*

Component of Career Development	Elementary School: Awareness	Middle School: Exploration	High School: Tentative Decision-Making
	• Character counts	• Time management and prioritizing tasks • Digital citizenship (ethical online use)	• Interviewing skills • Strengths identification
Career Aspirations and Awareness	• Foster a college-going school culture • Career and college door decorating • Career dress-up day • College colors day • Career ABCs • Career bingo	• High school graduation requirements • Introduce college lingo • Introduce career clusters • Career dreams collage • Awareness of postsecondary options • Career fair	• College website scavenger hunt • College fair • College dreams collage • Résumé writing • Informational interviews • Understanding the college admissions requirements (i.e., testing or GPA)
Career and College Exploration	• Career role models from community • Children's books about career • Career in my family and community	• O*NET exploration • Virtual college tours • Job shadowing • Connect self-awareness activities (above) to career • Careers by degree • Career interview	• Campus tours • Financial literacy (broad—not college specific) • Career research paper • College admission game
Career and College Decision Making	• Partner with feeder schools for college signing celebrations	• Short-term SMART goals • Six-year academic plan/transition to high school plan • Career and college options in my community	• Decision-making model of comparing options: What's best for me? • College app week • College "signing" day • 10-year class reunion
Academic Enrichment	• College geography • Early math and literacy skills • Establishing good study habits	• Connections between learning styles and career • Calculating the cost of college and ways to pay for it • Financial literacy • Understanding career salaries: mean vs. median, minimum vs. maximum, and cost of living • Create help wanted posters for specific careers	• Vocational courses • Work-based learning • Writing cover letters and personal statements • Résumé writing

(Continued)

TABLE 11.2 COMPONENTS OF CAREER DEVELOPMENT (*Continued*)

Component of Career Development	Elementary School: Awareness	Middle School: Exploration	High School: Tentative Decision-Making
Extracurricular Engagement	• Connect household chores to career • Early involvement in sports and hobbies	• Volunteering and community service • Commitment to sports and clubs (i.e., dependability and punctuality) • Connect hobbies to career interests	• Part-time jobs • Volunteering and community service • Leadership roles within sports and clubs (e.g., band section leader, class treasurer, or team captain)
College Affordability Planning	• Messages about college affordability • Family financial aid night	• Financial aid vocabulary • Family financial aid night	• FAFSA workshop • Connect to applicable scholarships and grants • Family financial aid night

things they like and dislike, such as music, play, sports, or friendships. Counselors can help students identify the identities that they hold, such as sister, friend, singer, artist, and so forth. They might help students promote confidence in themselves by showcasing these identities through a uniqueness collage or sand tray activity. A "uniqueness collage" involves having students identify what makes them an individual and different from anyone else. Younger children might focus on their physical characteristics and their family structure, while older students might share their favorite hobbies or special talents. In all cases, the collage can be completed in multiple ways. Students can draw or write these qualities, or they can use technology to create a slide show presentation with clip art and graphics. In the end, students can celebrate their unique qualities, find others who share similar traits, and consider how these characteristics can be used in their future careers.

MIDDLE SCHOOL

At the middle school level, self-exploration is critical as students are experimenting with new roles and identities. Imagine yourself as a middle school student. What did you like to do for fun? Where did you shine? Were there aspects of yourself that you were less sure of? Activities that recognize and celebrate different characteristics can be essential for the self-esteem development of middle school students. One activity for highlighting unique personal attributes is *creating a career coat of arms*. Although traditionally recognized in early modern age centuries, a coat of arms is a visual representation of the unique cultural characteristics and accomplishments of an individual. Students can craft their career coat of arms using colors, words, and images that represent their interests, skills, and values. They may also start to incorporate early career aspirations. This could be completed using traditional art supplies or graphic design software (i.e., PowerPoint or Canva). Alternatively, you might have students draw a future self-portrait that shows them working in an ideal career. They might include the setting (i.e., hospital, wilderness, or construction site), skills or tools needed, or other characters (i.e., students, coworkers, or animals).

Additionally, middle school is an excellent time to introduce tools that highlight students' interests, skills, aptitudes, values, and workplace preferences. In addition to the assessments and resources described in Chapter 5, Kuder Navigator and YouScience are two career assessments specifically designed for adolescents. Through this exploration, students can begin to see how these personal attributes might influence future career aspirations and plans.

TAKE A MINUTE

Earlier, we discussed Josiah, a middle schooler contemplating how to incorporate his values and interests into a future career goal. You have Josiah complete the career interests, skills confidence, and work values assessments within the Kuder Navigator career planning system. As expected, Josiah's results reveal his interest in creativity and business enterprise. However, he also scores high in the realistic interest code, which says he prefers working with his hands and problem-solving. His work values report shows a high score in achievement and independence.

- How might you work with Josiah to explore options for his future that align with his assessment results?
- How might Josiah explore these interests and values through early learning opportunities?

HIGH SCHOOL

In high school, self-exploration activities build upon earlier experiences as students begin to make connections to the world of work. Students can explore their identities as a professional person in the workplace. This might include exploration of their strengths and how to discuss them in a confident manner. One example of how to do this is to invite students to share a story with you or a peer. This story should be about a time in their life where they felt really proud of themself. As they're telling the story, ask them (or a peer) to listen for the strengths they hear. Were they strong in the face of adversity? Were they able to be flexible to meet the needs of the larger group? Were they creative in their problem-solving skills? "What are your greatest strengths?" is a common career and college interview question. Initially, students may not see themselves as determined, flexible, or innovative, so activities that highlight and provide language for intrapersonal strengths can be especially helpful for future career experiences.

As high school students develop, they become more aware of factors that might hinder their career goals. Some examples of barriers to career success are finances, discrimination, family responsibilities, and lack of role models, among others. Although counselors cannot remove barriers completely, they can provide information and resources about careers to students to help dismantle or reduce perceived obstacles. With a growing sense of autonomy, high school students may need specific activities that help them decipher what is within their control and what is not. For instance, while they may not be able to control the decisions of the college admissions board, they are able to earn good grades, study for their admissions exams, and volunteer within their community, which may contribute to them being a competitive applicant.

Transferable Skills

Across all levels, students must develop and strengthen transferable skills that are necessary for success in the world of work, regardless of the specific occupation selected. These characteristics include oral and written communication, teamwork, problem-solving and adaptability, respect, and technology skills, among others. These topics are already addressed in school settings, but counselors may additionally include career-related examples when teaching these concepts.

ELEMENTARY SCHOOL

Many transferable skills are commonly covered in the elementary counseling curriculum, such as trustworthiness, perseverance, and integrity. Counselors can intentionally include examples about the world of work within the lessons they provide on these topics. When introducing the trait of respect to students, counselors may ask students to think about respectfulness in the workplace: "Imagine you are now an adult and you work at a large company. The company wants to give an award for outstanding worker. You feel you have earned that award, but the company decides to give it to another worker. How would you show respect for the company's decision? How would you show respect to the worker who won the award?"

Oftentimes, elementary school teachers will assign classroom jobs to students, such as line leader (leads the line down the hallway), supply manager (passes out classroom supplies), or gardener (waters the classroom plants). By practicing these roles, students learn transferable skills, such as responsibility, commitment, and following directions. Counselors can help students identify the special traits needed to do these jobs well. This mock world of work allows students to develop early leadership and collaboration skills and learn how each person's job impacts the greater work environment.

MIDDLE SCHOOL

At the middle school level, counselors continue to build on the transferable skills addressed in elementary school while introducing higher-level tasks, such as time management, problem solving, and technology skills. Although it is common for students to use technology prior to middle school, adolescence is a key time for learning digital citizenship skills for ethical online use. Common Sense Media is a helpful resource for lesson plans and activities related to digital citizenship (www.commonsense.org). In addition to delivering lessons on digital drama, oversharing on social media, and trusting reliable information, counselors can incorporate a discussion about how these acts can impact students in the workplace. For example, counselors might show example fictional social media profiles and have students determine which person they would pick for the job based solely on their posts. Students might consider whether the person seems like a good fit for the job with careful attention to posts that suggest disrespectful language, risky behaviors, or a lack of trustworthiness.

Building upon the character skills introduced in elementary school, counselors may include elements of respecting and appreciating diversity in the workplace. Students must know how to work collaboratively with coworkers who hold different cultural identities from them. Further, counselors might introduce workplace discrimination laws to students and facilitate a discussion about the rights of employees. Here are a few examples counselors can use from Street Law (2015), an organization focused on teaching students about law and civics:

- A female employee gets pregnant. Her employer fires her because they don't want to pay for her maternity leave.
- A person in a wheelchair applies for a job in a warehouse. The job requirements say you must be able to lift 50-pound boxes onto shelves. The hiring manager assumes the person can't do that and refuses to hire him.
- A woman who works in retail has requested Saturdays off to observe the Sabbath according to her religious beliefs. The store repeatedly schedules her for Saturdays, despite the request.
- A man from Spain works for a computer company. In the break room and around the office, his co-workers always tease him by mimicking his accent and calling him derogatory Spanish names. He has complained to his boss, but the boss tells him to shake it off.

HIGH SCHOOL

In high school, students start to fine tune their transferable skills to be more specific to job-seeking behaviors. For instance, as they increase comfort and familiarity with technology, they may practice locating job information and completing job applications. Additionally, as written communication skills develop, counselors can work with students on composing business emails to future employers. Helping high school students identify their transferable skill strengths and growth edges can be another important activity. Counselors (both school and mental health) can help adolescents explore their top three skills and one or two they want to improve and engage in conversation about how these skills can be useful as they move into the world of work.

Leadership training is another important task for high school students. Learning how to effectively lead and manage others can easily connect to future career interests. Counselors can combine leadership skills with interviewing skills by creating mock job or scholarship interviews in which students need to describe the ways they lead *and* the ways they work as part of a team. For example, consider that the counselor is talking with Myia from the earlier vignette. Myia has strong leadership skills but struggles to let others be in charge of group projects and activities. The counselor might help Myia understand the value of being a strong team player as part of being a strong future worker.

Career Aspirations and Awareness

ELEMENTARY SCHOOL

Elementary school is the essential time to begin developing career aspirations and awareness. As students are learning about the world around them, it is important to instill messages about career and college success. Counselors might help students engage in early career experiences by promoting schoolwide career and college awareness campaigns. Such events might include a career dress-up day, wear your college colors day, classroom door decorating contest, and inviting teachers and community guests to share their career and college going stories. These events help foster a school culture that emphasizes a variety of postsecondary options. Importantly, care should be taken to demonstrate diversity in these models and activities, so all students, regardless of personal identities, feel included and are able to connect to role models and envision future selves. Therefore, inviting speakers with visible disabilities or those who learned about work through apprenticeships, rather than formal postsecondary education, fosters an inclusive environment.

Additionally, awareness activities can include increasing familiarity with potential career options and common terms. One activity is the career ABCs, where counselors ask students to name one career for each letter of the alphabet, such as A is for architect, B is for bus driver, C is for computer technician, D is for dental hygienist, and so on. Counselors can help students brainstorm careers from their community with a variety of educational backgrounds. In many instances, students may not be aware that the people they pass everyday are actually doing their career! Early awareness activities help students begin to think critically about the world of work around them.

MIDDLE SCHOOL

In middle school, career awareness builds on the early experiences of elementary school and includes additional language about high school and college specifically. School-wide career and college awareness campaigns continue into middle school but may be coupled with other events, such as a career fair or career speakers. The career fair could be grouped by career cluster or Holland code, so students can explore potential careers based on personality and interest. As counselors think about guest speakers to invite for career fairs, they may also include representatives from local high schools to share about vocational programs and career specific coursework.

As middle school students are increasing their awareness of the world of work, it is also important to increase their knowledge about high school and beyond. Middle school students should be exposed to local and state graduation requirements with discussion of how they tie to postsecondary options. Additionally, many students may not be aware of the different types of postsecondary options available outside of a four year college. Counselors can intentionally introduce, compare, and contrast options for students, including community college, vocational school, the military, apprenticeship, and more. All of this new information can be overwhelming for students, so counselors might try interactive classroom teaching strategies, such as Bingo, Jeopardy, or Kahoot!

HIGH SCHOOL

By the time students enter high school, we hope they have cultivated some career awareness and created some tentative goals for their career after high school. However, this is the time students increase their awareness of realistic postsecondary opportunities that will help them achieve their career goals. Counselors can help students increase their knowledge of postsecondary options through a college website scavenger hunt. Counselors prompt students to navigate college websites searching for key information, such as admission requirements, academic programs, and tuition costs. This activity also helps to reinforce the college terminology that was introduced in middle school. Additionally, counselors can invite representatives from a variety of postsecondary institutions to their career and college fairs to allow students the opportunity to ask questions and reduce anxieties they may feel toward the college admissions process.

Another important activity for high school students is to begin developing skills for obtaining a job. Counselors can help high school students build a cover letter and résumé and understand how to complete job applications. High school students may have limited formal work experiences, so counselors can use brainstorming and concept mapping activities, as seen below, to help students formulate ideas for their résumé. For additional resources, refer back to the career documents we discussed in Chapter 6.

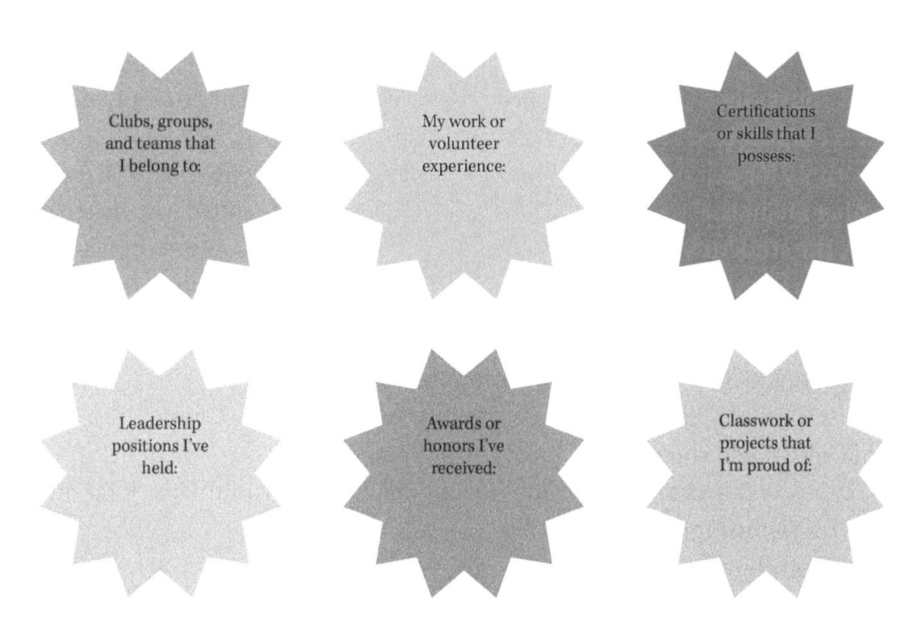

FIGURE 11.1. Activities

Career and College Exploration

ELEMENTARY SCHOOL

Given that the career focus for this group is about awareness, activities that expose students to a variety of occupations can be extremely beneficial. It is not necessary for elementary-aged students to deeply explore careers of interest, but rather, they can open themselves to the wide variety of options available to them. Some easy ways to accomplish this are to invite career role models from community or read children's books about career (e.g., *Snowmen at Work*, Buehner, 2012; *What Shoes Will You Wear?*, Cook, 2014; *Career Day*, Rockwell, 2000; *What do you do with an Idea?*, Yamada, 2014; *Peppa Pig and the Career Day*, Candlewick Press, 2018). Diverse representations of career help students connect with future possibilities. Recall Myia from the earlier vignette, who was receiving messages from family members about what she "should" do for a future career. As a counselor, you might use these children's books and community role models to help her envision herself in careers outside of the traditional gender stereotypes.

MIDDLE SCHOOL

By middle school, students have developed a general sense of their interests and skills, and counselors can help these young adolescents explore careers that specifically align with their personality. Utilizing the results from various self-exploration activities (i.e., interests inventories, skills and aptitude assessments), students can investigate careers on O*NET (www.onetonline.org). O*NET allows students to explore specifically by interest, abilities, and values. Students may research careers for education qualifications, typical work activities, and skill requirements. In addition to increasing a conceptual understanding of the world of work, it can be helpful for students to see and feel the world of work through various career and college experiential activities. These experiences can happen through virtual or in-person job shadowing or campus tours. These learning experiences are key steps in the career decision-making process that is emphasized later on in high school.

Another activity for exploring careers is to have students interview a family friend or community member about their career path. Ideally, this would be an adult who doesn't live in the same home as the student to ensure students learn about a career option that is new to them. Counselors can help students brainstorm questions prior to the interview. Possible questions might include:

- What do you do on a typical day at your job?
- How many hours a day do you work and how many days per week?
- In what setting do you work?
- What type of education or training do you need for your job? How long did it take to receive this training?
- How did you choose this career?
- What is the most important part of your job?
- What are your next steps in your career journey?

Following the interview, students may choose to share the information with others in the form of a paper or presentation. Additionally, counselors can discuss etiquette related to interviews, such as requesting a meeting time, engaging respectfully, and ensuring they thank the person at the end, with students. This practice helps reinforce skills transferable to future job settings.

HIGH SCHOOL

By high school, students need to be moving from exploration to tentative choices, so activities that help with decision-making or increase understanding of potential options are important. Although specific decision-making activities are discussed below, there are several topics that can help focus exploration activities and support eventual choices. For example, counselors can offer campus tour activities for those considering college. Many students lack the ability to visit colleges on their own or with family members, so counselors might create a college-going club that meets after school. Interested students can learn about postsecondary options and explore possible college majors. A day-long campus visit can be a culminating activity at the end of the school year. Counselors can select one or two colleges within driving distance and travel with the students for a formal campus tour and information session. Given that this may be the only opportunity some students have to visit a college, it is vital that counselors select schools that are attainable for students or that offer supportive services for those who might need them.

Counselors might also partner with English teachers to create a career research paper activity. Making the paper a class assignment increases student engagement and reaches all students. English teachers can offer feedback on grammar, theme identification, and overall writing, while counselors provide comments on career exploration next steps. This type of activity also reinforces the connection between school and career. We will address this further in the Academic Engagement section.

Career and College Decision Making

ELEMENTARY SCHOOL

At the elementary level, there is little expectation that students will be making decisions about their lifelong career goals. However, since awareness is the critical component for this age group, counselors can partner with local high schools during their college-going celebrations. Counselors might coordinate a "college café" where high school seniors are partnered with elementary students to talk about their plans after high school. As high school students are making decisions for postsecondary education, elementary students witness these behaviors and set early goals for themselves to achieve the same.

MIDDLE SCHOOL

The focus for career and college decision-making at the middle school level involves short-term goal setting and planning for the transition to high school. Counselors can assist students with creating goals that are specific, measureable, attainable, realistic, and time-oriented (SMART). Some appropriate goals for middle school students might be "to earn two postsecondary credits through dual enrollment courses before high school graduation" or "to maintain a 3.0 GPA throughout high school." Traditionally, counselors would complete a "four-year plan" with students transitioning to high school that laid out necessary coursework and activities required for high school graduation. However, we suggest expanding this planning activity to include the next six years, rather than four. This ensures that students at the middle school level are considering what paths they may take after high school. It is essential to engage in planning and goal setting early, so students know what they are working toward.

HIGH SCHOOL

High school is the most critical time for making decisions about career and college. Building upon earlier awareness and exploration activities, counselors can help students to narrow down their postsecondary options. One way to get students thinking about their hopes for their future is to ask them to envision themselves at their 10-year high school class reunion. Where do they hope to be in life? What do they want to be able to share with their peers? Are they living in their hometown, or have they moved away? What education have they received? The answers to these questions can be guides for developing a plan for their next steps. This activity can also be helpful for students who may be early on in their decision-making process or have recently encountered a setback.

TAKE A MINUTE

Let's revisit Parker's situation from before. Although he is worried and confused about his future now that he's suffered this injury, you are hopeful that you can help him determine his best option for after high school. In this book, we've discussed multiple approaches to career decision-making. Consider how you might help Parker, utilizing the following approaches.

- Drawing upon person–environment correspondence (Holland, 1985), how might you help Parker to revisit earlier self-exploration activities?
- Drawing upon social cognitive career theory (Lent et al., 1994), how might you increase Parker's self-efficacy for career decision-making?
- Drawing upon happenstance learning theory (Krumboltz, 2009), how might you help Parker shift his mindset from fixed to growth?

Counselors may also elect to host schoolwide events and recognition ceremonies for students who apply to college and receive admission. Many application deadlines fall within the fall semester, so counselors may host a "college app week" campaigns to provide students support and encouragement for meeting these deadlines. Activities might include workshops for revising personal statements or answering application questions. Counselors might create a display to recognize students' who successfully submitted their applications. In the spring semester, students begin to finalize their decisions about college admissions. High school counselors may host "signing day" events, where students are celebrated for making postsecondary decisions.

Academic Enrichment

Across all levels, teachers can provide examples of how written or oral communication skills are needed for career success. They can also demonstrate the link between math skills and future career activities. In fact, academics and career and college readiness can easily be intertwined throughout schools. Teachers can share these ideas with their students to reinforce the importance of communication skill development. Counselors might need to help teachers develop lesson extensions that offer concrete examples of the connection between academic skills and future careers, so specific examples for each school level are provided below.

ELEMENTARY SCHOOL

Connecting early learning experiences to future career goals helps students find value in their schoolwork. It also increases self-confidence and begins developing career self-concept and adaptability. Some activities for elementary students include college geography, math and literacy skills, and study habits. As students learn the 50 states, teachers can highlight a college in each state. They might explore the school colors or school mascot or, perhaps, learn about a famous alumnus of the school. This can be a fun extension to memorizing states and their capitals. School personnel, including teachers and counselors, can also remind students and their adult caregivers about the importance of math and literacy skills. Parents can share personal experiences of using reading and math in their jobs, teachers can offer ways that strong academic skills help students succeed in future careers, and counselors can use this information to reinforce the need to pay attention in class. For struggling students, this link to future goals can serve as a motivator or incentive.

Lastly, students can begin to learn strong study strategies and habits. Students can be taught about being organized, neat, and planful with their studies. If students do not find value in their academic work, a first step might be to connect study skills with hobbies or interests. For example, a student involved in community theater could share how they memorize their lines or learn the songs they sing. Then, these same skills can be translated into how they can help with schoolwork.

MIDDLE SCHOOL

Building connections between academic skills and future careers continues in middle school. A common middle school math concept is understanding measures of mean, median, mode, and range. Teachers can apply this to career development by having students look at the *Occupational Outlook Handbook* for median salaries of potential careers. They might facilitate a discussion about the following questions: Why do we use median versus mode to describe salary? What does the range of salaries mean? What's the difference between hourly wages and salary? Why does the salary change from one state to another? This conversation can help reinforce math concepts, while expanding on early financial literacy skills.

Another activity for academic enrichment in middle school is a college visit presentation. Students will research a college of their choice and present the resulting information in a slideshow, brochure, or poster. Teachers can ask students to identify several key pieces of information about the college, such as unique academic programs, extracurricular options, and admission requirements. Students can calculate the distance from the college to their hometown as well as the cost of tuition. They can research fun things to do in the city in which the college is located. Finally, they will develop a list of pros and cons for why a student might attend school there. This activity increases awareness about postsecondary options, while also developing oral communication, research, and presentation skills.

HIGH SCHOOL

At the high school level, academic connections to career become more explicit through vocational and work-based learning courses. Counselors can encourage students to enroll in these courses to further build their career-related skills. In many schools, high school vocational courses can lead students to the completion of an industry certification or license. Counselors may need to increase awareness of these options and help students see the benefits of acquiring this training during their high school career.

In addition to specific coursework related to career, teachers can incorporate career concepts into their curriculum. For example, business teachers can teach business etiquette skills, such as how to draft a professional email and how to build a resume using common computer applications. English teachers can help students write cover letters and personal statements, both of which are commonly required for job, college, and scholarship applications. Teachers can focus on grammar and sentence structure, while counselors help students identify key strengths and skills to include. Addressing these concepts in multiple academic settings can help reinforce the academic and career connection.

Extracurricular Engagement

Extracurricular experiences complement career development in a variety of ways. These experiences start as early as elementary school and continue building up to high school graduation and beyond. Through sports, hobbies, volunteering, and work, students learn new expertise, strengthen their soft skills, build confidence in themselves, and expand their networks. These skills are complementary to the educational training and qualifications necessary for career success.

SPORTS AND HOBBIES

Involvement in sports and hobbies begin in the elementary time period and oftentimes sooner. Although initial participation may be due to the caretaker's wishes, over time, students choose to participate in activities that align with their interests. Participation in sports and hobbies in elementary school might include self-exploration of likes, dislikes, and skills. As children find outlets that align with their skills and interests, they can build a sense of commitment, develop habits through practice, and fine tune their craft. Later on, they may also begin to take on leadership roles, such as team captain or band section leader.

TAKE A MINUTE

Let's consider Sienna, a seven-year-old girl with lots of energy. Her parents describe her as "always on-the-go" and "marching to the beat of her own drum." She loves doing flips and handstands on the furniture and being the creator of her own play.

- As her counselor, what sports or hobbies might you suggest for Sienna or her parents?
- How would you respond to the family's concerns about financial and transportation barriers to extracurricular activities?
- How do you see these early interests and personality traits playing out in potential careers?

CLUBS AND SERVICE

In addition to sports and hobbies, children and adolescents may engage in volunteering and community service. Since volunteer work can begin at any age, this is another avenue for students to learn about their interests and strengths, while building transferable skills. These activities may occur both within and outside of the school community. Oftentimes, schools will offer after school clubs that support students' service goals, such as student government, academic honor societies, and environmental club, among others. Community service is often a requirement for college scholarships or admission, and these opportunities, like sports, can help to expand students' networking options.

WORK

Children and adolescents can start to understand the responsibilities of holding a job at an early age through household chores and duties. Chores can be as simple as watering plants or feeding a pet. As they get older, responsibilities may increase with their developmental level. Caretakers can hold children accountable and discuss the consequences when one person doesn't follow through with their assigned tasks. These experiences can be beneficial as adolescents seek their first part-time jobs.

Adolescents choose part-time jobs based on a variety of reasons, such as interest, skill, or feasibility. For instance, a student who loves playing baseball may seek a part-time job at the baseball field collecting admission money or assistant coaching a youth team. Alternatively, another teen might be eager to start making her own money, so she gets a job at her local grocery store. Although the job doesn't necessarily align with her interests, she can walk to the store after school, rather than seeking transportation. In either case, part-time work demonstrates dependability, motivation, and work ethic to future employers and college admission personnel.

College Affordability Planning

College affordability planning involves understanding and navigating the complexities of paying for postsecondary education. Planning for the various costs associated with the college-going process must begin early and involve both students and their families. Family financial aid events can be held across K–12 settings to introduce families to the nuances of preparing and paying for college. As with students, it is important for caregivers to be aware of the many options available for postsecondary education (i.e., four-year college, community college, trade school, and apprenticeship). Since different options require and accept different types of scholarships and funding, caregivers must be aware of the distinctions. Early education from counselors surrounding this topic can help families expand their options for postsecondary education and allow transparency for attainable options.

ELEMENTARY AND MIDDLE SCHOOL

Counselors working with students might provide specific education surrounding terminology and procedures for securing money for college. As previously discussed, college-going beliefs are developed at an early age, and beliefs about college affordability are no different. Elementary school-age students may hear messages that "college is too expensive" or "not worth it" from family and community members, and counselors can play a role in dismantling beliefs that college is unattainable. At the middle school level, counselors can introduce relevant financial aid vocabulary to students, including, but not limited to, scholarships, grants, loans, and the Free Application for Federal Student Aid (FAFSA). Since many state and federal funding programs rely on high school academic performance, it is important for middle school students to have this information prior to beginning their high school transcripts.

HIGH SCHOOL

As students move into high school, counselors will focus more on connecting students to specific, applicable funding sources that align with their postsecondary goals. Many scholarships are available locally and nationally, but students often need assistance from counselors to locate and complete the applications. Counselors may consider hosting specific "office hours" or workshop events, in which students can receive hands-on support with these tasks. Additionally, counselors can encourage students to draw upon their self-exploration activities to seek out scholarships that relate to special talents or identities. Similarly, students often find scholarship opportunities within the networks they've developed through sports and community service.

Take Away and Use Today

Clearly, K–12 students need and benefit from career and educational development. This chapter provided a wealth of specific activities to engage students in developmentally and culturally appropriate ways. Although this chapter leans to work in schools, mental health counselors working with children and adolescents should attend to this topic with their clients as well. Whatever your setting, K–12 students are planning for the future and beginning to make important decisions about their future. Counselors cannot ignore this component of students' lives and, instead, must help them as they envision their future and enact their plans.

References

American School Counselor Association. (2021). *Mindsets and behaviors for student success: K–12 college- and career-readiness standards for every student.* https://www.schoolcounselor.org/getmedia/7428a787-a452-4abb-afec-d78ec77870cd/Mindsets-Behaviors.pdf

Anthis, K. (2021). *Child and adolescent development: A social justice approach.* Cognella Academic Publishing.

College Board. (2010). *NOSCA's eight components of college and career readiness counseling.* https://secure-media.collegeboard.org/digitalServices/pdf/nosca/11b_4416_8_Components_WEB_111107.pdf

College Board. (2014). *Empirical foundations for college and career readiness.* https://collegereadiness.collegeboard.org/pdf/research-foundations-college-career-readiness.pdf

Elementary and Secondary Education Act of 1965, Public Law No. 89–10. (1965). https://www.govinfo.gov/content/pkg/STATUTE-79/pdf/STATUTE-79-Pg27.pdf#page=1

Harter, S. (1999). *The construction of the self: A developmental perspective.* Guilford Press.

Hartung, P. J., Porfeli, E. J., & Vondracek, F. W. (2008). Career adaptability in childhood. *The Career Development Quarterly, 57*(1), 63–74. https://doi.org/10.1002/j.2161-0045.2008.tb00166.x

Holland, J. L. (1985). *Making vocational choices: A theory of careers* (2nd ed.). Prentice–Hall.

Krumboltz, J. D. (2009). The happenstance learning theory. *Journal of Career Assessment, 17*(2), 135–154.

Lent R. W., Brown, S. D., & Hackett, G. (1994). Toward a unifying social cognitive theory of career and academic interest, choice, and performance. *Journal of Vocational Behavior, 45*(1), 79–122. https://doi.org/10.1006/jvbe.1994.1027

Magnuson, & Starr, M. F. (2000). How early is too early to begin life career planning? The importance of the elementary school years. *Journal of Career Development, 27*(2), 89–101. https://doi.org/10.1023/A:1007844500034

Marcia, J. (1993). *Ego identity: A handbook for psychosocial research.* Springer–Verlag.

National Center for Education Statistics. (2021). *The condition of education report.* https://nces.ed.gov/pubs2021/2021144.pdf

National Forum on Education Statistics. (2015). *Forum guide to college and career ready data.* https://nces.ed.gov/pubs2015/2015157.pdf

Osipow, S. (1968). *Theories of career development.* Appleton–Century–Crofts.

Street Law. (2015). *Employment discrimination classroom lesson* [Lesson plan notes]. https://store.streetlaw.org/lessons/

Super, D. E. (1975). Career education and career guidance for the life span and for life roles. *Journal of Career Development, 2*(2), 27–42. https://doi.org/10.1177/089484537500200204

CHAPTER 12

Career-Focused Counseling in Emerging Adulthood

Melinda Gibbons, Kertesha Riley, and Chad Luke

CHAPTER GOALS

- Understand the unique career issues facing emerging adults.
- Identify concrete ways to assist emerging adults with their career-focused concerns.
- Understand differences in career development by educational choices in this age group.

OPENING VIGNETTES

Each of the following vignettes highlights a possible path after high school for emerging adults. They range from entry into the workforce to attending a four-year college.

Jon is entering his first year at his state's four-year college, Midwest University. His family has been reluctant about his choice because of the cost and since he will be the first in the family to attend a nontribal college. Jon would be participating in a summer bridge program, which also included a scholarship but would still need to work to support himself while in school. Jon has been interested in healthcare ever since he started volunteering at a health clinic on the reservation and has worked primarily with physicians. He isn't sure about his other options but decides to choose pre-med as his track for the program. Jon was looking forward to the summer bridge program for the opportunity to meet other new students and learn more about college life.

During an advising orientation for premed students, Jon learns that one of his pre-med courses includes a lab working with cadavers. In his culture, it is forbidden to touch dead bodies. Jon wants to become a doctor, so he can return to his community and continue doing work similar to his volunteer work at the clinic. He doesn't want to change his concentration, but he is unsure how or if he can complete this course requirement. Further, he is worried that his professors won't be understanding of this deeply held cultural belief. He decides to meet with an advisor to discuss his options.

Mia lives in the inner city and works at the neighborhood bodega as a cashier. Mia began the job part time while finishing up high school and continued on as a full-time employee after graduation. Mia lives at home with her dad, who helps her manage her chronic illness. He is supportive of Mia working because it gets her out of the house, but he worries that standing all day is contributing to Mia's flare ups.

The job at the bodega provides decent pay under the table but doesn't come with any benefits. Most of Mia's family members and friends work in similar jobs, so she never had the opportunity to explore different options for work.

Mia enjoys her job but is starting to get restless with the mundane nature of the work. Mia is also concerned about her dad, especially with his declining health from working in a factory for most of his life. Mia finished high school with average grades and really enjoyed her business classes, but she has no interest in going back to school. Mia wants to explore other work options but doesn't think she has the skills to do anything more. Now that she is entering her mid-twenties and hoping to eventually start a family, Mia realizes she may need to reconsider her current work situation.

David is a 25 year old is in his second year of taking courses at his local community college: Northern Tech. He began there several years after high school and has only completed a few courses due to working 30 hours a week to support himself and his parents. David's dad lost his job in sales due to the pandemic and now works in online customer service, making about half of his previous salary. David has aspirations of becoming a radiation therapist because he read online that the career only requires an associate's degree and has a median salary of over $85,000 a year. Only a few members of his extended family feel financially secure, so the financial reward is very important to him.

When David began at Northern Tech, he was given several placement tests, and the results showed he needed to complete a remedial math course before he could begin the required math course sequence for his degree, so that has also slowed down his progress. He is also worried about the upcoming practicum and internship requirements associated with his degree because they are 25–30 hours per week during regular work hours, meaning he will need to add these to his already busy schedule. He decides to talk with a counselor at his school about his anxiety and stress.

Imala is a 23-year-old Asian American woman, whose family immigrated to the United States from India when she was in fifth grade. Their goal was for Imala and her brothers to successfully enter college after high school and study to become either engineers or accountants. Imala has always struggled with her math and science courses and was diagnosed with a math learning disability in middle school; she feels like a disappointment to her family. After high school, Imala refused to continue her formal education and began working for a large clothing company. Her parents have strongly encouraged Imala to "return to school and make something of herself," but Imala believes she does not have the academic skills needed to succeed.

Imala's employer is offering scholarships for employees who want to earn an associate degree in business; in return, they must enter the company's leadership trainee program upon graduation, and work for the company for at least four additional years. They have approached Imala and offered the option to her, and she is considering it. She has been working with Chris, her counselor, for the past four months on her self-esteem and relationship issues, so she decides to bring up this opportunity with him at her next session.

REFLECTION ACTIVITIES AND QUESTIONS

1. What are your first thoughts about each of these clients? How do you understand their career-focused needs?

2. When you hear the term emerging adulthood, what comes to mind for you? What are the developmental tasks for people ages 18–29? If you are in this age group, what tasks are you encountering?

Introduction

Aisha sat across from me (Kertesha), almost as unsure of career-related counseling as I was. It was my first semester of what would become a year-and-a-half-long clinical experience in my university's career center during my master's program. Sheepishly, I will admit that this placement was not my first choice ... or second, or third even. Career didn't seem to be the juicy, emotional counseling that I was so excited to dive into as a new counselor-in-training. So when Aisha came in as a chemistry major not really enjoying her classes but still determined to go to medical school, I wasn't sure how to proceed. No matter what I asked her, there seemed to be uncertainty in her responses. Aisha was Indian American, and as I reflected on typical family systems in that culture, a new question came to mind: "Who else has a say in this decision?"

That question and what it revealed to me about Aisha helped me broaden our conversation from simply discussing her career issues to understanding the systems that shape her context. From there, we were able to talk about how much her family influences her beliefs about appropriate careers to pursue. A number of Aisha's family members were physicians—hence, the firm stance on continuing to medical school despite not being interested in the work of a physician. As we brought her family into the room, it became clear that helping others through medicine was the underlying value—not just becoming a doctor. With this perspective shift, Aisha forged a path that honored her interests while still aligning with her family values (we ended our time together with her considering a career in medical research!).

Now, almost a decade, and hundreds of students like Aisha, later, "Who else has a say in this decision?" still elicits such rich conversation about what's important to college students as they navigate their career journeys. The spectrum varies greatly—from family members and childhood dreams to anxiety or social media influencers to athletes or their friends. Yet, what is constant for this age group is the desire to keep their backgrounds, cultural identities, and values at the center of their career decision-making.

Our guess is that some of these tasks you identified about emerging adulthood include career development, relationships, and a belief that you are still trying to figure out what it means to be an adult. *Emerging adulthood* is a term first used to describe a unique developmental space occurring for young adults ages 18–29 (Arnett, 2007). During this time, people move from a school-only focus to a combination of school and work or work alone. The term was created to better describe the complex changes that occur during this time. Arnett (2007) proposed five primary aspects of emerging adulthood: *identity exploration*, *instability*, *focus on self*, *feeling of being in-between*, and *optimism* and openness to possibilities. Certain social constraints can negatively impact these developmental tasks. For example, emerging adults who live in poverty leave home earlier, struggle to maintain housing, are less likely to marry, or need to take on adult roles, such as parenting, earlier than those from more financially secure backgrounds (Berzin & De Marco, 2010). These experiences negatively impact opportunities for identity exploration and, likely, decrease optimism about the future. Recent research on emerging adulthood suggests it can be both a positive and negative time and is somewhat dependent on personality, relationships, and SES (Schwartz, 2016). These factors also impact career development during this time.

Emerging adults include both those who continue their education after high school and those who directly enter the workforce. Mitchell and Syed (2015) explored the differences between 30 year olds who had either graduated from college, completed some college, or did not attend college. They found that, by age 30, 24% of their participants had earned a bachelor's degree or higher (completed college), 34% had completed some college but less than a bachelor's degree (some college), and the remaining had completed either no formal education after high school or were limited to a technical degree (no college). Male, Latinx, and Native American participants were overrepresented in the no college group, and females were overrepresented in the some college group. Over 80% were employed full-time at age 30, with no differences by educational attainment. There were also no differences by education level related to marriage, with 62% of all 30 year-olds marrying by that age. One final, important difference was income level, which rose steadily by age for college graduates but plateaued by age 24 for those with no or some college only (Mitchell & Syed, 2015). So while there are some similarities by education level, there are also differences.

Why It Matters

It is vital that counselors recognize that not all emerging adults are alike. Even though theory suggests they encounter similar developmental milestones, they also differ based on cultural identities, educational paths, and occupational choices. While these considerations aren't novel or specific to this age group, understanding the unique factors of this age group is particularly important because of the value emerging adults place on integrating their identity into choosing and navigating career paths. Intentionally centering cultural factors facilitates trust and openness within the counseling relationship and lays out all considerations, so they can move forward with well-informed expectations and decision-making. If we are to assist all emerging adults effectively, we cannot clump them together simply based on age but must, rather, remember the impact of all of their experiences as well.

College Student Development Theory

Given that about half of those considered emerging adults continue their education after high school, it is important to understand college student development. As with most theories, multiple perspectives on college student development exist in the literature. A few theories, however, are particularly relevant for understanding the unique career development that occurs for 18–29 year olds, often referred to as emerging adults (Arnett, 2007). Self-authorship theory (Baxter Magolda, 2008) suggests that emerging adulthood is a time of internalized meaning-making, where people become authors of their own stories. Authorship involves truly understanding one's beliefs and values, while simultaneously considering the perceived validity of others' opinions and beliefs. Baxter Magolda (2008) completed a longitudinal study to better understand this process and found that successful self-authorship involved trusting one's internal voice, building a framework of understanding about how one engages in the world and moving from understanding to actually acting on one's beliefs. The path toward self-authorship can be complex or straightforward and is impacted by cultural identities and larger societal events. Ultimately, success in authorship is built on self-trust, authentic relationships, and acting on beliefs and values (Baxter Magolda, 2008).

Post-secondary education is also marked as a time of transition for emerging adults, particularly college students. Originally framed by Nancy Schlossberg (1981, 1984), transition theory looks at how an event results in changed assumptions, routines, relationships, and roles. Transitions may be anticipated or occur predictably (e.g., graduation from college). Others may be not predictable or scheduled, such as childbirth or illness. Even nonevents, or transitions that are expected but do not occur (e.g., being furloughed from a job), can significantly impact how emerging adults navigate this period of life.

Though the type, context, and impact of the transition must be considered, Schlossberg (1981, 1984) identified four major sets of factors that influence a person's ability to cope with a transition: situation, self, support, and strategies. The factor of *situation* refers to the overall environmental context when the transition occurs. Is the person experiencing other stressors during this time? *Self* relates to the person's ability to cope during the transition. Does the person have a sense of resilience and optimism? The factor of *support* relates to the perceived network of peers, family, and others who can help them cope. Does the person have others in their life they can turn to during the transition? Lastly, *strategies* refer to the behaviors a person engages in during the transition. Does the person have various coping mechanisms during times of stress (Schlossberg, 2011)? With so many overlapping transitions for emerging adults, Schlossberg's framework helps counselors understand the meaning of an individual's transition and further utilize that context within the counseling relationship.

Other recent theories place cultural and social structures as central to student development. Student development is viewed by these various postmodern theories as dynamic, shifting reactions to societal and cultural responses (Jones & Stewart, 2016). Abes et al. (2007) highlighted the multiple dimensions of the identity model, which combines background context, such as cultural and environmental influences, core personal attributes and characteristics, and how people make meaning of their experiences. In this model, the intersections of identities and salience of these various identities directly impact how college students engage in the world around them. In other words, context changes and influences identity all the time. Issues of power and oppression are always impacting views of self and overall development. These theories underscore the importance of cultural identity and societal context to promote a more layered and complex understanding of development in emerging adults.

Who Is Gen Z?

One way to deepen your understanding of career-focused counseling for emerging adults is to consider the current generation. Typically considered to be born between 1997 and 2012, Generation Z (or Gen Z) makes up the first truly global and digital generation, being one of the most racially and ethnically diverse generations so far (Rue, 2018). They are enrolling in college (two-year and four-year institutions) at higher rates than previous generations, while also being less likely to drop out of high school. This greater emphasis on education seems to also impact their experience in the workforce. They are less likely to work as teens or young adults. Some of the values they hold include a greater focus on family and societal change (Rue, 2018). Further, technology may be the biggest marker of Gen Z. Always "being on" and having constant access to information and others via the internet and social media, it is no surprise that mental health is also a major influence on beliefs and behaviors of this generation.

Developmental Tasks and Career-Focused Counseling

Using Arnett's (2007) five developmental tasks as a framework, we describe below the career-focused needs of emerging adults. A large, national survey revealed that these five tasks were endorsed by most emerging adults, whether in school or not (Arnett & Mitra, 2020). In each, we return to the case vignettes from the beginning of the chapter to highlight what counseling might look like.

IDENTITY EXPLORATION

Given that identity is often tied to career, it makes sense that this issue arises in career-focused counseling with emerging adults. Do you remember the discussion of intersectionality in chapter 3? Emerging adults as a whole are experiencing multiple activities that impact their identity development. They often move out of the family home for the first time, may be supporting themselves financially, are able to have some choice in their educational pursuits, and are continuing to learn what they like and what they do not like. The intersection of cultural identities, power and privilege, and career development impact this time of identity exploration.

These intersections make identity exploration in emerging adulthood very complex. Nearly all emerging adults in a national study indicated that they were trying to figure out who they really were during this time period (Arnett & Mitra, 2020). Some identity domains that can be particularly salient during this developmental period include political preferences, gender and sexuality, race and ethnicity, religious affiliation, and personal values and morals (Schwarz et al., 2013). For example, emerging adults may begin to engage in civic activities related to politics, while simultaneously being exposed to diverse political and ideological views of others—sometimes for the very first time. Similarly, religious and spiritual activities that were once decided by adult caregivers are now chosen by emerging adults. As they begin to choose their own religious or political beliefs, they may also begin to question the beliefs of those around them. Ultimately, their beliefs may mirror their family of origin or may diverge from them in significant ways. Racial and ethnic identity also continues to develop as emerging adults decide how much salience or importance they choose to place on this part of their being. For example, some young adults may seek out friends and colleagues with similar identities, while others may intentionally look for those who are quite different from them. These choices may impact their perception of discrimination and bias in the workplace.

Let's return to the case of Imala from earlier in the chapter. Career identity formation in Asian American emerging adults can be strongly influenced by family beliefs (Polenova et al., 2018). In particular, children of immigrant parents may face pressure regarding the type of career they should choose and the perceived value of that career. Those with less internal locus of control may delay their identity development, either by following their family's wishes or by ignoring them altogether. In either case, they may be reacting to family values and pressure, rather than developing their own identity and beliefs.

Imala refused to consider continuing her education, despite the wishes of her parents. In particular, her refusal is informed by low self-efficacy beliefs about her math and science skills, which directly relate to the careers endorsed by her family as appropriate and valued. Imala's career beliefs are also informed by being from Gen Z; she believes that making a positive contribution should be part of her career path and does not see accounting or engineering as being particularly meaningful. As she discusses this with her counselor, Chris, he asks if working at the clothing company offers meaningful work. Imala describes the new nonbinary clothing line they are currently marketing and how it is specifically meant to reduce gender stereotypes in how people choose to dress. Imala excitedly explains that she sees this as a major contribution to the world. She mentions that her friend Zola, who uses they/them pronouns, has struggled to find clothing that represents their gender identity, and this line has both size and gender inclusion, while still being affordable. Over the next two sessions, Chris helps Imala consider whether the leadership trainee program might be a positive career move for her, and Imala begins to realize that her work can be a way to positively contribute to the world. They practice how to discuss this topic with her parents, and Imala moves forward with accepting her company's offer.

TAKE A MINUTE

Consider how Imala's views of career are related to her being from Gen Z. How is her career identity and her generational identity tied together? How did the intersection of her cultural background and career development highlight different challenges for Imala?

INSTABILITY

A challenge for many emerging adults is the instability that occurs during this time. Over 80% of emerging adults see this time in their lives as full of changes (Arnett & Mitra, 2020). They often have multiple moves, various jobs, and changes in intimate relationships. Additionally, they may be trying to enter into their preferred career for the first time but encounter struggles, such as fit, meeting responsibilities, and being financially independent. According to a recent review of the literature (Grosemans et al., 2020), most college graduates expect to hold several jobs before finding stable and long-term employment. They see this as an inevitable part of their journey to finding a career that is a good fit and matches their career and personal goals.

Many emerging adults, whether in school or not, also expect to wait before being fully financially independent. About a third of 18–34 year olds still live at home, and less than one in three are financially independent by age 21 (Vespa, 2017). These statistics intersect with cultural differences, with Hispanic and Black emerging adults being more likely to live at home longer than their White or Asian counterparts. The constant role, family, work, and romantic shifts that occur during this time can lead to feelings of stress, anxiety, loneliness, or lowered self-esteem for emerging adults.

Let's return to the case of Jon to consider how instability might be a major issue. Jon meets with his academic advisor and is told that cadaver work is a standard part of the pre-med and med school process and cannot be avoided. His advisor encourages Jon to talk with a counselor about his concerns. During Jon's first meeting with new counselor, Patrice, he explains the situation and expresses his anxiety about his next steps. Jon admits that he already feels overwhelmed due to transitioning from high school to college, moving out of his family home, and interacting with people who don't understand his tribal background. Patrice listens and reflects that Jon seems to be struggling to cope with the unanticipated nature of these changes in his life and helps him recognize how his support system is limited in helping him.

As they continue to meet, Jon also describes the pressure he feels to represent his community and to be able to make a difference through his chosen career. However, he is adamant about never working with cadavers and recognizes the challenges this will present for him. Jon also reveals that he feels selfish for even coming to counseling; he knows that his community members encounter daily struggles, while he has been able to attend college and pursue a career of his choice. Patrice helps reframe this as a common feeling in emerging adults (Arnett, 2007), while helping Jon also recognize that he is in college to learn skills that will help his entire tribe, which seems quite selfless and altruistic.

> MHC: I hear what you are saying, Jon, and I want you to know that it is not uncommon for people your age to feel selfish for worrying about what major to choose or whether a career is the best fit. However, I also have heard you talk about the importance of giving back to your community through your future career. To me, that sounds quite selfless and altruistic.
>
> CL: Yeah, I guess so. I just don't want to let anyone down, and they are counting on me to become a doctor.
>
> MHC: Are they? Or are they celebrating your academic achievements and hoping you will return after graduation to be with your community?

CL: They want me to be happy and to contribute. Everyone needs to give back to the greater good, but no one has the right to dictate how we give back. The elders say I will find my path and know it to be my path. I just thought I already knew what my path was and it was the one predictable thing I could count on right now. But, I also believe it will work out. It has to.

Jon and Patrice meet occasionally over the next two semesters as he fully adapts to college life. From their sessions, Jon recognizes his need to build a support system on campus, while still maintaining a strong connection with his home community, so he finds a small group of friends who also come from collectivist cultural backgrounds. He also changes his major to "exploratory" and takes several classes to help expose him to other possible majors.

CL: I spoke to my professor about my career concerns and he told me a few things that were really helpful. First, he said there are some med schools that are using virtual cadavers instead of real ones. There are only a couple of them right now, but he said that the pandemic has actually helped increase the use of these virtual labs, since people couldn't meet in person. So I need to do more research on that. He also encouraged me to look at other health careers that could help my community, like being a dentist or pharmacist. This made me realize that I could still go into a health field, but it didn't have to be as a physician.

MHC: It sounds like you have started to embrace possibilities, rather than feeling overwhelmed by them.

CL: Yeah. I keep remembering what you said about taking time to make a decision and that I can still help my home without becoming a medical doctor. It's not giving up but rather figuring out what is best for me and for them, too.

TAKE A MINUTE

How does the case above demonstrate Schlossberg's theory? What are your overall thoughts about the vignette? What would you do differently?

FOCUS ON SELF

Related to identity development, emerging adults are trying on independence—often for the first time. Three-quarters feel this developmental time period is a time for focusing on self (Artett & Mitra, 2020). They may be identifying their own values separate from those held by their family or may be choosing where they want to live or with whom they want to interact for the first time. Family obligations, such as needing to provide emotional or financial support and a need to respect parent wishes regarding career paths, still influence emerging adults. In particular, those from Asian or Latinx backgrounds are more likely to feel this sense of obligation, which can have both positive and negative outcomes (Fuligni,

2007). For example, college students with high levels of family obligation and respect are more motivated academically and have higher educational aspirations. Those from immigrant backgrounds, in particular, are more likely to select majors that directly connect to well-paying future occupations, such as medical, business, or technical careers. These can be positive outcomes, but the result may mean delaying personal career exploration until later in emerging adulthood (Fuligni, 2007).

Clearly, focus on self is intertwined with the other themes of instability and identity exploration. However, focus on self also refers to a time of lacking obligation to others because most emerging adults are unmarried, without children, and without significant financial obligations. This perceived freedom gives emerging adults the opportunity to explore options and identify satisfying choices. Those from more privileged backgrounds have more opportunities to focus on self than those from marginalized groups, increasing the likelihood of positive outcomes for those who experience less discrimination and restricted options (Krahn et al., 2015). Therefore, counselors working with clients from marginalized backgrounds should be aware of restrictions to being able to focus on self, even though most emerging adults want to take this time to do so.

The case of Mia helps demonstrate these challenges. Mia had few college-educated role models, SES restrictions, and past and current health issues that have restricted her ability to focus on self. However, now that she is a bit older, she is beginning to recognize a desire to make planful choices that increase her financial independence. She wants to become the author of her own story, while still honoring and acknowledging her cultural heritage and current context. In a study of ethnically diverse, low-income emerging adults, Katsiaficas (2017) found most of the participants defined adulthood as having responsibilities and taking pride in doing them well. These included being responsible in work, making a living wage, and caring for family members and their local community. For these participants, taking responsibility was tied to a focus on self, meaning that considering what they wanted as individuals was directly connected to what important others needed.

To truly assist Mia, her counselor must recognize this interconnection of self-focus and caring for others. Rather than pushing Mia to only engage in what she wants, effective counseling must help Mia honor her need to help her father and stay connected to her local community, while also starting to consider what she wants from her future work and career.

FEELING OF IN-BETWEEN

Taking on adult responsibilities can be difficult for emerging adults. They may feel a sense of being in-between, where they want to be in charge of their personal and professional choices but still need to rely on others for financial and emotional support. Only about 44% of emerging adults feel like they have fully reached adulthood, while 50% feel only part of the way there (Arnett & Mitra, 2020). For example, a large study of emerging adults explored their most endorsed indicators of adulthood and whether they had achieved them (Sharon, 2016). For these participants, they had achieved some of these actions, such as accepting responsibility for their own actions and making independent decisions, but were still struggling with other perceived important milestones, such as no longer living with their parents or being financially independent. This gap between what is endorsed as indicators of adulthood and what is actually achieved leads to the feeling of in-between for emerging adults.

The phenomenon of imposter syndrome also connects to this feeling of in-between. Imposter syndrome refers to the feeling of being a fraud, despite successes in school or career, leading to feelings of stress, fear, and low self-esteem (Bravata et al., 2019). Most often explored in emerging adults from marginalized backgrounds, research has found that women and people of color are more likely to experience imposter syndrome related to education and work. Unfortunately, imposter syndrome also appears to negatively impact job and school performance and satisfaction (Bravata et al., 2019).

Counselors need to recognize that emerging adults from marginalized backgrounds may experience environmental contexts that contribute to imposter syndrome. In other words, when emerging adults receive environmental messages that suggest they are not good enough, talented enough, or the right fit for postsecondary education or certain careers, they may internalize these messages. Counselors can use the MSJCC (Ratts et al., 2016) to increase self-awareness and client worldview, regarding the systemic and environmental conditions that may promote feelings of "imposterhood." Then, they can help clients link these feelings to challenges they are facing with having to partially or fully rely on others for financial and emotional support. Using this frame can empower clients to recognize cultural and environmental influences, consider the power and privilege connected to these influences, and make next steps with a stronger and more internalized understanding of how their identities intersect with the world around them (Abes et al., 2007).

Let's revisit the case of David, our community college student. He is feeling anxious and stressed as he attempts to pursue training to become a radiation therapist. He admits he selected this career because of its possible financial reward—not because it necessarily fits with his interests, skills, or values.

> CL: I know I need to make money in whatever career I choose. I also know that I am not cut out for a four-year college and that my family couldn't afford to help me pay for it. I am working nearly full-time, while trying to go to school, and I just feel like I am failing everywhere.
>
> MHC: Tell me about your experience in high school. What type of student were you? How would your friends and teachers describe you?
>
> CL: I earned mostly As and Bs, but it was a small, rural school, and most of the students were not really strong academically. My teachers encouraged me to pursue college, but I knew I needed to work first to save up money and help support my family. The pandemic really hurt our financial situation, making it go from bad to worse.
>
> MHC: I hear a lot of "buts" as you reflect on your school experience. It almost sounds like you feel that you didn't really earn your successes or feel you have the right to pursue your passions.

CL: That's hard for me to hear. I know that others have told me that I am talented and capable and should choose a career that matches my interests or values, but I also see my reality. I also know that there are lots of people who don't believe someone like me, from a small town, with average abilities, and with no real career-related training, could actually make something of themselves. If I can at least make enough money to support myself and help my family, then that should be enough. It seems greedy to ask for anything more than that. Right now, I can't even do that and have to rely on others to support me.

MHC: Hmmm ... It seems like it might be worthwhile to explore where these beliefs come from and how your environment is influencing them. Additionally, I hear you not taking credit or ownership for your own talents and strengths, which may be getting in the way of achieving your goals. Would you be willing to explore these with me?

CL: Sure, if you think it will help.

TAKE A MINUTE

How is David demonstrating feeling in-between? What aspects of the imposter syndrome do you see in David? How might you use a career theory to empower David and help him recognize and evaluate environmental influences on his beliefs?

OPTIMISM AND OPENNESS TO POSSIBILITIES

Even with all of these challenges, emerging adults are known for their optimism and openness to possibilities. Most feel as though anything is possible and that this time of their lives is fun and exciting (Arnett & Mitra, 2020). Counselors are encouraged to build on this sense of optimism and openness to help emerging adults address their career-related issues and concerns. Arnett (2020) interviewed emerging adults about their view of their own future. Most of the participants were already married, employed full-time, and had completed some college, indicating they were in the later stages of emerging adulthood. In response to the question about whether their life is likely to be better or worse than their parents, nearly all felt their lives would be as good or better. Most also believed their financial well-being, career, and relationships would be at least as good or better than their parents (Arnett, 2020). In fact, when respondents said they believed their lives would be equal to their parents, they overwhelmingly added that they believed their parents' lives were happy and successful. In other words, nearly all of these emerging adults expressed optimism about their future and believed they would lead satisfying and positive lives.

Optimism about the future can be a powerful trait to build upon in counseling, but counselors need to be cautious about not dismissing systemic and environmental realities. Particularly for marginalized or minoritized clients, who already experience reduced opportunities and access, it is vital that counselors validate these real issues, while also encouraging empowerment and ownership of future selves. One way to accomplish this is to focus on career adaptability. Adaptability is demonstrated when clients look ahead to the future, feel volition in being able to make choices and a sense of ownership of those choices, and have confidence in their ability to explore available options. These characteristics are sometimes referred to as the 4 Cs: concern, control, curiosity, and confidence (as described in Chapter 9). Building on these characteristics, adaptability appears to result in increased career satisfaction, engagement in exploration and decision-making, hope, and overall life satisfaction (Johnston, 2018).

Ways to help clients increase career adaptability are plentiful. For example, counselors might help clients reduce anxiety or increase self-esteem, both of which help adaptability. Or they might provide psychoeducation on decision-making or goal attainment, which can increase a sense of control and confidence. Another option is to help clients assess and navigate perceived barriers, which simultaneously increases control and intentional pursuit of future goals. Helping clients consider ways to create opportunities for unplanned events (planned happenstance) is another avenue to increase career adaptability. Clients can take control of these possibilities and engage in exploration activities resulting from them. All of these examples help clients increase empowerment, build on their positive future outlook, and take ownership of their future.

Take Away and Use Today

Emerging adults have unique developmental characteristics that will likely connect with counseling needs and goals. Understanding what makes this group unique and how to best serve their needs positively influences the career-focused counseling you can provide for them. Remembering that not all emerging adults are continuing their education, that not all have similar opportunities or experiences, and that cultural identities intersect with this developmental stage is also important.

References

Abes, E. S., Jones, S. R., & McEwen, M. K. (2007). Reconceptualizing the multiple dimensions of identity: The role of meaning-making capacity in the construction of multiple identities. *Journal of College Student Development, 48*(1), 1–22. https://doi.org/10.1353/csd.2007.0000

Arnett, J. J. (2020). High hopes in a grim world: Emerging adults' views of their futures and "Generation X". *Youth & Society, 31*(3), 267–286.

Arnett, J. J. (2007). Suffering, selfish, slackers? Myths and realities about emerging adults. *Journal of Youth and Adolescence, 36*, 23–29. https://doi.org/10.1007/s10964-006-9157-z

Arnett, J. J., & Mitra, D. (2020). Are the features of emerging adulthood developmentally distinctive? A comparison of ages 18–60 in the United States. *Emerging Adulthood, 8*(5), 412–419. https://doi/org/10.1177/2167696818810073

Baxter Magolda, M. B. (2008). Three elements of self-authorship. *Journal of College Student Development, 49*(4), 269–284. https://doi.org/10.1353/csd.0.0016

Berzin, S. C., & De Marco, A. C. (2010). Understanding the impact of poverty on critical events in emerging adulthood. *Youth & Society, 42*(2), 278–300. https://doi.org/10.1177/0044118X09351909

Bravata, D. M., Watts, S. A., Keefer, A. L., Madhusudhan, D. K., Taylor, K. T., Clark, D. M., Nelson, R. S., Cokley, K. O., & Haag, H. K. (2019). Prevalence, predictors, and treatment of imposter syndrome: A systematic review. *Journal of General Internal Medicine, 35*(4), 1252–1275. https://doi.org/10.1007/s11606-019-05364-1

Fuligni, A. J. (2007). Family obligation, college enrollment, and emerging adulthood in Asian and Latin American families. *Child Development Perspectives, 1*(2), 96–100. https://doi.org/10.1111/j.1750-8606.2007.00022.x

Grosemans, I., Hannes, K., Neyens, J., & Kyndt, E. (2020). Emerging adults embarking on their careers: Job and identity explorations in the transition to work. *Youth & Society, 52*(5), 795–819. https://doi.org/10.1177/0044118X18772695

Johnston, C. S. (2018). A systematic review of the career adaptability literature and future outlook. *Journal of Career Assessment, 26*(1), 3–30. https://doi.org/10.1177/1069072716679921

Jones, S. J., & Stewart, D. L. (2016). Evolution of student development theory. *New Directions for Student Services, 154*, 17–28. https://doi.org/10.1002/ss

Katsiaficas, D. (2017). "I know I'm an adult when … I can care for myself and others": The role of social responsibilities in emerging adulthood for community college students. *Emerging Adulthood, 5*(6), 392–405. https://doi.org/10.1177/2167696817698301

Krahn, H. J., Howard, A. L., & Galambos, N. L. (2015). Exploring or floundering? The meaning of employment and educational fluctuations in emerging adulthood. *Youth & Society, 47*(2), 245–266. https://doi.org/10.1177/0044118X12459061

Mitchell, L. L., & Syed, M. (2015). Does college matter for emerging adulthood? Comparing developmental trajectories of educational groups. *Journal of Youth and Adolescence, 44*, 2012–2027. https://doi.org/10.1007/s10964-015-0330-0

Polenova, E., Vedral, A., Brisson, L., & Zinn, L. (2018). Emerging between two worlds: A longitudinal study of career identity of students from Asian American and immigrant families. *Emerging Adulthood, 6*(1), 53–65. https://doi.org/10.1177/2167696817696430

Ratts, M. J., Singh, A. A., Nassar-McMillan, S., Butler, S. K., & McCullough, J. R. (2016). Multicultural and social justice counseling competencies: Guidelines for the counseling profession. *Journal of Multicultural Counseling and Development, 44*(1), 28–48. https://doi.org/10.1002/jmcd.12035

Rue, P. (2018). Make way, millennials, here comes Gen Z. *About campus: Enriching the student learning experience, 23*(3), 5–12. https://doi.org/10.1177/1086482218804251

Schlossberg, N. K. (1981). A model for analyzing human adaptation to transition. *The Counseling Psychologist, 9*(2), 1–18.

Schlossberg, N. K. (1984). *Counseling adults in transition*. New York: Springer.

Schlossberg, N. K. (2011). The challenge of change: The transition model and its applications. *Journal of Employment Counseling, 48*, 159–162.

Schwartz, S. J. (2016). Turning point for a turning point: Advancing emerging adulthood theory and research. *Emerging Adulthood, 4*(5), 307–317. https://doi.org/10.1177/2167696815624640

Schwarz, S. J., Zamboanga, B. L., Luyckx, K., Meca, A., & Ritchie , R. A. (2013). Identity in emerging adulthood: Reviewing the field and looking forward. *Emerging Adulthood, 1*(2), 96–113. https://doi/org/10.1177/2167696813479781

Sharon, T. (2016). Constructing adulthood: Markers of adulthood and well-being among emerging adults. *Emerging Adulthood, 4*(3), 161–167. https://doi.org/10.1177/2167696815579826

Vespa, J. (2017). *The changing economics and demographics of young adulthood: 1975–2016.* U.S. Census Bureau.

CHAPTER 13

Career-Focused Counseling with Adults

CHAPTER GOALS

- Gain an appreciation for the many work-related transitions in adulthood.
- Identify the challenges and opportunities associated with these transitions.
- Consider how to best address the unique challenges adults encounter in the world of work.

OPENING VIGNETTES

Steve is a man in his early 60s, who has worked for the same company for the past 15 years. He has worked as a plant manager in several plants over his 40-year career in addition to periods of transition with leadership positions in other companies. He has been referred by his EAP (employee assistance program) for continued support, as he has had conflict with his supervisors during the past year. He describes feeling tired of the politics and the grind of management and that it's made him "testy" with those around him; he hastens to add that this does not extend to his supervisees—only his peers and boss. When asked what his goals for counseling are, he states that he feels like there is more he has to offer beyond "pushing papers and cracking the whip" with his supervisees to get more productivity from them. He wants a change but is sensitive that his age in particular will block him from making a switch.

Jill is a married mother with two school-aged children. She and her partner both work full-time, but Jill is typically responsible for much of the home and childcare responsibilities because her wife, Mardi, travels often for work. Over the past two years, Jill has felt increasingly overwhelmed with trying to balance her work and family responsibilities; she feels she never has time for herself and feels as though she is failing in all of her life roles. Mardi has tried to take on additional activities related to their children, but her travel schedule often means shifting schedules. While Jill does not blame Mardi, she does feel resentful about the uneven partnership and this has begun to impact their relationship.

REFLECTION ACTIVITIES AND QUESTIONS

The following is a list of characteristics of modern work life. Identify the ones you are aware of that have affected your life or the lives of those around you. What kinds of support would you like to have available to you or your loved ones to help you navigate these? What would you want from a counseling relationship, whether school or agency, to assist you in dealing with these?

- Job restructuring
- Downsizing
- Obsolete positions
- Retraining for skilled workers
- Technology
- Elimination of middle management
- Internationalization
- Aging of workforce
- Occupational insecurity
- Joblessness
- Stress at work
- Self-esteem
- Motivation
- Concentration
- Work relationships
- Communication
- Resentment
- Tardiness
- Psychological issues
- Burnout
- Career changes
- Alternative ways to work
- Work–life balance
- Dual-earner couples
- Family-friendly workplace policies
- Stay-at-home parent

Introduction

Adults experience many different types of transitions during their years at work, some of which are listed in the terms at the beginning of this chapter. You may be unfamiliar with some of these, so here is a short primer.

TABLE 13.1 ADULT CAREER CONCERNS AND DEFINITIONS

Term	Definition	What It Means
Job restructuring	Modification of job by an employer by changing or removing one or more responsibilities	You are giving more or less responsibilities that may or may not be tied to financial reward.
Downsizing	Permanent reduction of company's labor force by eliminating one or more positions or divisions	To save money, a company eliminates various positions and assigns the duties to other employees (see above).
Obsolete positions	Jobs that no longer exist due to technology advances or changes in social conditions	A job can now be completed via technology or is no longer needed in today's world.
Retraining for skilled workers	Typically trade or task-based jobs that need specialized skills to be completed	A job now requires additional training to learn the new technology or skills needed.
Elimination of middle management	Cost-saving plan to delegate more responsibility to upper management	A job removes those typically in charge of day-to-day routines and direct monitoring of employees.
Occupational insecurity	Concern about the future existence of a job	This is the perception that job may not exist for a variety of reasons, such as a recession, new management, or industry changes.
Burnout	Emotional, physical, and/or mental exhaustion due to ongoing work-related stress	This is the feeling of depression, lethargy, lack of control, health issues, dread, and/or lack of purpose.
Alternative ways to work	Options for full-time employment, such as contracting, job sharing, remote work, short-term contract work, or freelance work—sometimes referred to as the gig economy	Work does not conform to traditional norms; the position may be temporary or not offer benefits.

Job, work, career, vocation—whatever name it goes by—plays a key role in peoples' lives, from personal meaning and fulfillment to the satisfaction of providing the basic needs for oneself and one's family. The opportunity and ability to work is a privilege. This reality can be seen sharply in cases of job loss, unemployment, and underemployment. These events are existential threats to the material well-being of individuals as well as to their mental and physical well-being. Transitions require individuals to adapt, yet work-related traumas and distressing events can diminish an individual's adaptive capacities (Tabor, 2020). "Events such as involuntary job loss due to downsizing, breeches in employment contracts, workplace accidents and injuries can have a devastating impact" (p. 105). There are many ways to conceptualize career transitions. Pickerell and Neault (2019) described several types of transitions, including school-to-school (e.g., high school to college), starting over (e.g., working with refugees and immigrants), parental leave (e.g., transitioning to work after having a child), returning to work (e.g., following a leave of absence), career growth (e.g., transitioning to self-employment or other promotion), and retirement (e.g., leaving the workforce permanently and considering avocational activities or bridge employment). Additional transitions include school to work, whereupon graduating from high school, individuals immediately enter the full-time workforce, bridge employment for retirees, periods of unemployment, and chronic underemployment. This has been framed in the literature as the continuum of decent work to precarious work (Blustein et al., 2016). In this chapter we explore career-focused counseling with adults in transition, from the voluntary separation from work through career change, retirement, or role changes to job loss and termination or what has been called precarious employment. Each brings its own challenges, but all provide opportunities for growth and development.

TAKE A MINUTE

As you think back to the list at the beginning of the chapter, what did you feel? What do you imagine it would be like to work with these individuals? Working with adults will likely present as a mental health issue, yet the connection with career or work is undeniable. How would you begin your work with Steve or Jill? They both present with mental health-like distress, but they have career-related concerns as well. Career-related concerns can add complexity to the counselor role and identity for new counselors. Therefore, this chapter provides guiding principles to support counselors in feeling confident in responding to a host of client needs, such as those listed above. Workplace transitions, whether expected or not, can affect financial as well as psychological wellbeing.

Stress and Work

Work can be a source of both satisfaction and stress. When we feel satisfaction at work, this affective state positively impacts the other parts of our lives. We may feel happier, more secure, or more fulfilled. On the other hand, when people feel stressed by work, it can negatively impact our lives. Approximately 64% of adults in the United States identify work as a significant source of stress (APA, 2019). Forty percent cite job stability, and 60% identify money as significant sources of stress. Clearly, many workers are stressed out by work.

Home stressors also impact work. Family stressors, such as feeling overloaded or having to devote too much time to a family role can negatively impact work. Conflict within the family, such as overwhelming time demands, having too many tasks, or caring for a large number of dependents, can cause stress as well. Lower levels of perceived support from others, financial issues, and reduced internal locus of control also increase stress (Michel et al., 2011). Lastly, life circumstances, such as child and elder care, illness, and lack of family-friendly workplace policies, can negatively impact work–life balance.

Lack of access to decent work (see Chapter 3 for a review) can also increase stress. Decent work provides reasonable pay, some level of worker autonomy, fair treatment, and general safety. It also supports family and personal connections (Duffy et al., 2016). Often, the struggles faced by adults in the workplace challenge the concept of decent work. Perhaps, employment has become insecure or vulnerable. Or maybe the worker has lost benefits or income (Benach et al., 2014). These struggles negatively impact overall work satisfaction and the ability to connect with others or to feel a sense of purpose in the work being done.

Work–life balance includes role engagement in both work and home and minimal conflicts between these various roles. A more balanced work–life experience exists when people feel satisfaction across roles, believe they have enough time across roles, feel engaged in their roles, and are able to manage engagement in roles with minimal conflict (Sirgy & Lee, 2018). For most people, work–life balance is not something that exists all of the time. We all have situations that arise that require us to spend more time in a work role or a family role. Therefore, it is best to view work–life balance over time, rather than judging a specific moment.

Research demonstrates that when work–life balance occurs, people experience positive work, nonwork, and physiological outcomes (Sirgy & Lee, 2018). Positive work outcomes include increased job satisfaction and performance and lower burnout and absenteeism. Positive nonwork outcomes include higher life, marital, family, and leisure satisfaction. Positive physiological outcomes of work–life balance include: lower levels of exhaustion, anxiety, depression, marital distress, and hostility.

For those that do experience work-related stress, they cite a variety of sources for this stress (see Table 13.2). This stress can lead to negative physical, psychological, and occupational outcomes. Building on our neuroscience frame, the body has a significant response to stress. Stress hormones in the central nervous system impact metabolic, cardiovascular, and immune system responses (Ganster & Rosen, 2013). A review of studies on the impact of chronic stress at work revealed specific negative outcomes (Salvagioni et al., 2017):

- **Physical outcomes:** increased cardiovascular disease, high cholesterol, type 2 diabetes, and musculoskeletal pain
- **Psychological outcomes:** insomnia, depression, and anxiety
- **Occupational outcomes:** job dissatisfaction, increased work absences, and sick days

Stress is the brain's way of communicating to the body's support systems that a threat has been detected that requires specific action. The catalyst for this cascade of responses involves cortisol, the so-called stress hormone. Cortisol is the chemical

TABLE 13.2 SOURCES OF WORK-RELATED STRESS

Source of Work Stress	Percentage of U.S. Adults Identifying Source
Low salary	49%
Lack of growth opportunity	46%
Too heavy workload	42%
Unrealistic job expectations	39%
Long hours	39%
Job insecurity	37%
Work–life interference	34%

Note. Adapted from the APA Work and Well-Being Survey, 2018.

> current that carries response messages through the HPA axis. This system prepares the body to respond to threats. It performs this function very effectively ... in the short term. Over longer periods of time (prolonged stress states), Cortisol begins to exerts deleterious effects on the central nervous system. It degrades short-term memory, impairs concentration, disrupts digestion, and increases blood pressure (Garrett, 2015). It's important to note that all of these negative effects are highly facilitative in the short-term, when responding to environmental threats. However, when the system is "on" for extended periods, the consequences can become the focus of clinical attention. It is of critical importance that counselors recognize that this system activates whether the threat is real or perceived, because neurologically speaking, there is no difference. Consider the implications of prolonged stress, and its effects on the brain and central nervous system, on career-related tasks! (Luke, 2018)
>
> These negative outcomes can lead to the need for counseling services.

In an earlier chapter, we described the eight-factor metamodel, which described eight neuroscience-informed dimensions of counseling (Luke, 2016, 2018, 2020) to help frame the work of counselors relative to clients' and students' presenting concerns. In Table 13.3 we use the table from Luke (2018) to assist in clustering the challenges of career-related concerns from the reflection activity at the beginning of the chapter.

TABLE 13.3 CAREER CHALLENGES ACROSS THE EIGHT-FACTOR MODEL

Domain	Career Problem Examples	Observations
Relationships	• Relational conflict at work • Conflict at "home" over work • Intrapersonal conflict	Many career issues materialize *after* a job choice has been made, resulting in and from issues in interpersonal relationships; these issues are reciprocal with home and work—one affects the other.
Sociocultural milieu	• Social and cultural expectations about what work should be	Virtually every culture has their own expectations about productivity and contributions to the larger community, whether implicit or explicit, whether high or low; most bring these expectations into career decision-making.
Thoughts/ cognitions	• Self-defeating	Cognitive distortions underlie many, perhaps most, career-related issues, either as precursors to or results of career-related issues.
Emotions/affect	• Negative emotional experience of work	Emotions are real, though they don't always reflect reality; this does not preclude them from influencing and even exacerbating career-related issues.

(*Continued*)

TABLE 13.3 CAREER CHALLENGES ACROSS THE EIGHT-FACTOR MODEL *(Continued)*

Domain	Career Problem Examples	Observations
Behavior/ volition	• Poor or lack of motivation • Problematic behaviors at work	Most people make a change when the pain of stasis exceeds the pain of change; career-related issues in the behavior domain can be explicit (e.g., acting out, substance use, etc.) or implicit, as in passivity on the job or in seeking change.
Environment	• Work environment and impact of work on other environments (like home)	It is important to understand the individual's work environment (real and perceived) as well as their desired environment; in addition, examine how the home or other environments are impacting career-related issues.
Experiences	• Various negative experiences finding, maintaining, and transitioning through work	One of perhaps the most common and influential involves both early experiences related to the perception of work as well as individual experiences in and out of the workplace that shape perceptions and expectations.
Bio/genetic/ neuro	• Physical, cognitive, and emotional abilities that may be limited	A key component of diversity competencies involves ableness and its impact on work options; in addition, the brain changes in response to repetitive behaviors, so work transitions can be impacted by change across job types.

CASE VIGNETTE JILL

CL: I'm just overwhelmed by all of my responsibilities right now. I feel like I have given up all of my free time and just work and take care of others. It's exhausting.

MHC: It sounds like you feel out of balance and that work and home are competing for your time.

CL: Yeah (eyes tear up). Mardi tries, but she has to travel about 10 days of every month, so most of the day-to-day stuff is left to me. I make sure the kids do their homework and get to their afterschool activities, I pay the bills, I take care of the dog. Then, I go to work and I have so many responsibilities because we are short-staffed. They say that is just temporary, but it has been months with no additional support.

MHC: Can you tell me how your stress is affecting you physically?

CL: Well, I'm not sleeping because I think about work. And I can't find time to exercise, so I feel out of shape. Jogging used to be a stress reliever for me, but I can't find the time to do it. I also just feel bad.

MHC: Tell me what "just feel bad" means.

CL: I am irritable. I snapped at our youngest for no real reason the other day. And, I feel constantly annoyed with Mardi even though she is not really doing anything wrong. I'm just not happy right now, like I used to be.

MHC: You are feeling irritable, overwhelmed, tired, sad, and stressed out. That is a lot.

CL: This isn't how it is supposed to be.

Jill and her counselor talk about her expectations for work–life balance, and Jill reveals that she thought parenting and marriage would be easier and more fulfilling. Instead, she finds herself wishing she could spend more time alone or with friends. Her counselor keeps in mind what she knows about stress and its impact on physical and mental health and shares some of this information with Jill to normalize her feelings and offer a possible explanation for them. The counselor also uses career construction theory to help deconstruct and reconstruct the meaning Jill has attached to her work and home experience.

MHC: So a theme I hear from you is that home life and work life are supposed to look a certain way. They are supposed to be fun, fulfilling, and positive. I wonder if there is another way to look at that.

CL: Well, I guess a more accurate view is that I wish they were fun, fulfilling, and positive. I know life can't always be like that, but it should be at least some of the time, right?

Jill and her counselor continue to reconceptualize her view of work and home and eventually identify that Jill needs some aspects of her life where she feels able to make choices. She realizes that she has felt that things were being done to her rather than her having volition over her choices. As they move toward the end of counseling, Jill and her counselor work together to help her identify ways to increase volition. Jill talks with Mardi about what home responsibilities she can take on permanently, even with her travels. She also expresses her need to get back into jogging. Lastly, Jill approaches her work supervisor to discuss the need for redistribution of job duties. Many times, our clients find themselves thrust into situations that force change—change that they may never have initiated on their own. Yet, these times of transition can usher in reflection on one's path, along with the potential to redirect the course of life.

Challenges to and Opportunities for Older Adults

Older adults (age 55+) encounter unique challenges in the workplace. As you read the case of Steve, you may recall how it felt to be told you were too young or inexperienced to be considered for a job. This occurs quite often for high school students and young adults. The inverse can also be true for adults in transitions—except that, instead, they can be considered overqualified or too old. To be overqualified is to be perceived as expecting more compensation for the work than the position pays. It also means that job satisfaction may be lower for an overqualified individual, and they will be unlikely to remain in the position for long, or they will struggle to accept supervision from a potentially younger, less-experienced supervisor. Adults in transition may also be perceived as less able to be flexible in the workplace and to keep up with current trends; instead, they may be viewed as "set in their ways." In the first instance, overqualification may be a legitimate reason for not hiring an adult. However, the second instance is age discrimination and is legally protected. The Age Discrimination in Employment Act of 1967 (ADEA) offers legal protection for adults 40 years of age and older from discrimination on the basis of age.

It is vital, however, for counselors to be aware that just because a law exists, clients can still be victims of workplace discrimination—both real and perceived. Clients like Steve, who perceive that they have been passed over for promotions related to their age, need to understand their rights under the law. While CFC does not offer legal consultation, which is outside our scope of practice, we can provide clients with resources as they explore options for self-advocacy. In addition, counselors assist clients in processing these negative experiences as they look to rebuild a path to future success. Consider working with Steve through the lens of Krumboltz and Chan's (2005) steps for dealing with career transitions. They prefer the term "transition counseling" to "career counseling" because their emphasis is on career exploration—not merely decision-making, which is often overemphasized in career counseling. Some other important strategies for counselors include the following:

- **Expand the goal.** This means shifting from deciding to exploring what a satisfying life would look like.
- **Include all aspects of life.** This means eschewing a myopic view of work in favor of exploring personal and family issues related to work and the life one wants to live.
- **Make training more comprehensive.** While applied to counselors, this consideration is really the heart of CFC: addressing the individual while they consider the role work will play in the life they desire to create.
- **Deal with all transitions.** Career or work may be the focus at a given time in counseling, but transitions occur in ways that create a broader context in which career transition takes place. Counselors can and must address these as well.
- **Build a long-term relationship.** Making a career decision must not be the conclusion to counseling, nor should failure to make a decision represent a failed counseling experience.

STEVE IN SESSION

MHC: Thanks for coming in, Steve. How can I be of service?

CL: I don't know. My work says I have to come to six sessions.

MHC: Okay, so this is not exactly your idea?

CL: Right. At the same time, I probably could get some benefit out of talking.

MHC: That's my hope as well. I'm glad to hear whatever is on your mind.

CL: I think I'm burned out from my middle-management job. It's getting harder and harder to tolerate the pressure coming down on me to push my employees to perform more or better.

MHC: You're under pressure to put more pressure on your people?

CL: Yep.

MHC: Maybe there was a time this was easier for you but now it has become intolerable?

CL: (Nods)

MHC: I can see this is difficult for you ... (Waits)

CL: This can't be all my life means.

MHC: This has you asking big life questions.

CL: Definitely. I certainly never dreamed about being a middle manager.

MHC: What did you dream of?

CL: Huh?

MHC: What did you dream of doing or becoming?

CL: (Silent for some time) It's been a long time since I've thought about that kind of question. I always expected to provide for my family—and I have. But I never gave much thought to what *I* wanted.

MHC: Is that something you'd like to explore together in this space?

CL: I don't know. Don't we have to address my "insubordination" (uses air quotes)?

Expand the goal.

MHC: Could it be that the two are related? I mean, you seem disappointed in some aspects of your life, and it appears to be manifesting in your relationships with your bosses at work

CL: I guess I hadn't put those two things together.

MHC: I wonder how addressing this might improve other areas of your life.

CL: My wife would like me to be less stressed when I come home from home and not griping about it all the time.

Include all aspects of life.

MHC: How would that relationship be better if there was less stress and griping?

CL: I wouldn't know what to do with myself! My wife wouldn't either!

MHC: Could be a good problem to have. Maybe we can spend some time expanding on that

CL: That's it! I must quit my job!

MHC: There's a lot of energy there! Before you quit, perhaps we could talk for a bit about what you want from your work and from your life.

The counselor is addressing the role he wants work to play in his life.

CL: (Laughs) I won't quit today but I've thought of it many times.

MHC: I believe you. Could you tell me a little more about the areas of your life that you enjoy or would like to enjoy more?

Deal with all transitions.

CL: (Describes hobbies and interests he once held and the social activities he used to enjoy with his wife)

MHC: It sounds like you have a full life or at least the potential for one. I wonder if we could talk about what it might look like to reintroduce some of these things into your life over time.

CL: Sure. What do you mean?

MHC: You seem certain you could quit your job today, but before doing that (laughter) perhaps we can list something you want to include back into your life today, next week, in a month, and where you'd like to be in a year.

Build a long-term relationship with transition.

CL: That sounds doable. I'd also like to talk about my options for changing jobs and at my age.

MHC: Absolutely. Is that something you'd prefer to start with next session?

CL: Not necessarily. I can see how reintroducing things I enjoy can help a lot.

Retirement

The concept of retirement has evolved over time. Prior to industrialization and the move to city life for more people in the early 1900s, retirement was not really an option. People worked the land or shared work tasks with their local community. The Industrial Revolution and urbanization changed the world of work. People moved from their small towns to larger cities, which simultaneously decreased the likelihood of self-supported employment. The move to city life also increased life expectancy due to access to clean water and better health care. Also, until 1935 Social Security did not exist, making it difficult for people to consider retirement. The Social Security Act was created to pay retired workers over age 65 a regular income to support life after full-time employment (Social Security Administration, n.d.). So retirement as a viable option became available less than 100 years ago. Today, Social Security benefits are available in part starting at age 62, but full benefits are unavailable until age 67. However, Social Security benefits do not cover monthly expenses for many retirees, so they combine these payments with income saved for retirement.

Retirement is impacted by a variety of factors. For example, individual attributes, such as demographics, attitude, health, and finances, can impact decisions to retire. Those from marginalized or disadvantaged groups often have different retirement experiences due to issues of oppression or inequalities (Lytle et al., 2015). Job factors, such as employer flexibility, age stereotypes, and personal employment history, also impact retirement decisions (Shultz & Wang, 2011). Finally, family factors, such as partner working status and number or dependents, and economic factors, such as current economic trends, also influence the ability to retire.

Retirement can also look different for different people. Some may choose full retirement, where they leave their career and do not enter another job. Others may choose phased retirement, where their employer allows a voluntary and gradual progression out of work (Lytle et al., 2015). This may include flexible or decreased hours or extended leave opportunities. Still others may engage in bridge employment, where they transition from full-time occupation to part-time work with another employer. Lastly, workers may choose to delay employment. In fact, about 20% of workers ages 55–64 plan to work beyond the average retirement age of 64.

As noted above, retirement can be considered a transition time for older adults. They may change the way they spend their waking hours, increasing the time spent in leisure or family activities. Or they may continue to work but not in the career or field where they spent much of their adult lives. For those in physically demanding careers, they may be forced to retire from this work as their bodies age or physical health declines. In all cases, retirement requires adjustment to a new way of being.

Take Away and Use Today

The career- and life-related challenges of adulthood are myriad. The task of the counselor is to get inside of the client's lived experience to experience and express empathy for their experience. Validation of struggles is therapeutic, but because no counselor will experience for themselves everything that a client has, connecting early and thoroughly is vital. This chapter is but a brief introduction to the world of adult experiences with work. Be prepared to listen carefully, research thoroughly between sessions, and follow up with your clients. It is of equally vital importance that the further you as a counselor are from your client's age and stage of life, the more important it is that you listen more and talk less. Not only will you learn about your client, but you will build trust.

References

American Psychological Association. (2019). Stress in America™ 2020: A national mental health crisis.

Benach, J., Vives, A., Amable, M., Vanroelen, C., Tarafa, G., & Muntaner, C. (2014). Precarious employment: understanding an emerging social determinant of health. *Annual review of public health 35*, 229-253. https://doi.org/10.1146/annurev-publhealth-032013-182500

Blustein, D. L., Olle, C., Connors-Kellgren, A., & Diamonti, A. J. (2016). Decent work: A psychological perspective. *Frontiers in Psychology, 7*, 407. https://doi.org/10.3389/fpsyg.2016.00407

Duffy, R. D., Blustein, D. L., Diemer, M. A., & Autin, K. L. (2016). The Psychology of Working Theory. *Journal of Counseling Psychology, 63*, 127–148. http://dx.doi.org/10.1037/cou0000140

Ganster, D. C., & Rosen, C. C. (2013). Work stress and employee health: A multidisciplinary review. *Journal of Management, 39*(5), 1085–1122. https://doi.org/10.1177/0149206313475815

Garrett, B. (2015). Brain and behavior: An introduction to biological psychology (4th ed.). Sage.

Krumboltz, J. D., & Chan, A. (2005). Professional issues in vocational psychology. *Handbook of vocational psychology, 3*, 347–370.

Luke, C. (2018). *Career focused counseling: Integrating theory, research and neuroscience*. Cognella.

Luke, C. (2020). *Neuroscience for counselors and therapists: Integrating the sciences of mind and brain* (2nd Ed.). Cognella.

Luke, C., & Michael (2016). Interventions for veterans. In W. K Killam, S. Degges-White, & R. E. Michel, (Eds.), *Career counseling interventions: Practice with diverse clients* (pp. 225–239). Springer Publishing Company.

Lytle, M. C., Clancy, M. E., Foley, P. F., & Cotter, E. W. (2015). Current trends in retirement: Implications for career counseling and vocational psychology. *Journal of Career Development, 42*(3), 170–184. https://doi.org/10.1177/0894845314545785

Michel, J. S., Kotrba, L. M., Mitchelson, J. K., Clark, M. A., & Baltes, B. B. (2011). Antecedents of work–family conflict: A meta-analytic review. *Journal of Organizational Behavior, 32*, 689–725. https://doi.org/10.1002/job.695

Pickerell, D. A., & Neault, R. A. (2019). Maximizing career engagement across a lifetime of transitions. In J. Maree (ed.) *Handbook of innovative career counselling* (pp. 195–211). Springer.

Salvagioni, D. A. J., Melanda, F. N., Mesas, A. E., González, A. D., Gabani. F. L., & de Andrade, S. M. (2017). Physical, psychological and occupational consequences of job burnout: A systematic review of prospective studies. PLOS ONE 12(10): e0185781. https://doi.org/10.1371/journal.pone.0185781

Shultz, K. S., & Wang, M. (2011). Psychological perspectives on the changing nature of retirement. *American Psychologist, 66*(3), 170–179. https://doi.org/10.1037/a0022411

Sirgy, M. J., & Lee, D. J. (2018). Work–life balance: An integrative review. *Applied Research Quality of Life, 13*, 229–254. https://doi.org/10.1007/s11482-017-9509-8

Social Security Administration. (n.d.). Historical background and development of social security. https://www.ssa.gov/history/briefhistory3.html

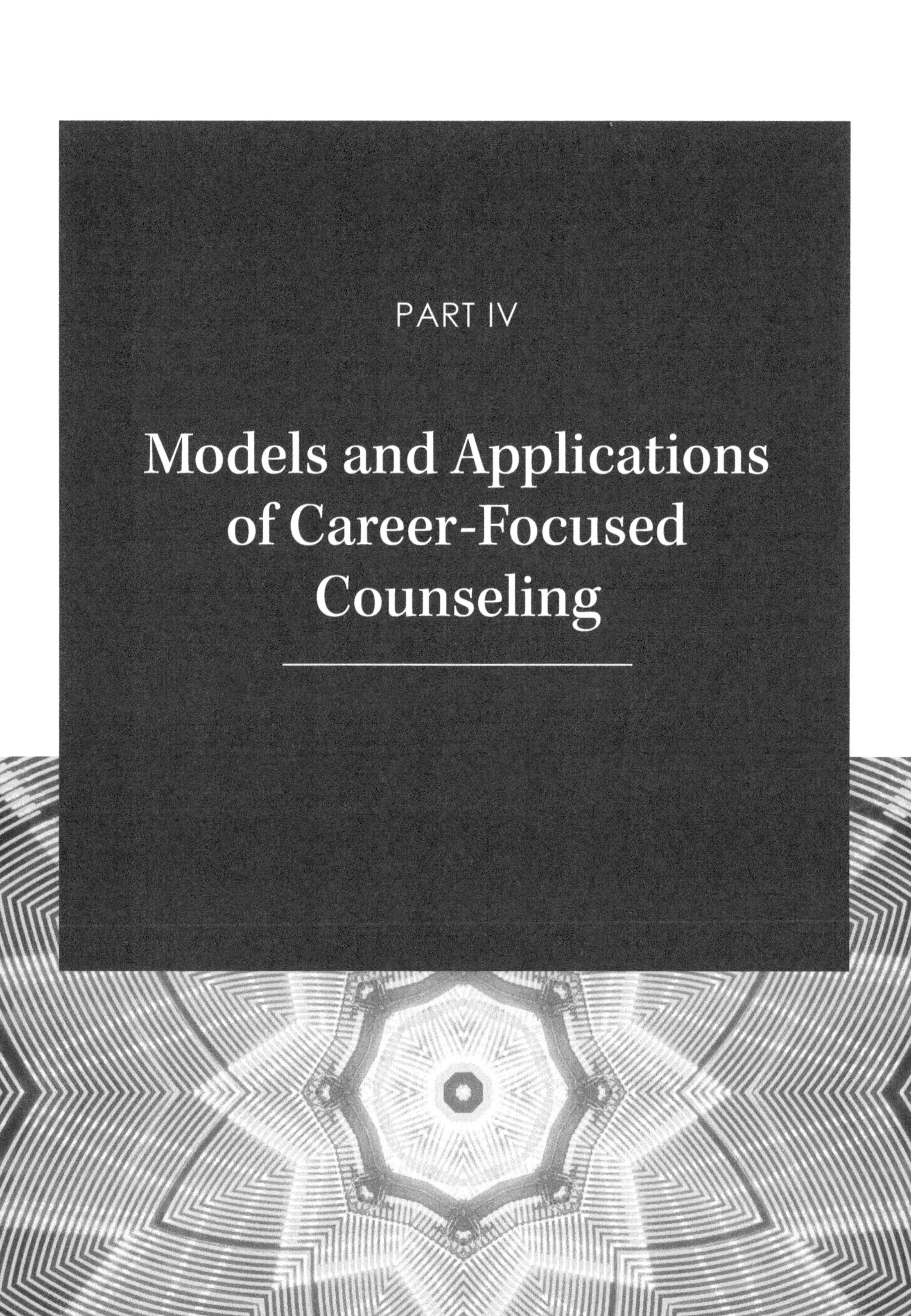

PART IV

Models and Applications of Career-Focused Counseling

CHAPTER 14

Career and Mental Health

Development vs. Diagnosis

CHAPTER GOALS

- Consider the mental health concerns that arise at different stages of development.
- Describe the interrelationships between career and mental health concerns.
- Provide a model for integrating career and mental health counseling across the lifespan.

OPENING VIGNETTES

Samuel is a 12 year old referred to the school counselor for difficulty concentrating and struggling to participate in activities at school. During a guidance lesson that is centered on career planning (e. g., field trips, worksheets, and exploration activities) he appears irritable. He has met with the school counselor on several occasions, but when asked about this afterward, he states that nothing is wrong and he does not understand why he is being singled out.

Marianna is a 17 year old senior in high school, referred to a counselor in the community for her apparent lack of motivation related to college and career planning. She states that she does not see the point, as she does not plan to go to college and just wants to graduate and get a job. She does not express any specific job interests, and her career assessments indicate undifferentiated results (no clear interests). Her counselor, seeing the results, recognizes immediately that Marianna's diffuse results on a career interest inventory fit a pattern that may indicate a depressed mood (even though the assessment is not a depression assessment) and recommends that Marianna see a mental health counselor.

Rami is a 23 year old working at a big box store following a series of jobs at a variety of retail stores. She is seeking career-focused counseling at a community counseling center because her life feels directionless. Feeling that she missed her opportunity to get a college degree, she believes it is "too late" for her to return to school and must now make the best of her work situation.

Carlos is a 57 year old who worked as a sales manager at a major brand car dealership at the start of the pandemic. He had worked his way from detailing cars in his teens to service, then sales, and, finally, sales leadership. He enjoyed his career, made a stable income for his wife and three children, was in line for a promotion to general manager of another dealership, and was active in his church and community. When the pandemic escalated and factories shut down, care manufactures closed plants and reduced shipments to dealerships. The dealership where Carlos worked lost much of their inventory as shipments slowed and traffic into the dealership also slowed as people lost their jobs. Suddenly, in the span of only a few months, Carlos found his salary cut in half. A year and a half into the pandemic, Carlos seeks counseling for mood concerns and lethargy as well as for career advice.

REFLECTION ACTIVITIES AND QUESTIONS

Counseling is an explicitly developmental and wellness-oriented profession. Yet, counselors often encounter people who are not well or for whom development has gone off-track. As you read this chapter and prepare for your work with students and clients, consider the following:

- How will I know when my student or clients difficulties are the result of development or a diagnosis?
- How can I determine which came first: the work-related issue or the mental health issue?
- How can I assess for diagnostic issues while focusing on develop in working on career-related issues?

Introduction

Mental health concerns affect work (Heppner et al., 1996; Pace & Quinn, 2000; Robitschek & DeBell, 2002), and work can cause and exacerbate mental health concerns (Anderson & Niles, 1995; Swanson, 2002); this is now well-established in the literature. The impact is reciprocal and includes work hours lost, under- and unemployment, and medical bills. It has also come to be more widely accepted that career and mental health are not easily separable in a counseling context: both must be addressed by counselors (Olesen et al, 2013; Osborn et al., 2016; Tang et al., 2021). As a reminder, the American Counseling Association includes *career goals* in its definition of professional counseling. This means that addressing career-related issues is not only in the purview of school and mental health counselors, it is a professional responsibility to be competent in this area of practice.

This chapter covers these reciprocal impacts across development with a focus on career and mental health across the lifespan. This means examining healthy and healthful developmental trajectories, while also seeking understanding of when development goes off track. Since the vast majority of mental health issues in adulthood emerge by about the age of 14, it is important to juxtapose healthy and unhealthy development and its reciprocal relationship with work and career. When exploring what happens when development runs off course, we maintain a focus on the individual's response to their environment and circumstances, rather than fixating on the diagnosis itself. In other words, these are people with developmental concern—not pathologies that conform to certain fixed views of what a person can and cannot do. We examine the difference between what can be called developmental career-focused counseling and diagnostic career-focused counseling.

TAKE A MINUTE

Think of a time when you were seeking employment. What were the range of emotions and thoughts you experienced? Were they positive, leaning toward excitement, anticipation, and optimism, or were they more negative, leaning toward dread, fear, and doubt? Now, consider how your experience might be different if you had an underlying mental health concern, such as anxiety, depression, or trauma. How might that affect your disposition and behavior related to the job search? You can see in this brief example of how a negative spiral could occur.

Career Development and Mental Health

Anxiety, depression, substance misuse, and stress-trauma that precede these life transitions both exacerbate the stress in these transitions and can decrease resilience in facing the challenges of these transitions. It is important to note that the trends related to emerging adulthood do not reflect generational character or that emerging adults are entitled or lazy; rather, this is their sociocultural milieu, wherein the rules have changed and, with it, what they expect from work. We cover specific career-related concerns in later chapters, so in this section, we introduce more general information related to mental health concerns in adulthood and their effects on career-related issues.

TABLE 14.1 POTENTIAL IMPACTS OF MENTAL HEALTH ON CAREER-RELATED DOMAINS

<table>
<tr><th></th><th>Work Performance</th><th>Career Decision-Making</th><th>Job Satisfaction</th><th>Protective Factors</th></tr>
<tr><td>Anxiety-Related Disorders</td><td>Hypervigilance, leading to fatigue and irritability</td><td>Avoidance, leading to premature commitment or delayed choice</td><td>Anxiety diminishes satisfaction in numerous life domains; career is a prime example</td><td rowspan="4">Work provides a creative outlet to relieve stress; increase sense of purpose and meaning; focus attention; inoculate against external, personal stressors; and opportunities for structure, productivity, and short and long-term rewards</td></tr>
<tr><td>Mood-Related Disorders</td><td>Decreased concentration, leading to limited attention to detail</td><td>Passivity or past orientation, impacting future planning</td><td>Depression limits perspective for deriving satisfaction from work</td></tr>
<tr><td>Stress- and Trauma-Related Disorders</td><td>Reactivity and distractedness, leading to errors</td><td>Chronic and acute stress, similarly impacting critical thinking and problem-solving capacities</td><td>As performance and engagement decrease, so does satisfaction</td></tr>
<tr><td>Addictions</td><td>Besides on-site inebriation, lethargy, paranoia, hangovers, and lateness</td><td>Long-term planning often gives way to short-term behaviors and making up for past behaviors</td><td>Work becomes a means to an end—often as a last resort</td></tr>
</table>

Note. From Luke, 2018.

In Table 14.1, we can see more clearly the overlap between career and personal counseling (Heppner et al., 1996; Pace & Quinn, 2000; Robitschek & DeBell, 2002) as well as the reciprocal effects on each other (Anderson & Niles, 1995; Swanson, 2002). Another way to consider the connections between career and mental health is in Table 14.1 (Luke, 2018). Note the wellness and developmental orientation of counseling in the list of protective factors.

When working with clients, it is important to be aware of these interrelationships in order to determine their influence on the other. It also highlights the importance of identifying strengths and protective factors for these—and all—clients and students. The issue then arises about whether to address career or mental health issues first. Fortunately, Anderson and Niles concluded:

> Although some career counseling theorists suggest that noncareer issues must be resolved before counseling for career decision making (e.g., Brown & Brooks, 1991), the findings of this study suggest that clients often choose to address both career and noncareer concerns throughout counseling. (1995, p. 244)

As you read this chapter and continue to reflect on your own career development, try to imagine a career-related issue that does not intersect with mental health. Counselors approach client issues from a wellness-based, developmental perspective, as described in Chapter 1. In the current context, development involves an ongoing process of growth and change, which, in turn, involves identifying and overcoming natural (and unnatural) barriers and challenges. Counselors facilitate this process by working to unlock the inherent potential in individuals and guide them to resources to accommodate areas of weakness. Career development is simply another domain of development that counselors facilitate. Because of this, every career issue is a developmental issue, and every developmental issue is an opportunity to benefit from counseling. Keep this in mind as you ask yourself the opening questions again (Luke, 2018).

Figure 1.1 (from Chapter 1) represents eight dimensions of human experience. As you can see, relationships form the hub of the model (wheel) and the sociocultural milieu forms the rim. All other dimensions can be understood in terms of these two dimensions. The sociocultural milieu as the rim emphasizes that all we are as humans is bound by cultural values and social norms, even, perhaps especially, in cases in which an individual resists those values or norms. One set of spokes on the wheel includes the traditional dimensions of thoughts, feelings, and behaviors. These are important in their own right but work together in harmony. Thinking or cognition is the mental activity involved in creating representations of reality. Thoughts are influenced by relationships and culture and, in turn, influence them. Thoughts are also connected closely with feelings and behaviors, and vice versa. Feelings, long thought to be merely the byproduct of cognition, are themselves important ways humans access truth. While heavily influenced by thoughts, their expression is informed by cultural norms and plays out in relationships. Behaviors are the acts, volitional and otherwise, that drive the human machine in day-to-day life. Behavior includes everything from scratching one's nose to exercising one's agency in relationships and the world of work—just to name a few. Behaviors exert an influence on both thoughts and feelings, even as they are affected by thoughts and feelings.

The second set of three spokes includes experiences (past and present); environment (past and present); and biology, genetics, and neurobiology. Experiences in this context refers to events in one's life that are both negative and positive. They can include small- and big-T traumas as well as positive experiences that foster resilience. Environments include early environments in which cultural norms and relational patterns affect the development of the child. Environments also include the current environment in which a person lives. For example, it matters for career-focused counseling and overall development if a child is living in poverty (environment) or experiences neglect. The biological dimension includes everything from genetics to health and wellness practices. This dimension really brings us back to the wellness orientation of the counseling profession. For example, a client may report not being able to concentrate long enough to research career possibilities. In some cases, the counsel, attending to biology and wellness, may learn that the client is not sleeping and is consuming copious amounts of caffeine. This brief wellness check helps avoid pathologizing what can be managed behaviorally. The interrelationships of these spokes has become a mainstay of neurodevelopment research, such that while it is true that we are influenced by our genetics, our genetic makeup is heavily influenced by the environment and our experiences. This is commonly referred to as epigenetics, and it effectively ends the nature versus nurture debate. This may be seen in the example of alcohol use disorder, or alcoholism to use the more common, yet pejorative, term. Alcoholism is 40–60% heritable, meaning that genetics heavily influence whether an individual develops an alcohol use disorder. However, this predisposition may never be realized if one never picks up a drink. Likewise, an early environment of stress or trauma experiences can "turn on" this genetic vulnerability.

Interestingly, the state of neuroscience is such that each of these dimensions has received significant attention in the literature. Every dimension has its neurobiological correlates. So what might this mean for career-focused counseling? Good question. The following table is updated from Luke (2018).

Career Development in Childhood

There is a growing movement in the fields of career development and education to begin career development at the earliest age possible or, more importantly, to recognize that career development begins very early in life whether we actively attend to it or not (Gottfrredson, 1981; 2005). It has been suggested that career development begins by age 18 month or even birth. This involves meeting children and, later, adolescents at their developmental level by aiding in exploration of self and work. In fact, whole models have been built around career development across the lifespan (e. g., Super, 1990 and others). This topic is so important that there is a chapter here dedicated to developmental models of career (Chapter 7), and there are chapters devoted to career development across K–12 settings (Chapter 11) and emerging adulthood (Chapter 12). So in this section we stay with healthy and unhealthy development patterns that affect and are affected by the world of work at a young age. The movement toward

TABLE 14.2 NEUROSCIENCE CORRELATES OF CAREER CONCERNS

Domain	Types of Work-Related Concerns	Neuroscience Correlates	Observations
Sociocultural milieu—Humans exist in layer upon layer of contexts (Bronfenbrenner, 1979) but may be best understood as the "subjective individual culture of one's life experience" (MacDonald, 1997, p. 199).	• Social and cultural expectations about what work should be	• Social and environmental effects on the brain (Crossley et al., 2018) • SES effects on the brain (Farah, 2018) • Relational context for social neuroscience (Clark-Polner & Clark, 2014)	Cultural expectations about productivity and contributions to the larger community, whether implicit or explicit, whether high or low; most bring these expectations into dealing with work-related concerns.
Bio/genetic/neuro—All that is human arises from neurobiological processes (Kalat, 2019) and biological functions (e.g., sleep, diet/nutrition, exercise, and overall physical health).	• Genetic vulnerability to stress; physical and emotional toll that stress takes	• Genetics passed down from previous generations; epigenetics/heritability of traits versus teleology (Berger et al., 2009) • Individual genetically-based variation in response to environment (Panksepp et al., 2017) • Interaction of genetics, lifestyle, and environmental factors (Lin et al., 2017)	A key component of diversity competencies involves ableness and its impact on work options; in addition, the brain changes in response to repetitive behaviors, so work transitions can be impacted by change across job types.
Relationships—Early and current connections with others, especially significant others—individual brains are best understood in the context of social relationships in terms of functioning (Kleinbub, 2017).	• Intrapersonal conflict • relational conflict at work • Conflict at "home" over work • Interaction of multiple roles, including work	• Brains are organized for complex socio-cognitive functioning (Clark-Polner & Clark, 2014). • Early attachment (relationship with caregiver) plays a significant role in neural development, from cognition to stress management (Gennaro et al., 2019; Kleinbub, 2017).	Counselors and clients exert a reciprocal influence on neurobiological functioning (Beckes, Ijzerman, & Tops, 2015).

(Continued)

TABLE 14.2 NEUROSCIENCE CORRELATES OF CAREER CONCERNS *(Continued)*

Domain	Types of Work-Related Concerns	Neuroscience Correlates	Observations
Environment—This includes both previous and current living situations and can be physical and emotional.	• Work environment and impact of work on other environments (like home)	• Early environments shape the development of all humans, facilitating or blocking growth in core domains of experience like cognition, emotion, relationships, and behavior (Suleiman & Dahl, 2017). • Implicit environmental cues evoke responses from individuals (Farah, 2018). • Modeling and mimicry in one's environment (Prochazkova & Kret, 2017) • Environmental context influences neural development and subsequent behavior (Suleiman & Dahl, 2017)	It is important to understand the individual's work environment (real and perceived) as well as their desired environment; in addition, examine how the home or other environments are impacting career-related issues.
Experiences—These can be both proximal and distal, and as the wealth of lab and practice-based research show, they can shape how our brain develops	• Various negative experiences finding, maintaining, or transitioning through work	• Experiences in cognition, emotion, behavior, and environment can directly impact the structure and function of neural networks in the brain (i.e., experience-dependent plasticity; Park et al., 2017; Ramamurthy & Krubitzer, 2018; Sweatt, 2016). • Acute experiences affect long-term memory (Clayton et al., 2019). • Environment affects brain function (Rogers et al., 2019).	One of, perhaps, the most common and influential involves both early experiences related to the perception of work as well as individual experiences in and out of the workplace that shape perceptions and expectations.
Thoughts/cognitions—This is a type of behavior but a distinct phenomenon as well. It encompasses language, perception, attention, memory, and other facets as well (Pulvermüller, Garagnani, & Wennekers, 2014).	• Self-defeating	• Cognitive appraisal to reduce depression in childhood maltreatment (Rodman et al., 2019). • "Thought circuits" aid the understanding of cognition (Pulvermüller et al., 2014). • The brain, body, and immediate environment in combination affect cognition (Matheson & Barsalou, 2018).	Cognitive distortions underlie many, perhaps most, career-related issues, either as precursors to or results of career-related issues.

(Continued)

TABLE 14.2 NEUROSCIENCE CORRELATES OF CAREER CONCERNS *(Continued)*

Domain	Types of Work-Related Concerns	Neuroscience Correlates	Observations
Emotions/affect—Positive core emotions include the following (Panksepp et al., 2017): • Seeking (enthusiastic interest) • Lust (passionate sexual arousal) • Care (devoted nurturance) • Play (prosocial joy) • Negative core emotions include the following (Panksepp et al., 2017): • Rage (anger) • Fear (threat-induced anxiety) • Panic (the psychological pain associated with separation distress)	• Negative emotional experience of work	• Emotions have been viewed as subordinate reactions to cognition or environmental cues, whereas more recent conceptions view them as fundamental to human functioning (Panksepp & Biven, 2012). • Koenig (2019) on the role of "neurovisceral regulatory circuits" as they relate to children and adolescents affective resilience	Emotions are real, though they don't always reflect reality; this does not preclude them from influencing, and even exacerbating, career-related issues.
Behavior/volition—This includes "perception, attention, emotion, memory, and more" (Purves et al., 2018, p. 726).	• Poor or lack of motivation • Problematic behaviors at work • "The question for counselors concerns whether one believes that behavior is primarily a response to a stimulus (behaviorism) or if it is a psychological phenomenon in which some mediating variable (e.g., will or cognitive) affects the outcome of a given stimulus" (Luke, 2020, p. 22).	• Kandel's (1976) seminal work on the neurobiological basis of behavior • Hebb's rule (1949) on neurobiology of learning • Ledoux et al. (2017) on the neurobiology of avoidance behaviors	Most people make a change when the pain of stasis exceeds the pain of change; career-related issues in the behavior domain can be explicit (e.g., acting out, substance use, etc.) or implicit, as in passivity on the job or in seeking change.

early career development is well-intentioned in most cases, but there is concern that career development in earlier ages may feed a colonialist mindset that dictates what success is and should look like for everyone.

Sharf discussed the career development of children under 12 in terms of developmental theorists from Piaget and Erikson to Super and Gottfredson. He describes several stage-related tasks and orientations related to children's development, career and otherwise, in terms of maturity (e. g., Super, 1980; Super, 1990; Savickas, 2002). These include curiosity, exploration, and information. Additional factors include key figures, locus of control, interests, time, and self-concept. It is vital that counselors working with children understand the developmental dynamics of these individuals. Landreth (2012) has asserted that children are not miniature adults (2012) and Sharf goes one step further, stating that, "children are not merely uninformed adults" (2013, p. 175). While most would agree with this position, acting on this insight in working with children takes self-awareness and insight into development (Byrd & Luke, 2021). For example, in the dimension of curiosity, children are innately curious, but this curiosity is often restrained by adults because of the energy and attention it can take to foster curiosity (Luke & Schimmel, 2022). In a school context, there are insufficient resources to permit all children to express their curious nature, while also managing a classroom of 25–30 students. One way curiosity may be fostered is connecting children's play to career themes. Unfortunately, this reflects an incomplete view of both play and career development. Play in children is not practice for adulthood; it is play for play's sake (Panksepp & Biven, 2012; Siviy, 2016). In fact, this is the definition of play itself. Play fosters brain development and must be accepted as such. Play has also been said to be a diagnostic tool in understanding child development and when it goes off track (Siviy, 2016). This is because play is primal (Panksepp et al., 2017). It is how children, in particular, understand the world around them and solve problems for themselves. This reality relates to the development of curiosity and how it leads to exploration. Exploration among children is the process of implementing play behaviors as they try on roles and engage risky behaviors in a safe way.

DEVELOPMENTAL CAREER-FOCUSED COUNSELING

Developmental CFC conforms to natural developmental patterns of cognitive, social, and emotional stages and tasks. For many children and adolescents, developmental CFC looks a lot like career guidance through the provision of career-related information, observing key figures in roles of interest, and beginning to implement a plan for turning a future orientation into concrete steps. This is where theorists like Piaget (1952), Erikson (1968), and Super (1990) come together to establish markers for healthy development and chronological, behavioral tasks that build in stages (i.e., the subsequent stage is contingent upon the previous one). As children and adolescents arrive at the next stage, often measured by grade level, achievement measures, and behavioral markers, the tasks for the next stage become clearer (Erikson, 1968). In terms of career development, the tasks at various stages have been articulated in the work of Super and Gottfredson. Super, for example, described the period of age birth to about 14 years old as the growth stage. Like all stage theories, the growth stage has a set of tasks that must be met before the child can fully transition to the next stage, exploration, regardless of age. Some of these tasks, for example, include building an identity (Super's self-concept) in relation to caregivers as well as taking on increasing levels of responsibilities through their dominant life roles, typically student and child. Gottfredson adds that during this period, or set of substages, children must also navigate the complexities of size and power, gender roles, value and valuation, and the self (2005). The point here is that all of these tasks fulfill stage requirements and prepare the child for the next stage, ultimately culminating in good citizenship (our term—in contrast to one life role in Super's work). Counselors can often support development through career guidance and access to resources that further move the child along their developmental trajectory.

DIAGNOSTIC CAREER-FOCUSED COUNSELING

The tasks and stages just described are challenging enough to navigate in and of themselves, but there are many instances in which development follows an alternate trajectory, and counselors often face a difficult choice: Suspend all growth-oriented work and address the crisis of mental health and development, or attempt to address both simultaneously. This is an incredibly complex challenge, so there is not one right response for all situations (mental health counselors know this all too well in deciding how to treat co-occurring disorders like addiction and mood disorders). The Centers for Disease Control and Prevention reports that ADHD, anxiety, depression, and behavior problems are the most common childhood mental health disorders (CDC, n.d.). These disorders produce a variety of cognitive, affective, behavioral, and social dynamics that occlude the view into necessary career development. These disorders, as discussed in Luke and Schimmel (2022), affect these individuals' relationships with parents, adults, and peers. Some are low intensity (like social anxiety that may be managed through behavioral interventions) to moderate (like the inattention and high energy of ADHD) to high intensity (like thoughts of death associated with a major depressive episode). While the same is true in adulthood, these disorders tend to emerge during childhood (ADHD and behavioral disorders) and adolescence (anxiety and mood disorders as well as substance misuse), and they appear during critical periods of development. These can greatly affect identity development and sense of self as well as future orientation that is essential from transforming fantasy to exploration and planning (Super, 1957). Other disorders diagnosed in early childhood, such as autism spectrum disorder (ASD) and intellectual disability (ID), can profoundly alter a child's ability and confidence to successfully complete these tasks, requiring the implementation of supports at school and at home.

SAMUEL IN SESSION

Samuel is struggling to maintain his attention in classes and has become increasingly irritable when prompted or invited to participate. While it is perfectly natural for a preadolescent to experience changes in their attention and interests, Samuel's challenges may be affecting his mood and overall performance in school. The school counselor sits down with Samuel to explore his struggles and to offer support.

SC: Thanks for coming by, Samuel. I wanted to follow up with you after our last meeting. I want to start by saying that you're not in any kind of trouble. I just want to check in to see how you are doing.

ST: (Shrugs)

SC: Do you know that you're not in trouble?

ST: (Shrugs again)

SC: How are you feeling today?

ST: I don't know.

SC: (Waits)

ST: It kind of feels like I am in trouble.

SC: Okay, thank you for sharing that. What does that feel like for you, thinking you're in trouble?

ST: (Shrugs) I'm kind of used to it.

SC: You've gotten used to being in trouble? Here or at home?

ST: Both. Somebody's always yelling at me.

SC: Oh, gosh. That sounds like it would be hard. What kind of things are you getting yelled at about?

ST: I don't know. Not paying attention, I guess. Forgetting to do chores or homework.

SC: So it's happening at school and at home. I mean, hopefully, you're not getting "yelled at" at school.

ST: I don't know. (Looking down most of this time)

SC: I'd like to ask you again how you're feeling right now.

ST: (Shrugs)

SC: If I had to guess, you seem sad.

ST: (Shrugs again but counselor waits) Yeah, I don't like getting in trouble all of the time. I just forget or get bored.

SC: What's hard about getting in trouble all the time?

ST: I keep letting people down. And I don't like my mom being mad or upset at me.

SC: That does sound hard. It also seems like you're trying not to have that happen but something is not working. How long has it been like this for you?

ST: I don't know.

SC: Was it like this at your elementary school? (Samuel is in 7th grade and switched to middle school a year and a half ago.)

ST: My other school was easy.

SC: So being here has been harder? What's made it harder for you?

ST: I miss my friends and people here are mean.

SC: Can you say more about "mean"?

ST: I don't have any friends and the kids here are rough. They're always giving me a hard time.

SC: I can imagine that's so difficult for you. Has this been going on for a long time?

ST: Ever since last year.

School counselor and Samuel go on to discuss bullying behavior by a student in Samuel's class as well as the difficulty in making friends. The counselor is empathic and expresses this to Samuel. The counselor suggests a support team meeting to bring in Samuel's mom and the school administration to explore solutions to this dilemma. One of the concerns includes Samuel's apparent internalizing of the struggles to make friends and of being bullied. A support team meeting can help identify supports in the school and in the community. For example, the school participates in a school-based counseling program, where a mental health counselor provides counseling to students in the school. The SC and MHC can work collaboratively to support Samuel and to treat the internal and external factors affecting his wellbeing. Together, they can determine what for Samuel is developmental and what may have become diagnostic.

Career Development in Adolescence

As noted in the previous sections on childhood, adolescent career development is touched on in Chapters 7 and 11. However, we feel it is important to first address fundamental understanding of adolescent development as well as the deviations and diversions from a normative (average) developmental trajectory. Adolescence is the ongoing search for identity in a world that tries to tell them what their identity is or should be (constant flow of advertisements on social media about the "right" kind of life). While not an indictment on social media and technology, children and adolescent's identity development is certainly influenced by these sources. Identity development is a series of challenges and tasks, leading to a hopefully clearer sense of who one is (Erikson,1968). One of the primary challenges related to career is the lack of clarity and completeness of this stage of development, even while they are expected to declare their career intentions. Super's observation and assertion that vocational identity is the projection of one's identity in the workspace has important implications for career development during adolescence. Our observations from career counseling practice is that individuals have to make career decisions with incomplete identity information and awareness. This leads to choosing a career path while identity is still being formed, resulting in a career self-identity fusion of sorts. In other words, work can significantly shape a person's identity. This is a function of the cultural context of modern society, which places an emphasis on early career development (i.e., elementary school), which is tantamount to making a career choice. This can be problematic, as emerging and ongoing research on stages of development, like Erikson's psychosocial stages, indicates that maturation takes place over a longer period of time, as seen in the additional stage of emerging adulthood (Arnett, 2000). This, no doubt, is in part due to longer life expectancy, and the decreased need for relatively early maturation needed for survival in a modern context. In other words, the incubation period of childhood and adolescence can be longer because they do not need to work as early to support a family. At the same time, however, socioeconomic forces have affected adolescents and emerging adults' ability to launch into a life that is financially costly.

DEVELOPMENTAL CAREER-FOCUSED COUNSELING

Identity development is a precarious path to adulthood, requiring the navigation of multiple tasks (Erikson, 1968; Marcia, 1966). Fortunately, cognitive, emotional, and social development occur during this time in ways that support the development of the whole person (Bowlby, 1988; Piaget, 1969). Career-focused counseling in this context recognizes the challenges inherent in forming a sense of self while looking toward a future with unprecedented decision-making demands. Only a small percentage of adolescents would have made such a high-stakes decision as those related to life after high school years. Notably, a similar dynamic can be found among college graduates, who are technically in the emerging adulthood stage (a somewhat nominal distinction). As a reminder, in this chapter we are exploring career-focused counseling outside the context of formal career programs that would be found in high school or vocational training programs, as those are considered in other chapters. Rather, we are focusing on the general developmental themes and the impact of alternative trajectories on work and career wellness. For example, when working with a teenager in an agency setting, we are working with the individual who is part of multiple systems.

DIAGNOSTIC CAREER-FOCUSED COUNSELING

Mental health issues emerge during adolescence in particular by about age 14 (CDC, n.d.). These include anxiety and mood disorders, and their effects on identity development can be profound. Anxiety and depression both can manifest as difficulty concentrating and making decisions, feeling unmotivated, and hopelessness about the future. Most of the referrals to an agency counselor will have as its presenting concern something around disruptions in mood or behavior—not career issues, in particular. This does not mean they are unrelated. During this time of identity formation, issues of work are necessarily connected. Seeking mental health counseling can be viewed as an opportunity for growth—not just symptom reduction or problem remediation. While we are not advocating that counselors respond to every teenage client with mood or behavior disruption with a career interest inventory, we are offering a reminder that education and work are essential domains for wellness and must be assessed and considered in the treatment plan. For example, career decision-making issues can affect one's mood and behavior, just as difficulties with anxiety, depression, stress, and substance misuse can make career development more difficult (Luke, 2018).

MARIANNA IN SESSION

As mentioned above, Marianna has been referred to a mental health counselor in the community because the school counselor is concerned that her symptoms may extend beyond those expected for this stage of development. The MHC talks with Marianna about her motivation in order to understand the extent to which the college or career issues are developmental in nature or reflect something diagnostic.

> MHC: Thanks for coming in today, Marianna. I hope we can take some time to get to know each other a little. If you have any questions before we begin, please feel free to ask them.
>
> CT: I guess I wonder if you've worked with many kids and if you think you can help.
>
> MHC: Those are great initial questions! I certainly see some children and many teenagers in my practice. Over time, I've seen many "kids" get what they wanted from counseling. I wonder what it is that you might want from counseling?
>
> CT: I'm not sure exactly. I know I want to feel better, but I just don't know how.
>
> MHC: That's actually a really good place to start. How does it feel that makes you want something better?
>
> CT: Well, I feel anxious all of the time—like butterflies in my stomach. It's hard for me to concentrate at school, and it sometimes gets in the way of having fun.
>
> MHC: That certainly sounds like important things in your life have been affected by this anxiety and makes sense that you'd like some relief. How long would you say it's been like this for you?
>
> CT: I don't know. I've noticed it a lot in high school. I started really worrying about performing in school and making friends and having to pick the right career path.
>
> MHC: So, since you're a senior now, it's been with you for a few years?
>
> CT: Yeah, I guess, but also in middle school some. I just worry about everything and get pretty overwhelmed.
>
> MHC: And it sounds like it has been difficult to control the worry.
>
> CT: Totally.
>
> MHC: Perhaps we could talk a little more about this, if you're willing.
>
> CT: Sure.

MHC: Can you think of anything in middle or high school that made life more difficult for you, like a significant event?

CT: Not really. I just noticed myself getting more and more anxious and less happy.

MHC: And have your friends or family noticed?

CT: Yeah, my friends worry but they're really anxious, too. My parents say they're concerned, but they don't seem to know what to do.

MHC: They don't know what to do to help you?

CT: Yeah. I don't blame them, because it's weird to just feel anxious and worried all the time.

MHC: I'm sure that feels strange or bad. What things would you say you worry about the most?

CT: I think it's been everything. I worry if my friends are upset at me, I worry that something bad will happen to my parents or my friends. I am so anxious about graduating and figuring out what's next—and everybody keeps asking me, so now I tell them I don't want to go to college, just to get them to back off.

MHC: It really does sound like this has affected many areas of your life and to a large extent. The good news is that there are lots of options for treating your anxiety. Would you be interested in working together on this?

CT: It would be great to feel better, so yes!

In this brief transcript, we see the counselor working to understand Marianna's concerns, assessing what might be developmental (e.g., career decision-making or high school transitions) and what might be diagnostic (i.e., some type of anxiety or mood disorder). This is important as it determines whether Marianna just needs support through her developmental journey or whether she needs more focused mental health intervention, which it appears that she does.

Career Development in Emerging and Early Adulthood

Described in detail in Chapter 12, the period of life from about 18 years old to the late 20s has come to be known as emerging adulthood (Arnett, 2000). During this period, transitions are made from the high school experience to work, vocational training, or higher education. It is a period of striking out on one's own through work or school, where increasing levels of independence are sought. This period of life is also a time wherein mental health issues become more florid, as the changing roles and contexts can exacerbate adolescent mental health concerns. For example, more intense psychological concerns emerge, such as psychoses and personality disorders. Depression and anxiety can also begin to more directly impact career futures, as they affect work and education (Luke, 2018). In fact, a defining feature of *DSM-5* diagnoses is that they affect school, work, or other significant life roles; therefore, a stage of life where work emerges as a primary life role, the connections between mental health and career are increasingly salient.

DEVELOPMENTAL CAREER-FOCUSED COUNSELING

This period of emerging adulthood is a transformative time in the lives of most individuals. It provides the resources and opportunities to implement life- and career-related decisions through job, training, and education selection. Arnett (2007) describes the improvements in quality of life in emerging adulthood, including declines in depression and increases in self-esteem. Arnett attributes this to the view that, "Emerging adults enjoy their self-focused freedom from role obligations and restraints, and they take satisfaction in their progress toward self-sufficiency" (p. 70). Research is also accumulating that a college degree is not necessarily the golden road to life satisfaction in emerging adulthood as it once was (Almeida et al., 2020). Emerging adults are making their own paths, and technology has only expedited this shift (Ackerman & Kanfer, 2020). Contrary to the fears that technology will replace humans, resulting in profound job loss, emerging adults are adapting by leveraging a technology and knowledge-based economy to the effect that unemployment has been historically low (Arnett et al., 2020).

DIAGNOSTIC CAREER-FOCUSED COUNSELING

Once again, the news is not all positive in emerging adulthood. In many ways, identity development (and concerns) persist through this period. "It is true that identity issues are prominent in emerging adulthood and that sorting through them and finding satisfying alternatives in love and work can generate anxiety" (Arnett, 2007, p. 70). For those with limited education and training, entry into the workforce can be challenging to say the least. For those with more education, the expectations of success are high, leading to stress and burnout. Add to this the fact that, increasingly, emerging adults impose high expectations on their work environment, expecting high pay and high satisfaction (Arnett, 2004). These individuals encounter work environments where "paying your dues" is the norm but feels quite foreign. Old ideas about inherent satisfaction in doing a job well are being replaced with expectations of meaningful work for high pay. The confrontation of this expectation by the realities of modern work life can be discouraging and lead to anxiety and depression (Luke, 2018).

Career-Focused Counseling in Adulthood

One of the most important features of effective career-focused counseling with adults at any stage involves the chicken–egg conundrum. When a client presents with career issues as well as mental health issues, it can be challenging to identify which came first. Since adults have largely achieved a higher level of development, in that the more formative stages are behind them and what awaits is transition and nuance, discerning which issues are developmental and which are diagnostic can be challenging. These challenges are exacerbated by the clinical presentation and its relation to career concerns. An additional complication is the global pandemic context through which career and work have changed significantly and, perhaps, permanently (Pfefferbaum et al., 2020). As we examine the line between development and diagnostics, the COVID-19 pandemic has significantly blurred the lines between the two. Whereas many adult workers around the world were in once stable jobs and industries, the global shutdowns of companies led to major shifts in unemployment to be sure but also shifts in the ways in which work is conducted and how workers communicate and connect. Rudolph et al. (2021) identified 10 topics for addressing pandemic needs with industrial or organizational psychology, which have important applications to counseling. These include occupational health and safety, work-family issues, telecommuting, virtual teamwork, job insecurity, precarious work, leadership, human resources policy, the aging workforce, and careers. These areas highlight the complexity of career-focused counseling in a pandemic context and how career and mental health cross between developmental issues and diagnostic ones.

DEVELOPMENTAL CAREER-FOCUSED COUNSELING

Adult development includes stages of generativity versus stagnation (ages 40–65) and integrity versus despair (ages 65–death; Erikson, 1968). During generativity versus stagnation, tasks include having a vital career and making material and relational contributions to family and society. It is a time where career has been somewhat established, childrearing is well underway, and the individual looks toward making contributions that will outlast them. For many adults, navigating this stage of life can reduce the occurrence of depression (Fadjukoff et al., 2016; Munley, 1975). This stage influenced Super's maintenance stage of career development (ages mid-40s to mid-60s; Super, 1990). During the maintenance stage, individuals work to improve their vocational position, either through promotion and advancement within an organization or moving on to other opportunities. This is a time of growth and stability in the world of work. The result of this stage when the tasks have been well completed is care, or a focus on others. If not successfully navigated, the result is stagnation, or a level of dissatisfaction with the direction of one's life, work, and relationships. This is also a time when counselors encounter clients seeking help.

Integrity versus despair is a stage of development in which individuals are moving toward retirement and reflecting on the course of their life. They ask if their life has been meaningful and if they will leave a lasting legacy. For Super, this is a time of decline in terms of work output or productivity. It is the time beyond working and earning a living and focusing on enjoying the fruits of one's labors. It is a time to shift to unpaid work and volunteering, spending time with family, and preparing for this last stage of life. The results of successfully navigating this stage of life is wisdom, or a conviction of a life well lived. When this stage is not successfully navigated, despair, or a belief that one has missed fulfilling their purpose in life, ensues.

DIAGNOSTIC CAREER-FOCUSED COUNSELING

To better understand the dialectic between career concerns and mental health concerns in adulthood and their implications for counselors, Luke (2018) provides a table conceptualizing

TABLE 14.3 SAMPLE CONCEPTUALIZATION OF DEPRESSION AND CAREER EFFECTS

Depression Criteria/ Symptoms	Implications for Career	Protective Factor
Depressed mood (i.e., sadness or hopelessness)	Affective: decreased motivation in goal orientation, so limited if at all follow through on exploration	Strengths- and interest-based assessments can illuminate possibilities, leading to hope
Decreased interest in what once was pleasurable	Cognitive: interest; affective: pleasure—limited reward for pursuing and attaining goals (feeds back into motivation); fixation on outcomes rather than on process	Bring back to process—not outcome-only pursuits; allows focus on here-and-now experience of joy-evoking activities without the pressure of a result
Appetite and weight loss or gain (i.e., an indicator of poor self-care motivation)	Difficult to perceive career-related tasks when mindful eating is not a priority	Short-term purpose (e.g., informational interviewing, shadowing, or visiting local career office) can trigger self-care (at least in the short-term)
Too sad to sleep or too sad to wake	Increased difficulty focusing on career related tasks when unrested; not waking to completed career-related tasks	Paradoxical intervention of forced waking to develop a list of interests, abilities, skills, etc., which can result in sleep (or helpful lists)
Slow movement or restlessness	Behavioral: either creating such a level of distraction from task or inaction toward task	Career development activities encourage focus and mindfulness
Feelings of being physically drained or exhausted	Basic life tasks take enormous work, so career-related tasks are pushed out of awareness	Small steps in career planning can lead to big results
Low self-worth or guilt that does not fit circumstances	Self-defeating thinking and feelings inhibit the belief that any of this (career-related behaviors) matters	Career-focused counseling encourages meaning-making—not meaning-finding; it must be created—not discovered
Trouble concentrating or making decisions	Cognitive: when the career-related task involves decision-making	Small, specific, concrete, short-term tasks in career development
Thoughts of death, thoughts of killing oneself, or attempts on one's life	In Durkheim's scheme, suicide is the permanent exit from a social system	Career engagement; while not a "cure" for suicide, it invites participation in the social system in tangible ways

the career effects of depression. This table is presented as Table 14.3. Note how the Implications for Career column can be a symptom of depression or a symptom of career-related stress and distress. These deleterious effects of depression on career and work are juxtaposed with protective factors for both depression and career.

In Carlos's case, his career was on track, and he was successfully navigating the tasks associated with healthy career and psychosocial development when the pandemic pulled the proverbial rug out from under him. As counselors, it is important to work with Carlos in navigating his current situation in light of the protective factors or resilience that he has cultivated in his life.

CARLOS IN SESSION

MHC: (second session) It is good to see you this week, Carlos. How are things?

CL: About the same. Should I get into it now?

MHC: I'm ready if you are. I'm interested to hear more about your experience.

CL: I've just been really irritable and frustrated lately. I don't sleep well, and I'm struggling to find any motivation to go to work. And I'm no fun to be around at home.

MHC: And this, you think, is mostly tied to the shift in your work situation last year?

CL: Yeah, I think so because things were good before that.

MHC: And you haven't seen any improvement in your mood; in fact, you seem to be feeling worse. Is that accurate?

CL: Yeah, I'm really trying to figure out if I should stay with this career or if I should make a change. They're saying the computer chip shortage isn't going to improve significantly for the next few years, and that's why cars are being manufactured and shipped.

MHC: Wow, I wasn't aware of that. So you're not seeing a light at the end of the tunnel just yet and are wondering about making a change.

CL: Yes. I'm really too old to do it, but the cut in pay and the decreased satisfaction have really hurt.

MHC: I haven't heard you use the word "hurt" before.

CL: Well, I had to lay off most of my sales force, so as tough as it's been for me, it was terrible sending those folks out into the world without a job. I had invested a lot into their professional development.

MHC: That really is another type of loss that adds to this.

CL: Yeah for sure. I know they got good unemployment checks for a while, but some of them have families and some are trying to build a career.

MHC: Like you.

CL: I thought my career was set. We were saving for retirement, and the kids were set for college.

MHC: It seems like the losses have added up for you, and they're more than just income.

CL: That's for sure.

MHC: It makes sense to me that you would feel despondent, if not outright depressed.

CL: You think?

MHC: Don't you?

CL: I guess I thought I was supposed to just deal with it since tons of people have been affected. I have felt weak for not being able to figure this out and make more money.

MHC: That's a heavy burden to carry and a lot of self-judgment. I wonder if I could share a couple of statistics with you. (MHC goes on to very briefly describe pandemic statistics and effects on mental health and well-being in order to normalize Carlos's sense of loss and self-criticism.) Could we look at some of the other factors in your life that have made you successful?

CL: Sure, I guess.

MHC: Here's what I have heard you say about your life: You have been a good financial provider for your family, you enjoyed being a support for your family, you found meaning in developing your sales staff, and you've been an active contributor to your church and community. Have I missed anything?

CL: I think that's right.

MHC: We can certainly explore alternative career paths, and we can also look at how to enrich your life through the things that build you up.

CL: That sounds good. I really don't want to change my career, but I was feeling desperate.

MHC: I could sense that. But most of the things that brought value into your life still seem to be available—if not exactly how you imagined they would be.

CL: That is true. I would really like to get back to being involved with my family and finding ways to develop staff.

MHC: Well, maybe we can work on those ideas while we also address the negative effects the past year has had on you?

CL: Sounds good.

Carlos's case is complex because of the global crisis that shifted his middle adulthood development. Using a strengths-based approach, the counselor can guide him back to the things that have worked for him in his life to get him to the level of success he has attained. Drawing on his values reminds him there are opportunities for him to continue to invest in others, if not like he had done prior to the pandemic. Carlos appears to be on the edge of the developmental and diagnostic career-focused counseling line. His counselor will work to determine if the toll over the past year has left him depleted to the point of diagnosis, or if this situation is a developmental hurdle that his previous success can help him navigate now.

Neuroscience, Culture, and Development

In this section, we take a closer look at four areas of mental health concerns through the lenses of neuroscience, culture, and development, building on the material presented earlier in this chapter. There is limited research in the literature on career and mental health, though there are some indications of increased attention (see Luke, 2018; the special issue of the *Career Planning and Adult Development* [CPAD], January, 2016).

Consider the eight-factor metamodel applied first to low mood, and imagine that a counselor viewed their role as providing a client with the low-mood "fix." They may tell them the problem is negative thoughts about themselves and situation (i.e., thinking); that they are emotionally unregulated (i.e., feelings); that the problem is behavioral inhibition, and they need to act when they feels depressed (i.e., behaviors); that they have a deficit in important connection with others (i.e., relationships); a result of systemic oppression (i.e., sociocultural milieu); caused by early attachment deficits (i.e., early environment); a result of trauma or toxic stress (i.e., experiences); or that it is a genetic predisposition or health issue (i.e., neuro/biology). Any one or combination of these factors may be true, but knowing this is not necessarily curative in and of itself. In fact, we would hope that the counselor uses restraint in explaining to the client why they are depressed or prescribing interventions right away. The reasons are twofold.

First and foremost, it is quite common in counseling that the presenting problem is not really the problem. Often, it is the safe response to the "What brings you to counseling?" question. It takes time and attunement to offer clients or students a safe space to explore their discomfort and, of primary importance, their own solutions. Anyone can dispense advice about depression or career issues; Instagram and TikTok are absolutely filled with these. Counseling is different in that it meets clients or students at their expressed need and invites them to greater exploration and self-understanding. The second reason is an extension of this first consideration and is the product of our hundreds of hours providing counseling for career concerns. On countless occasions, the presenting concern goes like this, "Can you help me with my resume?" and results in "I'm just so lost about what I should do with my life." The work of career-focused counseling involves engagement. We're not advocating for bait-and-switch marketing, where an individual comes in for a one-session issue, and we convince them to explore their childhood for the next two years. On the contrary, counselors acknowledge the expressed need and build credibility by having resources available. Just as Monte would not give LaKeisha exercise recommendations in the first (or any) session to help her depression, we would not want him to send her to a website for job search advice.

When we think of career development across the lifespan, it is important to understand and contextualize efforts to improve career and work trajectories for individuals. As the percentage of Americans with a bachelor's degree increases (U.S. Census Bureau, 2020), it is natural to make assumptions about the prevalence of Americans with a college degree. However, the reality is that, as of the 2020 census, less than a third of Americans have a college degree, and the numbers for historically underrepresented and marginalized groups is far less. At the same time, many studies of career development and testing of career theories and models take place on college campuses. While the data from these studies is highly valuable, they can paint an unrealistic picture of what career is and means to the "other," vast majority, of Americans without a degree. So as we explore career and mental health over the lifespan in this chapter, it is important to keep these higher education disparities in mind. While theory is indeed helpful for understanding groups, they may say less about the student or client sitting across from you. Researchers like Blustein and Richardson, on the other hand, have used their research to make advances in career development for all. Since other chapters deal with specific school context, our focus here is on mental health settings to make the applications concrete as well as to provide a resource for school counselors, whose primary role tends to fall outside of mental health counseling.

APPRECIATING DIVERSITY—LEVELS OF DIFFERENCES

> CFC draws upon the expertise of the counseling field to approach clients and students as individuals … and individuals in context. There are well-documented differences in mental health and career issues among large diversity groups, including groups differentiated by race, gender, and sexual orientation (MacDonald, 1997). Counseling cannot be fully effective when these issues are minimized or unattended to. At the same time, each individual's experience of these social markers impacts how and to what extent they will contribute to career and mental health issues. It is often the interaction of these factors that create the largest effect on a client's functioning (Slattery & Park, 2011). We also know that within group differences often exceed between-group differences (Pedersen et al., 2015). Additionally, challenges of a particular sub-group are subsumed under a larger social or other factor, such as socioeconomic status (Sue & Sue, 2003). This is especially true in CFC where poverty—driven by un- and under-employment, as well as downward pressure exerted by socio-political systems—create incredible—often virtually insurmountable—barriers to physical, mental, and vocational health and wellness (McAuliffe et al., 2008). As you read about mental health issues in this chapter, please keep these considerations in mind (Luke, 2018).

Swanson's (2002) baseline assumptions provide a guiding compass in the (re) integration of career and mental health into *CFC*:

1. Clients who seek help for issues that are primarily career related are similar on a number of relevant dimensions (e.g., psychological distress) to clients who seek help for other issues.
2. Counseling sessions for clients who seek counseling for primarily career related issues also contain noncareer content, and counseling sessions for clients who seek counseling for noncareer issues also contain career content.
3. Counseling primarily focused on career issues is more effective if salient noncareer issues also are addressed. Similarly, counseling primarily focused on noncareer issues is more effective if salient contextual career issues also are addressed.
4. Counselor and client in-session behaviors are fundamentally similar regardless of whether clients seek help for primary career issues or for noncareer issues (or, more broadly, whether the content of counseling sessions is career or noncareer in nature).
5. The nature and course of therapeutic change is similar regardless of the client's presenting issues.
6. The process of supervision is similar regardless of whether the counselor is delivering counseling that is primarily career or noncareer in nature. (p. 818)

Take Away and Use Today

Career-related concerns and mental health are linked by their mutual influence on one another. Counselors must be mindful of the impact of mental health on the various roles and stages of career development. Likewise, school counselors and career professionals must recognize the warning signs of mental health concerns and their impact on successful resolution of career-related tasks and make appropriate referrals. One of the purposes of this chapter is to emphasize that, because of the reciprocal influence of career and mental health, counselors must pause before referring out to a career specialist and, instead, address these issues in tandem.

References

Ackerman, P. L., & Kanfer, R. (2020). Work in the 21st century: New directions for aging and adult development. *American Psychologist, 75*(4), 486–498. https://psycnet.apa.org/doi/10.1037/amp0000615

Almeida, D. M., Charles, S. T., Mogle, J., Drewelies, J., Aldwin, C. M., Spiro, A., & Gerstorf, D. (2020). Charting adulthood development through (historically changing) daily stress processes. *American Psychologist, 75*, 511–524. http://dx.doi.org/10.1037/amp0000597

American Counseling Association (2014). *2014 ACA code of ethics*. https://www.counseling.org/resources/aca-code-of-ethics.pdf

Anderson, W. P., J., & Niles, S. G. (1995). Career and personal concerns expressed by career counseling clients. *The Career Development Quarterly, 43*(3), 240–245. http://search.proquest.com/docview/219436952?accountid=28833

Arnett, J. J. (2000). Emerging adulthood: A theory of development from the late teens through the twenties. *American Psychologist, 55*, 469–480.

Arnett, J. J. (2004). *Emerging adulthood: The winding road from the late teens through the twenties*. Oxford University Press

Arnett, J. J. (2007). Emerging adulthood: What is it, and what is it good for? *Child Development Perspectives, 1*(2), 68–73. https://doi.org/10.1111/j.1750-8606.2007.00016.x

Arnett, J. J., Robinson, O., & Lachman, M. E. (2020). Rethinking adult development: Introduction to the special issue. *American Psychologist, 75*(4), 425–430. http://dx.doi.org/10.1037/amp0000633

Bowlby, J. (1988). A secure base. Basic Books.

Bronfenbrenner, U. (1977). Toward an experimental ecology of human development. *American Psychologist, 32*(7), 513.

Erikson, E. H. (1968). *Identity: Youth and crisis*. W.W. Norton.

Fadjukoff, P., Pulkkinen, L., & Kokko, K. (2016). Identity formation in adulthood: A longitudinal study from age 27 to 50. *Identity, 16*(1), 8–23. https://doi.org/10.1080/15283488.2015.1121820

Gottfredson, L. S. (2005). Using Gottfredson's theory of circumscription and compromise in career guidance and counseling. In S. D. Brown & R. W. Lent (Eds.), *Career development and counseling: Putting theory and research to work* (pp. 71–100). John Wiley & Sons.

Hebb, D. O. (1949). *The organization of behavior*. Wiley & Sons.

Heppner, M. J., & Heppner, P. P. (2003). Identifying process variables in career counseling: A research agenda. *Journal of Vocational Behavior, 62*(3), 429–452.

Heppner, M. J., O'Brien, K. M., Hinkelman, J. M., & Flores, L. Y. (1996). Training counseling psychologists in career development are we our own worst enemies? *The Counseling Psychologist, 24*(1), 105–125.

Landreth, G. L. (2012). *Play therapy: The art of the relationship*. Routledge.

LeDoux, J. E. (2003). *Synaptic self: How our brains become who we are*. Penguin.

Luke, C. (2018). *Career focused counseling: Integrating theory, research and neuroscience*. Cognella Academic Publishing.

Luke, C., & Schimmel, C. J. (2022). *Applying neuroscience to counseling children and adolescents*. Cognella Academic Publishing.

MacDonald, G. (1997). Issues in multicultural counseling supervision. In: *Caring in an age of technology. Proceedings of the international conference on counseling in the 21st century* (6th ed.).

Marcia, J. E. (1966). Development and validation of ego-identity status. *Journal of Personality and Social Psychology, 3*(5), 551–558. https://doi.org/10.1037/h0023281

McAuliffe, G. (2008). Culturally alert counseling: A comprehensive introduction (Vol. 2). SAGE Publications.

Munley, P. H. (1975). Erik Erikson's theory of psychosocial development and vocational behavior. *Journal of Counseling Psychology, 22*(4), 314. https://doi.org/10.1037/h0076749

Olesen, S. C., Butterworth, P., Leach, L. S., Kelaher, M., & Pirkis, J. (2013). Mental health affects future employment as job loss affects mental health: findings from a longitudinal population study. *BMC Psychiatry, 13*(1), 1–9. https://doi.org/10.1186/1471-244X-13-144

Osborn, D., Belle, J., Gonzalez, A., & McCain, S. C. (2016). Linking career and mental health concerns through technology. *Career Planning and Adult Development Journal*. Retrieved from https://diginole.lib.fsu.edu/islandora/object/fsu:543800/datastream/PDF/view

Pace, D., & Quinn, L. (2000). Empirical support of the overlap between career and mental health counseling of university students. *Journal of College Student Psychotherapy, 14*(3), 4–50.

Panksepp, J., & Biven, L. (2012). *The archeology of the mind: Neuroevolutionary origins of human emotions.* Norton.

Panksepp, J., Lane, R. D., Solms, M., & Smith, R. (2017). Reconciling cognitive and affective neuroscience perspectives on the brain basis of emotional experience. *Neuroscience & Biobehavioral Reviews, 76,* 187–215. https://doi.org/10.1016/j.neubiorev.2016.09.010

Pedersen, P. B., Lonner, W. J., Draguns, J. G., Trimble, J. E., & Scharron-del Rio, M. R. (2015). *Counseling across cultures.* SAGE Publications.

Pfefferbaum, B., & North, C. S. (2020). Mental health and the COVID-19 pandemic. *New England Journal of Medicine, 383*(6), 510–512. https://10.1056/NEJMp2008017

Piaget, J. (1952). *The origins of intelligence in children.* International Universities Press.

Piaget, J., & Inhelder, B. (1969). *The psychology of the child.* Basic Books.

Robitschek, C., & DeBell, C. (2002). The reintegration of vocational psychology and counseling psychology Training issues for a paradigm shift. *The Counseling Psychologist, 30*(6), 801–814.

Rogers, C. R. (1959). A theory of therapy, personality, and interpersonal relationships, as developed from a client-centered framework. In S. Koch (Ed.), *Psychology: A study of a science. Vol. 3: Formulations of the person and the social context* (pp. 184–256). McGraw-Hill.

Rogers, D. R., & Whiston, S. C. (2014). Qualitative analysis of clinical notes do counselors ignore work and academic concerns? *Journal of Career Assessment, 22*(2), 207–220.

Rudolph, C. W., Allan, B., Clark, M., Hertel, G., Hirschi, A., Kunze, F., Shockley, K., Shoss, M., Sonnentag, S., & Zacher, H. (2021). Pandemics: Implications for research and practice in industrial and organizational psychology. *Industrial and Organizational Psychology, 14*(1–2), 1–35.

Savickas, M. L. (2002). Career construction: A developmental theory of vocational behavior. In D. Brown & Associates (Eds.), *Career choice and development* (4th ed., pp. 149–205). Jossey-Bass.

Sharf, R. S. (2013. Applying career development theory to counseling. Cengage.

Siviy, S. M. (2016). A brain motivated to play: insights into the neurobiology of playfulness. *Behaviour, 153*(6–7), 819–844. https://doi.org/10.1163/1568539X-00003349

Slattery, J. M., & Park, C. L. (2011). *Empathic counseling: Meaning, context, ethics, and skill.* Brooks/Cole.

Sue, D. W., & Sue, D. (2003). *Counseling the culturally diverse* (5th ed.). John Wiley & Sons.

Super, D. E. (1957). *The psychology of careers: An introduction to vocational development.* Harper & Bros.

Super, D. E. (1980). A life-span, life-space approach to career development. *Journal of Vocational Behavior, 16*(3), 282–298. https://doi.org/10.1016/0001-8791(80)90056-1

Super, D. E. (1990). A life-span, life-space to career development. In D. Brown, L. Brooks, & Associates (Ed.), *Career choice and development* (2nd ed., pp. 197–261). Jossey-Bass.

Swanson, J. L. (2002). Understanding the complexity of clients' lives infusing a truly integrative career-personal perspective into graduate training. *The Counseling Psychologist, 30*(6), 815–832.

Tang, M., Montgomery, M. L., Collins, B., & Jenkins, K. (2021). Integrating career and mental health counseling: Necessity and strategies. *Journal of Employment Counseling, 58*(1), 23–35. https://doi.org/10.3390/ijerph13080797

U.S. Census Bureau. (2020). Educational Attainment in the United States: 2019. *Current Population Survey Annual Social and Economic Supplement.* Retrieved from https://www.census.gov/newsroom/press-releases/2020/educational-attainment.html

CHAPTER 15

Career in Crisis

Chad Luke, Rachael Marshall, and Melinda Gibbons

CHAPTER GOALS

- Present the connection between crisis, trauma, mental health, and career development.
- Discuss career-focused counseling in a global context.
- Explore the history of the global economy and career counseling.
- Apply relevant theory such as trauma-informed care (TIC) to work with career-focused clients.

OPENING VIGNETTE

Qiu Li is a 24-year-old international student from China. She is a business major and found herself stranded in her dorm room during the pandemic. She was both worried about her family in China and dedicated to her studies. Due to institutional and federal policy changes, she was unsure if she would be able to stay in the United States and, if she left, if or when she would be able to return to complete her studies. The university also depopulated the campus except for international students, and all classes went online. While some students had the privilege to take time off, most international students had to continue classes or be sent back to their native home due to visa regulations. With varied responses to the pandemic, every country had different policies on quarantine, social distancing, and travel bans. Qiu Li comes to you with graduation in mind but feeling unable to gain employment. She is anxious about student, employer, and faculty interactions, and she is unsure where to start. She began her international school experience with so much hope, but now she feels lost and stuck.

REFLECTION ACTIVITIES AND QUESTIONS

Consider your time and experience with COVID-19—how it impacted yourself and those around you. What do you recall about the impact on work and career? What changes did you note as the world slowed and stopped?

Introduction

The world of work is ever-evolving, changing in response to global, technological, and environmental factors. Workers, too, must evolve in response to these ecological changes. Those who adapt can surf the waves and thrive, while those who cannot may be crushed by the weight of these changes. In this chapter, we address several work-related mutations and permutations within the world of work as well as the ways in which these changes affect workers. Some of the changes include new-wave globalization, job creation, loss as a result of technological advancements, and the effects of trauma and crisis on the ability to adapt. We also explore how crises and trauma are interwoven within the lives of individuals and are, therefore, essential knowledge domains for career-focused counselors. Included in this chapter is a description of the effects of the COVID-19 pandemic and the recent and future fallout for the world of work and of workers.

Career-Focused Counseling in a Global, Technological Economy

While the focus of this chapter is on COVID, the pandemic occurred within the context of our current world context. *Globalization* is the process by which businesses or other organizations develop international influence or start operating on an international scale. In a globalized economy, multiple systems are at work in career decisions, and these current systems were founded by colonization. A historical perspective of globalization demonstrates sociocultural and socioeconomic development. For example, the 14th amendment abolishing slavery was ratified on December 6, 1865, yet socioeconomic and legal values did not reflect this change. Juneteenth (June 19th, 1866—now a Federal Holiday) marks the first anniversary of the day that Black Americans in Texas first learned of the Emancipation Proclamation, a full two and a half years after its signing. Federal troops arrived in Galveston, Texas in 1865 to take control and ensure all enslaved people were freed. The Jim Crow era followed and impacted safety, social mobility, education access, and employment opportunities for Black Americans, while simultaneously ensuring that generational wealth was maintained in White communities through land ownership, entrepreneurial endeavors, and redlining policies.

However, despite race restrictive policy and White supremacist sociocultural values in the 1920s, Tulsa, Oklahoma arose as the "Black Wall Street" (Albright et al., 2021). Tulsa was nationally recognized for its affluent Black American community in the Greenwood District, with both thriving businesses and residential communities. On the morning of June 1, 1921, Greenwood was looted and burned by White rioters. The violence continued for 24 hours with 35 city blocks burned, 800 people treated for injuries, and what historians now believe may be as many as 300 people dead (Tulsa Historical Society & Museum, 2021; Messer, 2021). This was later referred to as the Tulsa Race Massacre, and while there were many examples of racial violence, this is an important example to help understand the complexities of how sociocultural norms, legal policy, and race and ethnicity impact the economics of the world of work.

One of the largest impacts on economic development was home ownership; nearly every Black-owned business and home was burned or destroyed. This resulted in the permanent destruction of assets, buildings, and capital integral to employment, economic freedom, and upward mobility. This also had impacts outside of Oklahoma, as the narrative after the event placed blame for the massacre on the Black community (in fall 1921, the *Tulsa World* ran an article entitled, "Grand Jury Blames Negroes for Inciting Race Rioting: Whites Clearly Exonerated"). This increased fears of future violence in response to Black economic success happening again with no consequences for White terrorists. Four decades of research demonstrate these side effects of racial trauma on career aspirations and expectations (Dillard, 1980; Evans & Herr, 1991; Leong & Leong, 2014). While aspirations can be higher or lower based on socioeconomic status, geography, and gender, goal completion expectations remain low (Evans & Herr, 1991; Leong & Leong, 2014). The ways in which policy, laws, and sociocultural consequences favor colonizers impact all individuals within globalized systems.

Globalized economies depend on continuous growth. While globalization has been shown to improve incomes of individuals around the world, some findings show that there are clear winners and losers predicted by colonization (Mills, 2009). Globalization has been shown to accentuate inequality both within and between countries and, conversely, disintegrate national borders and prompt economic integration for those that can either afford it or are powerful enough to engage with it (Mills, 2009). Globalization, therefore, presents both an opportunity for continuing pathways for those with power and privilege and the potential to carve new pathways for populations that have been marginalized and colonized in the past.

Globalization has also pushed and been pushed by advances in technology. Technology has increased the interconnectedness of all workers but has also exacerbated the inequities of separating those who can and cannot afford the most updated technology. New industries are created based on large technological advancements; however, new technology has also destroyed some jobs and markets. For example, mass production and assembly lines are becoming more automated with less individual workers needed, thinning positions that used to be considered "lifelong jobs." More automation creates the need for specialized professions, increasing the need for education and trade schools.

The changes in technology have not only impacted work but also education. Qiu Li's case illustrates how multiple systems can impact and complicate trauma for career focused clients. Technology has brought both advancements and challenges; while we can find information and people at the touch of a button, we can also find and spread misinformation and pain. The development of internet, mobile communications, and social networks influences lifestyle, daily life, learning modes, and career futures (Maree, 2017). This also creates opportunities to find information; companionship; discourse; and professional career, mental and physical health services (Galliott, 2017). The internet offers career counselors another avenue to provide services through the use of digital tests, resources, and online HIPPA compliant counseling services (Pordelan et al., 2018).

The consistent strain of an ever-evolving health care crisis and racial trauma make trauma-informed care (TIC) an important tool for career-focused counseling. TIC is a lens through which to view experiences that embraces the understanding that most people have experienced some type of trauma in their lives, including themselves. As the pandemic has impacted everyone globally, racial trauma contextualizes the experiences of clients, it is essential for TIC to be used to prevent retraumatization and help clients engage in self-care, "Caring for myself is not self-indulgence. It is self-preservation, and that is an act of political warfare" (Lorde, 1988, p. 103).

Qiu Li tells you that she experienced extreme stress during this time both with school and family. The initial stress of isolation and online learning was complicated by experiences of microaggressions, both on and off campus. As a business major, she had many team projects and needed more group communication. Her instructor allowed students to form groups on their own, but she felt like no group wanted to include her. Eventually, the instructor had to put her into a group, but she felt they accepted her reluctantly; none of her opinions were put into the final presentation, and her grade was lower than her group members, as they reported she did not turn on her camera and was quiet. She noticed many of her American friends seemed to cut ties with her suddenly, including her roommate.

The current labor market is more unpredictable than it was decades ago, or even two years ago; there are fewer safe spaces for young people to explore (Maree, 2020), there is less security, there are fewer linear trajectories (Larson, 2011), and there are far more career transitions (Herr, 2008). This unpredictability has been exacerbated and magnified by the impact of the COVID-19 pandemic (Akkermans et al., 2020). Maree (2020) explored how technological and industrial advancements impacted career helping professions, specifically illustrating the shared values of the time (see Table 15.1). We have adapted the table to include helping profession values and socioeconomic values to help understand this course of change and transition and the stress it brings.

Presently, career-focused counselors are engaging with multiple systems of privilege and marginalization within the working lives of themselves and their clients. Workers are challenged to blend work and life roles and become and remain employable, career resilient, and career relevant in a continuously changing world (Maree, 2020). Career-focused counseling is connected to mental health and wellness as well as global economy changes. Counselors must consider global occupational trends, technological advances, and social, cultural, and political changes in order to help clients adapt and thrive.

The main global challenges that impact workers are technological advancements and the ramifications of COVID-19. The changes in technology have not only created new industries and jobs but also created new ways to work. Qiu Li's case illustrates how multiple systems can impact and complicate trauma for career-focused clients. Technology has brought both advancements and challenges; while we can find information and people at the touch of a button, we can also find and spread misinformation and pain. The development of internet, mobile communications, and social networks influences lifestyle, daily life, learning modes, and career futures (Maree, 2017). This also creates opportunities to find information,

TABLE 15.1 HELPING PROFESSION AND SOCIOECONOMIC VALUES COMPARISON

Timeframe	Helping Profession Values	Socioeconomic Values
1770–1830: Industrial Revolution	Informal helpers or volunteers—one-size-fits-all approach; people expected to be the same (Savickas, 2011)	Eurocentric; land was central to make a living; work was an extension of the work from parents; children (workers) by and large stayed on the farms of their parents.
1830–1880: steam and railways	Vocational guidance—general information	Mass manufacturing was growing; increased work in cities; new job growth; less laws protecting workers
1880–1910: steel, electricity, and engineering	Helping model—career education and guidance; test used more to find matches to work and actualize themselves	Automation of work; increased specialized training to work; idea of promotion and "working up the ladder"
1910–1990: automobile, oil, and mass production	Authoring, creating, developing career identity; self-construction in chaos	Rapid technological and artificial intelligence development; less long term jobs; increased focus on networking and connection; workers' rights developments
1990–Present: information and telecommunications	Designers of "self"; career aided by technology; integration of self, work, and mental health; social justice	Wellness in work; tele-counseling and health services; new technology; focus on adaptability, resilience, and creativity; the rise of technology gave rise to more discussion on social justice and equity in work structures

companionship, discourse, and professional career, mental, and physical health services (Galliott, 2017).

Career-Focused Counseling in a COVID-19 Context

The quick spread of COVID-19 and new regulations to survive resulted in life-altering employment shifts across the globe. Workers internationally faced drastic vocational changes, such as sudden and unexpected job loss (U.S. Bureau of Labor Statistics, 2020) and adjustment to working and learning virtually and in isolation. Essential workers (those still working in person during the pandemic) faced both psychological stress from continuing their work with new regulations such as: social distancing, protective gear, and constant sanitizing and the emotional stress from the public health threat to themselves, friends and family (CDC, 2020). The COVID-19 outbreak exacerbated existing issues of racism in the U.S. higher education system. The rise in Sinophobia (anti-Chinese sentiment) during the Pandemic threatens to increase the number of racially traumatic experiences for Asian international students (Nam et al., 2021), like Qiu Li's experiences.

The Pandemic caused a *career shock* (Akkermans et al., 2020). A career shock is an event that is disruptive and extraordinary, caused by factors outside of an individual's control that trigger deliberate thought processes about career development (Akkermans et al., 2015). To be a career shock, an event must prompt a sensemaking process; not every event will cause reevaluation of career. For example, losing a coworker could be a career shock for one person but not another. In this same way COVID-19, racial trauma, grief, isolation, job loss or risk, and distance learning or working can feel like a career shock to some, but not everyone will intensely evaluate their current career.

With this in mind, how can counselors help? Research has shown that strengthening self-management and agency can promote healthy career decisions during a career shock (Seibvert et al., 2013) as can promoting safe environments (Hirschi & Valero, 2017). There is a dynamic interplay between career behaviors, personalities, competencies, and circumstances (Schneidhofer et al., 2019). Therefore, as counselors we can help clients focus on career identity, autonomy, and emotional and psychological management on an individual level to impact career behaviors. We can aid our clients in understanding their personalities and career competencies. Then, we can also do work to strengthen the environment surrounding our clients to make sure they feel safe—not just in our office but also across levels of policy and practice.

As stated before, trauma and career shock depend on each individual's response. Therefore, things like unemployment, work and mental health balance, wellness, work and family interface, and employment disparities can impact individuals differently. It is imperative that counselors work to help clients through a career shock or trauma by creating safe environments, individually and systemically, to process career decisions. With the mixture of racism and COVID-19 development, it is essential that career-focused counselors also work to support and develop policy to protect clients both institutionally and nationally.

Theory has evolved with world events, and the COVID-19 pandemic has created lasting changes to every facet of our global society. From the very start, career-focused counseling has worked to help people live better lives through occupational fit. Research has shown the interconnected nature of career and wellness (Blustein, 2006; Kramer & Chung, 2015; Whiston & Cinamon, 2015). Stress, anxiety, trauma, and ambiguity in work environments can impact mental health and wellness, and vice versa. For example, Ford et al. (2011) found, in a meta-analysis of multiple studies, that depression, anxiety, and fatigue were negatively correlated to work performance and that life satisfaction was positively related to work performance. We know that what happens in our lives impacts what happens in our work. After COVID-19, there is an increased interest in the importance of wellness in the realm of career.

The time of COVID-19 was not only a healthcare crisis but also inundated with racial trauma. The United States saw increases in racial violence, police violence, and anti-immigrant policy (Fallows, 2020). In the midst of the Pandemic, which disproportionately impacted Black, Indigenous, and People of Color (BIPOC; CDC, 2020), there were simultaneously protests against police violence and a significant increase in Asian hate crimes (Aydin, 2020; McCarthy, 2020). Counselors are, more than ever, dealing with the question of promoting wellness in others and oneself. Table 15.2 offers a summary of the impact of the pandemic.

TABLE 15.2 SUMMARY OF COVID-19 IMPACTS AND PRACTICE/POLICY RECOMMENDATIONS

Impact	Practice Recommendations	Policy Recommendations	TIC Considerations
Unemployment	• Be knowledgeable about current policies. • Educate clients about their rights and benefits. • Support clients through the process of accessing benefits. • Provide interventions that are appropriate for populations with restricted work choice. • Implement targeted interventions for specific worker groups (e.g., older adults).	• Support collective action on the part of career development professional organizations • Provide widespread and sustained economic support for unemployed workers. • Create social safety nets that include a paycheck guarantee. • Implement targeted interventions for specific worker groups (e.g., older adults).	• Create safe environments in session, and promote that safety in our professional organizations, economic systems, and policy. • Create specific opportunities for marginalized populations to feel safe.
Worker mental health & wellness	• Integrate mental health services into career counseling. • Use trauma-informed approaches to career counseling. • Use interventions that target basic survival, social, and self-determination needs.	• Expand mental health service delivery, especially access to telehealth services at the state and federal level. • Expand family and sick leave for essential workers at the state and federal level.	• Create connections between family, friends, networks, and support systems. • Promote TIC in multiple systems. • Target emotional management and regulation.
Work–family interface	• Recognize unique needs of each individual/family. • Assess for access to resources and the extent to which restricted access impacts work family relations.	• Create opportunities for decent work that affirms importance of family relationships. • Disentangle work from financial sustainability. • Provide financial and health care support for unpaid care workers.	• Evaluate and support healthy social systems, and aid clients in critiquing systems. • Aid clients in managing emotions, using coping techniques and by confronting emotions that are uncomfortable.
Employment disparities	• Work with community partners to assess needs. • Incorporate a critical lens into career counseling conceptualization and interventions.	• Work with community partners to assess needs. • Develop targeted supports for low-resourced communities. • Provide accessible COVID-19 testing and treatment centers. • Strengthen protections for essential workers.	• Expand safe spaces with community partnerships. • Evaluate connections and systems of oppression and support. • Promote infusing TIC into workers' rights and protections.

Note. Adapted from Austin et al. 2020, p. 488.

Trauma-Informed Career-Focused Counseling

An individual's ability to cope with a traumatic event (either directly or indirectly) is moderated by contextual factors, such as social support, personality variables, cognitive functioning, preexisting psychological conditions, behavioral capacities, and the duration and intensity of the trauma (Powers & Duys, 2020). Trauma is anything that has overwhelmed an individual's ability to process and integrate what has happened to them (Van der Kolk, 2003). Symptoms may include nightmares, flashbacks, inability to concentrate, headaches, panic attacks, and hypervigilance (Schnyder, 2016).

Racial trauma is a mental crisis that results when an individual (a) encounters an event or adverse incident that produces toxic stress (Anderson & Stevenson, 2020); (b) experiences the adverse incident in a way that is dependent on their individual genetics, neurodevelopment, health, resilience, and protective factors (Ota et al., 2019); and (c) demonstrates effects from this psychological trauma (Griffin, 2020). These factors can be dependent on how the individuals encounter and experience any type of trauma.

Trauma-informed care (TIC) can be used from individuals to policy makers to develop a strengths-based framework to improve wellness and decrease retraumatization. TIC is a way to organize responses to trauma by addressing physical, psychological, and emotional issues through what Bath (2008) termed "the three pillars of safety, connection, and emotion management":

1. **Safety:** Safety requires consistency, reliability, predictability, and transparency to boost safe environments. However, safety relies on connection to maintain positive interactions. Safety relies on connection.
2. **Connection:** Maintain positive interactions. These positive interactions support managing emotions.
3. **Managing emotions:** This fortifies an ability to engage in impulse control and self-regulation and produces opportunities for victimized individuals to gain empowerment and control. (Bath, 2008)

TIC ensures people are supported before, during, and after trauma and reduces the risk of retraumatization (Bath, 2008). TIC outlines vicarious trauma and trigger responses for both the client that has been victimized and the helpers working with them (Hopper et al., 2010). TIC emphases safety and encourages precautions to prevent retraumatization by promoting opportunities to rebuild control by creating safe environments (Hopper et al., 2010). TIC embraces a strengths-based approach, rather than a deficient-oriented model when engaging in the realm of trauma. Strength-based environments in TIC aid in the development of new coping skills and empowerment. Specifically, by creating environments and relationships built on safety, connection, and emotional management (Hopper et al., 2010).

Since TIC rests on the premise that everyone has experienced some sort of trauma, it also promotes the wellness of those practicing. For this entire chapter, you have read about stressful and anxiety-producing situations. Take a moment and check in with our body. Where is your stress sitting; sometimes we feel it in our shoulders as we scrunch them up to our neck; other times we feel it in our stomach, and we try to quell the feeling with food; and other times we feel it in our head and face and notice more headaches and tension. Trauma and stress sit with each of us, and we have to know how to engage with it in meaningful ways. To do this, we require safety, connection to others, and emotional management. Unless you have been traveling intergalactically, you have had some form of interaction with COVID-19, directly or indirectly, emotionally, psychologically, or socially, in some way the pandemic has shifted some part of your life. In this sense we have all experienced the trauma associated with the pandemic, and we all require safe places to explore our pain, connect to people willing to connect with us, and the ability to regulate our emotions (e.g., naming them, processing them, and holding space for them when appropriate). Trauma-informed care (TIC) is essential when encountering individuals in the time of COVID-19.

TAKE A MINUTE

Before moving into the next section that explores COVID-19 with more depth, take a moment and breathe ... in for 5, hold for 7, and out for 9. If you can, inhale through your nose and blow out through your mouth. Do this breathing 3–5 times. Then, take a moment to recognize the differences in your body.

QIU LI IN SESSION

Outside of the university she felt more fear in public—not just due to safety concerns but also due to the increase attached on Asian individuals. Qui Li noted feeling uncomfortable going outside and would try to stay in her room. "My daily life was just staring at a computer screen, writing endless assignments, and I started feeling sadder and sadder." On her last visit to the grocery store, while she was walking down the street, a man opened his car windows and yelled, "Go back" and then threw a paper cup at her. "I felt startled and threatened. The worst part was everyone saw it, and everyone ignored it. I felt completely alone."

A week later at a nearby university, a Chinese international graduate student was shot. After hearing of this, Qui Li started experiencing insomnia, headaches, and trouble concentrating. After this, she started paying extra for delivery and still leaves her dorm as little as possible.

As is often the case in career-focused counseling, sessions are rarely purely about career choice. Instead, career choice is embedded in layers of culture and experience.

> CO: Thank you for taking the time to expand on your experiences throughout this past year and a half. It could not have been easy to talk with a stranger about these things (Qiu smiles and looks down.). Could I ask how you are feeling about the decision to seek support for finding a starting point for work after graduation?
>
> CL: It's embarrassing to share these things as my experiences are shameful. I feel like I should be able to make career choices on my own.

CO: That's a lot that you're dealing with. You mentioned shame. I think of shame as embarrassment in public. Could you say more about that shame?

CL: My parents want me to move home to Beijing and find work, but want to try living here (the Northern United States). If I would move home I would make my family happy, I could find work and experience less anti-Chinese sentiment.

CO: I can sense your inner conflict in just listing those things, which on their own may be reasonable arguments to move back. But that's not what you want.

CL: I feel like there are more opportunities for professional success here.

CO: Okay. That seems like a strong reason to stay.

CL: But, the last year has been difficult and I don't feel confident like I once did.

CO: You've described a number of circumstances that would have that effect on most people, I think. CO recalls Qui's description of isolation on campus, estrangement from group members in class projects, verbal aggressions from people in the community in response to the "China virus."

CL: I used to be better at making decisions, like coming to the U.S. for my senior year of high school and then college. But these things have left me feeling unsure how to begin to make the transition from college to work.

CO: That really sounds like a difficult loss of confidence. How do you imagine that I might be helpful to you in this process?

CL: I'm unsure.

CO: That's totally natural. What was it that made you decide to make this appointment and follow through by coming in?

CL: What made me decide to come in was the graduation notice from the university. That cemented for me that I'm graduating soon and must make a decision. I've been having trouble sleeping, and I don't have an appetite since.

CO: Okay, so it sounds like this decision, or set of decisions, is beginning to affect your body because it feels somewhat urgent?

CL: It is urgent that I figure this out.

CO: I feel that from you. And you'd like some help taking the next steps to obtaining a job?

CL: Yes, I'm struggling to get started.

CO: May I start then by asking a simple-sounding question?

CL: Sure, go ahead.

CO: When it comes to work and what's next, what do you *want* to do?

CL: I want to get a good job.

CO: Okay, so any job will do?

CL: Well, preferably in my major: business.

CO: Okay, business is still pretty broad. What to do with business?

CL: I enjoy the idea of managing projects.

CO: Okay, great. What is it you like about that?

CL: I'm really organized and detail oriented.

CO: So a job where you would get to use those would be good for you?

CL: I think so, but I don't know what those jobs are. and I'm scared of getting rejected.

CO: Okay, that is good to know there are two big questions for you: What jobs will fit me? And will I get rejected? Both are important with potentially scary answers.

CL: Definitely! What if there are no jobs suited for me, and I have to take whatever, and I fail at that?

CO: (Noticing that Qiu is pink-faced and seems stressed about the clarification of her fears) I wonder if we could take a second to pause to do something very different? (Qiu nods.)

Counselor now takes her through a brief grounding exercise to help her feel safer and calmer in the moment. They spend the remaining part of the session, using the information Qiu has provided to conduct basic Web searches, beginning with CareerOneStop to generate leads on where Qiu can begin to explore before their next meeting. She leaves the session with a detailed, concrete plan (suits her style) to explore highly conventional career options (from Holland code). Notice that throughout the interaction, the counselor is working to establish a basis for *safety* and *connection* to build capacity for *managing emotions*.

Neuroscience, Culture, and Development

Stressful events are generally remembered well, but exposure to an aversive experience has also been reported to impair the acquisition, storage and retrieval of novel information?" (Alfarez, et al., 2003, p. 1928). Stress-trauma is both an external event where demand exceeds resources as well as an internal experience of both perception and physiology (Garrett, 2011). There is the stress that people bring with them to the work situation (i.e., trauma history), positive stress (i.e., globalization), tolerable stress (i.e., technological advancements), and toxic stress (i.e., work in a time of COVID-19). Stressors can include stress that winds us up (i.e., acute/immediate), stress that wears us down (i.e., chronic/over time), stress that feeds on itself (i.e., stress about stress; attitudes), and contextual stress. One research paradigm used to understand stress in these dimensions is chronic variable stress (CVS), where "CVS is ... recurrent physical, psychological and social stress that is unpredictable and unavoidable" (Cordner & Tamashiro, 2016). "When the individual feels safe and the system is working as intended, the prefrontal cortex is in control. This is the so-called top-down process, wherein responses to environmental cues are balanced between environmental awareness and cognitive appraisal. In essence, it is the brain's rational response system ... the brain under threat from stress ... Reactions to these threats do not require rational responding but instead speed in moving toward safety" (Luke & Schimmel, 2022). Stress shrinks the dendrites in the DMS, where goal-directed learning and memory are governed, and increases the dendrites in the LMS, where habitual learning and memory is governed leads to compulsivity (Taylor et al., 2014). When people are put in situations where they experience recurrent physical, psychological, and social stress that is unpredictable and unavoidable (e.g., the COVID-19 pandemic), their capacity for goal-directed learning and memory diminishes, resulting in increased habitual learning and memory, which leads to fight, flight, freeze, or faint reactions. This leads to difficulties in decision-making behaviors. Purves et al. (2018) describe behaviors this way: "[B]ehavior is not limited to motor actions but also includes perception, attention, emotion, memory, and more. ... [B]ehavior depends not just on sensory input, but on remembered information, goals, and prediction about what might happen. ... Estimating the value of an option involves perceiving sensory properties, identifying the situation, and retrieving information about past experiences with similar contexts from memory (pp. 724–727). Given the events of the world over the last century and, in particular, the last two years, it is important that we ask how this might look with career or work-related behaviors. Therefore, chronic variable stress (Cordner & Tamashiro, 2016) and the stress continuum of positive, tolerable, and toxic (Shonkoff et al., 2012) serve to inform the discussion of global, technological, and pandemic-related stress. These stressors can be seen in the cycle of global and technological changes, which affect workers both positively and negatively.

Take Away and Use Today

Now more than ever counselors must be trauma-informed in order to practice well. Trauma in career-focused counseling wears many guises, including workplace shifts resulting in un- or underemployment, global shifts in health or economics, personal history of trauma that affects work life, abrupt shifts in technology, and much more. Many of the clients and students with whom we work live in contexts that are disruptive to the developmental processes of career and work; therefore, counselors must be ready to respond by seeing into the presenting concern and supporting the whole person.

References

1921 Tulsa Race Massacre. Tusla Historical Society and Museum. Retreived from https://www.tulsa-history.org/exhibit/1921-tulsa-race-massacre/

Akkermans, J., Brenninkmeijer, V., Schaufeli, W. B., & Blonk, R. W. (2015). It's all about CareerSKILLS: Effectiveness of a career development intervention for young employees. *Human Resource Management, 54*(4), 533–551. https://doi.org/10.1002/hrm.21633

Akkermans, J., Richardson, J., & Kraimer, M. (2020). The COVID-19 crisis as a career shock: Implications for careers and vocational behavior. *Journal of Vocational Behavior, 119*. https://doi.org/10.1016/j.jvb.2020.103434

Albright, A., Cook, J. A., Feigenbaum, J. J., Kincaide, L., Long, J., & Nunn, N. (2021). *After the burning: the economic effects of the 1921 Tulsa Race Massacre* (No. w28985). National Bureau of Economic Research.

Anderson, R. E., & Stevenson, H. C. (2019). RECASTing racial stress and trauma: Theorizing the healing potential of racial socialization in families. *American Psychologist, 74*, 63–75. https://doi.org/10.1037/amp0000392

Aydin, S. (2020). *Why universities need to actively combat Sinophobia*. University World News. https://www.universityworldnews.com/post.php?story=20200616105836478.

Bath, H. (2008). The three pillars of trauma-informed care. *Reclaiming Children and Youth, 17*(3), 17–21.

Blustein, D. L. (2006). The psychology of working: A new perspective for career development, counseling, and public policy. Erlbaum.

Center for Disease Control and Prevention (2020). *Health equity considerations and racial and ethnic minority groups*. U.S. Department of Health and Human Services. https://www.cdc.gov/coronavirus/2019-ncov/community/health-equity/raceethnicity.html

Cordner, Z. A., & Tamashiro, K. L. K. (2016). Effects of chronic variable stress on cognition and Bace1 expression among wild-type mice. *Translational Psychiatry, 6*(7), e854–e854. https://doi.org/10.1038/tp.2016.127

Dillard, J. M. (1980). Some unique career behavior characteristics of blacks: Career theories, counseling practice, and research. *Journal of Employment Counseling, 17*(2), 288–298. https://doi.org/10.1002/j.2161-1920.1980.tb01206.x

Evans, K. M., & Herr, E. L. (1994). The influence of racial identity and the perception of discrimination on the career aspirations of African American men and women. *Journal of Vocational Behavior, 44*(2), 173–184. https://doi.org/10.1006/jvbe.1994.1012

Fallows, J. (2020). A reporter's notebook. A 2020 time capsule. *The Atlantic*. https://www.theatlantic.com/notes/all/2020/03/trump-time-capsule-2020/607897/

Ford, M. T., Cerasoli, C. P., Higgins, J. A., & Decesare, A. L. (2011). Relationships between psychological, physical, and behavioural health and work performance: A review and meta-analysis. *Work & Stress, 25*, 185–204. https://doi.org/10.1080/02678373.2011.609035

Galliott, N. Y. (2017). Online career guidance: Does knowledge equate to power for high school students? *Journal of Psychologists and Counsellors in Schools, 27*(2), 190. https://dio10.1017/jgc.2017.7

Garrett, B. (2011). Brain & behavior: An introduction to biological psychology (3rd ed.). Sage.

Griffin, G. (2020). Defining trauma and a trauma-informed COVID-19 response. *Psychological Trauma: Theory, Research, Practice, and Policy, 12*(S1), S279. http://dx.doi.org/10.1037/tra0000828.

Herr, E. L. (2008). Social contexts for career guidance throughout the world. In J. A. Athanasou & R. Van Esbroeck (eds.) *International handbook of career guidance* (pp. 45–67). Springer.

Hirschi, A., & Valero, D. (2017). Chance events and career decidedness: Latent profiles in relation to work motivation. *The Career Development Quarterly, 65*(1), 2–15. https://doi.org/10.1002/cdq.12076

Hopper, K., Bassuk, E. L., & Olivet, J. (2010). Shelter from the Storm: Trauma-informed care in homelessness services settings. *The Open Health Services and Policy Journal, 3*(1): 80–100.

Kramer, A., & Chung, W. (2015). Work demands, family demands, and BMI in dual-earners families: A 16-year longitudinal study. *Journal of Applied Psychology, 100*(5), 1632. https://doi.org/10.1037/a0038634

Larson, R. W. (2011). Positive development in a disorderly world. *Journal of Research on Adolescence, 21*(2), 317–334. https://doi.org/10.1111/j.1532-7795.2010.00707.x

Leong, F. T., & Leong, F. (2014). *Career development and vocational behavior of racial and ethnic minorities.* Routledge.

Lorde, A. (2017). A burst of light: Living with cancer. In A. Lorde (ed.) *Feminist theory and the body* (pp. 149–152). Routledge.

Luke, C., & Schimmel, C. J. (2022). *Neuroscience for child and adolescent counselors.* Cognella.

Maree, J. G. K. (2020). How global change necessitates innovation in career counseling: Linking economic, industrial, psychology, and career counseling waves. In J. Maree (ed.) *Innovating Counseling for Self-and Career Construction* (pp. 67–84). Springer. https://doi.org/10.1007/978-3-030-48648-8_4

Maree, K. (2017). Utilizing career adaptability and career resilience to promote employability and decent work and alleviate poverty. In K. Maree (ed.) *Psychology of career adaptability, employability and resilience* (pp. 349–373). Springer.

McCarthy, S. (2020). *Coronavirus: Chinese students battle rising tide of prejudice in US but fear they may not be welcomed home.* The Coronavirus Pandemic. https://www.scmp.com/news/china/article/3079877/coronavirus-means-chinese-students-battle-rising-tide-prejudice-us-fear

Messer, C. M. (2021). Causes of the Tulsa Race Massacre. In *The 1921 Tulsa Race Massacre* (pp. 33–53). Palgrave Macmillan.

Mills, M. (2009). Globalization and inequality. *European Sociological Review, 25*(1), 1–8. https://doi.org/10.1093/esr/jcn046

Nam, B. H., Marshall, R. C., Tian, X., & Jiang, X. (2021). "Why universities need to actively combat Sinophobia": racially-traumatic experiences of Chinese international students in the United States during COVID-19. *British Journal of Guidance & Counselling*, 1–15. https://doi.org/10.1080/03069885.2021.1965957

Ota, M., Nemoto, K., Ishida, I., Sato, S., Asada, T., Arai, T., & Kunugi, H. (2019). Structural brain network correlated with the resilience to traumatic events in the healthy participants: An MRI study on healthy people in a stricken area of the Great East Japan Earthquake. *Psychological Trauma: Theory, Research, Practice, and Policy.* Advance Online Publication. https://doi.org/10.1037/tra0000517.

Powers, J. J., & Duys, D. (2020). Toward trauma-informed career counseling. *The Career Development Quarterly, 68*(2), 173–185. 10.1002/cdq.12221

Pordelan, N., Sadeghi, A., Abedi, M. R., & Kaedi, M. (2018). How online career counseling changes career development: A life design paradigm. *Education and Information Technologies, 23*(6), 2655–2672. https://doi.org/10.1007/s10639-018-9735-1

Purves, D., Augustine, G. J., Fitzpatrick, D., Hall, W. C., Lamantia, A. S., Mooney, R. D., Platt, M. L., & White, L. E. (2018). *Neuroscience* (6th ed.). Sinauer Associates.

Savickas, M. L. (2011). Reshaping the story of career counselling. In K. Maree (ed.) *Shaping the story* (pp. 1–3). Brill Sense. https://doi.org/10.1163/9789004406162_002

Schneidhofer, T. M., Hofbauer, J., & Tatli, A. (2019). A bridge over troubled water. In H. Gunz, M. Lazarova, & W. Mayrhofer, (eds.). *The Routledge companion to career studies*. Routledge.

Schnyder, U., Bryant, R. A., Ehlers, A., Foa, E. B., Hasan, A., Mwiti, G., Kristensen, C. H., Neuner, K., Oe, M., & Yule, W. (2016). Culture sensitive psychotraumatology. *European Journal of Psychotraumatology, 7*. https://doi.org/10.3402/ejpt.v7.31179

Shonkoff, J. P., Garner, A. S., Siegel, B. S., Dobbins, M. I., Earls, M. F., Garner, A. S., McGuinn, L., Pascoe, J., & Wood, D. L. (2012). Committee on early childhood, adoption, and dependent care. The lifelong effects of early childhood adversity and toxic stress. *Pediatrics, 129*(1), e232–e246. https://doi.org/10.1542/peds.2011-2663

Taylor, S. B., Anglin, J. M., Paode, P. R., Riggert, A. G., Olive, M. F., & Conrad, C. D. (2014). Chronic stress may facilitate the recruitment of habit-and addiction-related neurocircuitries through neuronal restructuring of the striatum. *Neuroscience, 280*, 231–242. https://doi.org/10.1016/j.neuroscience.2014.09.029

U.S. Bureau of Labor Statistics. (2020, December). *Employment recovery in the wake of the COVID-19 pandemic*. https://www.bls.gov/opub/mlr/2020/article/employmentrecovery.htm

Van der Kolk, B. A. (2003). *Psychological trauma*. American Psychiatric Pub.

Whiston, S. C., & Cinamon, R. G. (2015). The work-family interface: Integrating research and career counseling practice. *The Career Development Quarterly, 63*(1), 44–56. https://doi.org/10.1002/j.2161-0045.2015.00094.x

CHAPTER 16

Career-Focused Counseling with Specific Populations

CHAPTER GOALS

- Increase the understanding of the career-related needs of persons with substance use disorder and a history of incarceration.
- Increase the understanding of the career-related needs of veterans and military personnel and their families.
- Increase understanding of unique career-related concerns of first-generation college students.

OPENING VIGNETTES

In this chapter, we introduce you to three clients—J. T., Jack, and Dina—each with distinct histories and experiences. We recognize that no vignette can fully encompass the characteristics and needs of any one member of these populations. The purpose of the vignettes is to spur your thinking about the personal and work-related issues for each of these groups. Note that we have combined two groups due to their significant overlap: persons with substance use disorders and persons with a history of incarceration.

JT

JT is a 35-year-old veteran, who served eight years in the Air Force, in which he was a mechanic. He was deployed to several international locations during his time. While working on a piece of equipment, a large machine fell on him, injuring his back and left leg. His injury resulted in him being unable to continue in his role as a mechanic, and he was subsequently medically discharged from the Air Force, ending his military career and aspirations. While he has regained some function in his leg, he lives with chronic pain, which limits his ability to work. In addition, he says that since then he has lost his job, career, and sense of purpose. He seeks counseling to explore what could be next for him, though he admits feeling hopeless a lot of the time.

Jack

Jack is a 33 year old seeking counseling as a condition of his parole. He was released from prison two months prior, following serving two and a half years of a three year sentence for larceny. Jack reports that he has been in and out of jail or on probation since his teens, primarily for theft. He describes growing up in poverty, turning to drugs at age 14 and theft to fund his "habit." He states that while in prison, he took a few courses and found that he enjoyed learning and working with his hands. Now, he says, he would like to change his past behaviors and set a better example for his children. He is concerned, however, about continuing his education and finding stable employment as a convicted felon.

Dina

Dina is a 20-year-old college student. She has dreams of becoming a nurse after graduation but is currently struggling with her science and math coursework. She tearfully tells her advisor that all her peers seem to "magically understand the math and science concepts taught in class," while she "struggles daily." Dina is starting to reconsider her career and college plans and wonders if she should just drop out and attend the local community college to become a certified nursing assistant (CNA). She doesn't want to disappoint her family, though, as she is the first to graduate from high school and attend college.

REFLECTION ACTIVITIES AND QUESTIONS

School counselors: For those of you who are or are training to become school counselors, the material in this chapter may seem less relevant to your work. But consider the following: How does my student's parents' history of being a veteran, a person who misuses substances, is on probation or parole, or is first-generation or no college, inform how I might provide CFC with them? Where are the potential developmental gaps or opportunities in working with these students?

Mental health counselors: In what ways can you use the information in this chapter to better serve your clients, without objectifying them because of their respective identities?

Introduction

The purpose of this chapter is to provide descriptions of career-focused counseling with individuals representing various special populations. "Special," as it is used here, is not a euphemism for these groups; it is a call to be mindful of certain potentially shared experiences, barriers, and opportunities for individual members of these groups. Each section will begin with its own case vignette to illustrate each type of special group: veterans, previously incarcerated individuals, first-generation college students, and individuals with substance use disorders. However, it is very important to keep in mind that these cases are examples of the types of people the counselors will see in their practice, but they are not intended to represent all individuals in these dimensions of human experience. For example, when reading about a person with a particular substance abuse issue, the approach described is not intended to make assumptions about all people with those particular substance abuse issues. Instead, the case applications are intended to guide your thinking and decision-making about individual and group differences among a variety of special populations in counseling. So for this chapter, we briefly examine the career-related concerns and challenges for individuals who are associated with the military, individuals with substance use disorders, and first-generation college-goers. It is also important to keep in mind the basics of counseling and the basics of career-focused counseling that apply to all persons. We hope that you will keep this in mind instead of thinking, when a member of this population arrives in your office, "Oh, I have to do something different here." Rather, use the information in this chapter to help you support the individual who is in front of you. It would be difficult for this one chapter to include case examples for every subcategory of special populations outlined here. Instead, we extend the description offered in Luke (2018) of challenges and opportunities for career development in working with individuals who fall within the categories outlined in this chapter.

Let's address this from the outset in this chapter: The groups identified here are members of our larger society, deserving of our respect and support while finding their place in the world, in general, and the world of work, in particular. Each group has its own strengths and needs, and it is the responsibility of the counselor to respond to the needs of these individuals, while recognizing and respecting their strengths. In each section, we offer a guiding vignette to inform your thinking as you prepare to practice with these individuals. We also offer a reflection activity for each to aid you in recognizing any implicit bias or preconceived notions related to these groups. Next, we provide some background information on each group to situate the work of career-focused counseling in a meaningful context. Each section also contains information and practice strategies for addressing the challenges and opportunities associated with each group.

TAKE A MINUTE

Showing respect: How do you show respect for someone you know little about? Think of a time when you met someone for the first time who was a member of a group you knew little about? How did you express interest while showing respect? Did you move toward or away from them?

Woodside and Luke (2019) describe three ways of learning about someone new. The first way is the most harmful one: *morbid curiosity.* This is when a counselor (or anyone for that matter) asks insensitive questions of a person for their own gratification and to the detriment of the individual. For example, when working with persons with disabilities, we have heard many times that one of the first questions people will ask is about their sex life: Can they, and how? This is a prime example of morbid curiosity. For those of us in counseling or training to be counselors, this can seem like an extreme example and something we would never do. And yet, counselors do ask insensitive, self-gratifying questions of clients and students to the detriment of the personhood of the individual. Regardless of whether you, as the reader, think you would ever ask such questions, it is important to note that your clients and students have been asked invasive questions that were harmful. Other examples of morbid curiosity for the populations discussed in this chapter include asking a veteran if they ever killed anyone, asking a person with a substance use disorder if they have ever "shot up" or "lost their kids," or even a person with a criminal record what their crime was. These questions sate the curiosity of the person asking, which is counter to the purposes of counseling.

The second type of expression of interest is *careless curiosity.* Careless questions are asked spontaneously, without pausing to reflect on why the question is being asked and how the response will better inform counseling. Careless curiosity is complex because it is not inherently harmful, but neither does it advance the counseling process. Clients and students have a habit of answering counselor questions because they were asked—not because they should answer. This places a lot of responsibility on the counselor to be intentional when asking or gathering information. For example, when working a person who uses a wheelchair, and they describe going grocery shopping, examples of careless curiosity include asking, "How do you get items that are on the top shelf?" or asking a veteran, "Did you get to shoot a .50 cal?" or, in a career context, asking a person with a substance use disorder about getting fired from their last job: "Oh, were you using on the job?". These types of questions can harm the relationship, as once again, the questions are geared toward the counselor—not the client.

The third way to express interest is respectful curiosity. *Respectful curiosity* is 100% oriented to the client or student and their expressed needs. These expressions of interest communicate a desire to make contact with the client or student's lived experience, to enter their world, and to walk with them through the difficult or challenging circumstances that brought them in. As counselors, we are naturally curious, but this curiosity must be carefully cultivated. The opportunity to make contact with another human being is a real privilege that must be safeguarded. You can spot an expression of respectful curiosity because, often, there will be a preface or qualifying statement that precedes it. As you ask yourself what it might mean to be respectfully curious, consider these examples:

- **Military or family member:** "You've mentioned the benefits of being in the military and the work you did there. Are there things you won't miss that you'd hope are different in civilian work?"
- **Person with substance use disorder:** "You mentioned being fired from your previous job. Do you see any connections between that job loss and your substance use?"
- **Previously incarcerated person:** "I appreciate your willingness to share small parts of your experience leading up to and while in prison. Is there anything you want me to know that would help me better understand you and how I might be of service?"

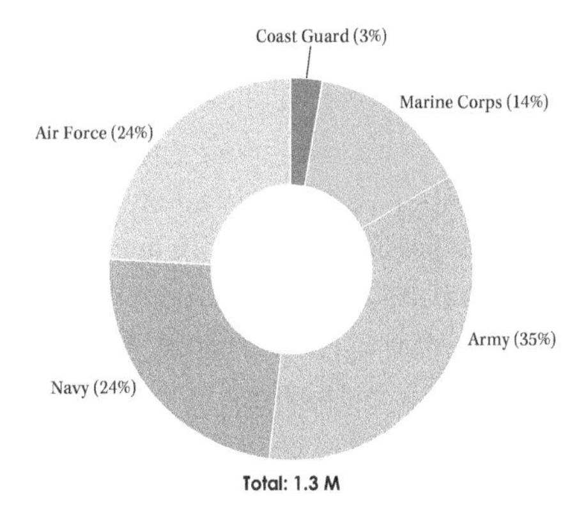

FIGURE 16.1. Active-Duty Personnel by Service, 2018

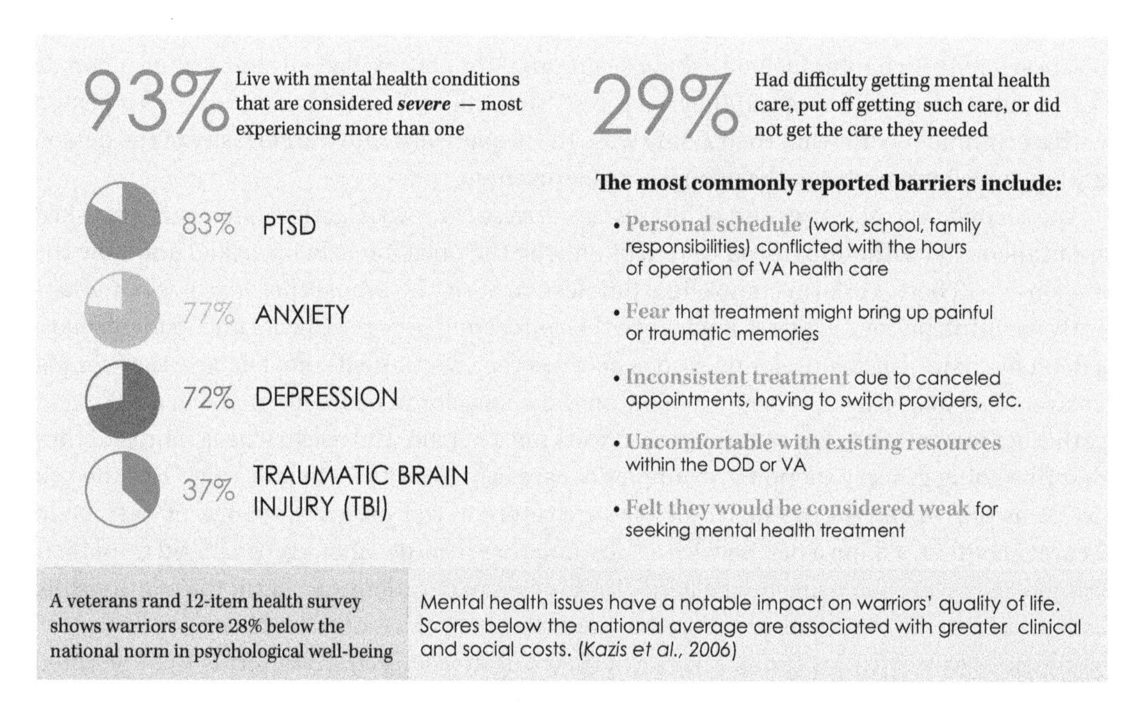

FIGURE 16.2. Mental Health of Veterans

We invite you to keep these types of curiosity expressions in mind as you read more about each of these groups in the pages that follow.

Military: Active, Veterans, and Spouses or Families

MILITARY BY THE NUMBERS

The first thing you will notice in this section is the title. Career-focused counseling is not just about working with veterans but also active, retired, spouses and partners, and family members of service members. This is because military culture is an important component of military identity that extends to family and loved ones. Additionally, the challenges of transitioning from military to civilian employment affects the individual as well as their family, adding pressure and challenge to finding work. In this section, we highlight several important considerations for working with veterans (an umbrella term used here) to work productively within that cultural frame. Further, the intent of this section is to assist in identifying any biases or preconceived notions you may have regarding this population.

TAKE A MINUTE

It is important to begin by considering your own experience of even the terms "military" and "veteran." Think about the images you have of the military based on your personal experience as well as exposure to depictions of the military and, in particular, veterans in movies and the media.

1. What are your visceral thoughts about veterans, active duty military, and their families?
2. Do the images in popular culture lead you toward a positive impression, negative, or other?
3. What are your attitudes about military, military service, and warfare?

It is easy to get caught up in popular culture's depiction of the military and news coverage of isolated incidents that affect views of veterans. Our attitudes and preconceived notions about these individuals can affect our ability to work with them. For instance, many movies and shows depict veterans as angry and violent, always seeking retribution, psychologically unstable, and a threat to the community or suffering from PTSD, which makes them fragile and dangerous. These depictions take individual episodes and magnify them such that it can appear that this is the reality of all military veterans and lead to misconceptions. Luke and Michael (2016) discussed myths about veterans that counselors need to attend to in their work with this population:

- All military personnel are angry and aggressive—they have to be—and, therefore, so are veterans.
- All veterans have PTSD and are therefore likely to "go off" at work.
- All veterans have trouble reintegrating back into civilian life and, therefore, back into the workplace.
- The skills needed to be successful in the military are vastly different from the skills needed to succeed as a civilian employee.
- All veterans are "high maintenance" in that they have a lot of physical and mental health issues to contend with.
- You can be successful without good people skills.
- There is a perfect job waiting out there for you.
- Working hard and keeping your nose clean will guarantee success. (p. 228)

As the list indicates, there are assumptions that veterans may make about the civilian world of work, but many more that the civilian population has about veterans (e.g., may not have good people skills, may demand respect because of their service, may be mentally unstable, etc.). The development of career readiness and adaptability have been shown to affect life satisfaction among veterans in college (Ghosh et al., 2019).

The reality is that veterans, particularly combat veterans with PTSD, are more likely to harm themselves than others, whether through homelessness or suicide. Veterans have significantly higher rates of PTSD (13.4 for women, 7.7% for men; Lehavot et al., 2018). These issues are especially complicated by other marginalized statuses (Bartee & Dooley, 2019; Greer, 2017).

In the case of transitioning from military to civilian life, whether through retirement or discharge, veterans face a host of challenges. Career development is a key challenge, but it exists in the context of other challenges. Bobeck et al. (2013) identified issues of "culture shock, identifying transferable skills, lack of job preparation and job search skills, and financial concerns" (p. 658)—not to mention all the other challenges that life brings to all people (Simpson & Armstrong, 2009). While these challenges are important and must be given consideration when working with veterans, it is critical that counselors also recognize the wealth of knowledge, skills, and experience these individuals possess that can be used to support their transitions (Luke, 2018). Luke describes four challenges specific to veterans that are important considerations in career-focused counseling:

1. Not understanding the world of work as it exists outside of military culture and structure. Many of those enlisted personnel who find success or a home in the military are either drawn to or become acclimated to the military culture. This includes a clear chain of command, rigid rules and structure and often swift consequences for noncompliance. These individuals have become highly proficient in these environments, drawing satisfaction from attention to detail. During the transition back to civilian life, many veterans find the world of work to be the opposite: ambiguous rules and leadership, unclear expectations, and capricious maintenance of standards (Killam, Weber, Michael, & Luke, 2016). This represents hardships that most civilians will never confront (though it is very true that these work environments cause others stress, as well).
2. Not feeling understood by the civilian population, as well as being viewed with mixed emotions by the populace. It is an unfortunate reality that stereotypes of military veterans pervade society's collective unconscious. Popular press and media present many veterans as unstable, raging killers, most of whom have post-traumatic stress disorder (PTSD). This is unfortunate for many reasons, not the least of which is that this inaccurate portrayal leads civilians to view veterans with an unhealthy level of skepticism. The majority of veterans transition back to civilian life and are productive members of society. Adding to the complicated picture of veterans is the pop psychology notion of PTSD. It is important for counselors to know and actively inform others that PTSD is not something you pick up from military service. It is a complex diagnosis and one not lightly assigned. For example, the lifetime prevalence of PTSD in the general population is between 6.8–7.8 percent. In one study of Gulf War Veterans, the prevalence of PTSD was estimated to be 10.1%, while the prevalence of those serving in Operation Enduring Freedom and Operation Iraqi Freedom was 13.8%. Granted, these are high rates—almost double the general population—but not a rate that represents a specific threat to others. In fact, a common feature of PTSD is depression and anxiety, yet the popular narrative is of the angry combat veteran looking to pick fights with co-workers. Now imagine that you are the veteran in the room, coping with all the transitions in your life, while trying not to read into the looks from others who wonder if you are a Rambo waiting to explode.

3. Finding a sense of identity—individual and vocational—outside of the military. Many enlisted personnel entered the military right after high school and, therefore, had limited opportunities to continue their education (Killam, Weber, Michael, & Luke, 2016). The period of emerging adulthood (18–29 years of age) is a critical time for identity and career development. Consistent with the developmental upheaval of this time period, veterans between the ages of 18–24 have the highest rates of unemployment (Boutin, 2011), in some cases approaching triple the national average (Robertson & Brott, 2013). The military and, at times, unemployment becomes the context in which these developmental tasks are approached.
4. Degree of concomitant stress and distress that accompany both transition from military to civilian life and the impact of their experiences in the military. While it is imprudent to stereotype veterans and their experiences, it is prudent to assess for complicating factors when engaged in CFC. Veterans do struggle with transition to civilian life, and this can result in stress, depression, anxiety, financial problems, homelessness, and disability—visible or invisible. Two additional complicating factors include combat veterans and veterans with disabilities (Clemens & Milsom, 2008). (Luke, 2018)

CFC Interventions

Keim and Day (2016) describe an intervention designed to help veterans address issues of transferring military skill development to the civilian world of work (as cited in Luke, 2018):

Activity Directions

1. Ask the clients to briefly list the types of training, leadership experiences, and skills they developed while in the military on a piece of paper.
2. Explain that you are going to do an activity together to help them better understand how employers understand these skills and what terms they use for the same experiences.
3. State for the client: If you think of developing your career like building a house, you already have a strong foundation of training that prepared you for your military occupation. The framework of that house was built with skills and experiences that are particular to military service, and therefore you use military terms to describe what you did. Let's use these sticks to represent the frame of the house—its walls, supports, and roof. Label each of the main skills that you demonstrated in your military position on one side of each stick.
4. When this part of the activity is completed, assist the client to identify similar terms used in the civilian world to describe the experience or skill set described on each of the sticks.
5. The client would then label the stick on the opposite side with the civilian term. Putting these together by taping them to a piece of paper in the shape of a house,

the client can then see how he or she has "reframed" the career house that the client has already made in his or her own life. The client can then see it literally from the employer's perspective as well.

6. These new terms for military skills and experiences can be used to assist the client to develop a résumé that fits a civilian job expectations and descriptions. (p. 235)

J. T. IN SESSION (THIRD SESSION)

MHC: Hey, J. T. Thanks for coming in. How are things?

CL: I'm hanging in there. I've used the mobile app we talked about last time: Insight Timer. Not sure it's helping, but it gives me a better way to start the day than what I was doing.

MHC: I appreciate that you tried it and have seen some benefit, even if it was unexpected.

CL: Yeah, I've never really been into meditation and stuff like that, but some of the talks are interesting.

MHC: That's great. Last week we discussed your challenge with considering careers outside of the military that would let you use your skills but would also be accessible for you with your pain.

CL: Yeah, it really sucks to have lost my career and income. I was a pretty good mechanic.

MHC: And it sounds like the losses really stacked up: mobility, pain-free status, job, income, sense of purpose.

CL: That last part has been hardest to shake. I was a damn good provider for my family, and now I lay around on the couch all day.

MHC: And you'd like to be able to change that, for them and also for yourself.

CL: Definitely. It's just hard to know what to do next.

MHC: You mentioned what a good mechanic you were.

CL: Yes, I was E-7 so I oversaw other mechanics.

MHC: And I think you said that E-7 was Master Sergeant rank, right.

CL: You remembered.

MHC: You also mentioned that you had not accessed your GI Bill funds for education. I wonder if you have considered training to train others.

CL: I did one time. The problem is that in the transition from military to civilian life, my experience doesn't matter. I have to start over and learn things the civilian way.

MHC: That seems discouraging and daunting, like civilians don't acknowledge or respect your experience.

CL: That's exactly what it is like! People say shit like "thank you for your service" but then ignore my training and experience.

MHC: That's a mixed message for sure. I wonder to what degree this has held you back in developing your civilian career.

J. T. would be considered an at-risk veteran (Robertson & Hayden, 2018), due to his disability and discharge status. As we can see in this transcript, the counselor works hard to understand and acknowledge the work- and life-related struggles. The counselor evokes his feelings related to his injury and transition to civilian life. While J. T. has access to resources (e.g., the GI Bill), he is also stuck in accepting the vastly different world he has to now live in. The counselor can certainly provide resources and suggestions and try to help him translate his military experience to civilian on his résumé, but it is of primary importance that J. T. finds a place or person that understands and appreciates his circumstances. Counselor empathy and the therapeutic alliance are what will be needed to support him in his difficulty in accepting the civilian world of work.

Previously Incarcerated Adults

In this section, we discuss the challenges associated with employment and career development for adults who have been incarcerated. The relationship between a person and their criminal record is a complicated one, as Griffith et al. (2019) found in their systematic review of 10 years of interdisciplinary research on the subject. What is clear is that previously incarcerated persons are at high risk of unemployment, homelessness, and recidivism. Strength-based approaches have been advocated for helping these individuals in making the transition to success (Snodgrass, et al., 2020).

INCARCERATION BY THE NUMBERS

The 2018 *Key Statistics* report from the Bureau of Justice Statistics (2021) indicates the following: 1.4 million people were incarcerated in federal and state facilities; just under 1 million were on parole; 3.5 million were on probation; and from May to June 2020, over 200,000 inmates in local jails for misdemeanors were given expedited release due to COVID-19 (BJS). Perhaps the most sobering data from the BJS is one recidivism. In a nine-year follow-up study of released prisoners, the BJS reported:

- The 401,288 state prisoners released in 2005 had 1,994,000 arrests during the 9-year period, an average of 5 arrests per released prisoner. Sixty percent of these arrests occurred during years 4 through 9.
- An estimated 68% of released prisoners were arrested within 3 years, 79% within 6 years, and 83% within 9 years.

- Eighty-two percent of prisoners arrested during the 9-year period were arrested within the first 3 years.
- Almost half (47%) of prisoners who did not have an arrest within 3 years of release were arrested during years 4 through 9.
- Forty-four percent of released prisoners were arrested during the first year following release, while 24% were arrested during year-9 (BJS, 2021)

This is significant in thinking of the role of counselors engaging in career-focused counseling with previously incarcerated individuals. The first level of concern for these individuals is finding work, any work, but the second level of concern likely more directly impacts recidivism, which is finding decent work (Blustein et al., 2016). It is one thing for an individual to find an employer willing to hire a person who is on probation or parole; it is another to find one willing to offer decent work. The problem is that "any work" often means low-wage, unskilled work in environments that place the individual at risk for returning to previous behaviors.

Persons with Substance Use Disorders

SUBSTANCE MISUSE BY THE NUMBERS

Substance use and misuse pose significant health and vocational risks to individuals. By the numbers, the statistics are staggering. According to the National Center for Drug Abuse Statistics (n.d.) there have been 700,000 drug overdose deaths in the United States since 2000. The federal budget for drug control in 2020 was $35 billion, and almost 20% of people have used illicit drugs at least once. "Drug use is highest among persons between the ages of 18-25 at 39% compared to persons aged 26-29, at 34%. 70% of users who try an illegal drug before age 13 develop a substance abuse disorder within the next 7 years compared to 27% of those who try an illegal drug after age 17. 47% of young people use an illegal drug by the time they graduate from high school." The importance of these statistics is that given the frequency and demographics, counselors must be aware of and prepared to assess for substance use disorders. The co-occurrence of addiction and incarceration are staggering, with 50% of incarcerations due to substances.

Fortunately, education and career adaptability can increase an individual's hope for the future, which can aid in getting and remaining substance free (Di Maggio et al., 2021; Merrin et al., 2020). At the same time, unemployment can increase the risk of substance use disorders (Compton et al., 2014). For example, Luke (2018) discussed this in a career-focused counseling context:

> Career-focused counselors face unique challenges when engaging in CFC with those struggling with addiction (Comerford, 1999; Henkel, 2011; Wood & Cato, 2012). There is a dearth of professional literature on how counselors can begin to address the

> complexities of these issues when intertwined. For this section, it is important perhaps to begin with an overview of addiction, both in terms of the DSM-5 diagnostic criteria as well as its clinical presentation. First and foremost, addiction is a behavior or set of behaviors. Also, this chapter addresses use disorders, rather than intoxication and withdrawal. In addition, the focus is on substance addiction, as opposed to process addictions, e.g., pathological gambling, pornography, Internet, etc., in part due to space limitations, but also because, from a neurological perspective, substance and process addictions are virtually indistinguishable (Fetting, 2011). Regardless of its precursors—and there are many—addiction is addiction because of the behavioral expression.
>
> It takes only a cursory look at the diagnostic criteria for a "use" disorder to see the connections between addiction and career issues. By definition, in fact, addiction negatively impacts work-related activities (see criteria 5 and 7), not to mention the indirect impact of other criteria (3, 4, and 9). Likewise, career issues that are left unaddressed or unresolved lead to negatively coping behaviors, including alcohol/substance use (Henkel, 2011). (Luke, 2018)

Especially troubling is the relationship between substance abuse and unemployment and, in particular, their reciprocal nature. Azagba et al., (2021) reported findings indicating that unemployment increases substance misuse. For example, Compton et al. (2014) assert that substance misuse can lead to problems in employment, even as they found that unemployment leads to problematic substance use. Counselors must be attuned to the potential for a student or client's vulnerability to substance misuse due to employment issues, whether work-related stressors or unemployment. Likewise, work related issues may also place these individuals at risk for substance misuse. It is important that counselors explore with clients the role of substances in their lives, as substance misuse may be a primary driver of unmet career-related goals.

The degree of overlap between previously incarcerated individuals and addiction makes it incumbent upon counselors to consider their presence and possible interaction. Let's consider the situation in which Jack finds himself.

JACK IN SESSION

> MHC: Thanks for coming in, Jack. It's nice to meet you. I know you referred to me from your IOP (intensive outpatient) counselor to discuss work. How can I help?
>
> CL: Well, we discuss triggers for relapse in groups and a big one for me is boredom and not staying busy. And I need a job to help with both.
>
> MHC: It sounds like you know yourself pretty well, both in terms of risk factors and also support. That's a great place to begin.

CL: The problem is that I have a criminal record and most of the jobs I can get are blue collar, construction jobs, but there's a lot of drug use around those jobs.

MHC: Oaky, so you can find work, but the work environment can also be a trigger?

CL: The trigger is being around alcohol all of the time and being around guys I know are high. It just makes me want to use.

MHC: That sounds pretty difficult.

CL: It's actually worse than that. I have to have a job before I can finish IOP, and I have to finish IOP to get off probation.

MHC: That's a heck of a lot of pressure on you, then.

CL: Yep. That's why I'm here. I need you to help me find a job.

MHC: You want to share some of that pressure with me (smiling).

CL: That's what you're here for, right? To help me get a job? If not, this is a waste of both our time.

MHC: Well, Jack. I really appreciate you being clear about your expectations for our work together. In your mind, how do you picture me helping?

CL: Don't you have a list of jobs for me or something?

MHC: OK, so helping you through this would mean me providing you with a list of jobs? Has that helped you in the past?

CL: What do you mean?

MHC: You've said that you have been able to get plenty of jobs, but they set you up for failure. How would a list of jobs from me change anything for you?

CL: Maybe you know of jobs that would not have me working around addicts all day.

MHC: Oh, OK, so it's finding a better environment for you to work in then?

CL: Yeah.

MHC: I wonder if we could work together to identify types of work that are available for folks with a felony on their record that would also provide a "safe" environment for you to help you stay clean?

CL: That'd be great.

MHC: Great! Let's get started.

First-Generation College Students

First-generation college students (FGCS) can be defined in several ways, ranging from parents or adult caregivers with no postsecondary education to those whose parents or caregivers did not earn a four-year college degree. Of undergraduate students enrolled in 2016, 24% had parents with no postsecondary education at all, and 56% had parents without a bachelor's degree (RTI International, 2019). In either case, FGCS are more likely to be African American or Hispanic, less likely to attend college full-time, and more likely to have dependents. They are also less likely to persist in college or to earn a degree in a timely manner compared to their peers (RTI International, 2019).

FGCS also differ from their peers related to career and academic preparation and needs. Prospective FGCS, or K–12 students who would eventually be the first in their families to attend college, experience differences in college-going beliefs quite early. Gibbons and Borders (2010) found that seventh grade prospective FGCS reported lower college-going self-efficacy beliefs and a significantly larger list of potential barriers to postsecondary success compared to their peers. Relatedly, a study of ninth graders found nearly half of prospective first-generation college students noted that finances would be a significant barrier to college-going, and almost one in five had already discarded their plans to attend college (Gibbons et al., 2006).

For those who do successfully enter college, challenges with adjustment and persistence exist. They often struggle to balance their family and school needs as they try to stay connected to and supportive of their families, while also trying to connect with the college experience (Gibbons et al., 2019). Both two- and four-year FGC students experience challenges with academic preparedness as they begin college. Those who start at a two-year college are less likely than their peers to transfer to a four-year college, and even if they do, they are less likely to complete their bachelor's degree (Ampaw et al., 2015). FGCS are also less likely to earn degrees in engineering or computer science, even though these are two of the fastest growing careers; in fact, they are less likely to be offered jobs in any field they interview for upon graduation (Eismann, 2016). This last discrepancy is likely due to challenges in formal writing and lack of a strong professional network. Together, these challenges lead to difficulty with college adjustment and persistence, making this group unique in their career development needs.

Not all the information on FGCS is grim, though. Researchers have identified several key interventions that help bridge the gap between barriers and ultimate success in college. For example, helping FGCS create networks of mentors and role models can help increase overall adaptability and success (Tate et al., 2015). Demystifying the college process by providing concrete information on the language of college (e.g., major, minor, Pell grant, and syllabus) and explaining how to tackle college assignments empowers these students (Collier & Morgan, 2008). Proactively offering writing (Conefrey, 2018) and math skill-building opportunities (Dika & D'Amico, 2016) helps to increase academic self-concept, while also filling any learning gaps. FGCS currently succeeding in college have offered advice to those just beginning. They recommend preparing for change, preparing early for college (Gibbons et al., 2019), finding ways to persevere, and relying on their strong work ethic (Gibbons & Woodside, 2014). Overall, social and academic capital can overcome the challenges new FGCS face.

DINA IN SESSION (SECOND SESSION)

> MHC: So I'd like to pick up from where we left off last week. You were talking about your academic struggles and your fear about letting down your family.
>
> CL: Right. I have wanted to go to college for as long as I can remember, and my parents have worked hard to help me get here. I feel like the degree is for all of us, not just for me, and that is great, but it is also a lot of pressure. My mom doesn't know that I am failing chemistry and getting a low grade in calculus. I don't want to disappoint her but maybe I just do not have what it takes to be successful in college.
>
> MHC: You mentioned that your high school had limited advanced science and math classes for you to take, right? I know that many of your peers took calculus and AP chemistry in high school, so I imagine some of the material might be review for them rather than new information like it is for you. That is not a reflection on your ability but rather on your access to academic resources and opportunities.
>
> CL: I guess that's true. In my study group, I'm the only one who only had one year of chemistry in high school, and most of my friends in calc took it in high school as well. But how am I supposed to make up for all this missed learning? I feel like I am being set up for failure.
>
> MHC: I can see how frustrated you are. I wonder if we might look at some of the resources available on campus for students struggling with their courses.
>
> CL: Yeah, that might be a good idea. I need to find a way to attend more tutoring sessions, but it is so hard to find the time because of my job and having to take care of my younger brother on the weekends. And starting next year, the nursing program requires me to have a weekly internship, so I need to find time to fit that into my schedule as well.
>
> MHC: I think it is also really important to remember that navigating college life can sometimes be like learning another language. You have to understand not just the words but also the nuances of those words. What I mean is, just reading the material is sometimes not enough. You also need to understand the reasons for what is being asked, how the material is structured, and so on. I believe it is a skill that can be learned, but it is not something we are born knowing.

Dina and her counselor talk about ways to ask for help that don't feel like weakness. They also discuss strategies to help with Dina's time management and self-care. Her counselor works hard not to diminish the real struggles Dina is facing, while also helping her increase her coping skills and self-confidence. In a later session, they discuss skills she learned from the university's academic success center.

> CL: So talking with the academic success coach has actually been really helpful. He helped me reorganize my study schedule, so I actually get more accomplished in less time. Who knew there were so many strategies to studying successfully? He also gave me the contact information for a nursing instructor, who was the first in her family to attend college. She and I have a meeting set up for next week to talk about how she accomplished her goals.
>
> MHC: It sounds like you are really using your resources and becoming more comfortable with asking for the help you need.
>
> CL: Yeah. I think I just needed to accept that asking for help is not a weakness. I told my mom about talking with you and she was actually really proud of me. She told me that she knows how hard I work and that, sometimes, even hard workers need a little support.

Neuroscience, Culture, and Development

In-group bias is a well-documented phenomenon that affects our ability to connect with those outside our group. Research from psychology, sociology, and neuroscience highlight the effects of this in human behavior, from Schadenfreude to overt aggression toward outgroup members. The evidence indicates that members of a group struggle to identify with members of other groups. This is magnified in situations where status is involved. For example, high status groups are particularly resistant to understanding the experience or having empathy for low-status groups and group members. It is even the case that members of low-status groups show bias toward other low-status members—even when they are both in the same group. This affects the ability of counselors (themselves a high-status group based on education and role) to empathize with other groups. In the case of the groups described in this chapter, most are viewed as low status. Now, no one wants to view themselves as having implicit bias toward members of these groups any more than we want to consider individuals in these groups as lower status than us, or anyone. Yet, these and many other groups are viewed this way.

The way this can manifest itself in counseling is through what Luke and colleagues (Woodside & Luke, 2019; Luke, 2020) refer to as projective sympathy. Projective sympathy is the process of imagining what one would feel if they were going through something they observe in others, then assuming that is how the other person feels. Behaviorally, I might respond to the person based on my projection. For example, I might be in the grocery store and see a person using a wheelchair, trying to reach items on the top shelf. As an automatic process, I might think to myself, "I would feel frustrated and helpless if that was me. I'll bet they feel helpless.

I should help them." In reality, the observed individual may have a great deal of experience resolving situations like this themselves or seeking assistance when needed. They likely feel empowered to meet their own needs both because they have the power and because this is their lived experience, not mine. When I project my anticipated feelings on another person, I limit my ability to make contact.

Take Away and Use Today

Resources for individuals in the groups described in this chapter are some of the best kept secrets in career-focused counseling. Therefore, it can be helpful to set up a scavenger hunt of sorts with these (and all) clients or students. It starts with identifying success Web search strategies. It may sound simple, but success in locating resources depends on utilizing successful Web search strategies to identify and curate helpful resources. For example, blogs, such as MindTools (see https://www.mindtools.com/pages/article/internet-searching.htm) can frame searches for clients and students and give them a leg up on finding the resources they need. For many clients, mobility and transportation can be limiting factors in being part of a community, so online communities can serve to fill these gaps. In the scavenger hunt, clients and students can identify resources for employment, education, transportation, community, and other categories. They can bring what they find back to the next session, and the counselor and client can review together.

References

Ampaw, F., Partlo, M., Hullender, T., & Wagner, N. (2015). Do community colleges promote postsecondary and labor market success for first-generation students. *Journal of the First-Year Experience and Students in Transition, 27*(1), 9–28

Azagba, S., Shan, L., Qeadan, F., & Wolfson, M. (2021). Unemployment rate, opioids misuse and other substance abuse: quasi-experimental evidence from treatment admissions data. *BMC psychiatry, 21*(1), 1-9. https://doi.org/10.1186/s12888-020-02981-7

Bartee, R. L., & Dooley, L. (2019). African American veterans career transition using the transition goals, plans, success (GPS) program as a model for success. *Journal of Veterans Studies, 5*(1). http://doi.org/10.21061/jvs.v5i1.122

Blustein, D. L., Olle, C., Connors-Kellgren, A., & Diamonti, A. J. (2016). Decent work: A psychological perspective. *Frontiers in Psychology, 7*, 407. https://doi.org/10.3389/fpsyg.2016.00407

Boutin, D. L. (2011). Effective vocational rehabilitation services for military veterans. *Journal of Applied Rehabilitation Counseling, 42*(2), 24.

Bureau of Justice Statistics (2021). *Key Statistics, Total Correctional Population.* Retrieved from www.bjs.ojp.gov

Bureau of Justice Statistics (2021). *2018 Update on Prisoner Recidivism: A 9-Year Follow-up Period (2005–2014).* Retrieved from https://bjs.ojp.gov/library/publications/2018-update-prisoner-recidivism-9-year-follow-period-2005-2014

Clemens, E. V., & Milsom, A. S. (2008). Enlisted service members' transition into the civilian world of work: A cognitive information processing approach. *The Career Development Quarterly, 56*(3), 246–256.

Collier, P. J., & Morgan, D. L. (2008). "Is that paper really due today?": Differences in first-generation and traditional college students' understandings of faculty expectations. *Higher Education, 55*, 425–446. https://doi.org/10.1007/s10734-007-9065-5

Compton, W. M., Gfroerer, J., Conway, K. P., & Finger, M. S. (2014). Unemployment and substance outcomes in the United States 2002–2010. *Drug and alcohol dependence, 142*, 350–353. https://doi.org/10.1016/j.drugalcdep.2014.06.012

Conefrey, T. (2018). Supporting first-generation students' adjustment with high-impact practices. *Journal of College Student Retention: Research, Theory, & Practice, 23*(1), 139–160. https://doi.org/10.1177/1521025118807402

Di Maggio, I., Montenegro, E., Little, T. D., Nota, L., & Ginevra, M. C. (2021). Career adaptability, hope, and life satisfaction: An analysis of adults with and without substance use disorder. *Journal of Happiness Studies*, 1–16. https://doi.org/10.1007/s10902-021-00405-1

Dika, S. L., & D'Amico, M. M. (2016). Early experiences and integration in the persistence of first-generation college students in STEM and non-STEM majors. *Journal of Research in Science Teaching, 53*(3), 368–383. https://doi.org/10.1002/tea.21301

Eismann, L. (2016, November 1). *First-generation students and job success.* National Association of Colleges and Employers. https://www.naceweb.org/job-market/special-populations/firstgeneration-students-and-job-success/

Ghosh, A., Kessler, M., Heyrman, K., Opelt, B., Carbonelli, M., & Fouad, N. A. (2019). Student veteran career transition readiness, career adaptability, and academic and life satisfaction. *The Career Development Quarterly, 67*(4), 365–371. https://doi.org/10.1002/cdq.12205

Gibbons, M. M., & Borders, L. D. (2010). Prospective first-generation college students: A social–cognitive perspective. *Career Development Quarterly, 58*(3), 194–208. https://doi.org/10.1002/j.2161-0045.2010.tb00186.x

Gibbons, M. M., Borders, L. D., Wiles, M. E., Stephan, J. B., & Davis, P. E. (2006). Career and college planning needs of ninth graders—as reported by ninth graders. *Professional School Counseling, 10*, 168–178. https://doi.org/10.5330/prsc.10.2.vj457656056x55w7

Gibbons, M. M., Rhinehart, A., & Hardin, E. (2019). How first-generation college students adjust to college. *Journal of College Student Retention: Research, Theory, & Practice, 20*(4), 488–510. https://doi.org/10.1177/1521025116682035

Gibbons, M. M., & Woodside, M. (2014). Addressing the needs of first-generation college students: Lessons learned from adults from low-education families. *Journal of College Counseling, 17*, 21–36.

Greer, T. W. (2017). Career development for women veterans: Facilitating successful transitions from military service to civilian employment. *Advances in Developing Human Resources, 19*(1), 54–65. https://doi.org/10.1177%2F1523422316682737

Griffith, J. N., Rade, C. B., & Anazodo, K. S. (2019). Criminal history and employment: an interdisciplinary literature synthesis. *Equality, Diversity and Inclusion, 38*(5), 505–528. https://doi.org/10.1108/EDI-10-2018-0185

Lehavot, K., Katon, J. G., Chen, J. A., Fortney, J. C., & Simpson, T. L. (2018). Post-traumatic stress disorder by gender and veteran status. *American Journal of Preventive Medicine, 54*(1), e1–e9. https://dx.doi.org/10.1016%2Fj.amepre.2017.09.008

Loprest, P., & Maag, E. (2007). The relationship between early disability onset and education and employment. *Journal of Vocational Rehabilitation, 26*(1), 49–62.

Luke, C. (2018). *Career focused counseling: Integrating theory, research and neuroscience.* Cognella Academic Publishing.

Luke, C. & Michael, T. (2016). Interventions for veterans. In W. K Killam, S. Degges-White, & R. E. Michel, (Eds.), *Career counseling interventions: Practice with diverse clients* (pp. 225–239). Springer Publishing Company.

Merrin, G. J., Ames, M. E., Sturgess, C., & Leadbeater, B. J. (2020). Disruption of transitions in high-risk substance use from adolescence to young adulthood: school, employment, and romantic relationship factors. *Substance Use & Misuse, 55*(7), 1129–1137. https://doi.org/10.1080/10826084.2020.1729200

National Center for Drug Abuse Statistics (n.d.). *Drug Abuse Statistics: Key Findings.* Retrieved from https://drugabusestatistics.org

Robertson, H. C., & Brott, P. E. (2013). Male veterans' perceptions of midlife career transition and life satisfaction: A study of military men transitioning to the teaching profession. *Adultspan Journal, 12*(2), 66–79.

Robertson, H. C., & Hayden, S. C. (2018). Serving all that served: career development among at-risk veterans. *Career Planning & Adult Development Journal, 34*(4).

RTI International. (2019). *First-generation college students: Demographic characteristics and postsecondary enrollment.* NASPA. https://firstgen.naspa.org/files/dmfile/FactSheet-01.pdf

Simpson, A., & Armstrong, S. (2009). From the military to the civilian work force: Addressing veteran career development concerns. *Career Planning & Adult Development Journal, 25*(1), 177–187.

Snodgrass Rangel, V., Hein, S., Rotramel, C., & Marquez, B. (2020). A researcher–practitioner agenda for studying and supporting youth reentering school after involvement in the juvenile justice system. *Educational Researcher, 49*(3), 212–219. https://doi.org/10.3102%2F0013189X20909822

Tate, K. A., Caperton, W., Kaiser, D., Pruitt, N. T., White, H., & Hall, E. (2015). An exploration of first-generation college students' career development beliefs and experiences. *Journal of Career Development, 42*(4), 294–310. https://doi. org/10.1177/0894845314565025

Woodside, M., & Luke, C. (2019). *Practicum in counseling: A developmental guide.* Cognella Academic Publishing.

CREDITS

Fig. 16.1: Source: https://www.cfr.org/backgrounder/demographics-us-military.

Fig. 16.2: Adapted from source: https://www.woundedwarriorproject.org/media/ssdj3mez/2020-annual-warrior-survey_executive-summary.pdf.

Final Thoughts

As our journey of understanding the role of work in client's lives comes to an end, we know that your actual learning has only just begun; your current and future clients will continue to help you understand the complex connections between work, career, and life. For now, we want to leave you with a few highlights:

1. **Career and personal counseling are intertwined** to the point that the separation is really almost superficial. Career, at least how we define it in the United States, is a central part of our lives. Not everyone ascribes personal meaning to the work they do, but most of us do spend the majority of our waking hours planning to enter the world of work, engaging in the world of work (paid or unpaid), or navigating away from the world of work. As a result, the way we spend our waking hours impacts all of the other parts of our lives: our relationships, our leisure time, our homemaking, and so on. We hope that, at a minimum, you now recognize the need to ask your clients about their career development and their current engagement in the world of work.
2. Relatedly, **career counseling is counseling**. Whether you are providing career resources to your client or educating them on career options or helping them find meaning in the work they do, it is all a form of counseling. As counselors, we use skills, such as active listening, paraphrasing, empathy, unconditional positive regard, and reflection to create a therapeutic alliance with our clients. Whether you are providing counseling or career-focused counseling, it is all counseling at its core. We hope that this textbook has helped you find the "counseling" in career-focused counseling.
3. We use a **career-focused counseling theory to serve as a frame** for our work to help clients grow and change. While this theory may not be your primary theoretical orientation, it should align with it enough, so as your clients disclose career-focused needs, you can easily shift to a career-focused theory that still aligns with your way of being with clients. As you read the multiple chapters on theories of career counseling, you hopefully found at least one that was similar to your overall theoretical orientation and added it to your theory frame.
4. **Career is impacted by culture**. There is no one-size-fits-all experience of career development and engagement; our environment, family-of-origin, cultural backgrounds, and cultural identity salience impact the role of work in people's lives. Part of providing ethical services for clients involves a sense of cultural humility and cultural competence. Our clients come from complex backgrounds, have influential experiences that impact their development, and create a worldview perspective that is uniquely based on these experiences. They are the experts of their own lives, and in career-focused counseling,

like all counseling, we must offer a safe space for clients to share their salient identities and consider how their past experiences impact their current and future career paths.

5. **Understanding neuroscience** helps you provide better career-focused counseling. We know that knowledge of how the brain works helps us understand how to help our clients, and this is true of career-focused counseling as well. Counselors are not neuroscientists, nor should they try to be, but understanding the human experience as a brain-based experience will increase your empathy, skills, and effectiveness in working with clients. This includes the neurobiology of stress and its impact on decision-making, the neuroscience of identity and its implications for career choice, and the neurobiological foundations for wellness and resilience and how they underpin the work of counselors.

Putting It All Together: The Final Take Away and Use Today

What's next? Hopefully, you were able to start implementing your learning with clients. If not, our guess is that you will be working with clients quite soon. Remember to utilize the skills and knowledge you learned in this course and apply it to your work. Remember that the role of work in people's lives impacts each of your client's lives as well. Remember that theory, counseling skills, and a therapeutic relationship are key to helping clients grow and change, ultimately achieving their goals.

Index